THE ROUTLEDGE COMPANION
TO POSTCOLONIAL STUDIES

The Routledge Companion to Postcolonial Studies offers a unique and up-to-date mapping of the postcolonial world and is composed of essays as well as shorter entries for ease of reference. Introducing students to the history of the major European empires and the cultural legacies created in their wake, this book brings together an international range of contributors on such topics as:

- the colonial histories of Britain, France, Spain and Portugal
- the diverse postcolonial and diasporic cultural endeavours from Africa, the Americas, Australasia, Europe, and South and East Asia
- the major theoretical formulations: poststructuralist, materialist, culturalist, psychological.

With a comprehensive A to Z of forty key writers and thinkers central to contemporary postcolonial studies and featuring historical maps, this is both a concise introduction and an essential resource for any student of postcolonial culture, whatever their field.

John McLeod is Reader in Postcolonial and Diaspora Literatures at the School of English, University of Leeds. He is the author of numerous books, including *Beginning Postcolonialism* (Manchester University Press, 2000) and *Postcolonial London: Rewriting the Metropolis* (Routledge, 2004).

Also available from Routledge

Post-Colonial Studies: The Key Concepts (second edition)
Bill Ashcroft, Gareth Griffiths and Helen Tiffin
978–0–415–42855–2

Cultural Theory: The Key Concepts (second edition)
Edited by Andrew Edgar and Peter Sedgwick
978–0–415–39939–5

Fifty Key Contemporary Thinkers (second edition)
John Lechte
978–0–415–32694–0

THE ROUTLEDGE COMPANION TO POSTCOLONIAL STUDIES

Edited by
John McLeod

Routledge
Taylor & Francis Group

LONDON AND NEW YORK

First published 2007
by Routledge
2 Park Square, Milton Park, Oxfordshire OX14 4RN

Simultaneously published in the USA and Canada
by Routledge
270 Madison Avenue, New York, NY 10016

Routledge is an imprint of the Taylor & Francis Group, an informa business

© 2007 John McLeod

Typeset in Times New Roman by
Book Now Ltd, London

Printed and bound in Great Britain by
TJ International Ltd, Padstow, Cornwall

British Library Cataloguing in Publication Data
A catalogue record for this book is available from the British Library

Library of Congress Cataloging in Publication Data
A catalog record for this book is available

ISBN10: 0–415–32496–3 (hbk)
ISBN10: 0–415–32497–1 (pbk)
ISBN10: 0–203–35808–2 (ebk)

ISBN13: 978–0–415–32496–0 (hbk)
ISBN13: 978–0–415–32497–7 (pbk)
ISBN13: 978–0–203–35808–5 (ebk)

CONTENTS

CONTENTS

CONTRIBUTORS

Alice Brittan is Assistant Professor of Postcolonial Literature in the Department of English at Dalhousie University, Canada. She has published in *Australian Literary Studies*, *Tydskrif vir Letterkunde*, and twice in *PMLA*. She is currently working on a book manuscript called 'Empty-Handed: traffic among strangers'.

Kai Easton is Lecturer in African Literature and Diaspora Studies at the School of Oriental and African Studies, University of London, UK. She has previously taught at the Universities of Sussex, UK, and Rhodes, South Africa, and was until recently a Mellon postdoctoral fellow in English at the University of KwaZulu-Natal, South Africa. Her book on J. M. Coetzee is forthcoming from Manchester University Press. Her most recent publication is 'J. M. Coetzee's *Disgrace*: Reading Race/Reading Scandal' in *Scandalous Fictions: the twentieth-century novel in the public sphere*, edited by Jago Morrison and Susan Watkins (Palgrave Macmillan, 2006).

Charles Forsdick is James Barrow Professor of French at the University of Liverpool, UK. His recent publications include *Victor Segalen and the Aesthetics of Diversity* (Oxford University Press, 2000), *Travel in Twentieth-Century French and Francophone Cultures: the persistence of diversity* (Oxford University Press, 2005), and *Francophone Postcolonial Studies: a critical introduction* (Arnold, 2003; co-edited with David Murphy). He is currently completing books on representations of Toussaint Louverture and on the travel writing of Ella Maillart, and is co-editing (with David Murphy) a volume entitled *Postcolonial Thought in the Francophone World*.

Luz Mar González Arias is a Senior Lecturer in the English Department at the University of Oviedo, Spain. She has worked on the inscription of female corporeality in the Irish text, as well as on contemporary revisions of Greek mythology by Irish women poets and playwrights. She has a special interest in postcolonial theories and literary practices, and has published a number of articles in international journals as well as two books, *Otra Irlanda: La estética postnacionalista de poetas y artistas irlandesas contemporáneas* (Universidad de Oviedo, 2000; trans. *Another Ireland: the postnationalist aesthetics of contemporary Irish women poets and visual artists*) and *Cuerpo, mito y teoría feminista: Revisiones de Eva en autoras irlandesas contemporáneas* (KRK ediciones, 1998; trans. *Body, Myth and Feminist Theory: contemporary revisions of the myth of Eve by Irish women writers*).

John McLeod is Reader in Postcolonial and Diaspora Literatures in the School English, University of Leeds, UK. He is the author of *Beginning Postcolonialism* (Manchester University Press, 2000), *Postcolonial London: rewriting the metropolis* (Routledge, 2004), and *J. G. Farrell* (Northcote House, 2007), and co-editor (with David Rogers) of *The Revision of Englishness* (Manchester University Press, 2004). He is a member of the Editorial Board of *Moving Worlds: a journal of transcultural writings* (www.movingworlds.net).

Anshuman Mondal is Senior Lecturer in English at Brunel University, UK and Deputy Director of the Brunel Centre for Contemporary Writing. He is the author of *Nationalism and Post-Colonial Identity: culture and ideology in India and Egypt* (RoutledgeCurzon, 2003), and *Amitav Ghosh* (Manchester University Press, 2007). He is currently writing *Young British Muslim Voices*, which will be published by Praeger in late 2007.

Stephen Morton is Lecturer in Anglophone Literatures and Cultures in the Department of English, School of Humanities, University of Southampton, UK. He is the author of *Gayatri Spivak: ethics, subalternity and the critique of postcolonial reason* (Polity, 2006) and is currently completing a study of postcolonial modernity in the fiction of Salman Rushdie.

David Murphy is Senior Lecturer in French at the University of Stirling, UK. He has written widely on African literature and cinema, as well as on the relationship between francophone studies and postcolonial theory. He is the author of *Sembene: imagining alternatives in film and fiction* (James Currey, 2000), and is co-author (with Patrick Williams) of *Postcolonial African Cinema: ten directors* (Manchester University Press, 2007). He is also the co-editor (with Charles Forsdick) of *Francophone Postcolonial Studies: a critical introduction* (Arnold, 2003).

Máire ní Fhlathúin is Lecturer in English at the University of Nottingham, UK. She has published on a range of topics in colonial/postcolonial literature and culture, particularly on British India. Her edition of Rudyard Kipling's *Kim* was published by Broadview Press in 2005.

Melanie Otto is Lecturer in Postcolonial Literatures in English at Trinity College Dublin, Ireland. She completed her PhD at the University of Wales, Swansea, concerning utopian space in Kamau Brathwaite's video-style work, which she is currently preparing for publication with Africa World Press. Her research interests include Caribbean literature and women's writing.

James Procter is a Senior Lecturer in the School of English at Newcastle University, UK. He is the author of *Dwelling Places: postwar black British writing* (Manchester University Press, 2003) and *Stuart Hall* (Routledge, 2004), and editor of *Writing Black Britain, 1948–1998* (Manchester University Press, 2000). He is also the Principal Investigator on a three-year AHRC-funded project, 'Devolving Diasporas' (www.devolvingdiasporas.com).

Mark Shackleton is currently Acting Professor at the Department of English, University of Helsinki, Finland, and is co-director of the University of Helsinki Literature project 'Cross-Cultural Contacts: Diaspora Writing in English'. He is author of *Moving Outward: the development of Charles Olson's use of myth* (University of Helsinki, 1993) and has edited a number of volumes on North American studies, including *Migration, Preservation and Change* (Renvall Institute Publications, 1999), *Roots and Renewal: writings by bicentennial Fulbright Professors* (Renvall Institute Publications, 2001), and *First and Other Nations* (Renvall Institute Publications, 2005). He has published widely on Native North American writing, including articles on Tomson Highway, Thomas King, Monique Mojica, Gerald Vizenor, Louise Erdrich and Simon J. Ortiz. His forthcoming publications include (as editor) *Diasporic Literature and Theory – Where Now?* (Cambridge Scholars Press).

Claire Taylor is Lecturer in Hispanic Studies in the School of Cultures, Languages and Area Studies at the University of Liverpool, UK. She is the author of *Bodies and Texts: configurations of identity in the works of Albalucía Ángel, Griselda Gambaro, and Laura Esquivel* (Maney, 2003), as well as several articles covering topics in Latin American literature and culture. Her research interests include Latin American women's writing; Latin American cinema, especially the films of María Luisa Bemberg; Latin American popular culture; issues in postcolonial studies; and Latin American cyberculture. She is currently working on a jointly-edited book and associated project on Latin American Cyberculture, and a three-year project on Women, Gender and Discourse in collaboration with researchers in the Universidad del Valle, Colombia.

Abigail Ward is Lecturer in Postcolonial Studies at Nottingham Trent University, UK. She is currently working on a monograph on representations of slavery in the selected works of Caryl Phillips, David Dabydeen and Fred D'Aguiar. She has published essays on Phillips's work in *Perspectives on Endangerment*, edited by Graham Huggan and Stephan Klasen (Georg Olms Verlag, 2005), and in *Moving Worlds: a journal of transcultural writings*, 7: 1 (2007). Her article on Dabydeen's poem 'Turner' appears in the *Journal of Commonwealth Literature*, 42: 1 (2007), while her essay on his novel *A Harlot's Progress* is published in the *Journal of Postcolonial Writing*, 43: 1 (2007). Her chapter on Fred D'Aguiar's Bloodlines is included in the collection *Revisiting Slave Narratives II* (Les Carnets du Cerpac, 2007), edited by Judith Misrahi-Barak.

FOR CAITLIN, LYDIA AND MADELEINE

'DÈYÈ MÒN, GENYIN MÒN'

ACKNOWLEDGEMENTS

I am extraordinarily grateful to Rosie Waters at Routledge for the chance to contribute to the Routledge Companion series, for being such a generous and wise editor, and a source of strength (again). She has been a pleasure to work with, as have her colleagues at Routledge, especially Aimee Foy and Liz Thompson. I do hope this book repays the faith which Rosie has invested in me and this project.

The contributors to the *Routledge Companion to Postcolonial Studies* deserve a special 'thank you' for their endless patience, intellectual energies and their promptness in responding to my editorial queries. Each has advised me in different ways, and at different points, about this book, and I hope they will take a collective pleasure in its strengths and achievements (its weaknesses are, of course, entirely my own responsibility). I've learned a great deal from each of them, and I am deeply grateful that they have given their expertise to this book so willingly and cheerfully. Thank you.

In editing this book I found myself continually indebted to the Brotherton Library at the University of Leeds, especially its truly unique collection of Commonwealth and postcolonial texts which has been created by scholars and library staff over several decades. It remains a privilege to work as one of the robust team of postcolonial scholars at the School of English at Leeds, from whom I continue to learn: Sam Durrant, Dave Gunning, Graham Huggan, Ananya Jahanara Kabir, Stuart Murray and Brendon Nicholls. Professors Shirley Chew and David Richards continue to offer me support, guidance and their example, for which I remain deeply grateful. Friends and colleagues have also helped me bring this book to fruition in more ways than one: Alison Creedon, Rachel Evans, Tracy Hargreaves, Robert Jones, Katy Mullin, Alex Nield, Francis O'Gorman, Matthew Pateman, Sandra Ponzanesi, Mark Taylor-Batty and Andrew Warnes. Thanks too to Dorothy Desir, whom I met in Bellagio, Italy, in the summer of 2003, and from whom I learned the Haitian proverb which aptly prefaces a book of this nature (and which translates in English as: 'Beyond the mountain there are many mountains').

Julie Adams has lived with this book from the day it was first discussed, and I continue to be indebted to her in so many ways. Indeed, she was instrumental in securing the picture for the cover, 'Belief in Renewal', by the late Maori artist John Bevan Ford (for more about Ford's painting, see *Moving Worlds: a journal of transcultural writings*, 4: 2, 2004). My fantastic parents, Veronica and James

McLeod, remain my primary source of inspiration. Finally, I must acknowledge the care and support of my sister and her husband, Linda and Brian Joy, and their three children: Caitlin, Lydia and Madeleine. This book is for my nieces, with much love (enjoy the mountains, you guys).

CREDITS FOR FRONTISPIECE MAPS

Robert Aldrich, *Greater France: a history of overseas expansion* © 1996 Macmillan, reproduced with permission of Palgrave Macmillan.

Leslie Bethell, *Spanish America after Independence c.1820–c.1870* © 1987 CUP, reproduced with the permission of Cambridge University Press.

Norrie MacQueen, *The Decolonisation of Portuguese Africa: metropolitan revolution and the dissolution of empire* © 1997 Longman. Reproduced with permission of Pearson Education.

Denis Judd, *Empire: the British imperial experience from 1765 to the present* © 1996 HarperCollins. Reproduced with permission of David Higham Associates.

A NOTE ON THE TEXT

As you read through the essays in this book, you will discover that the authors quote from a wide variety of important cultural texts, critical studies, scholarly articles and collections of essays. You will find the full details of each quoted reference in the Bibliography of Works Cited (pp. 231–43) at the back of the *Companion*, which collects together in one place all of the references made by the different contributors in this book.

In addition to this resource, at the end of each individual essay there is a brief bibliography which details some recommended further reading concerning the topics covered in the individual section, which we hope you will find useful in continuing and developing your engagement with the range and scope of post-colonial studies.

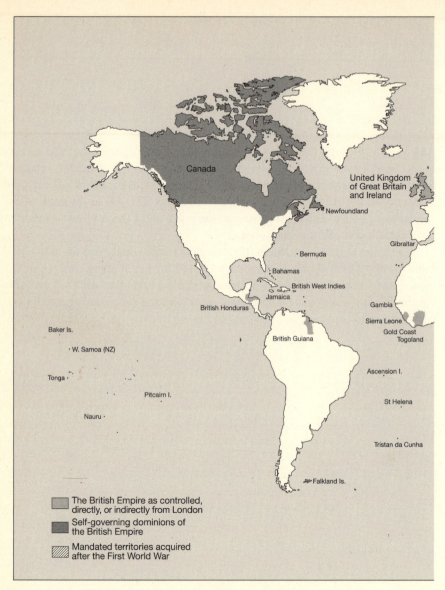

The British Empire as controlled, directly, or indirectly from London

Self-governing dominions of the British Empire

Mandated territories acquired after the First World War

Map 1 The British Empire at it greatest extent, 1920.

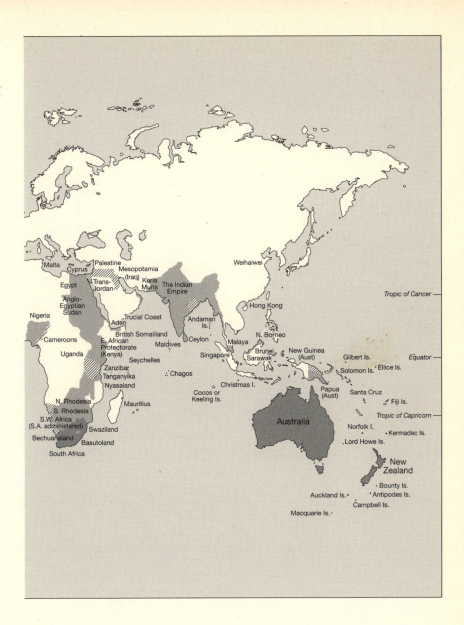

Malta
Cyprus
Palestine
Trans-Jordan
Egypt
Anglo-Egyptian Sudan
Nigeria
Cameroons
Uganda
Zanzibar
Tanganyika
Nyasaland
N. Rhodesia
S. Rhodesia
S.W. Africa (S.A. administered)
Bechuanaland
Swaziland
Basutoland
South Africa

Mesopotamia (Iraq)
Kuria Muria
The Indian Empire
Trucial Coast
Aden
British Somaliland
E. African Protectorate (Kenya)
Seychelles
Chagos
Mauritius
Maldives
Andaman Is.
Ceylon

Weihaiwei

Tropic of Cancer

Hong Kong

N. Borneo
Malaya
Singapore
Brunei
Sarawak
New Guinea (Aust)

Gilbert Is.
Solomon Is.
Ellice Is.
Equator

Cocos or Keeling Is.
Christmas I.
Santa Cruz
Papua (Aust)
Fiji Is.

Tropic of Capricorn

Australia

Norfolk I.
Kermadec Is.
Lord Howe Is.

New Zealand

Bounty Is.
Auckland Is.
Antipodes Is.
Campbell Is.
Macquarie Is.

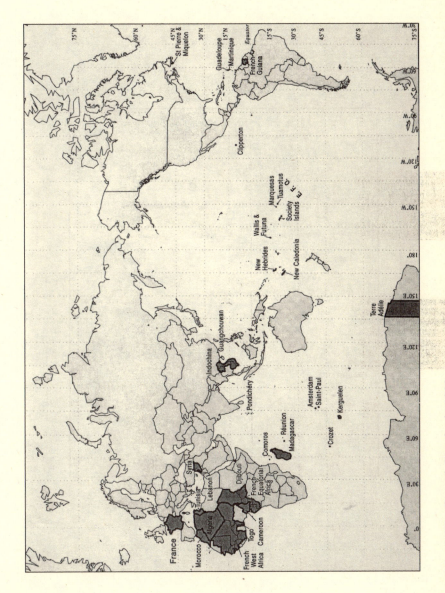
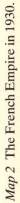

Map 2 The French Empire in 1930.

Map 3 Latin America in 1830.

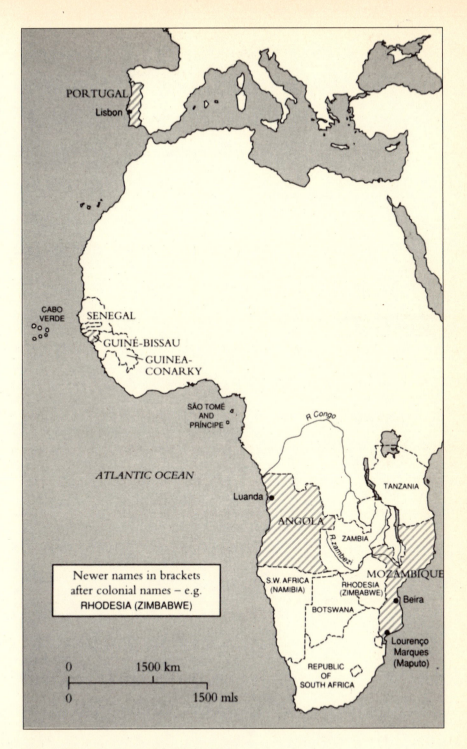

PORTUGAL
Lisbon

CABO
VERDE
SENEGAL
GUINÉ-BISSAU
GUINEA-
CONARKY

SÃO TOMÉ
AND
PRÍNCIPE

ATLANTIC OCEAN

R Congo

TANZANIA

Luanda

ANGOLA
ZAMBIA

R. Zambezi

MOZAMBIQUE

Newer names in brackets
after colonial names – e.g.
RHODESIA (ZIMBABWE)

S.W. AFRICA
(NAMIBIA)

RHODESIA
(ZIMBABWE)

Beira

BOTSWANA

Lourenço
Marques
(Maputo)

0   1500 km

0   1500 mls

REPUBLIC
OF
SOUTH AFRICA

Map 4 The Portuguese Empire in Africa.

1
INTRODUCTION

JOHN MCLEOD

POSTCOLONIAL STUDIES: SOME KEY ISSUES

In the opening chapter of J. G. Farrell's novel *The Singapore Grip* (1978), the narrator offers a panoramic vista of 1930s Singapore which contrasts the affluent European suburb of Tanglin, home to many colonial settlers, with the crowded, unruly and vibrant enclave of Chinatown and the docks, where the majority of the Tamils, Malays and Chinese live and work. Two different populations co-exist in the same location, and their two contrasting experiences of the city inevitably are intimately connected. Yet colonial Singapore is also a deeply divided city: the maintenance of an apparent hierarchy and distance between people is central to its colonial existence, as the narrator notes with pointed irony:

> up here in Tanglin people moved in a quiet and orderly way about their daily affairs, apparently detached [. . .] from the densely packed native masses below. And yet they moved, one might suppose, as the hands of a clock move. Imagine a clock in a glass case; the hands move unruffled about their business, but at the same time we can see the workings of springs and wheels and cogs. That ordered life in Tanglin depended in the same way on the city below, and on the mainland beyond the Causeway, whose trading, mining and plantation concerns might represent wheels and cogs while their mute, gigantic labour force are the springs, steadily causing pressures to be transmitted from one part of the organism to another . . . and not just at that time or just to Tanglin, of course, but much further in time and in space: to you thousands of miles away, reading in bed or in a deck chair on the lawn, or to me as I sit writing at a table.
>
> (1984: 12)

I have quoted this passage at length because we might use it to begin to discern the shape, range and some of the key concerns and problems which often preoccupy postcolonial studies. In particular, Farrell's words point to at least four issues which scholars in the field, new and old, are minded to take into consideration when engaging in postcolonial thought.

First, Farrell invites us to attend to the *demographical and geographical consequences* of European, and in this instance British, colonialism: its irreversible impact beyond Europe on lived, and built, environments, population change and demographics. Colonialism was so often a matter of terrain: seizing lands, attacking and disenfranchising the existing inhabitants of those lands, and changing the function, prior purpose and meanings of the now-colonized

1

terrain. As the Martinician intellectual Frantz Fanon described it at the beginning of his book *Les Damnés de la Terre* (1961, trans. *The Wretched of the Earth*) the colonized location is often a perversely organized one, geographically divided to cement and maintain the imaginary differences between colonizer and colonized. In contrasting the elegant and spacious European quarters often found in colonial towns with the haphazard, impoverished and cramped enclaves of the colonized, Fanon writes that '[t]his world divided into compartments, this world cut in two is inhabited by two different species' (1967: 30). The divisive territorial consequences of colonialism express and underwrite other kinds of distinctions and discriminations which often mark out colonized people as lacking the same the levels of humanity, and human rights, as the European colonizers. Colonialism transformed place, reorganizing and restructuring the environments it settled; and it also changed the people involved – on all sides – who lived in colonized locations.

Second, Farrell's sentences attend to the *material and economic realities* of colonialism. The colonized 'native masses' were often co-opted into a vast European capitalist machine which had begun to expand in the late sixteenth century, and which enabled the European colonial powers and the many individuals who pursued the aims and objectives of colonialism to amass vast fortunes and unimaginable wealth. Nearly always this involved the exploitation of, and trade in, the colonies' natural resources – the mass production of foodstuffs, the mining of precious metals and fuels – as well as its disenfranchised people. Colonialism could not have prospered without the Atlantic slave trade, which engendered the forced migration of millions of African people to the Americas as captives of Europeans; or the system of indentured labour which brought South and East Asian people to the Caribbean; or the genocidal annihilation of indigenous people in North and South America, the Caribbean and the South Pacific, whose presence hindered the capitalist designs of European entrepreneurs, keen to make their fortunes (note that this is not an exhaustive list). Colonial wealth would not have been possible without the killing, enslavement and exploitation of colonized peoples – the multitude whose interests and rights were more often than not ignored by colonial authorities. To be blunt, the fortunes and success of modern Europe – perhaps of modernity itself – depended squarely on the pecuniary pursuits of empire. Empire, colonialism and colonized peoples are not marginal, or additional, to the history of Europe, but lie at its very heart; just as the European nations have irreversibly altered the histories of the terrain and populations they colonized.

Third, Farrell points to the *unequal imaginative distinctions* between the beneficiaries of colonialism and the disenfranchised natives which normalized a sense of detachment between (in Albert Memmi's terms) the colonizer and the colonized. If the colonizers were deemed civilized, then the colonized were declared barbaric; if the colonizers were thought of as rational, reasonable, cultured, learned, then the colonized were dismissed as illogical, awkward, naïve, ignorant. European colonialism required, and made possible, inequalities

Power

of power that pivoted around apparently real yet ultimately imagined differences between colonizer and colonized.

These invented differences, which encouraged and supported endless physical acts of dispossession and cruelty, were both complex and stark. The simultaneous contempt for, and reliance on, the colonized – for labour, local knowledge, identity – made the relationship between the colonizer and the colonized at times a strangely intimate one, notable for its ambivalence and contradiction, although the operation of power in the colonies was not necessarily less effective because of this. Without the exertions of colonized peoples, colonialism could not succeed: in many parts of the world the colonizers *depended* on the energies, input and skills of the colonized to make possible the wealth they pursued. Reflecting on the education of Indian peoples in 1835, the British poet and politician Lord Thomas Macaulay argued that '[w]e must at present do our best to form a class who may be interpreters between us and the millions whom we govern; a class of persons, Indian in blood and colour, but English in taste, in opinions, in morals, and in intellect' (2006: 375). This sentiment demonstrates the extent to which colonial powers paradoxically needed the very people whom they often considered 'infrahumans' (Gilroy 2004a: 49) to succeed in their colonial aims, as well pointing out the extent to which colonialism irrevocably transformed the identities of those involved, and *on both sides*. The terms 'colonizer' and 'colonized' are not simply words which substitute precisely for, in this instance, 'British' and 'Indian'; rather, they describe particular *new kinds of identities*, inseparable from each other, that are generated by the establishment of colonialism. As Memmi points out, 'the colonial situation manufactures colonialists, just as it manufactures the colonized' (1990: 122). *Colonial relations*

loving British?

yes.

To enter into colonial relations, willingly or by force, then, is to be changed irrevocably. For Europeans travelling to colonial lands as well as those disenfranchised by Europe's empires, colonialism required and shaped certain kinds of behaviour, described and imposed new models of identity, and recodified cross-cultural relationships through European-derived models of difference and inequality. These colonial relationships, often characterized by an ambivalent mix of dependency and disdain, consequently were much more complex and variable than that implied by the simple, stark polarity of colonizer and colonized. And we must not forget those Europeans who admired the cultures of colonized peoples, or protested against their exploitation, as well as those colonized individuals who willingly serviced colonialism and prospered moderately themselves through their careful complicity with colonialism. That said, the unequal oppositional power relations required by colonialism unavoidably structured the lives of those who were caught up in the fortunes of empire, regardless of their position or point of view. Memmi's deliberate abstraction of that relationship in his binary couplet of the colonizer and the colonized importantly recognizes the primacy of these Manichean power relations which (re)produced the conflicted realties of colonial life.

Fourth, and finally for now, the quotation from Farrell's novel suggests that there remains an important hinge between distant times and places – in this instance, Singapore of the 1930s and 1940s – and the period after the decline of the European empires (Farrell was writing in the mid-1970s, by which time decolonization in the British empire was well established). This linking is both a historical or material one, and a cultural one too. The administrative and governmental realities of European colonialism may no longer be in the ascendancy at the end of the twentieth century with the coming of independence in many nations across the globe, yet *colonialism's historical and cultural consequences remain* very much a part of the present and still have the capacity to exert 'pressures' today. This is not to suggest that, despite the decline of the European empires in the twentieth century, nothing has changed. As Michael Hardt and Antonio Negri argue, the new, globalized world order of the twenty-first century is no longer primarily defined by the competing imperial aspirations of Europe's 'Great Powers', who furthered their fortunes and ambitions primarily through acts of colonial settlement. That period of history is over. Yet as they also point out, today '[t]he geographical and racial lines of oppression and exploitation that were established during the era of colonialism and imperialism have in many respects not declined but instead increased exponentially' (2000: 43). As others also point out, the world today remains firmly indebted to the history, geography and imagination of European colonialism – indeed, for Hardt and Negri, colonialism has not so much stopped as been surpassed by a new political, juridical and economic global structure, which they term 'Empire'. Think of contemporary globalization, the North's primacy over the South, or the militaristic 'war on terror'. Or consider current transnational economic inequalities, patterns of migration and demographic change, racism and its murderous consequences the world over, poverty and disease in Africa, the unresolved military conflicts in Palestine, Afghanistan, Kashmir. Each has *at least* a part of its origins in the consequences of colonialism, and remains hinged to that history in a changed and changing world today.

As Farrell's sentences importantly remind us too, not only do these consequences continue to impact on the way in which we, in our different positions, experience the world and its relative opportunities; they also impact on how we *regard* and *represent* the world. Farrell's passage closes with our attention firmly focused on the acts of *reading and writing*, and reminds us that even today these seemingly innocuous activities cannot be separated from – indeed, they may be(come) complicit in – the business of colonialism, as well as its aftermath. Postcolonial studies lays a challenge at our door: as well as needing to understand the material consequences of European colonialism, in the past and present, we must also become *inquisitive about the ways in which we come to this understanding*, through the knowledge we make and the language and terms we use in making it.

The realm of culture – of reading, writing and representation – does not exist fully beyond the social, historical and material matters of the globe. As Edward

W. Said has suggested, culture may well normalize, legitimate and encourage European colonialism:

> Neither imperialism nor colonialism is a simple act of accumulation and acquisition. Both are supported and perhaps even impelled by impressive ideological formations that include notions that certain territories and people *require* and beseech domination, as well as forms of knowledge affiliated with domination: the vocabulary of classic nineteenth-century imperial culture is plentiful with such words and concepts as 'inferior' or 'subject races', 'subordinate peoples', 'dependency', 'expansion', and 'authority'.
>
> (1993: 8)

At one level – not the only one, of course, but an important one nonetheless – colonialism was a matter of representation. The production of culture (literature, music, painting, etc.) could also reproduce imperial ideological values, and cultural creativity contributed greatly to lubricating the machine of colonization. Of course, as Said also argues, cultural practices could equally work to challenge, question, critique and condemn colonialist ways of seeing; but the crucial point to grasp is that the act of representation itself is also securely hinged to the business of empire. As Said's list of vocabulary hints, the very language we use may well be complicit in perpetuating forms of knowledge which support a colonialist vision of the world. Indeed, many of those who pursue postcolonial studies believe that by challenging and changing the ways in which we make the world meaningful, we might find new conceptual modes (however modest) of *resisting, challenging* and even *transforming* prejudicial forms of knowledge in the past and the present. The serious political and ethical goals of postcolonial studies often find their genesis in this transformative reflex.

Terrain, people and their relationships, capital and wealth, power and its resistance, historical continuity and change, representation and culture, knowledge and its transformation: postcolonial studies often involves a prolonged engagement with these issues, and several others besides, in a number of related cultural contexts – either individually, or (as is more frequent) in interdisciplinary clusters. Again, the above is not an exhaustive list, but it does open a vista on the varied and diverse work which is often regarded, or names itself, as part of the rhetoric of postcolonial studies. *The Routledge Companion to Postcolonial Studies* will also open up a number of vistas on selected European empires, postcolonial locations, conceptual reformulations and key contemporary writers and thinkers in the field, as a way of engaging the reader with the important historical and cultural consequences which persistently preoccupy the field.

HINGING THE POSTCOLONIAL

Postcolonial studies is similar to all modes of academic enquiry, in that it involves asking certain kinds of questions about selected aspects of the world.

Although it often focuses on locations with a history of colonialism and often tries to understand the world at different times from something like the point of view of its subjugated peoples, it is not a field of study which is exclusive to selected nationalities, cultures or races. The postcolonial may well be seen by some as 'the discourse of the colonized' (Ashcroft 2001: 12) in Bill Ashcroft's reductive but forceful phrase; but it is not illegible to, nor protected from critique by, any group of people. To borrow the words of Paul Gilroy, addressed primarily to the descendents of African slavery, the insights gained from the history of anti-colonial and anti-racist resistance 'will belong to anybody who is prepared to use them. This history of suffering, rebellion, and dissidence is not our intellectual property, and we are not defenders of cultural and experiential copyright' (2004a: 61).

In short, postcolonial studies has the potential to assemble new communities and networks of people who are joined by the common political and ethical commitment to challenging and questioning the practices and consequences of domination and subordination. Anyone can do it. We all come to things from our own positions, of course, and we are each of us enabled and blinkered by the location of our standpoint; but we all have something to learn from, and contribute to, postcolonial studies.

The transformative potential of the field is available – perhaps even necessary – for us all. J. G. Farrell, for example, was an Oxford-educated writer who spent a significant amount of his childhood in Ireland (his mother was Irish, his father was English), and always felt a little remote from Britain. In choosing to write about colonized Singapore in *The Singapore Grip* (part of his famous 'Empire Trilogy' of novels), Farrell was attempting to contest the ideological and cultural arrogance of empire from a Marxist-inspired critical position, primarily by satirizing the British colonial classes. He used his unique position to enable meaningful, combative critique, even if he was limited by this position too – famously, Farrell could not articulate the fall of Singapore in 1942 from the situation of its subjugated peoples, or on their terms, and so his writing remained at a remove from the 'discourse of the colonized'. This does not prevent his work from being read in terms of the postcolonial, of course (indeed, the imperious and inappropriate judging of people, places and cultural endeavours as legitimately or authentically 'postcolonial' – or not – is a major irritating distraction in the field). 'Postcolonial' more often that not describes something which one *does*, rather than something which one *is*. It is not a rosette of identitarian authenticity or ideological purity – many postcolonial thinkers are highly sceptical of such claims to authenticity – but is better considered as a challenging critical practice which demands the attention of us all.

According to Terry Eagleton, postcolonial studies is 'the most flourishing sector of cultural studies today' and 'has been one the most precious achievements of cultural theory' (2003: 6). Yet its emergence has been dogged from the beginning by scepticism, fierce criticism and, at times, hostility. Robert Fraser has remarked of postcolonial literature that it has 'grown up in full exposure to academic curiosity from its very inception' (2000: 217). The same might be said, too, of postcolonial studies, which has been subjected since its relatively recent emergence to far-reaching, prolonged and often heated critique – indeed, over fifteen years ago, in 1992, Anne McClintock poured cold water on the term by lamenting its 'panoptic tendency to view the globe within generic abstractions voided of political nuance' (1993: 293) and chiding it for being 'prematurely celebratory' (1993: 294).

Many such debates have sprung from the difficulties we encounter when trying to delimit, or at least demarcate, the remit of postcolonial studies. It is not always clear exactly what constitutes the proper terrain of the postcolonial, and there is perpetual disagreement concerning the approaches we take. Should postcolonial studies be concerned only with the historical fortunes and cultural legacies of those locations colonized by Europeans? Should it take its intellectual inspiration primarily from non-European modes of thought, or risk being compromised by its 'complicity' in Western ways of thinking? It is hard to discover consensus in postcolonial studies regarding those 'particular aspects of the world' and 'certain kinds of questions' which I mentioned above. Consequently, engaging in postcolonial studies often involves becoming involved in a shifting and inordinately unstable intellectual environment while encountering a high degree of scepticism inside the field – and, despite Eagleton's remarks, especially outside it too.

Much of the impact and controversy surrounding postcolonial studies arises from its commitment to think about, and at times theorize in complex ways, the relationship between cultural practices and the historical and political consequences of colonial settlement. This relationship has been examined often in three distinct areas. First, critics have investigated the ways in which European cultural and intellectual practices – the novel, poetry, opera, painting, anthropology, etc. – symbolized or contested the historical practice of colonialism as it happened. Second, a great deal of work concerns how once-colonized cultures have formulated their own responses to the history of colonialism and resistance to it, especially during, and in the wake of, decolonization. A third area of concern is the contemporary unequally globalized condition of the world, and the enduring exploitative cultural and national relations which suggest that, if the practice of colonial settlement belongs to yesterday, imperial pursuits continue determinedly today in the guise of transnational corporations, global capitalism and the 'war on terror'.

But even these three areas together suggest something of the difficulties involved in delimiting the terrain of postcolonial studies. Postcolonial analyses have been both geographically specific (once-colonized countries, particular European empires) and universal (globalization, migration). They have looked at the fortunes of European colonization and the history of decolonization and revolution in the past, as well as the new imperial and neo-colonial realities of the present. To complicate matters further, in recent years there has been an attempt to consider as postcolonial a number of cultural figures, historical periods and geographical areas which, at first sight, might seem to have very little to do with the business of postcolonial studies – as evidenced by collections such as Ania Loomba and Martin Orkin (eds), *Post-Colonial Shakespeares* (1998); Ananya Jahanara Kabir and Deanne Williams (eds), *Postcolonial Approaches to the European Middle Ages* (2005); and Jane Aaron and Chris Williams (eds), *Postcolonial Wales* (2005). It seems that, increasingly so today, postcolonial studies is not neatly delimited by a stable sense of geography, historical period or primary object of focus. What is it, then, which makes so many diverse areas of study, sometimes surprisingly so, 'postcolonial'?

The answer, clearly, does not lie in declaring a common historical, cultural or intellectual purview which acts as an adhesive that bonds different kinds of colonial contexts or postcolonial studies. Discontinuity, heterogeneity and diversity are perhaps the field's recurring markers. Yet postcolonial studies is not simply disparate and incoherent either; to be a field it must have some recurring elements or goals. One way of discerning the field's possible cohesion lies, I believe, in the *configuration* of that relationship between the material world and how we conceptualize it, which I mentioned towards the end of the previous section. Or, to put it differently, postcolonial studies requires us to recognize and explore the inseparable relationship between history and culture in the primary context of colonialism and its consequences.

Robert J. C. Young helps us to delineate this cohesive critical standpoint when he explains that the postcolonial condition specifies 'a transformed historical situation, and the cultural formations that have risen in response to changed political circumstances' (2001: 57). In his view, the radical practice of postcolonialism thus 'names a theoretical and political position which embodies an active concept of intervention within such oppressive circumstances' (57). Thinking postcolonially demands not only that we foreground particular kinds of historical conditions and cultural practices in our studies, but that we do so in order to expose and question the prevailing assumptions we might find there. *How* we look is as important as *what* we look at. As Bart Moore-Gilbert has argued, postcolonial criticism can be understood as primarily preoccupied with forms which 'mediate, challenge or reflect upon the relations of domination and subordination – economic, cultural and political – between (and often within) nations, races or cultures, which characteristically have their roots in the history of modern European colonialism and imperialism and which, equally characteristically, continue to be apparent in the present era of neo-colonialism' (1997: 12). This preoccupation occurs at a critical vantage which ultimately refuses to accept the legitimacy of the relations of domination and subordination. It is an attitude – both political and ethical – which is epitomized by Bill Ashcroft's announcement that the postcolonial can be thought of as a range of discursive practices and struggles which formulate 'ways of contending with various specific forms of colonial oppression' (2001: 12).

With these thoughts in mind, we might well find a shared investment in the *goals* of postcolonial studies across the work of diverse writers and thinkers:

goals of postcolonial studies

resistance, transformation, antagonism, disobedience and, ultimately, the end to all forms of intercultural domination. To enter into postcolonial studies is to engage in a self-conscious process of contestation; it is to contend often with both the *form* and *content* of prevailing knowledge. It involves learning how to look critically at the world, and the knowledge and representations that have been made about it.

For these reasons, we might begin to think about the postcolonial as a *hinged* concept, which articulates together particular historical and material conditions on the one hand, with strategic, often contestatory ways of representing, knowing and transforming such conditions on the other. It does not glibly mean 'after colonialism', as implied by the misleading axis of the hyphen in 'post-colonial' (which is one reason why we never use this spelling in this book). Rather, it is a term which describes, evaluates and helps to configure a *relationship*: between reality and its representations; between what we study and how we study it; between thought and action. It is a concept which helps us to frame and ask questions often from a particular, interested vantage, and which secures a utopian ethics at its heart. Bearing in mind our image of the hinge, we might say that the postcolonial turns in one direction towards the realms of historical experience, political upheaval and acts of dissidence; while in an other direction it revolves towards transgressive, disobedient and transformative forms of knowledge, modes of representation and ways of seeing. These forms of knowledge are negotiated through cultural endeavours *and* the critical approaches we might take to them.

The relationship between history and culture, reality and its representations, society and aesthetics, has often troubled postcolonial studies. David Theo Goldberg and Ato Quayson have raised the following question: '[i]s postcolonial theory the content of particular social referents, or the form of the discursive application of theories?' (2002: xvi). Although they worry about the banal simplification of the postcolonial if it is regarded plainly as the 'oscillation' (xvi) between these two related realms, I would suggest that their question actually poses a potentially rich way of opening up the tensions and possibilities of the postcolonial. As Stuart Hall reminds us, and as we have been considering, the postcolonial has both chronological and epistemological dimensions – in other words, it has a relationship with the particular historical periods of European colonialism and decolonization on the one hand; while on the other hand it also involves a challenge to the prevailing knowledges concerning the world and its myriad cultures which both resourced and resulted from European colonial practices. These different, yet hinged, realms often exist in a tense relationship. I agree with Stuart Hall when he writes that 'the tension between the epistemological and the chronological is not disabling but productive' (1996b: 254). In continually pushing at the limits of historical *and* epistemological confinement and propriety, postcolonial studies continually challenges – sometimes at a certain risk – the very forms of knowledge which partly have enabled its emergence and existence. Its responsibility to history pulls against its tendency to

9

'locate itself everywhere and nowhere' (Goldberg and Quayson 2002: xvi); while its epistemological possibilities push against the confinement of postcolonial studies strictly to those locations and moments affected by the consequences of European colonialism and decolonization. The sense of pulling or pushing *against* – which I think of as a kind of torsion, a twisting away from a fixed location which can never be fully unhinged – explains the often brigandly kinesis of the postcolonial, its refusal to be securely located or remain neatly 'in place'. So those of us who pursue postcolonial studies have a responsibility to eschew reductive models of the postcolonial which too tightly tether it to a particular approach, or groups of people, or set of locations.

Proceeding with Hall's sense of a productive tension *within* the postcolonial, then, I would contend that the term enables us generally to think about the relationship – which is by no means a happy or harmonious one – between, on the one hand, the geographical and historical factuality of the world during and after the decline of European colonial settlement, and, on the other hand, the new knowledges that have emerged from the imaginative and intellectual opposition to colonialist discourses across time and place, and which enable us to regard differently, and critically, the world at large. The postcolonial acknowledges both a concrete reality (the material world) and particular ways of regarding that reality (culture, representation, knowledge). As you will discover, in various thinkers' use of the term, the emphasis may fall more on one rather than the other, or perhaps across both simultaneously. Consequently, the sense of what is meant precisely by 'postcolonial' can vary quite dramatically between different critics. We must allow for these differences, perhaps even encourage them, while keeping a grip on the political and ethical purposes of the postcolonial which engender so much wide-ranging work in the field.

THE EUROPEAN EMPIRES

The Routledge Companion to Postcolonial Studies has been designed specifically to stimulate our sense of the material and conceptual aspects which are hinged at its core. It has also been structured in such a way as to contest some of the prevailing orthodoxies in the field which, towards the end of the first decade of the twenty-first century, are perhaps becoming a little dated.

Since the 1980s the bulk of work in the field has taken place in a predominantly anglophone intellectual environment. Although much postcolonial theory draws on a markedly francophone body of critical materials and thinkers – Louis Althusser, Jacques Derrida, Frantz Fanon, Michel Foucault, Albert Memmi – postcolonial thought in its early years impacted most notably in British and American cultural studies and, most importantly, the study of English and English-language literatures. Some of the field's most influential thinkers – such as Homi K. Bhabha, Edward W. Said, and Gayatri Chakravorty Spivak – write in English and have spent a significant amount of time using English literary examples when explicating their ideas. Bhabha's *The Location of Culture* (1994) engages with E. M. Forster's *A Passage to India* (1924) and Salman Rushdie's *The Satanic Verses* (1988); Said's *Culture and Imperialism* (1993) has long readings of Jane Austen's *Mansfield Park* (1814) and Rudyard Kipling's *Kim* (1901); while one of Spivak's early ground-breaking essays, 'Three Women's Texts and a Critique of Imperialism' (1985), explores work by Charlotte Brontë, Jean Rhys and Mary Shelley. In addition, postcolonial studies also in part grew out of the older field of Commonwealth literature studies, which took as its primary subject the new literatures in English written by those in, or from, countries with a history of British colonialism (McLeod 2000). So the term 'postcolonial' achieved its primary currency in English and anglophone scholarly contexts, where it established its centre of gravity by the beginning of the 1990s.

In recent years, however, significant work in postcolonial studies has appeared in (for example) francophone, hispanic and lusophone intellectual contexts. The field's centre of gravity is shifting, so that postcolonial studies is now more generally alert to the *different European empires*, and their legacies, which shaped European colonialism and made it a *variable* phenomenon – as well as the wide variety of postcolonial cultural practices throughout the world which have emerged from French, Spanish, Portuguese, Dutch and (not just) British colonialism, and often, but not exclusively, in (versions of) these transplanted European languages and artistic conventions. Recent postcolonial initiatives in francophone studies, for example, have been inspired by an unhappiness with the anglophone bias in the field, as well as the prevailing tendency to presume that the critical and conceptual models pursued in anglophone postcolonial studies can be neatly applied to non-anglophone historical contexts: the French colonization of Algeria, for example, or the Spanish and Portuguese conquest of Latin America. As the editors of an important recent collection, *Francophone Postcolonial Studies* (2003), put it, such specific colonial histories 'do not seem to correspond directly to any equivalent history in the Anglophone world, and [. . .] must consequently be more carefully analysed in order to escape the worst generalizing tendencies of postcolonial theory' (Forsdick and Murphy 2003: 6).

The Routledge Companion to Postcolonial Studies responds to these recent initiatives by ranging across four different European empires and their historical and cultural legacies: the British empire, the French empire and the Spanish and Portuguese empires. It does so cautiously: as Gayatri Chakravorty Spivak reminds us, 'there is something Eurocentric about assuming that imperialism began with Europe' (1999: 37). Indeed, the British empire in India represents only a relatively recent, and short-lived, example of a much wider history of history of conquest in South Asia dating back to, and beyond, the Mughal dynasty established in the sixteenth century. So we must be aware from the start that the colonial empires that we look at in this book collectively represent *one particular European conjuncture*, from a certain period in history, of an imperial structure – and which may not be the only one, or the most significant, to impact on certain postcolonial locations.

Hence, in Part I of this book, 'Colonial empires', a sense of the particularity *and* conjunction of selected examples of European colonial settlement will emerge comparatively. Much European colonial endeavour occurred competitively, with the different empires aspiring to match the achievements of others, and sometimes antagonistically, with European nations fighting each other over colonized territories. Many of the colonies in the Caribbean, for example, suffered more than one European master: Trinidad was a Spanish colony before the British took control in 1797, and featured a large French settler population, while St. Lucia changed hands several times between the warring British and French in the late eighteenth century. In a similar fashion, much political resistance to empire was built transnationally, with independence movements in one location often inspiring or suggesting effective dissident resources to those in another. As Elleke Boehmer has explained, for example, Irish nationalist support for the Boer minority in Southern Africa during the second Anglo–Boer War (1899–1902) productively 'opened the self-involved enclaves of Irish nationalism to inspiration from beyond the Irish diaspora' (2002: 26).

The selective focus on the British, French, Spanish and Portuguese empires of course does not exhaust European colonial projects. The Netherlands, Belgium, Germany, Italy and Denmark also were involved in colonial settlement. The Dutch were probably the world's premier colonial power in the seventeenth century, and had colonies in the Caribbean, Latin America, Southern Africa, South and East Asia and the South Pacific. Belgium maintained several colonies in sub-Saharan Africa from the late nineteenth century. Germany's brief colonial endeavours lasted from 1883 to 1919, when the newly-formed nation pursued imperial ambitions in Africa and New Guinea in the South Pacific, until stripped of their colonies after the end of the First World War (1914–18) by the Treaty of Versailles (1919). The Italian empire emerged in the late nineteenth century and included parts of East Africa (such as Eritrea and Ethiopia) and the Middle East. Denmark had small colonial settlements in India, Africa and the Caribbean. There are two reasons why this book focuses in particular on the empires of only four European nations. First, it is simply not possible to cover adequately in a book of this size and nature all examples of European colonialism. Rather than dwell briefly on an exhaustive range of examples, it may well be wiser and more productive to look in detail at four major examples of European empires, in order to come to an informed and nuanced understanding of the varied mechanics of European colonialism (which may be used to help readers when they consider further colonial contexts). Less is more, perhaps. Second, to my mind the most influential work in postcolonial studies seems to be emerging from scholars working with anglophone, francophone, hispanic and lusophone materials. As part of the ambition of this book is to open up a sense of what constitutes postcolonial studies as a field of enquiry and debate, it seems sensible to foreground these particular contexts as they predominantly preoccupy the field today. This is *not* to say that important work has never occurred in other contexts – postcolonial studies of locations with a history of Dutch colonialism quickly disprove that mistaken view. But taking the risk of being selective enables us to dwell more deeply, and with more patience, than would be possible in an encyclopaedic and inevitably fleeting engagement with the entirety of European colonialisms.

POSTCOLONIAL LOCATIONS

The second motivation for the design of *The Routledge Companion to Postcolonial Studies* concerns the frequently inadequate attention to the specifics of location in some postcolonial scholarship. Often this has been due to a rather excessive preoccupation with postcolonial theory – the new modes of representing and knowing the world made possible in postcolonial studies – at the expense of an attention to the geographical and historical specifics of colonial settlement, resistance to empire and the difficult fortunes of many once-colonized locations since independence from European rule. To return to the image of the hinge we used above, we might say that the concentration on conceptual, cultural and epistemological issues has sometimes uncoupled them from the historical and material realities of countries with a history of colonialism. In truth, it is very difficult to unhinge the cultural from the material in postcolonial studies, but at times this has seemed to be the case, especially to many critics of the field.

Indeed, many new readers in postcolonial studies are often put off by the excessive engagement with, and sometimes quite baffling vocabularies of, postcolonial theory. A lot of postcolonial scholarship has tended to work exclusively with some of the key terms popularized by the field's most visible intellectuals, which are often rendered in a synoptic and unsubtle fashion. The common and cheerful application of Said's model of Orientalism, Spivak's critique of the subaltern and the native informant, and Bhabha's discussion of ambivalence and hybridity to the work of a range of writers and artists from William Shakespeare to Salman Rushdie, has given the impression that this is indeed *all that happens or needs to happen* in order for one to 'do' postcolonial studies. Questions about the concrete conditions from which such creative endeavours emerge and which they might critically represent, or the historical and cultural specifics of postcolonial locations, are not always raised. Indeed, perhaps the biggest accusation levelled at postcolonial studies is its alleged tendency happily to liquidate historical, political and cultural considerations in the pursuit of theoretical innovation and conceptual novelty.

Taking seriously the challenging ideas proposed by thinkers such as Bhabha, Said and Spivak is certainly an important and time-consuming critical task, not least because their work has been enormously suggestive and resourceful, and represents a significant and disruptive contribution to the humanities in general. It is not possible to engage with postcolonial studies without them, perhaps; and in recent years several excellent books have appeared which introduce some of the key postcolonial theoretical manoeuvres (Childs and Williams 1997; Gandhi

1998; Moore-Gilbert 1997; Quayson 2000; Young 1990, 2001). But we are not going to get very far if we confine ourselves purely to this wing of the postcolonial hinge. The reading of, say, a novel by Michael Ondaatje with recourse only to synoptic renderings of postcolonial theory, readily available in primers and collections of explanatory essays, perhaps releases us from the responsibility of, on the one hand, engaging with the novel's relationship with cultural specifics and historical context, and, on the other hand, from drawing on other disciplines: history, anthropology, language studies, geography, economics, to name a few. As Elleke Boehmer importantly argues, '[t]o do justice to a text's grounding either in the now, or in the past, it may be necessary to draw on specialized knowledge: to find out about local politics, for example, to read up on ritual practices, or to learn to decipher unfamiliar linguistic codes' (1995: 246). This takes time, of course, and perhaps involves the acknowledgement on the part of some readers that they initially approach a cultural text from a position of ignorance and unawareness, rather than as sophisticated, aware and culturally *literate* readers. As Boehmer vitally suggests, postcolonial studies often involves us going beyond immediate generic or disciplinary boundaries, perhaps engaging with new kinds of knowledge, in order to remain sensitive to the cultural specifics of the materials we are studying.

Therefore, Part II of this book is called 'Postcolonial locations' and introduces some of the historical, geographical and cultural particularities of different regions of the colonized world. Several of the chapters here take the opportunity to think comparatively across different European empires, as in Chapter 5: Africa: North and sub-Saharan and Chapter 8: The Caribbean, for example. Many contributors approach postcolonial locations with proper regard to the hinged concerns of postcolonial studies. Hence, in the chapters in this Part the emphasis falls on key incidents and significant cultural resources, representations and endeavours which have both characterized and transformed the ways that different locations have been formulated and regarded imaginatively. These chapters are *not* exhaustive as histories of cultural accounts of postcolonial terrain – how could they be? – but rather act as critical accounts of the representation of concrete places which invite readers to begin to explore the richness, diversity and key issues which they introduce.

POSTCOLONIAL FORMULATIONS

As I have explained above, postcolonial theory has come to dominate the scene of postcolonial studies, and despite its sometimes challenging vocabularies it demands and rewards the critical attention of those who pursue postcolonial studies. Part III of *The Routledge Companion to Postcolonial Studies*, 'Postcolonial formulations', engages with some of those theoretical materials and debates which define four particular strands of conceptual innovation in the field.

I have chosen to use the term 'formulations' rather than 'theory' in this section for two reasons. First, the prevailing critical work concerning postcolonial theory tends to get tangled up in deciphering the key terms of the three major figures of Bhabha, Said and Spivak, with occasional reference to other important thinkers. It is something of an orthodox manoeuvre in the field to equate postcolonial theory exclusively with the work of the aforementioned three thinkers (ironically referred to by some as the 'Holy Trinity'), to the extent that other voices are neglected. The choice of the term 'Postcolonial formulations' at one level, then, signals an attempt to think beyond the more exclusionary vista surreptitiously implied by 'postcolonial theory'. So, in the third part of *The Routledge Companion to Postcolonial Studies*, the contributors focus on a number of important thinkers whose work has helped to formulate different kinds of critical and theoretical approaches (for a prolonged and detailed engagement with the work of the 'Holy Trinity', see, instead, Young 1990 and Moore-Gilbert 1997). These approaches have been organized for reasons of convenience and coherence into four conceptual tendencies – poststructuralist, culturalist, materialist, psychological – although, as we will see, there is often some overlap between, and debate across, these different approaches.

Second, the choice of the phrase 'Postcolonial formulations' is also motivated by the desire to keep before us that sense of the postcolonial as hinging together the material and epistemological realms, and to emphasize the fact that the seemingly rarified intellectual and conceptual pursuit of postcolonial studies may often be earthed to the realities of empire and its consequences. Let me explain with an example. In his introduction to Albert Memmi's book *Portrait du Colonisé précédé du Portrait du Colonisateur* (1957; trans. *The Colonizer and the Colonized*), Jean-Paul Sartre reflects on Memmi's vexed and complex cultural position: Memmi was born into a Jewish family in Tunisia, spoke Arabic and wrote in French, had grown up in a French colony, and was later educated in France. For Sartre, Memmi's study of the colonizer and colonized was not a history of the vexed colonial relations in Tunisia, nor an aloof or disinterested example of philosophical contemplation far from the vicissitudes of colonial life. It was another kind of book entirely, mixing together observation and critical reflection. 'Memmi's book is not a chronicle', writes Sartre. 'The author may feed on memories, but he has assimilated them all. The book is rather the formulation of an experience' (in Memmi 1990: 20). Sartre uses the word 'formulation' to hinge the realms of philosophical reflection and practical knowledge, and thus reminds us that perhaps even the most seemingly abstract postcolonial thinking may have purchase on – and may even have been moulded by – a particular kind of experience of the colonized world.

For these reasons, we must also think about the intellectual and philosophical pursuits of postcolonial theory as unbreakably hinged to social and historical realities – indeed, they may constitute *creative responses to them* within the context of academic discourse. For example, when Spivak responds to Benita

Parry's criticism of her work (and that of Homi K. Bhabha and Abdul JanMohamed) as dangerously 'writing out the evidence of native agency' (Parry 2004: 20) and silencing the voices of colonized peoples in the past, she comments that '[Parry] has forgotten that we are natives too' (Spivak 1999: 190). Spivak is *not* claiming here a privileged authenticity for her work because she happens to be a Bengali woman. Rather, her comment bears witness to the ways in which postcolonial intellectuals, in their critical approaches and use of conceptual vocabulary, have formulated an engagement with colonialism and its consequences which *cannot* be disconnected from their investment – experiential, political or ethical – in the material world.

To sum up, the choice of the term 'formulations' has been made to emphasize the ways in which postcolonial critical thought in its various modes remains hinged with the concrete and historical factuality of colonialism and its consequences, no matter how disorienting, abstract and (at first sight) baffling might appear the new critical languages which have been created as a consequence. That said, it must also be acknowledged that, for some, the new languages created to (re)evaluate and transform the world have actually made it *more* difficult to put the ethical and political goals of the postcolonial into practice beyond the academy. The possible value of new conceptual and theoretical formulations remains a hotly debated part of postcolonial studies. The 'Postcolonial formulations' section will allow us to encounter some of these current debates, as well as engage with some of the key concepts which have entered the *lingua franca* of postcolonial studies.

FROM A TO Z: SOME CONCLUSIONS

Finally, Chapter 18 of *The Routledge Companion to Postcolonial Studies* engages with forty contemporary writers and thinkers in postcolonial studies, drawn from a number of locations and historical contexts. This A–Z list may suggest coverage, but actually it is in keeping with the general spirit of the book in focusing on selected examples as a way of raising key issues while pointing to a much wider terrain. This chapter does *not* intend to define a fixed canon of postcolonial intellectuals and practitioners; although in claiming that certain figures are key to the field, it inevitably runs the risk of selectivity, censure and the accusation of cleaving the field into major and minor figures. In the spirit of this book, it is a section which is intended to act as a companion to your ongoing studies, and which will take you beyond and at times back to these figures, rather than as a complete or definitive roll-call of postcolonial thought. In addition, its selective yet varied list of thinkers also helps to emphasize the fact that postcolonial studies can be so much more than the theoretical insights, and vocabulary, of a small coterie of, albeit important, intellectuals and that its range these days takes us beyond the strictly anglophone aspect of the field which, as I have explained, has tended to dominate the scene of postcolonial studies in previous years.

Let me make one final, concluding comment. To proceed in postcolonial studies we often need to acknowledge the initial *limits* of our knowledge and approach, as well as our (perhaps unchosen, even unaware) complicity in the very modes of oppression which postcolonial studies critiques. *The Routledge Companion to Postcolonial Studies* is no exception: collectively, the work you will find in this book is similarly engendered, as well as bounded, by the locations, languages and insights of its contributors. All of us, regardless of how we consider our subject position or our relationship to colonialism and its legacies, study from a position of possibility *and* limitation. Our fortunes are also our confinements. Yet as Bhabha has famously put it, the boundary is a place of emergence, rather than the terminus of sense: 'the boundary becomes the place from which *something begins its presencing*' (1994: 5). In pursuing postcolonial studies, we would be wise to remember the example of J. G. Farrell's work with which I began: that no matter how well-intentioned we might be, or keen to bear witness to and learn from the experiences of those disenfranchised by colonialism, we must contend with our limits, perhaps even push against them, in pursuing our goals. But happening upon our limits can be a fertile, transformative experience.

It is not at all fanciful, then, to suggest that in marking out a terrain of study, in a deliberately approachable fashion, *The Routledge Companion to Postcolonial Studies* in part attempts to expose its readers (in their different ways) to that which they might not know, and suggests at the same time that the pursuit of new knowledge frequently involves a vigilant and critically self-conscious attention to the ways in which we often make knowledge about the world. As I hope is clear, proceeding from a sense of one's limits is ethical, exciting, inspiring and conscientious. There is little lasting value, and virtually no transformative potential, in merely learning new names. We have to think, and sometimes think again, if we wish to join the political and ethical purpose of the postcolonial. We should be willing to learn, and to unlearn. We must be ready for, and open to, transformation and change.

RECOMMENDED FURTHER READING

Ashcroft, Bill, *Post-Colonial Transformation* (London: Routledge, 2001).

Boehmer, Elleke, *Colonial and Postcolonial Literature* (Oxford: Oxford University Press, 1995).

Forsdick, Charles and Murphy, David (eds) *Francophone Postcolonial Studies: a critical introduction* (London: Arnold, 2003).

Harrison, Nicholas, *Postcolonial Criticism: history, theory and the work of fiction* (Cambridge: Polity Press, 2003).

Lasso, M., Thurner, M. and Gurerro, A. (eds) *After Spanish Rule: postcolonial predicaments of the Americas* (Durham, NC: Duke University Press, 2003).

Loomba, Ania, *Colonialism/Postcolonialism* (London: Routledge 1998).

McLeod, John, *Beginning Postcolonialism* (Manchester: Manchester University Press, 2000).

Moore-Gilbert, Bart, *Postcolonial Theory: contexts, practices, politics* (London: Verso, 1997).

Quayson, Ato, *Postcolonialism: theory, practice or process?* (Cambridge: Polity Press, 2000).

Young, Robert J. C., *Postcolonialism: a very short introduction* (Oxford: Oxford University Press, 2003).

Part I
COLONIAL EMPIRES

2
THE BRITISH EMPIRE

MÁIRE NÍ FHLATHÚIN

From the first English colonial ventures in the sixteenth century to decolonization in the late twentieth century, the British empire lasted around four hundred years, and included areas of land on all five continents. Its development cannot be attributed to any one cause: successive British governments, companies and individual colonists participated in the empire for profit, for national prestige, to escape conditions in their home countries and occasionally from an idealistic desire to share with the rest of the world the benefits of British civilization. Their interventions, and their interactions with colonized people, shaped the course of the world's history.

THE FORMATION OF BRITAIN

The Norman invasion of England in 1066 started a slow process of conquest and assimilation during which England, Wales and Scotland gradually became incorporated into 'Great Britain'. In the reign of Henry VIII of England, the 'Acts of Union' with Wales (1536 and 1543) ended centuries of Welsh resistance to English domination. When Henry's daughter Elizabeth I died childless in 1603, James VI of Scotland succeeded to the throne of England. Although this 'union of crowns' left both kingdoms still legally independent of one another, it marked the inception of a new political entity: a conglomerate of territories (the kingdoms of Scotland and England, and the principality of Wales) ruled from London. In a deliberate attempt to merge the national identities of Scots and English, James had himself proclaimed King of Great Britain in 1604. A century later, 'Great Britain' became the legal title of the state founded by the Act of Union between England and Scotland in 1707.

THE FIRST PHASE OF EMPIRE

The first Anglo-Norman incursions into Ireland in the twelfth century were largely an extension of the Norman conquest of Saxon England. As in the case of Wales, the establishment of English domination over Ireland was a gradual process, reaching its final stages under the Tudor dynasty. Since the coronation of King John in 1199, English monarchs had included in their titles a claim to the status of 'Lord of Ireland'. This was revised to 'King of Ireland' by Henry VIII, who induced the Gaelic aristocracy to accept him as overlord. His government also encouraged the 'plantation' of parts of the country, when large tracts of

21

land were taken over by settlers from elsewhere in the British Isles. The English claim to Ireland acquired further momentum under Elizabeth I, as successive military campaigns carried out by her commanders ended in defeat for the Gaelic forces at the Battle of Kinsale in 1601, and the death or surrender in the following years of the Gaelic lords of Ulster. Lands confiscated from the dispossessed aristocracy became the site of further plantations by English and Scots settlers. Subsequently, Ireland was both an English colony and a subjugated element of the British state. It was nominally a separate kingdom until 1801, and afterwards subject to direct rule.

The growth of English power in Ireland also had broader effects. English became established as the language of government and of economic advantage, setting in motion the long decline of the Irish language. (Scots Gaelic and Welsh were similarly affected to varying degrees, although all three Celtic languages still retain some native speakers.) Indigenous systems of economic and social organization were replaced by those on an English model. The indigenous élite classes were dispossessed or downgraded, replaced with a colonial aristocracy, although some individuals and families retained part of their wealth. These features of colonial domination in Ireland were to recur throughout the period of empire. Just as Scots had become settlers in Ireland, so many of the subordinate agents of the British empire – soldiers, civil servants and missionaries – were later drawn from Ireland, and some of the governing classes from Anglo-Ireland. English became a language of the élite and governing classes across the empire, although it never replaced indigenous languages in Africa or India to the extent that it did in Ireland.

The early seventeenth-century episodes of colonization in Ireland can be regarded as the first signs of British imperial activity, and they set a pattern for much of the later expansion of the British empire, particularly in the North American colonies. At a time when the term 'British' still signified no more than James I's desire to promote a feeling of community among the subjects of his two diverse kingdoms, the Irish plantations brought together English and Scots people in the common enterprise of settlement on foreign ground. The historian Nicholas Canny argues that the colonization of Ireland served in this way to consolidate British national identity (1998: 12). Through the process of colonialism, the evolution of Britain and its expansion into the British empire happened together.

THE ATLANTIC EMPIRE

The next phase of imperial expansion is normally referred to as the 'first empire', the 'Atlantic empire' or the 'mercantile empire' – the last term derives from Britain's perception of its colonies as an important source of raw material and a potential market. The first colonial ventures into North America were organized by the commercial and financial dealers of London, with the encouragement of the English government. The London Virginia Company was licensed by James I in 1606 and landed its first settlers in Jamestown in 1607. The Virginia colonists led a precarious existence in their first years, dependent on the indigenous Amerindian inhabitants of the area for food supplies; most of them died of starvation. The colony endured, however, and was joined in the course of the seventeenth century by other colonies spreading across the east coast of North America. They became a destination for English, Scots and Irish settlers, and for other European migrants, during the seventeenth and eighteenth centuries.

Notwithstanding the early weakness of the colonists, the balance of power in North America soon shifted in their favour. The Amerindians lived by agriculture and hunting; their communities were susceptible to disruption both materially and culturally by interaction with the newcomers. Traders and fishermen entered into commercial dealings with coastal villages, using alcohol and luxury goods as exchange media, while explorers (many still looking for Christopher Columbus's imagined route to Asia) travelled inland. The diseases carried by these Europeans spread quickly and with traumatic effect among the Amerindian population. The later arrival of increasing numbers of colonists, and their practice of agriculture, further strained relations between the two sides. The Amerindians found themselves gradually dispossessed of increasing tracts of their traditional grounds as the settlers moved westwards. Entire communities and language groups died out, both north and south of the present border between Canada and the USA. In the nineteenth century, those who had survived were relocated to reservations.

The Atlantic empire also included extensive territories in the Caribbean – collectively called the West Indies – where British rivalry with Spain drove the colonial enterprise in the early seventeenth century. Some of the islands, such as Barbados and Nevis, were settled or colonized during this period; others were later taken over from Spanish colonizers, such as Jamaica and Trinidad. The rivalry continued until victory over France and Spain in the Seven Years War (1756–63) consolidated Britain's position in the area. For European settlers, the wealth of Caribbean territories lay in their sugar plantations, a lucrative but labour-intensive industry. The indigenous inhabitants (Arawaks and Caribs) had for the most part died out, victims of disease and exploitation when the islands were first visited by Europeans. Following Cromwell's campaigns against supporters of the exiled king Charles II in the 1650s, Scots and Irish prisoners were transported to the West Indies, but white emigrants willing to work the plantations were otherwise in short supply. British plantation owners, like their Spanish and Portuguese counterparts, turned to another source of labour: Africa.

THE SLAVE TRADE AND THE END OF THE ATLANTIC EMPIRE

By the late seventeenth century the transport of African slaves to Europe and the Americas was already in progress, carried out mainly by Portuguese traders. It capitalized on the economic conditions prevalent throughout much of Africa, where indigenous economies already included the use of slaves or indentured labourers, and where rulers were anxious to acquire European manufactured goods. The triangular Atlantic slave trade linked Britain, West Africa and the West Indies from the mid-seventeenth century until British involvement in slave trading was outlawed in 1807. Ships loaded with trade goods sailed from British ports to the African coast and exchanged their cargo for people supplied by local authorities. The slaves were carried across the Atlantic (the crossing known as 'the middle passage', where overcrowded conditions contributed to disease) and sold in the West Indies. Losses caused by high rates of mortality on the seas were offset by the profits to be made on individual slaves. The triangle was completed when the now-empty slave ships were used to carry sugar, cotton and other products of the West Indian plantations back to Britain.

The practice of slavery was made illegal in all British territories in 1833, and its abolition exacerbated the economic decline of the West Indian plantations, already vulnerable to French and Spanish competition. Chinese and Indian workers were subsequently recruited as indentured labour throughout the nineteenth century, replacing the freed slaves on the plantations and contributing to the multiracial and multi-ethnic mix of the Caribbean region.

The Treaty of Paris, negotiated following the Seven Years War, left Britain the sole colonial power in North America. While the northern half of the continent, present-day Canada, remained under British control, the 'thirteen colonies' along the eastern seaboard were no longer willing to do so. In the aftermath of the war, their identity was self-defined in opposition to the British government, whose defence and taxation policies were now seen as oppressive. The American revolution began in 1775, and the Declaration of Independence was signed a year later; Britain finally recognized the United States of America in 1783.

With this defection, the most basic principles on which the empire was founded seemed to be under threat. The influential economist Adam Smith, writing *The Wealth of Nations* in 1776, decried the whole idea of empire as a means of creating and protecting trade, arguing that 'Great Britain derives nothing but loss from the dominion which she assumes over her colonies' (2001: 55–56). His view was borne out by the fact that the newly independent states of America continued to be a lucrative market for British commerce. Although the British retained their Canadian and West Indian colonies, the Atlantic empire was drawing to an end. The second phase of British imperial expansion would take place in other areas of the world.

AUSTRALIA AND NEW ZEALAND

James Cook's three voyages of exploration between 1768 and 1779 laid the foundations for the colonization of Australia and New Zealand, and stimulated British trade and missionary activity across the Pacific islands. This was, from the beginning, a new kind of colonization. While the North American settlements had been founded on land purchased from its Amerindian occupants, Cook claimed a swathe of territory along the east coast of present-day Australia for Britain on the grounds that it was *terra nullius*, empty or uncultivated land (see also Chapter 6: Australasia). This claim implicitly disregarded the indigenous inhabitants and their relationship to the land (albeit a relationship unfamiliar to Cook and his contemporaries); it remains a contentious issue to the present day. The British government used its new territory as a destination for convicts transported overseas, replacing the lost American colonies. The 'First Fleet' of convicts and their guards sailed into Botany Bay in 1788, beginning an eighty-year period during which criminals, rebels and some free settlers, mainly from England and Ireland, were landed in New South Wales. Most were never to return; convicts became landholders once their time was served. The islands of what is now New Zealand, also a destination for European settlers and freed convicts from Australia, were annexed in 1840.

The settlers of Australia and New Zealand, like the American colonists before them, rapidly assumed distinct regional identities, in a process of separation from the 'mother country' aided, for Australians in particular, by the emerging national myth of tenacious survival in a hostile landscape. They did not sever their connection with Britain, however, but became largely self-governing 'dominions' by the early years of the twentieth century. The First World War (1914–18) was a turning-point for Britain's relationship with these and its other colonies of settlement. In 1919, Australia, New Zealand, Canada and South Africa all signed the Treaty of Versailles (establishing the League of Nations) as independent states, and in so doing claimed a status in international law formally recognized by the British Parliament's 1931 legislation (known as the Statute of Westminster) to grant the dominions full independence. It should be noted that this had no substantial impact on the lives of the original inhabitants of these territories; they, like the Amerindians of the USA, found their colonized state unaffected by the new freedom of their colonizers. Even as the former colonies developed their own national identities, sometimes in strong opposition to Britain, the ties of economic advantage, culture and race-identification linking the white-settler-descended populations proved stronger in most cases than any notion of shared partnership with indigenous people.

THE SECOND EMPIRE: INDIA

Although the English East India Company (EIC) was granted its royal charter in 1600, it was over two hundred years later that the Indian sub-continent became a significant location of British colonial activity. The Mughal dynasty, rulers of India since 1526, found their power declining during the eighteenth century; while the emperor still reigned in Delhi, strong local centres of government were emerging in the rest of the country. The British traders of the EIC, like their French and other European counterparts, had long maintained a presence on the Indian coastline. Now, British and French armies manoeuvred for territory, each forming alliances with Indian rulers, and each depending partly on Indian recruits to maintain their forces. British victories in a series of actions between 1746 and 1761 established the EIC as the predominant European force in India. Robert Clive, who had already distinguished himself in action against the French, took charge of Bengal, agreeing to pay the Mughal emperor a fixed annual fee in return for full control over the state's revenues. With this move into administration, the EIC began its gradual transformation from a trading company into a semi-autonomous state, at first one of many and then the reigning power in India. From its original centres in Calcutta, Madras and Bombay, the EIC's sphere of control was expanded through military action, and through strategic, one-sided alliances with Indian rulers. It eventually covered the sub-continent, and extended to Burma, Ceylon and part of present-day Malaysia, where the 'White Rajah', James Brooke, ruled the kingdom of Sarawak. The East India Company Regulating Act of 1773 had the effect of bringing the EIC under state control; it lost its monopoly on trade in 1813, and functioned thereafter as a branch of the British government.

Unlike the white settler colonies of North America and Australasia, the Indian sub-continent never became a destination for large numbers of British emigrants. Most of those who made the journey travelled as employees of the EIC, and returned once their employment was at an end. Nevertheless, the presence of British people, and the imposition of British rule, had substantial effects on the indigenous societies of India. Bengal suffered economic decline and famine in its first years under EIC government. Across India, changes in the relationships between landholders, farmers and the state tended to disadvantage the old aristocratic classes, as well as leading indirectly to the growth of a strong middle class, especially in Bengal. The activities of missionaries – who succeeded in disseminating Western education where they often failed in making converts – and the EIC's need for English-speaking intermediaries both contributed to the rise of the English language.

By the mid-nineteenth century, the EIC's long-standing practice of managing states through 'protective' alliances had been replaced by a drive to impose direct rule. Under the 'doctrine of lapse', the British administration took over control of kingdoms where a ruler had died without a recognized male heir; other territories, including the rich and historically powerful kingdom of Oudh, were annexed on the grounds that they had been mis-governed. The disaffection thus produced among the élite classes contributed to the 1857–58 insurrection against British rule traditionally, if controversially, known as the 'Indian Mutiny'. Although the rebels held their ground for a time, and inflicted substantial losses on their opponents, the rising failed in its objective of dislodging the British. The EIC's government was replaced by direct rule from Britain, and India remained the most prized of British overseas possessions in the nineteenth century.

EMPIRE AND IMPERIALISM IN THE NINETEENTH CENTURY

Britain maintained a relatively untroubled grasp of its imperial possessions after 1858. Its main European competitors, Spain and France, had both suffered a decline in fortunes in the early nineteenth century: Spain lost many of its South American territories to revolutionary action, while the Napoleonic wars ended in French defeat in 1815. Afghanistan became the scene of disconcerting British losses in the Afghan wars of the 1840s and 1870s but, despite these reversals, British power in the area remained sufficient to deflect the threat of Russian advances towards the north-west frontier of India. The Treaty of Nanking provided for British commercial ventures to be granted access to China in the wake of the First Opium War (1839–42); it also gave Britain possession of Hong Kong. Although China was never colonized or directly subject to British rule, it remained part of the 'informal empire' of British influence until the rise of Japan altered the balance of power in the region at the end of the nineteenth century.

Imperialism was a potent idea in domestic British culture at this time. The 'Great Exhibition of Works of Industry of all Nations' (1851), intended to show-case Britain's industrial strength, brought the empire to London and reinforced its British audience's perception of their own national identity as an imperial power. In the following decades, works such as Charles Dilke's *Greater Britain* (1868) and J. R. Seeley's *The Expansion of England* (1883) identified empire with Britishness, or more specifically with Englishness, and argued for the value to Britain of its overseas possessions as well as the special fitness of the English to rule over other people. John Ruskin, an influential writer on aesthetics and society, spoke of the destiny of England in his inaugural lecture at Oxford University in 1870. He declared that England

> must found colonies as fast and as far as she is able, formed of her most energetic and worthiest men; – seizing every piece of fruitful waste ground she can set her foot on, and there teaching these her colonists that their chief virtue is to be fidelity to their country, and that their first aim is to be to advance the power of England by land and sea
>
> (1903: 37)

Some of those men and women who travelled overseas – from Scotland, Wales and Ireland as well as England – may have done so in pursuit of this ideal; others were motivated by the prospect of a better life, and assisted (or in some cases compelled) by local authorities, landlords and charitable associations who saw emigration as relieving Britain of unproductive members of its communities. British imperialism was both idealistic and pragmatic.

EMPIRE IN AFRICA AND THE MIDDLE EAST

From the 1880s onwards, amid a global economic recession, British imperialism acquired a new impetus: Japan, Russia, the USA and European countries such as Belgium and Germany were beginning to develop the means to compete as imperial powers, building modern navies and targeting the 'unclaimed' territories of Africa. British settlements in Africa were for a long time confined to four relatively small areas: Gambia, the Gold Coast (part of present-day Ghana) and Sierra Leone, founded in 1787 as a refuge for freed slaves. The fourth and most important was the Cape Colony: a Dutch settlement since the seventeenth century, it was taken over by the British in 1795. Other European countries maintained similarly limited holdings. Already, however, the social and economic fabric of Africa had been affected by interactions with Europe, not least through the slave trade. As explorers and missionaries – some, like David Livingstone, celebrities whose exploits were widely followed in their home countries – moved inwards from the coastal settlements in the mid-nineteenth century, Africa became the focus of European interests, both commercial and humanitarian.

The 'scramble for Africa' in the 1880s and 1890s saw the continent partitioned into European colonies: Egypt, the 'Central African Federation' (Northern and Southern Rhodesia, and Nyasaland), Nigeria and British East Africa were all among the territories that became part of the British empire. British defeat of the Afrikaners, longstanding rivals in Southern Africa, during the Second Boer War (1899–1902) led to the establishment of the Union of South Africa, incorporating the old Cape Colony. The practice of 'indirect rule,' particularly in sub-Saharan Africa, emphasized the role of indigenous rulers and traditional institutions, but these were incorporated within a larger colonial administration under British control. Indigenous institutions and practices, although they retained their outward form, acquired new meanings and functions within the apparatus of imperial government (as Bernard Cohn demonstrates in his analysis of British India (1987: 640–41)).

At the outbreak of the First World War, the British empire, including the self-governing dominions of Australia, New Zealand and Canada, extended over much of the surface of the globe. The colonies and dominions contributed largely to the British war effort. Following the defeat of Germany and the fragmentation of the Ottoman empire, Britain acquired other territories in the Middle East, administered under a League of Nations mandate. These included the new state of Iraq (an amalgamation of three Mesopotamian provinces) and Palestine, envisaged as a homeland for Jewish people.

THE END OF EMPIRE

Even while this final expansion was taking place, the first signs of the empire's eventual disintegration were becoming visible, most notably in Ireland. During the nineteenth century, a series of campaigns for reform on issues such as the disenfranchisement of Catholics, and the ownership and control of land, demonstrated the growing dissatisfaction of many Irish people with their status within the United Kingdom. British laissez-faire economic policies were widely blamed for the catastrophic effects of the Irish famine of 1845–51, which caused the loss of a large part of the population through death and emigration. Nationalist politicians, drawing their strength largely from the Catholic middle and lower classes, pursued their goal of 'Home Rule' for Ireland through the last decades of the nineteenth century and into the twentieth. In 1912, the British Parliament voted in favour of a Home Rule Bill; this was opposed by many in the north-east of Ireland, with its inbuilt Unionist majority of the population descended from Scots and English settlers. The law came into effect in 1914, but was suspended because of Britain's involvement in the First World War. In the meantime, Irish nationalists gathered to the militant Sinn Féin party, with public sympathy for their cause exacerbated by the British imprisonment or execution of the rebel leaders of the 1916 Easter Rising. Three years of guerrilla action against British forces ended with an agreement between the rebels and the British government that Ireland should be partitioned. The twenty-six counties of the Irish Free State became self-governing in 1922, initially acknowledging the British monarch as head of state, and from 1949 as the Republic of Ireland with no constitutional ties to Britain. Six of the counties of Ulster remain part of the present United Kingdom of Great Britain and Northern Ireland.

The rise of nationalism in Ireland was paralleled by a similar resurgence in anti-colonial feeling in British India. The evolution of a proto-national identity across the Indian sub-continent was, paradoxically, fostered by British-inspired technological innovations (notably the expansion of the railways and of print industries) which had the effect of practically and psychologically unifying the large spaces of India during the nineteenth century. At the inaugural meeting of the Indian National Congress (1886), delegates expressed Indian aspirations to self-determination as well as Indian loyalty to the British crown. India's participation in the First World War was generally supported as likely to be rewarded with Indian *swaraj*, or self-rule. When this did not materialize, Hindu and Muslim disaffection with British rule increased, as did their mutual antagonism. The peaceful resistance movement led by M. K. Gandhi drew many Indians into anti-colonial activities. By the outbreak of the Second World War (1939–45), British withdrawal from the sub-continent was all but inevitable. British India finally gave way to independence and partition in South Asia with the formation of the states of India and Pakistan in August 1947. In the same year, Palestine – now in a state of irresolvable internal conflict between Arabs and Jews – was returned to the United Nations. Ceylon (now Sri Lanka) became independent in 1948.

There were other indications at this time of Britain's waning strength in the post-war world. Although Britain had conceded Egyptian independence in 1922, the commercially important Suez Canal between the Mediterranean and the Red Sea remained under the control of its British and French owners until President Nasser of Egypt nationalized it in 1956. The military response undertaken by Britain, France and Israel was condemned by the USA, in a sequence of events eventually leading to the collapse of the British government of the day.

This episode, known as the 'Suez crisis', underlined the relative weakness of Britain, and the new influence of the USA. Britain no longer had either the will or the means to maintain an overseas empire. Across the world, British colonies underwent a more-or-less peaceful transition to independent states. The Federation of Malaya left British control in 1957. Most of the West Indian colonies (including Jamaica, Trinidad, Guyana and Barbados) became independent in the 1960s; many of Britain's Pacific Island colonies also became independent in the 1960s and 1970s.

The British empire in Africa similarly disintegrated over a period of little more than twenty years. Ghana became independent in 1957, Nigeria in 1960 and Sierra Leone in 1961. In Kenya, Mau Mau rebels attacked white settlers and fought to overthrow British rule during the 1950s. A state of emergency was imposed and the rebellion quashed, but Jomo Kenyatta, who had been convicted of Mau Mau membership and imprisoned by the British authorities, became the first prime minister of an independent Kenya in 1963. The independent state of Tanzania was formed when the former colonies of Tanganyika and Zanzibar merged in 1964. Uganda, Malawi (Nyasaland), Zambia (Northern Rhodesia), Gambia, Lesotho, Botswana, Mauritius and Swaziland all became independent states during the 1960s. Ian Smith's unilateral declaration of independence for Rhodesia in 1965 started a period of civil war, with Smith's white minority government opposed by much of the population. The country finally gained international recognition, under its newly-elected black leader Robert Mugabe, as the state of Zimbabwe in 1980.

Britain's overseas possessions are today few in number, and most have control over their own domestic affairs. The defeat of Argentina in the Falklands War of 1982 secured the British possession of the group of islands called the Falklands or the Malvinas. Gibraltar, on the coast of Spain, also remains British, although Spain has long maintained its claim to the territory. Bermuda voted against independence in 1995. Other British territories include Anguilla, the Cayman Islands, Montserrat, the British Virgin Islands and Pitcairn Island. The symbolic 'end of empire' was reached in 1997, when the British governor of Hong Kong, Chris Patten, handed control of the island back to China. A recent movement towards devolution of power within the United Kingdom has resulted in control of some domestic affairs being returned to the Scottish Parliament, and the Assemblies of Wales and Northern Ireland.

THE AFTERMATH OF EMPIRE

Although those remaining fragments of the empire comprise together only a minute fraction of the land and people once dominated by Britain, the legacy of British imperial domination remains. On the continent of Africa, and in the Middle East, the state borders established in the process of colonization and the later negotiation of independence frequently diverged from long-established ethnic or regional boundaries, resulting in conflict both within and between the newly-independent states. All Britain's colonies have been transformed by the economic, political, technological, cultural and linguistic impact of colonial domination. The British monarch remains head of the Commonwealth, an association of states which were, in most cases, once British colonies.

The domestic social and political landscape of Britain was also affected by the end of empire, in an unexpected coda to the history of British interactions with the rest of the world. Reversing the journey made by generations of British emigrants, people from the colonies and former colonies travelled to Britain after the Second World War. The British Nationality Act of 1948 conferred the status of 'citizen of the UK and colonies' on all Commonwealth citizens, thereby also granting them the right to live and work in the UK. Immigration to the UK from the West Indies and the Indian sub-continent increased in the 1960s. It was met with a hostile response from many of the indigenous inhabitants, their fear of economic competition compounded by their long-established sense of the racial superiority of white people. The legal right to citizenship was eroded and then removed by further legislation, but not before many immigrant communities had become established in British cities. Their continued presence, and their contribution to the cultural life of an increasingly multicultural country, serve as a reminder of Britain's imperial past.

RECOMMENDED FURTHER READING

Bayly, C. A. (ed.) *Atlas of the British Empire* (New York: Facts on File, 1989).

Boehmer, Elleke (ed.) *Empire Writing: an anthology of colonial literature 1870–1918* (Oxford: Oxford University Press, 1998).

Brooks, Chris and Faulkner, Peter (eds) *The White Man's Burdens: an anthology of British poetry of the Empire* (Exeter: University of Exeter Press, 1996).

Colley, Linda, *Britons: forging the nation 1707–1837* (London: Pimlico, 1992).

Judd, Denis, *Empire: the British imperial experience from 1765 to the present* (New York: Basic, 1997).

Louis, Wm. Roger (*Gen.* ed.) *The Oxford History of the British Empire*, 5 vols (Oxford: Oxford University Press, 1998–2000).

Marshall, P. J. (ed.) *The Cambridge Illustrated History of the British Empire* (Cambridge: Cambridge University Press, 1996).

Samson, Jane (ed.) *The British Empire* (Oxford: Oxford University Press, 2001).

3

THE FRENCH EMPIRE

CHARLES FORSDICK

The history of the French empire, like that of most processes of colonizing activity, is a complex and fundamentally uneven one. Characterized by expansion and contraction, decline and resurgence, instability and yet startling longevity, the French colonial enterprise lasted over four centuries and encompassed territories spread across five continents. At its height, in the inter-war period, the empire affected the lives of over one hundred million colonized people, living in an area that exceeded eleven million square kilometres. Although the empire is seen to have come to a formal conclusion with the peace treaty that ended the Algerian War (1962), evidence of its afterlife is still clear: in France's continued relationships (political, cultural and linguistic) with its former colonies; in the various territories (such as Martinique, Guadeloupe and Reunion Island) that have been integrated constitutionally and administratively into France; and in France's slow and often reluctant adjustment to its own status as a postcolonial nation state.

The continued impact of the French empire in contemporary Europe and beyond reveals the extent to which colonialism was not a monolithic process that can be reduced to and understood within clear-cut chronological limits. It is essential to avoid presenting the French empire as a single entity, resulting from a systematic programme of expansion and control. There were indeed at least two French empires, one – centred in the *vieilles colonies* (old colonies) – acquired under the *Ancien Régime* and radically reduced following the French Revolution, and another, inaugurated by the beginning of military activity in Algeria in 1830 and rapidly expanded as the century progressed, which developed into a vast French Republican empire in Africa, Indochina and the Pacific.

These successive periods of colonial expansion were far from discrete. Some of the oldest colonial territories have, for instance, had an almost unbroken connection with France since their acquisition in the seventeenth century. The nineteenth century, through the abolition of slavery, witnessed major changes in the plantation colonies of the Caribbean and Indian Ocean which had, during the previous century, been a source of great wealth. French expansion into sub-Saharan Africa radiated primarily from trading posts which had been instrumental in the earlier Atlantic trade in goods and enslaved people. To this chronological and geographical complexity, marked by clear continuities and discontinuities, is to be added a comparative dimension, for the French empire is but one (if admittedly significant) part of a globalized imperial project in which most of the major European powers were involved. Although, in the fifteenth and sixteenth centuries, the Spanish predominated in the transatlantic exploration of the New World, by the 1600s the principal rivalry over the acquisition of new territory was between England and France. This situation continued for several centuries, as is evident not least in the diplomatic and military manoeuvring during the 1775–83 American War of Independence (when the French supported the rebel colonists), as well as in the scramble to colonize Africa in the later nineteenth century. Any account of the French empire is, therefore, to be read in the light of other imperial histories, although it is important to recognize the distinctiveness of these differing national traditions. The French empire, in its nineteenth-century Republican manifestation, was, for instance, associated with a 'civilizing mission', underpinned by a belief in the superiority of French civilization. France's long-term impact was, however, more limited than that of Britain, Spain and Portugal, all of whom have been overtaken by their former colonies in terms of size and population.

THE 'OLD COLONIES': THE *ANCIEN RÉGIME* EMPIRE

During the reign of François I (1515–47), the French undertook their first significant overseas explorations. Jacques Cartier's three voyages to Canada between 1534 and 1542, during which he sailed up the St Lawrence to indigenous settlements at present-day Quebec City and Montreal, initiated the processes of settlement of 'New France'. The colony developed from the early 1600s, predominantly on the East coast of the country and around Hudson Bay, after Samuel de Champlain had founded Quebec in 1608. The first colonists led dangerous and uncertain existences, dependent for their livelihoods on trapping and the trade in furs, often developing alliances with indigenous peoples to ensure their survival. With the promotion of settlement, the population increased, and the French gradually expanded their sphere of influence into the Great Lakes area and further southwards, down the Mississippi, to New Orleans. The French territories in North America remained precarious: at the end of the War of the Spanish Succession in 1713, Acadia (present-day Nova Scotia and its surrounding regions) was surrendered to Britain, resulting in the forced emigration half a century later of many settlers to Louisiana (see Chapter 7: Canada). The Seven Years War against Britain (1754–63) proved even more damaging, for it led to the abandonment of any French claims to Canada and the loss of territories in Louisiana and Florida to the Spanish. The 1763 Treaty of Paris left France with Saint-Pierre and Miquelon, two small but strategically located islands off the coast of Newfoundland, which are still French territories today. Quebec, with a population of seven million, remains a French-speaking region in the predominantly anglophone zone of North America.

France's first overseas empire was not restricted to the American continent. The French willingness to abandon the North American territories was indeed linked to a desire to maintain their more lucrative Caribbean possessions in the same hemisphere. Companies chartered by the French government had begun exploration of the region's economic potential in the early seventeenth century, occupying a number of islands including Martinique, Guadeloupe and Saint-Domingue (Haiti). Colonists were recruited to develop sugar (and subsequently coffee) plantations for the export of produce to France. Contact with Europeans decimated the Amerindian population, and the principal workforce was acquired from West Africa, initiating two centuries of French involvement in the slave trade. The French Atlantic ports of Bordeaux, La Rochelle and Nantes prospered as a result of this commerce, and the population of enslaved people in the French Caribbean increased progressively, reaching half a million by the mid-eighteenth century. Although South America was principally colonized by the Spanish and Portuguese, the French took possession of Guyane in 1637, almost a century after Jean de Léry's voyage to the area. Guyane proved resistant to efforts at colonization (which increased after the loss of the North American territories). It remained, as a result, underpopulated, with settlers defeated and often killed by extreme weather conditions, tropical diseases and the dense rainforest that covers much of the country.

The expansion of the French slave trade led to the seventeenth-century development of trading posts in West Africa, most notably on the island of Gorée and in Saint Louis. Trade also underpinned French interests in the islands of the Indian Ocean: the uninhabited Ile Bourbon (Reunion Island) was occupied in 1642, and the Ile de France (Mauritius) settled, after the earlier withdrawal of the Dutch, in 1715. Both became prosperous plantation economies, with the former also serving as a significant centre for trade. Various efforts to settle Madagascar were unsuccessful, but, in the face of strong British competition, the French succeeded in maintaining five *comptoirs* (trading posts) in India, the most notable of which were Pondichéry (established in 1673) and Chandernagor (1688).

REVOLUTION AND THE EMPIRE

The French Revolution (1789–99) and subsequent Napoleonic Wars had a major impact on France's overseas territories. With Canada ceded to the British, the late eighteenth-century *Ancien Régime* empire consisted of the *comptoirs* in India and West Africa, Saint-Pierre and Miquelon, and the increasingly prosperous islands of the Caribbean and Indian Ocean. Although Reunion Island, and the French commercial footholds in India, were temporarily lost to the British, these were returned to France under the Treaty of Paris settlement (1814–15). The principal impact of the Revolution and its aftermath was, therefore, on the Caribbean, where the political upheaval in mainland France had effects which were undoubtedly unimagined, perhaps even unimaginable, by the revolutionaries of 1789. By the late eighteenth century, the islands of the francophone Caribbean – and in particular the largest of these, Saint-Domingue – had become a rich and productive plantation economy. Their societies were rigidly stratified, with a small minority of white planters controlling the activity of the majority enslaved black population. This racial mix was complicated by the existence of two additional groups, the *petits blancs*, a poor white population, consisting of various artisans, sailors and tradesmen, and an increasingly large free coloured ('mulatto') population, whose ownership of property created increasing resentment among the whites.

In the context of debates begun by the French Revolution, tensions between these groups soon reached crisis point, triggering extreme political upheaval in the Caribbean itself. Although the Declaration of the Rights of Man (1789) purported to offer equality for all, the majority of those proclaiming it never imagined that it would apply to the colonies. Indeed, although the elected French assemblies were granted the right to legislate on colonial issues, these remained a low priority, not least because the status quo overseas ensured continued affluence in the plantations. News of the Revolution crossed the Atlantic fast, however, and settlers in the Caribbean colonies began to question the role they would play in selecting government and exercising power. The planters, sympathetic to the King and hostile to the Revolution, toyed with the idea of self-government, whereas the *petits blancs* sought to exploit their sympathy for the revolutionary cause in order to permit a redistribution of power and property in their favour. Further tensions emerged, surrounding the voting rights of the free coloured population, and these led to inter-ethnic violence.

The principal issue, however, underpinning these other debates, concerned the future of slavery, whose abolition seemed implicit – to metropolitan abolitionists, and to the enslaved population itself – in the revolutionary slogan of 'liberty, equality, fraternity'. A slave revolt broke out in Saint-Domingue in August 1791 where, under the leadership of the former slave Toussaint Louverture, the rebels were progressively transformed into a revolutionary army (Dubois 2004). The black troops briefly fought on the side of the Spanish (colonizers of the other half of the island of Hispaniola), but, with the abolition of slavery in 1794, they rallied to the French and contributed to the defeat of the British, who had captured Martinique and Guadeloupe and occupied parts of Saint-Domingue itself. Under Toussaint, the economy and infrastructure of the island were slowly restored, until Napoleon, irritated by his Caribbean general's increasing shift towards independence, sent a major force to restore slavery and French control. Although Toussaint himself was arrested in 1802 and died in France, anti-colonial resistance remained fierce, and the independence of Haiti (formerly Saint-Domingue) was declared in January 1804 by Jean-Jacques Dessalines. Despite violent struggle, especially in Guadeloupe, slavery was reimposed elsewhere in the francophone Caribbean (and abolished only in 1848).

On the one hand, Haiti's defiance was punished by France with diplomatic ostracism followed by crippling reparations to planters; on the other hand, Martinique, Guadeloupe and Guyane were progressively drawn into a closer relationship with France, culminating in their eventual departmentalization in 1946. Napoleon's defeat in Saint-Domingue scuppered his colonial ambitions in

North America. Territory along the Mississippi valley, restored to France by the Spanish in 1803, was almost immediately sold to the USA in the Louisiana Purchase. Expansion into Egypt had already failed, and plans to challenge the British for dominance in India remained undeveloped. France thus emerged from the Napoleonic Wars greatly diminished as an imperial force. Remnants of the first empire – primarily in the Caribbean, the Indian Ocean and India – were retained, but these were rapidly to be eclipsed by territories conquered during a second wave of post-revolutionary colonization, conducted under the successive régimes, monarchical, republican and imperial, that shaped nineteenth-century France. In consolidating a centralized nation state, republican France simultaneously subjected its various regions to an internal colonialism similar in many ways to its external counterpart.

NORTH AFRICA AND THE MIDDLE EAST

Napoleon's invasion of Egypt in 1798, resulting in a brief period of French rule, is to be read more in the context of Franco–British rivalry and French designs on the Indian subcontinent than as a systematic attempt to begin colonization of North Africa. Once peace had been restored in Europe in 1815, the French nevertheless began, through diplomacy and trade, to expand their sphere of influence into the Maghreb, seeking new markets for goods and cheap sources of raw materials. The French assault on Algiers in 1830 was more the result of domestic concerns, as the increasingly unpopular Restoration monarchy attempted to consolidate support at home by flexing its muscles overseas. The conquest of Algiers, although not sufficient to protect Charles X's power, was nevertheless popular in France, signalling the beginning of a progressive 'pacification' of Algeria that would not be complete for a further eight decades. Resistance was led by a number of indigenous chiefs, most notably Abd el-Khader, but the aggressive campaigns of General Thomas-Robert Bugeaud terrorized the local population and paved the way for the transfer of much land into the hands of European settlers, many of whom arrived from Alsace-Lorraine after 1870. By 1900, these *pieds noirs* constituted one-sixth of the population. (Their economic exploitation of the country would continue until independence in 1962.) The last thirty years of the nineteenth century saw the rapid development of legal, administrative and economic structures that favoured settlers to the detriment of the indigenous population and transformed Algeria into a department of France.

French expansion into other areas of North Africa was slow to develop and differed from the intensive colonization that characterized colonial activity in Algeria. Using as their alibi a border incident during which Tunisian tribesmen had killed several Algerians, French troops landed in Tunisia in 1881, turning the country into a 'protectorate'. Morocco, on the other hand, was increasingly exploited in terms of trade. Parts of the country were occupied by Hubert Lyautey's troops in 1903, consolidating the French sphere of influence in the area, but almost triggering a major European crisis since the German Kaiser favoured continued Moroccan independence. This Morocco retained until 1912, when France inaugurated a protectorate, having in return permitted German occupation of part of the French Congo. Often fierce local resistance was only subdued in the 1930s, by which time decolonization was only two decades away. As Robert Aldrich trenchantly remarks: 'Conquering an empire was, in the case of some colonies at least, the major part of the imperial adventure' (1996: 88). The Moroccan crises nevertheless reveal the close relationship between expansionist politics and international rivalry, demonstrating the ways in which European tensions were often played out on a colonial stage.

The colonization of the Maghreb developed the consular and commercial presence of the French around the Mediterranean rim, a presence well established even before the invasion of Algeria. Although it was primarily the British who held sway in Egypt, France added further territories to its empire in the aftermath of the First World War (1914–18), when it was granted mandates by the League of Nations over Syria and Lebanon. While these involved administrative as opposed to sovereign powers, the mandates reflected longstanding French interests in the area, which the French now treated in very much the same manner as their other colonies. Under the mandate, Lebanon was expanded into Syria, creating resentment among the Syrian population and triggering an unsuccessful insurrection in 1925–27.

SUB-SAHARAN AFRICA AND THE INDIAN OCEAN

French expansion into sub-Saharan Africa differed radically from the progressive acquisition of the Maghreb. Except for a few *entrepôts* and *comptoirs* in Saint-Louis, Gorée, Dakar and Rufisque, originally associated with the slave trade, French activity in the area before the nineteenth century had been minimal. In the process dubbed the 'scramble for Africa', however, European rivalry between the 1880s and the First World War precipitated the rapid and fundamentally haphazard conquest of much of the rest of the continent, carved up over a period of thirty years into colonies that often had no relation to pre-existing ethnic and tribal boundaries. There were major obstacles to this colonization, most notably tropical disease, local resistance, impenetrable terrain and domestic apathy (or even hostility) towards colonial expansion. Under the influence of a number of single-minded and often charismatic explorers and military officers, the process was nevertheless pursued relentlessly, bringing about the destruction of the existing political, social and cultural infrastructure of millions of Africans' lives. The French aim was to extend influence from its holdings in Senegal and on the Gulf of Guinea in order to gain control of French Western Africa (AOF). It also acquired colonies in French Equatorial Africa (AEF), including most notably the French Congo and Gabon. Togo and Cameroon, a former German colony and protectorate respectively, passed to France under mandates from the League of Nations after the First World War.

Initial expansion began under Louis Faidherbe, Governor of Senegal (1854–61, 1863–65), who expanded French control inland from its existing coastal possessions. The extension of the imperial sphere into the Casamance and along the Southern Rivers Region along the Guinea coast provided new platforms for trade, but much of the acquisition of AOF (consisting of the now independent states of Senegal, Mauritania, Mali, Burkina Faso, Guinea, Ivory Coast, Benin, Togo and Niger) was motivated by the desire to thwart British and German expansionism. The landscape and climate of Niger, for instance, made this vast and sparsely populated colony particularly unattractive in commercial terms, but its location – linking northern and central Africa – granted it a strategic importance.

The French Equatorial African colonies (present-day Cameroon, Gabon, Chad, Central African Republic and Congo) were less extensive, of less economic interest and, as a result, attracted less attention than the AOF. Incursion into this region began in Gabon in 1839, when the French negotiated rights to a port and trading station at Libreville. This, and other settlements which were gradually occupied, became the base for movement inland, an expansion seen most notably in Pierre Savorgnan de Brazza's treks in the 1870s and 1880s, which established the boundaries of what would become the AEF. Fully reported in the French press, de Brazza's exploration brought African colonialism to the attention of a wider public, who were accordingly introduced to the complex rivalries in the area between France, Britain, Belgium, Portugal and Germany. This competition for territory culminated in the definitive Berlin Conference of 1884–85. Tensions persisted, however, and Franco–British competition led to the Fashoda incident in 1898. As the French sought to establish control over an area of Africa that would stretch from the Atlantic to the Red Sea, they pushed from Mali into Chad, and from there moved into Sudan where they were opposed by the British who were themselves attempting to establish a north–south corridor from the Mediterranean to the Cape. Fashoda is a further example of the impact of European rivalries on the conduct of imperial expansion.

Once territories were annexed for France, colonial administrators were often at a loss as how to develop them into colonies. Much of the AEF was eventually handed over to private companies, granted concessions to develop a commercial infrastructure. Building of the Congo–Ocean railway here was, however, slow, laborious and dependent on the brutal treatment of a primarily indigenous workforce. Despite the success of commercial forestry, the rubber and ivory trades failed to generate the profits anticipated.

France's colonies in sub-Saharan African were, therefore, concentrated in the west, although Djibouti, the one French holding in eastern Africa, had a particularly strategic importance given its location on the Red Sea. Madagascar in the Indian Ocean – on which French attempts at settlement in the 1600s and 1700s had failed – was finally annexed in the 1890s, as were the Comoros Islands in 1912.

ASIA AND THE PACIFIC

After Africa, the second major zone of French post-revolutionary expansion was in the Asia-Pacific region, contact with which was increasingly facilitated by the opening of the Suez Canal in 1914. The Pacific islands had, since the eighteenth-century publication of accounts of Polynesia by travellers such as Bougainville and La Pérouse, played a major role in the French exotic imaginary. At the same time, British predominance in the Pacific as a result of its Australasian colonies served to highlight France's clear commercial and geo-strategic weaknesses in the region. Once it became apparent that the British were keen to develop their own interests in the area, initial missionary activity in the Pacific islands was supplemented with military and diplomatic intervention.

It is very difficult to conceive of a unified 'French Pacific', so fragmented is the region in terms of its island geography as well as its complex cultural and linguistic make-up. The Pacific territories were concentrated in three groups. In Polynesia, the naval officer Dupetit-Thouars occupied the Marquesas Islands for France in 1842, establishing in the same year a French protectorate in Tahiti (eventually annexed in 1880). These formed the core of the French Oceanic establishments (EFO). In Melanesia, the islands of New Caledonia were declared French in 1853 and progressively turned into a settler colony and site of a penal institution for French criminals and political prisoners. Authority was then extended to the adjacent Loyalty Islands. Finally, in Wallis and Futuna (situated between Tahiti and New Caledonia), France created a missionary-administered protectorate in 1842 to forestall the ambitions of other major powers. The plantation colony of the New Hebrides, a Melanesian archipelago to the north of New Caledonia, reveals the international rivalry by which claims to the region were regulated. Occupied by French, British and Australian colo-nists, the islands were turned into a Franco–British condominium (often described as a 'Pandemonium') in 1905. This ambiguous status was retained until the islands' independence (as Vanuatu) in 1980.

The fragmented archipelagos of the Pacific contrast starkly with Indochina, where the French – after several centuries of commercial and missionary activity in Asia – established their showpiece colony under the Third Republic (1870–1940). Fearing the consequences of the British acquisition of Hong Kong in 1842, France sought to bolster its presence in the area. The trigger for annexa-tion was concern about the safety of French missionaries in Vietnam, and a mili-tary campaign in 1858 permitted the establishment of a permanent base in Indochina. Progressive expansion ensued, with the Mekong expedition of 1866 initiating the French assimilation of Cambodia. Activity intensified after defeat in the Franco-Prussian War, as if the domestic loss of Alsace-Lorraine might be compensated for by the acquisition of new territory overseas. There was marked nationalist resistance, particularly in Vietnam, but the political boundaries of Indochina were formally established in 1887 with the creation of the *Union indo-chinoise* (to which Laos was added in 1893). Although the Vietnamese monarchy was permitted to survive, Cochinchine was ruled by a Governor General based in Saigon, whereas Annam, Laos and Tonkin had the status of protectorates. Through education and urban planning, France endeavoured to transform Indochina into a modern colony, a rich source of mineral resources and crops, and a base for trade throughout Asia and the Pacific (Cooper 2001).

THEORIES, INSTITUTIONS AND IDEOLOGIES

Until the early twentieth century, by which time it might be argued that the end of empire was already foreseeable, there was no programmatic, centralized agenda for colonial expansion. Driven by the interests of commerce or evangelism, overseen by explorers and soldiers with individualist (even maverick) tendencies, the imperial frontier had often been extended in reaction to the ambitions of rival powers or as a result of mutual agreements among them. Imperial expansion did not occur in an ideological vacuum, but its haphazard and often opportunistic progress reveals the lack, at least initially, of any underlying systematic thought. Diplomatic incidents were often used to justify intervention, but, as the cases of Algeria and Indochina make very clear, expansionism was often motivated by the need to demonstrate the re-establishment of international authority to an anxious French domestic audience. There remained a distinct lack of consensus concerning the uses of the colonies, with attitudes to empire ranging from apathy to open hostility. Jules Ferry was one of the first, in the 1880s, to rationalize the motivations for colonial expansion in terms of commerce, political rivalry, and cultural and moral superiority. Scepticism and indifference persisted, as a result of which, in the late nineteenth century, a distinct *parti colonial* (colonial lobby) emerged, grouping pro-colonial politicians, explorers and geographers. The motivations of members of the lobby were diverse, although commercial interests were a strong factor. Convinced of the economic and strategic value of the colonies, its members argued for an extension of France's power and for a maximization of the empire's economic potential for France. Underpinning this policy was an unswerving belief in the superiority of French civilization over indigenous cultures, a guiding principal of colonial expansion that was transformed into the moral imperative of the *mission civilisatrice* (civilizing mission).

The growing awareness of the need to justify conquest and then to govern newly conquered territory led to the emergence of a much clearer colonial policy, supported by institutions that would ensure its execution. A school for administrators, the *École coloniale*, was set up in 1887 (although it was not until 1912 that it became an obligatory pathway to colonial service); a dedicated Colonial Ministry was created in 1894 (although it did not have responsibility for Algeria and the protectorates, and was forced to share major responsibilities with other ministries, such as Finance and War); and finally, during this period, a colonial education system was developed, consisting principally of rural primary schools (whose aim was to deliver some French language skills to indigenous children), and technical schools designed to staff the colonial economy.

Until the late nineteenth century, the predominant concept governing French colonial policy – and evident in the spread of colonial education – was 'assimilation', a belief that through the imposition of a single colonial policy all overseas territories could be transformed into elements of a 'Greater France'. Raymond Betts explains its popularity: 'Not only did assimilation appeal to the French love of order, belief in man's equality, and ever-present desire to spread French culture; it also appeared to provide for a uniform colonial administration' (2005: 8). The practical difficulties of applying this would-be universal model to a diverse range of colonial situations led to the emergence in the early 1900s of a more flexible policy, known as 'association', according to which – as was often the case in the British empire – control should be exercized through existing indigenous administrative and political structures. For the majority of colonized people outside a small indigenous elite, the loosely theoretical mode of administration in vogue in fact made little difference at an everyday level, not least because the universalist pretensions of French republican ideology persistently favoured some form of *francisation* (Frenchification) of colonized peoples (Deming Lewis 1962).

THE INTER-WAR YEARS: THE APOGEE OF EMPIRE?

By the end of the First World War, the French empire had achieved a stability largely unimaginable over the previous century. Although the colonial project was still subject to the challenge of indigenous resistance, especially in places such as Morocco (where the Rif War erupted between 1919–26) or Syria (where the Druze Uprising occurred in the 1920s), the rapid expansionism that characterized 'New Imperialism' had come to an end. In the Versailles peace settlement of 1919, various territories were added to the empire under League of Nations mandates, but principal efforts were channelled henceforth into ensuring that the French public was broadly sympathetic towards, even supportive of, the maintenance of a substantial overseas presence.

The involvement of thousands of indigenous soldiers – *tirailleurs indigènes* – in the 1914–18 conflict had caused the first mass displacement of colonized people to France itself. Inter-ethnic tension emerged after the war, caused especially by concerns over French unemployment, but these colonial troops proved to be the vanguard of an increasingly visible black presence in France – and especially in Paris – in the 1920s and 1930s (Miller 1998). The troops themselves, witness to horrific scenes at the Front, were forced to reassess the image of France projected through the propaganda of the 'civilizing mission'; at the same time, their involvement in the conflict developed the persistent sense of a 'dette de sang' (blood debt), in the light of which the colonies began to expect new rewards and recognition. Paris of the 1920s was the home of a number of early anti-colonial activists, such as Lamine Senghor (from Senegal) and Ho Chi Minh (from Vietnam).

Under the supervision of Maréchal Lyautey, the French government agreed to the organization in 1931 (just over a century after the invasion of Algeria) of a huge Colonial Exhibition in Paris whose aim was to persuade the inhabitants both of France and of the colonies of the benefits of empire. The *mise en valeur* (economic development) of the colonies demanded substantial financial investment, and one of the principal aims of the Exhibition was to persuade the public of the benefits of such expenditure and of the entrepreneurial colonialism it would underpin. The park at Vincennes was transformed into the empire in miniature, with the 'authenticity' of exhibits provided by indigenous extras who had been brought to Paris for the event. Over eight million tickets were sold to visitors who were more likely to have been entertained by exotic distractions than educated by the Exhibition's more serious displays. Although this demonstration of imperial power is often seen as the apogee of empire, it is important to note that the Colonial Exhibition was disrupted by anti-colonial protests: not only the Surrealist counter-exhibition, organized by André Breton and colleagues, but also a demonstration by Indochinese students against the brutal suppression of the Yen Bay rebellion in Vietnam in 1930. Indeed, in most locations throughout the history of the empire colonization had been met by indigenous resistance. This tendency was consolidated throughout the inter-war period as an early anti-colonial movement – associated with intellectual developments at the same time, such as Negritude – began to gain international coherence, credibility and strength (Wilder 2005).

ANTI-COLONIAL MOVEMENTS AND THE END OF EMPIRE

The impact of the Second World War (1939–45) on the French empire was considerable (Thomas 1998). During the conflict, most colonies had been brought under the Vichy regime by collaborationist officials (Jennings 2001), whereas a few others had rallied to the Free French, often providing troops who were instrumental in the liberation of France in 1944–45. France emerged from the war a radically altered country, and during the next fifteen years it witnessed the collapse of the empire it had spent the past century building. France recognized Syrian independence in 1946, and Lebanon had already gained its independence after British forces had confronted the pro-Vichy administration in Beirut in 1943. Seeing such inevitable shifts, General de Gaulle had convened a conference at Brazzaville in 1944, at which the idea of the '*Union française*' (French Union) had been developed. Aiming to avoid self-government and even independence in the colonies, this institution offered various constitutional reforms while ensuring that post-war France would maintain control over its colonies. In 1946, links between France and the 'old colonies' in the Caribbean and Indian Ocean were strengthened as they were granted the status of 'overseas departments', beginning a destructive process of economic and cultural assimilation that continues today.

With indigenous involvement in government limited, there was increasing anti-colonial resentment and desire for self-determination. As colonial intellectuals such as Aimé Césaire made clear, the Second World War had been a struggle against Fascism, a totalitarian doctrine which – like colonialism – depended on the dehumanization and brutalization of people on ethnic grounds. In the aftermath of the conflict, it became apparent that the days of empire were numbered (Betts 1991). In Indochina, Vichy administration during the war and Japanese occupation in 1945 led to the dislocation of the country, the north of which was administered by Ho Chi Minh. Although the French attempted to rule the colony as part of the *Union française*, their efforts in 1946 to retake the north of the region triggered the eight-year Indochinese War. France's humiliating defeat at Dien Bien Phu in 1954 led the USA to assume the role of anti-communist protector of South Vietnam, but resistance to French colonialism continued elsewhere (see Chapter 12: South and East Asia). The Indian *comptoirs* were ceded to India in 1954, and Morocco and Tunisia were granted their independence in 1956. All of France's sub-Saharan African colonies negotiated their independence in 1960, except for Guinea, which had opted to leave the *Union française* in 1958.

Unlike in Indochina, this independence was achieved through predominantly peaceful means, although for much of the post-war period, anti-colonial resistance often met with fierce repression. The massacre prompted by a nationalist uprising in Madagascar in 1947 led to the deaths of up to ninety thousand Malagasy victims, but it was the Algerian War of Independence that would have the greatest impact on domestic and colonial politics, plunging France itself into political crisis. Nationalist feeling – accentuated by the massacre of pro-independence demonstrators carried out by French troops in Sétif on VE Day – had been evident in Algeria since the end of the Second World War. The War of Independence finally broke out in 1954, after which the increasingly violent French 'pacification' of insurgents relied on the widespread use of torture. When the conflict began to affect mainland France in the 1960s, any remaining public support rapidly subsided. The conflict ended with the Evian Accords in 1962, by which time victims of the War of Independence numbered approximately half a million (Horne 2002).

THE AFTERMATH OF EMPIRE

Despite the widespread desire of both colonizer and colonized to draw a veil over the often traumatic process of decolonization, 1962 did not signal the absolute end of the French empire (Aldrich 2005; Lebovics 2004). Algerian independence led to the displacement to France of thousands of people, not least many *pieds noirs* and *Harkis* (French-sympathizing Algerians). Indeed, it is arguable that postcolonial France witnessed an ethnic diversification which was more rapid than ever, with North African workers travelling to staff the country's accelerated industrialization, and many citizens from the French Caribbean also undertaking journeys of economic migration. France retains its overseas departments and territories, although a violent pro-independence struggle in 1980s New Caledonia triggered the island's progressive change of status. At the same time, the French influence persists over former colonies, even going as far as – in the cases of the Ivory Coast and Haiti – recent military intervention. French involvement in the 1994 Rwandan genocide remains contested, but it is becoming increasingly apparent that France provided support to the majority (francophone) Hutu population. 'La Francophonie', grouping countries where French continues to have some role in communication, is seen by many to be France's means of wielding an indirect, neo-colonial influence over its former colonies.

From the 1980s onwards, French literature and cinema have revealed a certain nostalgia for empire, but there was consternation when on 23 February 2005 a law was passed obliging educators to teach students the positive aspects of French colonialism. Protests by prominent historians led to the suppression of the clause in question, but colonial history and postcolonial memory – long eclipsed by public debate over Vichy – have become increasingly visible topics of discussion. Confessions about the use of torture in Algeria have led to the wholesale reassessment of the impact of the War of Independence, and a recent public commission on the memorialization of slavery has, in addition, permitted new reflection on the role of the francophone Caribbean in the development of modern France. Equally, the November 2005 uprisings in France's suburbs revealed the persistent tensions generated by the end of empire. The supposed colour blindness of French Republican ideology, with its insistence on the universal application of principles of equality, fails to account for the practical exclusion of young people of immigrant origin from mainstream society, as well as for the 'glass ceilings' that continue to block their social progress.

While France itself struggles, in these ways, to come to terms with its own postcolonial status, one of the principal legacies of the French empire has been the emergence, across five continents, of a wider francophone world. It is undeniable that the constituent parts of this world, often still dominated by France, are joined by asymmetrical relations of power. The globalized dynamics of this francophone space suggest, however, that any neo-colonial links co-exist with a more ambiguous postcolonial interdependency. With the rise of English as a global language, the links between 'francophone' countries are likely to become more historical and cultural than explicitly linguistic. France draws from its former colonies a symbolic capital essential to the maintenance of its profile as an international force. At the same time, the diversity and autonomy of these former colonies are witness to France's subjection to a process undergone by the countries responsible for the other European empires, that of progressive 'provincialization' (Chakrabarty 2000).

RECOMMENDED FURTHER READING

Aldrich, Robert, *Greater France: a history of French overseas expansion* (Basingstoke: Palgrave, 1996).

Betts, Raymond, *France and Decolonisation* (London: Macmillan, 1991).

Deming Lewis, Martin, 'One Hundred Million Frenchmen: the "Assimilation" Theory in French Colonial Policy', *Comparative Studies in Society and History*, 4 (1962), 129–53.

Dubois, Laurent, *Avengers of the New World: the story of the Haitian revolution* (Cambridge, MA: The Belknap Press of Harvard University Press, 2004).

Forsdick, Charles and Murphy, David (eds) *Francophone Postcolonial Studies: a critical introduction* (London: Arnold, 2003).

Horne, Alistair, *A Savage War of Peace: Algeria 1954–1962* (London: Pan Macmillan, 2002 [1977]).

Lebovics, Hermann, *Bringing the Empire Back Home: France in the global age* (Durham, NC: Duke University Press, 2004).

Miller, Christopher, *Nationalists and Nomads: essays on francophone African literature and culture* (Chicago, IL: University of Chicago Press, 1998).

[The author wishes to acknowledge the kind assistance of Patrick Crowley and Kate Marsh.]

4

THE SPANISH AND
PORTUGUESE EMPIRES

CLAIRE TAYLOR

IBERIANS IN THE AMERICAS: CHRISTOPHER COLUMBUS AND THE CONQUISTADORS

The processes of Spanish and Portuguese empire building in the Americas famously began on 12 October 1492 when Christopher Columbus first set foot upon a small island in the Bahamas. Columbus had set off from Spain with the backing of the Catholic monarchs, Ferdinand of Aragón and Isabella of Castile, with the aim of reaching the Indies, and was convinced that he had secured a lucrative western trade route to the mainland of Asia.

From that moment on, the conquest and subsequent settlement of the American continent by Iberians began. After Columbus's initial voyage and his return to Spain to convey news of his venture to the royal court, the Spanish monarchs entered into their enterprise of empire building. Eager to legitimize their venture with the Catholic Church, the monarchs successfully sought a papal Bull from Pope Alexander VI which granted them dominion over all lands that would be 'discovered' by Spaniards. As Mario Góngora comments, these Bulls, which gave the monarchs 'full, free and all-embracing authority and jurisdiction' over the lands also established 'in a most emphatic manner, the obligation of sending missionaries at the king's expense' (1975: 34), indicating how, from an early date, the twin projects of conquest and conversion to Christianity were intertwined. A further crucial development in these early stages of conquest was the Treaty of Tordesillas of 1494, which intended to negotiate between the rival Iberian powers, giving Portugal a free reign in Asia and Africa while confirming Spain's rights in the New World. In fact, however, since the American land mass reached much further east than anticipated, the treaty had the effect of giving Portugal the rights to as yet unexplored Brazil (Lockhart and Schwartz 1983).

After Columbus's initial explorations of the Americas, two of the most prominent names associated with the subsequent conquest and colonization of Latin America are Hernán Cortés and Francisco Pizarro. Cortés is renowned for the conquest of Mexico and for the defeat of the powerful Aztec empire which reigned there, led by the famous emperor Montezuma. Cortés had arrived in the Caribbean island of Hispaniola in 1504, and in 1519 led an expedition to the Mexican mainland, heading inland and eventually reaching Tenochtitlán, the capital of the Aztec empire (the site of current-day Mexico City). After a series of abortive attempts, Cortés's political cunning and his capitalizing on rivalries between the Aztecs and some of their traditional enemies led to his successful taking of the Aztec capital on 13 August 1521 (for detailed accounts of Cortés's battles and conquest of Mexico see Thomas 1993).

Cortés is also famous for his association with one of the iconic figures of Mexican history and national identity: a woman called Malintzin, also known as 'La Malinche' who spoke Nahuatl, and who, according to accounts, became Cortés's interpreter and mistress. She was to provide Cortés with vital information that proved strategic in his battles against the Aztecs. La Malinche still functions as an important figure in discussions of Mexican national identity even today, and can perhaps be seen as heralding one of the first examples of hybridity in that, symbolically, the union of Cortés and La Malinche provided the first generation of Mexicans – people of mixed Spanish and indigenous origin. At the same time, her status as collaborator with the invading Spanish forces has led to her being branded a traitor by many and a source of Mexican shame rather than pride (see Octavio Paz's excellent 1950 study, *El laberinto de la soledad* (trans. *The Labyrinth of Solitude*), in particular the chapter 'Los hijos de La Malinche', for more detail on the significance of this figure).

While Cortés had increased the lands of the Spanish crown and made conquests towards the north, there were also explorers who went south, the most famous of these being Francisco Pizarro, who during the 1520s led two expeditions down the west coast of South America. On his return to Spain he told of the gold and riches worn by the inhabitants of these lands, and secured the king's permission to conquer the land and become its governor. In December 1530 Pizarro set sail from Panamá, reached what is now the coast of Ecuador, and from there went inland, waging war on the Inca empire. The Inca empire was in chaos due to a dispute over succession, and also the fact that its people were fast succumbing to a strange disease – the smallpox that the Spaniards had brought with them to the New World. Pizarro and his men seized the emperor, Atahuallpa, on 16 November 1532, and slaughtered an estimated seven thousand Indians, before finally going on to take Cuzco, the capital of the Inca empire, some months later.

With this conquest, the two most powerful empires in the Americas – the Aztecs and the Incas – were dismantled, and the Spanish empire in the New World had begun to establish itself in earnest.

PORTUGUESE ENDEAVOURS

Initially, Portugal was primarily concerned to pursue its more profitable overseas dominions in Africa and India, so Portuguese colonization in the Americas had been slower to get underway than that of the Spanish. However, while Spanish ventures of discovery and conquest were restricted, geographically, to the Americas and the Philippines, Portuguese endeavours ranged from India to China, Africa, Indonesia and some Atlantic islands. This meant not only a far wider Portuguese presence globally, but also that the Portuguese encountered a vast range of cultures, religions and commercial practices, all of which has led historian A. J. R. Russell-Wood to declare that the complexity of Portuguese overseas expeditions 'makes the Spanish experience in the Americas and the Philippines pale by comparison' (1993: 10).

From Vasco da Gama's ground-breaking voyage, rounding the Cape of Good Hope to the trading post of Calicut in India in 1498, Portuguese expansion overseas was primarily motivated by commercial concerns, with a view to controlling some of the major trade routes for gold, silver, spices and other commodities. A series of strategic overseas outposts were established by the Portuguese, including one in Goa on the west coast of India in 1510, Malacca in the Malay Straits in 1511, Hormuz on the Persian Gulf, and Colombo in 1518. These strategic posts, backed up by a series of smaller *feitoras* or fortified trading posts, meant that the Portuguese became major players in Asian and Indian trade routes. The profitability of these endeavours to the south and to the east meant that Portugal was slower to take up the opportunities for expansion and conquest in the Americas.

With regard to expansion in the Americas, the first Portuguese to set foot on American soil was Pedro Alvares Cabral in 1500, who was blown off course while on a trip to South Africa and landed on the Brazilian coast, although for more than two decades neither Spain nor Portugal was aware that this in fact constituted part of the same continent as the Spanish 'discoveries' (Williamson 1992). During the first years of Portuguese presence in the region, Portuguese interest was focused on the rich quantities of Brazil wood which were to be found in the region, and this provided the basis for Portugal's trading posts which were set up on the coastline. Portugal took little interest in this overseas colony until some thirty years later, when French attempts to rival Portuguese trading in the region prompted the Portuguese crown to establish its rule there more firmly, sending Martim Afonso de Sousa and some four hundred men to found a colony in 1530. Subsequently, between 1533 and 1535 the region was divided into fifteen captaincies, with the *donatorios* (captains) who ruled over each one having great power, including the privilege of awarding parcels of land known as *sesmarias* to other settlers.

What must be remembered, however, was that the Iberian conquest of the Americas was not simply the imposition of Spanish or Portuguese rule on an empty continent; in fact, America was inhabited by a variety of well-established civilizations, some of whom – the Incas and the Aztecs – had their own extensive and highly organized empires. The Inca empire in South America stretched from present-day Chile to Peru, and functioned through an efficient tribute system. The Aztec empire of present-day Mexico, meanwhile, had clear divisions between nobles and the lower classes, and its capital Tenochtitlán was estimated to be larger than any European city of the time. Therefore, while the actions of the invading Spaniards and Portuguese were acts of colonization, historians have pointed out that the process taking place was not a simple imposition of empire onto the indigenous subjects. An existing imperial system was in place for much of the Americas prior to Iberian settlement.

MYTHS AND CONCEPTUALIZATIONS OF THE AMERICAS

While the battles of the early conquistadors and the acts of colonization were foremost in the shaping of the relationship between Europe and the New World, a further and highly significant process was taking place at the same time, namely, the depiction of this New World in the letters, chronicles and diaries of those who were encountering it. To use Edmundo O'Gorman's now-famous phrase, the Spanish, far from describing America, were engaged in the 'invention of America'; that is, 'the historical appearance of America lay in considering the event as the result of an inspired invention of western thought and not as the result of a purely physical discovery' (1961: 4). O'Gorman's compelling argument, which has since been elaborated on by a variety of historians, proposes that the Spanish, rather than objectively describing an already existing America which they encountered, in fact actively created America, as they fashioned it according to their own European preconceptions. Initially, this invention of America can be seen in Columbus's insistence on identifying the geographical and cultural features he encountered with accounts of Asia, thus imposing pre-existing models on America.

Second, and more enduringly, even once the existence of America as a separate entity was confirmed, the accounts of conquistadors and settlers still maintained a predominantly European framework within which to see the New World. While there were some notable attempts to convey the newness and difference of the Americas in a way sensitive to the context (such as Bartolomé de las Casas's *Short Account of the Destruction of the Indies*, published in 1552), the majority of those who encountered and described America and its inhabitants tended to repeat stereotypes of otherness. Examples of the Europeanizing lens through which the conquistadors and their successors viewed the Americas can be seen in a series of recurring motifs or myths which shaped the conquistadors' motivations for exploring and settling the continent.

One of the legends which was associated with America from Columbus's first voyages to the continent, and which has proved one of the most enduring, is that of the cannibal. Columbus made several references to the existence of man-eaters in the islands he visited in his letters and in his *Journal*, yet the veracity of these accounts, and of the wave of subsequent reports of cannibals that followed, have been the subject of much debate. As historians have shown, Columbus already held the pre-conceived idea that he would encounter man-eaters in the Indies, and he insisted on identifying the terms that the inhabitants of the Caribbean islands taught him – *caníbales*, *canimas* and *caribes* – as denoting man-eaters, despite the fact that he was unable to speak their language (Palencia-Roth 1993).

Columbus sent reports of the existence of cannibals in the Spanish Indies to the monarchs, which eventually led to the 'Cannibal Law' of 1503, granting Spaniards the right to capture and sell any man-eating Indians they encountered. The significance of this law lay in the fact that previously the enslavement of Indians had been forbidden; now, the Cannibal Law provided a way to make slavery legal. Michael Palencia-Roth has further noted how this led to a rash of supposed encounters with cannibals, thus enabling the Spanish who encountered them to take them as slaves (1993: 42–43). In this way, the identification of certain peoples as cannibals was not a disinterested one, but one invested with political connotations.

A further myth frequently associated with Latin America, and whose legacy still remains in the name given to the continent's longest river, is that of the Amazons. The myth of the Amazons is an ancient legend derived from classical traditions and refashioned throughout medieval Europe. Mention of the existence of Amazons, the fearful tribe of women who assumed the role of warriors and rejected the rule of men, is made as early as Columbus's letter of his first voyage, in which he suggested there were such women living on some of the Caribbean islands (for a transcription of this letter see Zamora 1993). Other subsequent conquistadors were to follow suit, including Francisco de Orellana, who sailed the length of the great river in the American continent and gave it the name 'Amazon' due to the attacks on him by women warriors (Williamson 1992). Again, the figure of the Amazon was not one without its colonizing framing as, in the words of Restrepo, 'the erotic and dangerous figure of the Amazon [. . .] revealed a deep European fear of an inverted social order' (2003: 53), thus enabling the native Amerindians to be coded as savage and uncivilized. However, Beatriz Pastor Bodmer has noted that the Amazonian myth does not function solely through the attribution of savage and dangerous characteristics to the inhabitants of the Americas, but that it was also employed in connection with the conquistadors' thirst for gold, since, 'according to the medieval version of the myth, the Amazons lived in Far East Asia and consequently were associated with the fabulous treasures presumed to exist there' (1992: 156). Thus, the continuing myth of the Amazons fulfilled a dual function: that of presenting the native American societies as barbarous, uncivilized and as violating the accepted social order on the one hand; and that of encouraging European quests for gold and riches on the other.

The obsession with man-eaters and wild women exemplified in the cannibal and Amazon myths can be associated with a wider set of preconceptions that the Iberians brought with them to the New World, which belong to European traditions of the barbarian. In terms of Portuguese colonialism in the New World, Cecelia F. Klein has noted the tendency of early sixteenth-century explorers and their illustrators to represent the native women of Brazil as a type of female counterpart of the man-eating 'wild man' of European lore, and thus repeating pre-existing European stereotypes (Klein 1995). Moreover, the issue of the representation of women that Klein tackles is pertinent with regard to a continent frequently depicted by its European conquerors as female. This tendency can be seen in works such as Jan van der Straet's 'America' (*c.* 1600), in which, in Peter Hulme's words, 'in line with existing European graphic convention the "new" continent was often allegorized as a woman' (1986: xii). The depiction of America as female and the conquering Europeans as male is a constant in colonial images, and indicates the gendered nature of colonial imagery.

Yet not all of the powerful myths shaping Spanish and Portuguese conceptions of the Americas had a basis in European mythology or preconceptions. One of the most influential myths – and arguably the most enduring, given that the term still has currency in both modern-day Spanish and English – is one which, although it resonated with European desire for gold, has its genesis in the New World rather than the Old: El Dorado. The myth of El Dorado, which according to Enrique de Gandía's *Historia crítica* (cited in Pastor Bodmer 1992) first arose around 1534, was inspired by tales of a Chibcha ceremony in Guatavita (now in present-day Colombia), in which the Chibcha chief, covered in powdered gold, throws gold and other precious objects into the bottom of the lake. As Pastor Bodmar notes, the myth originally referred to this specific setting and ceremony, but soon became the term to describe a marvellous location with untold treasures and quantities of gold. Thus, this localized legend – which in itself has never been definitively corroborated – fuelled a whole range of myths which inspired hundreds of conquistadors to hunt for the elusive city of gold.

SOCIETY IN THE SPANISH AND PORTUGUESE EMPIRES

From the mid-sixteenth century onwards, as the efforts of the Spanish were increasingly directed towards settlement and the establishment of colonial society proper, the New World entered into what James Lockhart and Stuart B. Schwartz have termed the 'mature colonial period' (1983: 122), lasting from approximately 1580 to 1750. The vast territories belonging to Spain were divided into two viceroyalties: the viceroyalty of Nueva España (New Spain), covering the northern section of Spain's empire, from Panamá to Mexico, was ruled from Mexico City while the viceroyalty of Peru, covering Spain's lands in South America, was governed from Lima. The structure of society within the viceroyalties was hierarchical, with the highest ranking official being the viceroy, and the immense areas that he ruled over being divided into smaller administrative areas administered by *audiencias*.

A series of decrees and laws governed life in the Spanish colonies. In the early states of conquest and settlement, the famous *Requerimiento* of 1513 was set down, a legal document which stipulated that natives should submit to the Spaniards and accept the Christian faith. The document was to be read out each time the advancing Spaniards came upon a community of Indians, and failure of the Indians to comply would mean that the Spaniards were permitted to wage war on them. In effect, the *Requerimiento* placed the Indians in an impossible situation, since it meant that unless they submitted to Spanish rule voluntarily, they could be legally brought under their rule by force. Indeed, the

Requerimiento was subject to so many abuses by the Spanish, frequently involving the enslavement of the Indians, that it led to the abolition of slavery by New Laws in 1535, although, in practice, slavery continued in some regions of the Americas until as late as the mid-eighteenth century (see Góngora 1975).

While the *Requerimiento* was instrumental in conquering Indian communities and annexing their lands, other laws came into place to govern colonial life and work practices. The most infamous of these institutions was that known as *encomienda*. *Encomienda* was a system of enforced labour in which Amerindians were obliged to work for, and also in some cases pay goods to, a Spanish *encomendero*, a holder of the right to *encomienda* (for a more detailed discussion of this phenomenon, see Lockhart and Schwartz 1983: 68–71). While, in theory, the Indians were entitled to wages for their work, in practice payment was soon abandoned as their labour was considered an obligation. However, as Laura A. Lewis notes, while initially the power given to the *encomenderos* was wide ranging, over time the Crown began to limit their rights, less out of sympathy with the Indians' plight than out of a need to protect their own interests and prevent the *encomenderos* from becoming too powerful (Lewis 1996).

In addition to the regulation of colonial society by the state, the rule of the Spanish and Portuguese in the Americas was also upheld through another important institution: the Catholic Church. Associated with the conquistadors from the outset, the Church played a vital role in colonial society in the setting up of schools, universities and hospitals, as well as religious establishments. While the most notorious of the Church's institutions was the Inquisition, which began to operate in 1569 in Lima and Mexico City, scholars such as Luis Fernando Restrepo caution against overemphasizing this institution (Restrepo 2003). In addition to its educational and charitable roles, however, the Church was strongly committed to evangelism, with almost all of Latin America being converted to Roman Catholicism during the colonial period.

RACE AND GENDER IN THE AMERICAS

Since Columbus's first encounters with the native inhabitants of the Caribbean islands, the question of racial differences, and how to organize society in relation to race, preoccupied the colonial society. As a whole, colonial society in the Spanish colonies was hierarchized along racial lines: at the top of the social scale were those of Spanish parentage, either *peninsulares* (Spaniards from Spain), or *criollos* (creoles, or those of Spanish parentage born in the Americas). Even within this top echelon of society there were significant divisions, with the *peninsulares* frequently being awarded the most influential administrative and ecclesiastical positions, and the *criollos* holding positions in landowning.

Below those of Spanish ancestry was the growing group of mixed-race inhabitants of the Indies, constituted in the main of people of Spanish and Indian parentage – although this group also included significant numbers of people of Spanish and black parentage, with, to a much smaller degree, some of mixed

Indian and black parentage. It was this growing class of mixed-race inhabitants that most concerned the colonial society in its urge to classify and assign a fixed place to all its members. As several historians have noted, there developed a series of complex denominations to describe the different possible combinations of racial mixes (see Góngora 1975: esp. 161; Burkholder and Johnson 2001; Andrien 2002). The burgeoning list of terms, such as the *zambo* for a person of mixed Indian–African heritage, the *mestizo* for someone of Indian–European heritage, and the *castizo* for a person of *mestizo*–European heritage, illustrates the anxieties that colonial society felt over the status of such individuals. Yet, clearly, demarcations along racial lines were difficult to maintain as the number of mixed-race inhabitants grew. By the mid-seventeenth century, men and women of mixed origin were the largest population in most urban areas and a growing number of them began to hold skilled jobs in mines and manufacturing.

While the mixed-race population held an intermediate position in society, the indigenous population occupied the lowest rungs of the social ladder. Although initially there was some differentiation between those of a high rank within their own communities and those of a lower rank, in a relatively short space of time Spanish conceptions of the Indians tended to reduce them to a uniform mass. Indeed, the term 'Indian' itself is a European imposition since, as Lockhart and Schwartz note, it 'did not correspond to any unity perceived by the indigenous peoples' (1983: 31), and was thus an attempt to homogenize the racially and socially diverse peoples of the Americas under one catch-all term. Within Spanish colonial society, the few members of the indigenous communities who did manage to retain some of their power and status did so in the main because they proved useful to the functioning of the colonial system; that is, they worked as supervisors overseeing the labour of other Indians working for the Spanish, or the collection of tribute payments to the Spanish.

In terms of legislation, initially in the Spanish Indies there was an attempt to enforce a separation of the Spanish and Indian populations, known as the policy of the two republics. Royal orders in 1523 created two authorities: the *República de los indios* (Indian Republic) and *República de los españoles* (Spanish Republic). However, this did not mean independence and equality for the indigenous communities, but rather the opposite; this 'rudimentary apartheid policy' (Liss 1975: 43) meant that the Amerindian communities were conceived of as inferior to the Spanish ones, and also that their members could be more easily controlled. Moreover, legal and other writings continued to depict the Amerindians as inferior, frequently through strategies of infantilization and feminization (Lewis 1996).

Still lower within the hierarchy were the black members of colonial society, who had arrived in colonial Spanish America during the conquest and initial settlement, and who were, for the most part, brought to the colonies as slaves from Africa. Black peoples were prevalent in the Caribbean in particular, in the islands and throughout the mainland Caribbean coast, where the indigenous population had been all but wiped out and where the slave trade flourished.

Black slaves were also prominent, however, in New Spain, where disease had caused a sharp decline in the indigenous population, which again led to the introduction of increased numbers of black slaves. As Colin Palmer has noted, during the early colonial period, two-thirds of all Africans imported to Spanish America were destined for New Spain (Palmer 1976). Although the status of the black population of the Americas improved slowly over time with some slaves eventually able to purchase their freedom, slavery nonetheless was to become relatively widespread, with even some affluent indigenous households owning black slaves.

In terms of the racial stratifications of the Portuguese empire, the situation in Brazil was broadly similar to that within the Spanish colonies, in that the elite were composed of the white Europeans, the lower classes of the indigenous and black peoples, with those of mixed race lying somewhere between these two. In a similar way to the Spanish colonies, those of Portuguese birth held the majority of the important posts in the colonial administration and in the church hierarchy, while the *mazombo* or American-born Portuguese were the landowning class. However, that is not to say that the situation in Brazil was identical to that in the Spanish Indies, and there were several factors which meant important differences between the racial make-up of the two empires. First, since the indigenous communities in Brazil were not as highly organized as the Incas or the Aztecs, their members did not benefit from the same role of go-between accorded to indigenous supervisors and overseers in the Spanish colonies. Second, the indigenous population in Brazil died out almost completely due to enforced labour, disease and military defeat, resulting in a much stronger and earlier slave trade than in Spanish America and meaning a greater black presence in Brazil.

The issue of gender, meanwhile, intersected with that of race in colonial Latin American society. Since the initial Iberian conquerors and settlers were for the most part men, the shortage of Spanish and Portuguese women in the Iberian colonies led to these women being highly protected and controlled in colonial society. As Laura A. Lewis has commented, the status of women within colonial society was closely linked with the notion of honour, itself highly implicated in issues of race. Such women were seen by the colonial elite as the 'last line of defense for an elite intent on maintaining its dominance over mixed-races, blacks and Indians by protecting Spanish lineages, the very basis of Spanish authority, from "bad blood"'(1996: 76). In this way, the curtailment of women's freedom – above all, Spanish and Portuguese women's freedom – was intimately bound up with the attempt to control racial 'purity' and prevent interracial relations. Patricia Seed's detailed analysis of marriage in New Spain in particular has shown that although a considerable number of interracial sexual relations did occur, mixed-race children tended to be born out of wedlock due more to prejudice than to any legislation prohibiting interracial marriages (Seed 1988). Throughout the sixteenth and seventeenth centuries these status distinctions remained, but from the latter half of the seventeenth century onwards, as the mixed-race population began to grow, so too did the number of legitimate inter-racial marriages. As Seed has shown, by the end of the colonial period in New Spain approximately 25 per cent of the total population of was 'racially mixed' (25).

INDEPENDENCE

The Spanish and Portuguese empires in the New World were soon rife with divisions along ethnic and class lines, which sowed the seeds for independence movements which came to fruition in the nineteenth century. However, with a few notable exceptions – the French colony of Haiti being a case in point – the drive to overthrow colonial rule in the Americas came less from the indigenous communities than from the creoles. The growing resentment of the creole middle classes against the ruling Spanish and Portuguese elites provided the impetus for independence and the emergence of a specifically Latin American identity. A variety of factors contributed to the struggles for independence: the growing size of the population in the Americas; radical ideas stemming from the American War of Independence and the French Revolution; the increasingly disgruntled creole elite; the Napoleonic wars in Europe (see Bushnell and Macaulay 1994). Some earlier uprisings are notable – although historians caution against designating these 'precursors of independence' (Skidmore and Smith 1992: 29) – such as the 1780 indigenous revolt led by Tupac Amaru II, who claimed to be a direct descendent of the Incas. Tupac Amaru II led an army of some eighty thousand men, and was engaged in nearly two years of fighting in southern Peru and Bolivia, but was ultimately defeated.

The more lasting attempts at independence, however, came in the nineteenth century. In New Spain, while Mexico City itself remained under royalist control until 1821, in the provinces a rebellion took place in 1810, headed by the creole priest Miguel Hidalgo. Known as the *Grito de Dolores* (The Cry of Pain), Hidalgo's call to arms on 16 September is nowadays celebrated as Independence Day in Mexico. However, although garnering substantial support from *mestizos* and Indians, and making significant gains, Hidalgo was defeated near Guadalajara early in 1811 and executed. He was succeeded by José María Morelos, who proposed a new vision of society, calling for 'a new government, by which all individuals, except *peninsulares*, would no longer be designated as Indians, mulattoes, or castas, but all would be known as Americans' (Skidmore and Smith 1992: 32). The 1813 Congress of Chilpancingo declared Mexico's independence from Spain, although two years later Morelos was captured, tried and executed.

Further south, in the viceroyalty of New Granada, the most famous independence figure was Simón Bolívar, a wealthy creole born in 1783 in Caracas, who came to be known as *El Libertador* (The Liberator). Vowing in 1805 to free his homeland from Spanish rule, Bolívar led the resistance in Venezuela, and in July 1811 the Venezuelan congress declared independence. However, the rebellion was crushed and Bolívar exiled, returning two years later to continue his campaigns. By early 1819 Venezuela was firmly back in Bolívar's hands, at which point he moved east to New Granada, defeating royalist forces decisively at the Battle of Boyacá in August 1819. In December of that same year the independence of all the provinces making up the viceroyalty of New Granada was declared. Bolívar later advanced to Peru, and thence to Upper Peru, where rebel leaders declared him president for life and renamed the country after him – Bolivia.

Further south still, in the River Plate region the key independence figure was José de San Martín, born in what is now Argentina. In early 1817 San Martín led an army of five thousand across the Andes to attack royalist troops in Chile, where he won the major victory known as the Battle of Chacabuco, and entered Santiago, leading to independence for Chile. San Martín then proceeded to liberate Peru, entering Lima in mid-1821, and formally declaring Peru's independence on 28 July of that year. From there he went to Ecuador where he had a historic meeting with Bolívar, but the two leaders, unable to agree on tactics, went their separate ways.

For the Portuguese-ruled colony of Brazil, however, the gaining of independence from its colonial master was a different story. As Skidmore and Smith note, this was partly due to Brazil's relative size, being a country far more populous and wealthy than Portugal itself (1992: 35). In addition to this, Brazil had an altogether different relationship to its colonial master since, when Napoleon's forces invaded the Iberian peninsular in 1807, the entire Portuguese government decamped to Brazil. Thus, Brazil found itself in the somewhat unusual situation of being the colonial periphery governing the metropolis. The stability and unity that Brazil enjoyed, in contrast to the lengthy civil wars taking place in the Spanish viceroyalties, meant that, although some fighting did take place, the process of independence for Brazil saw far less bloodshed than that of its Spanish American counterparts. Brazil's independence is formally dated from the famous *Grito de Ipiranga* (Shout of Ipiranga) of 1822, when the monarch Dom Pedro rejected Portugal and proclaimed the independence of Brazil, establishing the first truly independent monarchy in Latin America.

It is important to note, however, that independence for the majority of the Latin American nations meant the transfer of power to a creole élite, rather than to the indigenous communities. (The first country to gain independence in the region was the former French colony of Haiti in 1804 after a slave uprising, proving a striking exception to the rule in that its leaders were the black slave underclass, who effectively expelled Europeans from the island.)

Portugal's colonies in Africa and India, meanwhile, although smaller and less geographically united than vast Brazil, were to prove more long-lasting, only gaining independence in the twentieth century. Portugal's principal African colonies of Mozambique and Guinea, which had developed from trading posts, had originally based their economies on a variety of commodities, but by the early seventeenth century they had become focused on the slave trade as the most profitable endeavour. The official abolition of slavery by Portugal in 1836 threatened these colonies as they had come to rely on a single export and, indeed, there were initially rumours in both Angola and Mozambique of severing links with Portugal itself and joining independent Brazil (Newitt 1981). However, independence did not come about as a result of the crisis caused by abolition; indeed, as Newitt has noted, this crisis in fact led to Portugal's policy to extend and consolidate its African territories, a policy which predates the general European 'scramble for Africa' by some decades.

Instead, independence for Portugal's major colonies in Africa and India was to come in the twentieth century. The first major Portuguese colony to pass into the hands of the indigenous population was Goa, a small Portuguese enclave on mainland India. After India's independence from the British was declared in 1947, Portugal initially refused to relinquish its control of Goa, although a United Nations General Assembly ruled in favour of self-determination in the 1950s. In 1961, the Indian army entered Goa, and Portugal finally recognized the sovereignty of India over Goa in the early 1970s.

In Africa, Portuguese Guinea (later named Guinea-Bissau after independence), was the first major colony to liberate itself from Portuguese rule. The African Party for the Independence of Guinea and Cape Verde (PAIGC) waged war for independence during the 1960s and by 1973 the PAIGC controlled most of the country, independence being declared on 24 September of that year. As for Portugal's two other principal African colonies, Mozambique and Angola, although independence movements in these countries were well underway, it was events in Portugal itself that precipitated their independence, in the shape of the military coup of April 1974. The instability this caused, along with liberalization and an increase in political organizations (Cabrita 2001: 72), led to the transfer of power in Mozambique to the nationalist Frente de Libertação de Moçambique (Frelimo: Front for the Liberation of Mozambique) in September 1974, with official independence being declared in 1975. In Angola, meanwhile, power was handed to a coalition government in 1974, with official independence being declared on 11 November 1975, the day on which the Portuguese left the capital.

In the post-independence era, relations between the Iberian nations and their former colonies have been in a state of flux. In the aftermath of its own Civil War (1936–39), Spain found itself in the position of sending refugees to a variety of Latin American countries, and an estimated number of three and a half million Spaniards emigrated to Latin America in the 1930s and 1940s. Today, the flow of migrants is in the opposite direction, with a notable influx of Ecuadorians, Colombians and other Latin American nationalities into Spain in recent years, attracted by improved living and working conditions. It is worthy of note that, within this context of changing relationships between metropolis and former colony, the 1992 quincentenary celebrations of Colombus's voyage to the Americas were the scene of intense debate on the nature of his venture, and even of the terms used to describe it. The controversy which arose over the use of the word 'discovery' and its implicit Euro-centric bias – the Americas were already populated by extensive civilizations who had no need of Europeans to 'discover' their own existence – led to the search for alternative terms such as 'encounter' to define the endeavour more precisely. Such debates are reflective of the continuing legacies of colonialism, and of the ongoing negotiations between Iberian nations and their former colonies.

RECOMMENDED FURTHER READING

Birmingham, David, *Frontline Nationalism in Angola and Mozambique* (London: Currey: 1992).

Burkholder, Mark A. and Johnson, Lyman L., *Colonial Latin America*, 4th edition (New York: Oxford University Press, 2001).

Góngora, Mario, *Studies in the Colonial History of Spanish America*, trans. by Richard Southern (Cambridge: Cambridge University Press, 1975).

Hulme, Peter, *Colonial Encounters: Europe and the native Caribbean, 1492–1797.* (London: Methuen, 1996).

Jara, René, *1492–1992: rediscovering colonial writing* (Minneapolis, MN: University of Minnesota Press, 1989).

Lockhart, James and Schwartz, Stuart B., *Early Latin America: A history of colonial Spanish America and Brazil* (Cambridge: Cambridge University Press, 1983).

Pastor Bodmer, Beatriz, *The Armature of Conquest: Spanish accounts of the discovery of America, 1492–1589*, trans. by Lydia Longstreth Hunt (Stanford, CA: Stanford University Press, 1992).

Russell-Wood, A. J. R., *A World on the Move: the Portuguese in Africa, Asia, and America, 1415–1808* (New York: St. Martin's Press, 1993).

Williamson, Edwin, *The Penguin History of Latin America* (London: Penguin, 1992).

Part II
POSTCOLONIAL LOCATIONS

5

AFRICA: NORTH AND SUB-SAHARAN

DAVID MURPHY

Attempting to define 'African literature' is a problematic exercise. Does one include 'Arabic' North Africa alongside 'black' sub-Saharan Africa? Does one include writing in both 'European' and 'indigenous' languages? How does one compare under a single heading texts by authors from Muslim, Christian and animist backgrounds? What does a writer from the desert-like landscape of Mali have in common with an author from the coastal, urban landscape of Lagos? In light of this diversity, the Nigerian novelist, Chinua Achebe, has written that 'you cannot cram African literature into a small, neat definition. I do not see African literature as one unit but as a group of associated units' (1975: 91). Achebe's call to examine African literature in terms of both its specificities and its generalities is a sensible one. Consequently, rather than attempting to provide an overarching explanation of postcolonial Africa, this chapter has the more modest ambition of examining certain dominant features of postcolonial literature from north and sub-Saharan Africa partly as a way of discerning a number of prevalent historical and cultural issues at large.

Discussion of postcolonial African literature often makes assumptions about the existence of a unified 'African' culture but closer inspection reveals a far more complex and problematic picture. The term 'African literature' covers a huge range of languages, cultures and colonial contexts, so this chapter will chart both connections and divergences between postcolonial African writers across the continent. In addressing the colonial legacy it is critical to bear in mind that, although empire may have been a shared experience for most of Africa, the experience of empire itself was far from uniform. Generalizations based on the specific colonial history of one part of the continent can lead to confusion: for instance, Senegal and Algeria are often cited as typical of France's colonial policy of assimilation, as they were both partially integrated within the structures of the French state. However, this was not the case for any of France's other African colonies and such a comparison hides the reality that Algeria was France's sole settler colony, with over one million Europeans, while Senegal was a colony of domination with a relatively small French military and bureaucratic presence. Thus, for the student approaching African literature, it is necessary to remain attentive to difference when attempting generalizations about the continent.

The choice of corpus for this chapter has been guided by a number of pragmatic criteria; the focus will be on the novel, which is the dominant, modern literary form, and discussion will be limited to texts in English, French,

Portuguese and Arabic, as few texts written in 'indigenous' sub-Saharan African languages exist in translation. The chapter will necessarily be limited to a few case studies discussing the work of prominent authors. However, the emphasis will be on tracing stylistic and thematic connections rather than on establishing an African literary canon that promotes a few, key authors. The texts discussed in this chapter should therefore be seen as starting points for a much wider reflection on postcolonial Africa.

CRITICAL MODELS

Within the primarily anglophone field of postcolonial studies, the analysis of African literature has largely meant the analysis of writing in English, although the exemplary comparative writings of critics such as Simon Gikandi (1987; 2003) and Abiola Irele (2001) are noteworthy exceptions to this rule. There is a large body of criticism on French-language literature but postcolonial studies has tended to focus solely on a small number of key francophone texts that have been translated into English. Writing in Arabic, Portuguese and 'indigenous' African languages has received even less attention, which can no doubt be explained by the marginal nature of these literatures and languages both within the global world order, and, consequently, within the university system. One might generalize then that experts of 'postcolonial African literature' are usually experts of the literature of *one* of the languages of Africa (the author's knowledge of French and English has, of course, guided the choices in this chapter).

If knowledge of African literature is often limited by language, then there is also a historical barrier to its study. Many critics have focused exclusively on the post-Second World War period, as though African literature had emerged solely in this period as a response to the tyranny of colonialism. A number of African languages existed in written form before colonialism, and there is, of course, a very long history of North African writing in Arabic. Even in the European languages, there exist important forerunners from the eighteenth century onwards: the autobiography of Olaudah Equiano (1789), a freed West African slave, provides an early example of the ambiguous and hybrid identities of Africans initiated into European culture; in Senegal, the mixed-race cleric David Boilat wrote a monumental study of his homeland, *Esquisses sénégalaises* (1853), in which he displays great respect for 'indigenous' culture but he also believes wholeheartedly in the civilizing powers of European culture. There is therefore a pressing need to develop a better historical understanding of African literature, in order to create a more complex genealogy of current postcolonial preoccupations.

Even where there was no written tradition, there exists in all parts of Africa a strong oral tradition of storytelling. Early critics of African texts in European languages often tried to incorporate these works into the literary traditions of Europe. However, increasingly, the exploration of the ways in which 'orality' (or 'orature') has shaped African literature has become central to literary criticism.

There have been many sophisticated and intelligent analyses exploring the connections between European literary traditions and the influence of oral narrative structures (Quayson 1997), although some of this criticism can be rather simplistic and prescriptive, viewing the extent of a text's orality as evidence of how 'authentically' African it is (arguments about the question of authenticity have been central to much critical work). As Eileen Julien has warned, the existence of oral traces within a text by itself cannot be taken as proof of its 'authenticity': African authors employ many diverse narrative strategies often engaging with orality in an oblique fashion, if at all (Julien 1992).

Language

The fragmented map of contemporary Africa bears witness to the frenzied 'scramble for Africa', which saw the major – and even some of the minor – European powers colonize much of the continent in the late nineteenth century: Britain, France, Germany, Belgium, Italy, Portugal and Spain all possessed African colonies at one time. Many postcolonial African writers have adopted the languages of their former colonizers, while others have chosen to write in 'indigenous' African languages such as Arabic and Swahili; in this polyphonic context, a singular notion of postcolonial African literature is thus deeply problematic.

In his controversial book, *Decolonising the Mind* (1986), the Kenyan author, Ngugi wa Thiong'o, argues that African authors must abandon European languages if they are genuinely to 'decolonize' their cultures; for Ngugi, using a European language forces the African writer to write primarily for a foreign audience, a process reinforced by the domination of African publishing by European-based publishers such as Heinemann (although after the failed attempts of the 1970s, new African-based publishers have emerged in the 1990s). Ngugi himself opted to write in his native language Gikuyu, claiming that this would allow him to speak directly to his compatriots. A similar unease about writing in European languages has been evident among a number of African writers: the Algerian writer Rachid Boudjedra abandoned French in favour of Arabic in the 1980s; Senegalese author Boubacar Boris Diop published a recent novel in Wolof after twenty years of writing in French; white Angolan writer José Luandino Vieira writes in a hybrid mixture of Portuguese and Kimbundu; the prominent Senegalese novelist Ousmane Sembene has found another way round the language 'problem' by leading a dual career as a French-language writer and a film director, shooting his films in 'indigenous' African languages.

This ambiguity about language should be seen as a reflection of the linguistic pluralism of most African countries; many African authors are bilingual (or multilingual), brought up in a 'native' language but schooled in a European language. The counterargument to Ngugi is that English, French and Portuguese have themselves become African languages, a position elaborated by Chinua

Achebe in the essay cited above. For Achebe and others, this is partly a prag-matic issue; Africans generally learn to write in one of the former colonizers' languages, and literature in indigenous languages has no significant, local audi-ence (equally, there are generally low literacy rates in Arabic-speaking coun-tries), while English, French and Portuguese give access to a readership across the continent, as well as globally. More importantly, African authors have often made great strides to 'Africanize' their language, adapting English, French and Portuguese to the rhythms and cadences of indigenous languages, although African writing in French has often been relatively 'classical' in approach, due to the normative nature of the education system inherited from the French empire.

AFRICAN LITERATURE (1900–1967)

This section begins with a discussion of North African literature in Arabic, as its evolution is different to the emergence of African literatures in European languages and it is also emblematic of dominant thematic and stylistic preoccu-pations of writing in the former colonizers' languages. African writing in English, French and Portuguese emerged as a result of the colonial 'encounter' with Europe; and although there is a much longer and illustrious Arabic literary tradition, primarily associated with poetry, the dominant European form of the novel emerged in the twentieth century as the principal forum for literary expression (Allen 1995). There has been an important and substantial body of work in Arabic from the countries of the Maghreb – including Mahmüd al-Misadi (Tunisia) and Mohammed Choukri (Morocco) – but it is Egypt that occupies a central position in modern Arabic writing. The 'New School' of Egyptian writing emerged in 1917, and the work of its leading practitioners, such as Mahmud Tahir Lashin, is emblematic of the ambiguous position of the colo-nized intellectual trapped between the culture of the British oppressor and that of the uneducated masses (Al-Nowahi 2000). Similar ambiguities would be traced by later generations of writers across the continent: Mouloud Feraoun (Algeria), Camara Laye (Guinea), Cheikh Hamidou Kane (Senegal), Chinua Achebe (Nigeria).

The most celebrated Egyptian novelist is Naguib Mahfouz (second African winner of the Nobel Prize for Literature in 1988); his Cairo trilogy – *Bayn al-Qasrayn, Qasr al-Chawq, Al-Sukkariyya* (1956–57, trans. *Palace Walk, Palace of Desire, Sugar Street*) – is a hugely ambitious portrait of Egyptian society from the First World War to the nationalist revolution of 1952. In a realist mode, he charts the vast changes undergone by Egyptian society as it emerged from decades of British rule. His depiction of the tyrannical but charming father figure provides a complex critique of patriarchal power within the emerging postcolonial world, one that finds echoes in much postcolonial writing. Another important example of this is to be found in the work of a fellow North African author, the Moroccan Driss Chraïbi, who paints a similar portrait of the Arab father in *Le Passé simple* (1954, trans. *The Simple Past*) but in a rather more ironic, ambiguous and experimental fashion.

The first transnational (and transcontinental) literary movement in Africa was that of Negritude, which emerged in the 1930s, and is most closely associated with the Senegalese poet-president Léopold Sédar Senghor. Bringing together writers from francophone sub-Saharan Africa and the French Caribbean, Negritude sought to restore pride in black African culture through a celebration of what it described as its sensual, emotional nature, as opposed to the dour rationalism of Europe (see also Chapter 8: The Caribbean). Critics of Negritude have rightly highlighted its occasionally simplistic vision of African culture and its adoption of European parameters for the assessment of the continent but this does not detract from the power of this literary re-imagining of Africa for an entire generation of francophone authors. As the Martiniquan theorist Frantz Fanon argues in *Les Damnés de la Terre* (1961, trans. *The Wretched of the Earth*), his hugely influential analysis of decolonization, Negritude's decision to embrace African culture – however abstract and idealized – was a crucial step in developing a nationalist, anti-colonial consciousness.

A key element in this process of celebrating African culture was the literary adaptation of tales from the oral tradition. The best example of this process is the collection of folk tales by the Senegalese author Birago Diop, *Les Contes d'Amadou Koumba* (1947, trans. *Tales of Amadou Koumba*) in which the author tells stories about Leuk the Hare, Bouki the Hyena and other well-known characters from the West African oral tradition, as well as writing original short stories, framed within the structures of the oral narrative. In anglophone Africa, the most startling example of oral narrative style is Amos Tutuola's *The Palm Wine Drinkard* (1952), which tells the fantastic story of a hapless hero who embarks on a quest in the land of the dead; deploying the oral motifs of circularity, repetition and exaggeration, Tutuola also writes in a deeply inventive language, breaking grammatical rules and creating neologisms.

Francophone African writing of the 1950s and 1960s produced much autobiographical fiction. Mouloud Feraoun's *Le Fils du pauvre* (1950, trans. *The Poor Man's Son*) and Camara Laye's *L'Enfant noir* (1953, trans. *The African Child*) are two classic examples of somewhat nostalgic narratives recounting the experiences of African children who enter the French colonial education system, undertaking a physical voyage from their villages to the city – and in Laye's case to the metropolitan centre – which is also an emotional and spiritual journey, gradually distancing them from their uneducated compatriots. A darker vision of the colonial education system is found in Cheikh Hamidou Kane's *L'Aventure ambigué* (1961, trans. *Ambiguous Adventure*). Kane's tragic hero, Samba Diallo, is torn between the 'spirituality' of African culture and the 'rationality' of Europe. The intellectual and spiritual voyage from Koranic school to French school creates a split personality that leads to madness in the case of *le fou* – an ex-soldier in the colonial army traumatized by his experience of war – and to death for Samba Diallo, when he is murdered by *le fou* for refusing to renounce the influence of Europe.

Chinua Achebe's novel *Things Fall Apart* (1958) includes an anglophone perspective on colonial education. One element of its narrative tells of a son growing apart from his father's traditional culture when he is enrolled in the missionary school. This provides an instructive comparison between the francophone and anglophone colonial contexts. Samba Diallo's obsession with learning the colonizer's language has been repeated in many francophone African texts. However, in Achebe's text it is religion that is a determining factor in alienating educated young Africans from their parents. The secular French Republic won over its African schoolchildren with the all-encompassing embrace of its universal language and values, not the loving embrace of Jesus (there were very few French Catholic schools).

Kane and Achebe highlight the ambiguities produced by the colonial encounter, but there was also a very strong vein of anti-colonial nationalist writing, especially in French, whose primary concern was to imagine a new nation that might replace the old colonial order: *Nedjma* (1954) by the Algerian author Kateb Yacine is a highly complex, mythical narrative of Algeria's struggle for independence; Ousmane Sembene deploys a romantic realism to create an epic, anti-colonial narrative in *Les Bouts de bois de Dieu* (1960, trans. *God's Bits of Wood*), which casts the struggle against colonialism in Marxist terms; Ngugi wa Thiong'o charts the Kenyan struggle for nationhood in similarly realist style in his novels *Weep Not, Child* (1964) and *The River Between* (1965). For such writers, anti-colonial nationalism was a revolutionary process, bringing about the creation of new societies, and new types of African. They identified with Fanon's depiction of the postcolonial writer as an active participant in this social, cultural and political transformation.

Most African writers of this period belonged to a relatively privileged elite, which had access to European schooling (Tutuola and Semebene are exceptions, as they had little formal education). Within this elite, there were virtually no women and, consequently, there were few women writers until the 1960s. Anglophone Africa saw the emergence of women writers about a decade earlier than francophone Africa, perhaps because the British had promoted greater female participation in education. The Nigerians, Flora Nwapa and Buchi Emecheta, and the Ghanaian Ama Ata Aidoo all began their careers in the 1960s, although they were marginalized within a male-dominated literary establishment.

The belated decolonization of Portugal's African colonies in the 1970s, after bitter wars of independence, means that their anti-colonial writing largely appeared towards the end of, and after, the period under discussion here (Peres 1997). Many of the most important lusophone authors were also heavily involved in the independence movement: the Angolan resistance leader, Agostinho Neto, was a renowned poet; Angolan author José Luandino Vieira was imprisoned for his part in the resistance movement. Another key lusophone writer is Amílcar Cabral, leader of the resistance movement in Guinea-Bissau and the Cape Verde islands. A theorist rather than a creative writer, Cabral has become an important figure in postcolonial studies for his analysis of the process of decolonization in English-language collections such as *Return to the Source* (1973) and *Unity and Struggle* (1980). He has thus become a lusophone counterpart to Frantz Fanon, who wrote primarily about Algeria's traumatic war of independence against France (1954–62), and to anglophone writers/independence leaders, such as Jomo Kenyatta (Kenya) and Kwame Nkrumah (Ghana).

AFRICAN LITERATURE (1968–2004)

It has become commonplace in criticism of African literature to argue that the post-independence period has been marked by a shift away from anti-colonial certainties to a more troubled questioning of the newly independent African nations. There is no precise moment at which this shift occurs, although 1968 has a particular resonance within the francophone context as that year witnessed the publication of two hugely important texts: *Les Soleils des indépendances* (trans. *The Suns of Independence*) by Ahmadou Kourouma (Ivory Coast) and *Le Devoir de violence* (trans. *Bound to Violence*) by Yambo Ouologuem (Mali). Kourouma's novel employed a startlingly hybrid French, laden with direct translations from Malinke, in relating the tragicomic tale of a former prince fallen on hard times in the new Africa of the one-party state. Ouologuem's was an even more striking novel, using an array of styles in a devastating satire of the African nobility, cast as the true oppressors of the common African. For the influential Ghanaian critic Kwame Appiah, Ouologuem's novel represents a 'post-national' stage in African writing, when the dream of national liberation from empire was replaced by the nightmare of so many failed independent African states (1992: 150–52).

This 'post-national' stage saw satire, ambiguity and hybridity become the dominant motifs of much African fiction from the 1970s onwards. There was also a pronounced move away from realist narratives to more fragmentary and experimental styles. The previous generation of writers had sought to develop narratives of resistance against empire and to imagine a national consciousness for the emerging African nations. However, the ethnic tensions, widespread poverty and oppressive regimes in many emerging African nations, as well as the continuing dependence on Europe, led many writers to question the whole nationalist project in their writing. These young authors related fragmented stories, often employing a range of narrative voices, which has seen them classified by some critics as 'postmodern', in that they reject the linear, realist narrative styles of the nationalist generation, which are deemed to have employed simplistic binary oppositions between Africa and Europe in order to create a unified picture of the new African nations. Instead, these younger authors are seen by many critics to represent the ambiguities at the heart of the postcolonial nation state.

However, it would be incorrect to present their work as the 'true voice' of post-independence African writing, just as it is far too generalizing to claim that all nationalist literature is reductive in its portrayal of the nation after colonialism. Many of the anti-colonial generation of writers, far from simplistically repeating the certainties of the anti-colonial struggle, also sought to chart the problems of independence. Chinua Achebe's novel, *No Longer at Ease* (1960) relates the story of an idealistic young Nigerian student who returns from university in Britain and becomes mired in corruption and disillusionment. The work of Sembene – *Voltaïque* (trans. *Tribal Scars* 1962) and *Xala* (1973) – and Ngugi – *A Grain of Wheat* (1967), *Devil on the Cross* (1982) – also charts the problems besetting post-independence Senegal and Kenya respectively from a specifically Marxist-inflected standpoint. Their work forms an important rejoinder to those who would see all postcolonial fiction as post-ideological: they denounce the ongoing western domination of Africa but not at the expense of a complex portrayal of the competing voices within postcolonial African nations.

At the other end of the political spectrum to Sembene and Ngugi are the many 'traditionalist' writers, frequently publishing with 'local' African publishers, whose work often bemoans the incursion of western modernity into Africa, and instead promotes a return to 'authentic', traditional values. In her pioneering work on Ghanaian popular fiction, Stephanie Newell argues that this 'local' African work is often viewed as simplistic by postcolonial theorists, who instead celebrate the work of 'international' African authors based in the West, whose texts are seen to explore Africa within the context of a globalized hybridity (Newell 2000). However, for Newell, 'local' texts are as aware of 'global' trends in ideas as their 'international' counterparts; they just treat these matters in a very different fashion.

What then of this important, internationally published, 'post-national' African fiction, which has been at the heart of postcolonial theory's analysis of contemporary Africa? If Kourouma and Ouologuem launched this tradition in francophone Africa, then Wole Soyinka – first African winner of the Nobel Prize for Literature in 1986 – and the Ghanaian Ayi Kwei Armah are central to its anglophone development. In his poetry, plays and novels (such as *The Interpreters*, 1965), Soyinka explores, in grimly comic fashion, the sense of despair at the corruption and repression at the heart of many post-independence regimes. Armah's novels, in particular, *The Beautyful Ones are not yet Born* (1968), have become emblematic of a profoundly pessimistic vision of post-independence Africa, which foregrounds images of dirt, decay and disease as metaphors for the failure to transform the oppressive social conditions inherited from the colonial era.

One can draw a direct line from Armah's writing to a whole strand of African fiction, which has attempted to represent the complete disintegration of post-independence nation states in countries such as the Congo, Somalia and Mozambique. In francophone African fiction, many authors from the former

Belgian Congo (Democratic Republic of the Congo, formerly Zaire), such as V. Y. Mudimbe have presented nightmarish visions of a society suffering from the mental and physical exactions of both colonialism (*L'Écart*, 1979) and the neocolonial order (*Le Bel Immonde*, 1979). Mudimbe's work undoubtedly reflects the legacy of the extreme brutality of the Belgian colonial regime, which led directly to three decades of corrupt rule by the dictator Mobutu Sese Seko. On the other side of the Congo River, in the former French Congo, Sony Labou Tansi's novels, especially *La Vie et demie* (1979), satirize the corruption of African governments in a highly complex narrative style, which combines fantasy and black humour to great effect.

Mia Couto's extraordinary short novel, *A varanda do frangipani* (1996, trans. *Under the Frangipani*) is a highly imaginative and complex tale of the legacy of thirty years of violence in Mozambique, the war against the Portuguese colonizers being followed by a brutal civil war between rival nationalist groups. In a multilayered, dreamlike narrative (the main character has been dead for two decades), Couto writes of a murder investigation in an old Portuguese fort, which leads to an exploration of the ambiguities of guilt, heroism and identity in the aftermath of war. Perhaps the most celebrated writer of the traumas that have befallen many post-independence African states is Nuruddin Farah, whose 'Blood in the Sun' trilogy, *Maps* (1986), *Gifts* (1993) and *Secrets* (1998), explores the fault-lines of Somalian national identity, which saw the country slide from war with Ethiopia to a disastrous civil war, which effectively destroyed the entire state infrastructure. *Maps*, in particular, has become a cornerstone of postcolonial studies' analysis of the nation: the novel's chief protagonist, Askar, is an orphan from the disputed border territory of the Ogaden, who is raised by a 'foreign', Ethiopian woman, Misra. The ambiguity of his origins, his national identity and even his gender – his close identification with Misra leads him to bleed as though menstruating – is cast in opposition to the certainties of Somalian nationalist discourse on the unity of the greater Somalian nation.

Farah's exploration of the links between sexuality, gender and the nation is also present in many other important African texts. In his striking novel *L'Enfant de sable* (1985, trans. *The Sand Child*), the Moroccan novelist Tahar Ben Jelloun relates the story of a female child raised as a boy by her father, distraught at the fate that has previously brought him seven daughters and no sons. In this landscape of blurred gender, Ben Jelloun deploys an ambiguous, polyvocal narrative as he seeks to dramatize the unequal status of women within postcolonial North Africa. The Sudanese Arabic-language author, Al-Tayyib Salih, charts the physical and sexual violence of colonialism in his landmark novel, translated as *Season of Migration to the North* (1966), which represents the traumatic legacy of colonialism through the actions of Mustafa Sa'eed, who travels to London where he carries out acts of sexual aggression (both physical and psychological) in revenge for the violence of colonialism. The major Algerian novelist Assia Djebar has used her fiction – *Femmes d'Alger dans leur appartement* (1980, trans. *Women of Algiers in their Apartment*) and *L'Amour, la fantasia* (1985, trans.

Fantasia: an Algerian Cavalcade) – to explore the specific histories of women under French colonial rule, as well as their contribution to the war of independence, which has often been denied or effaced by male-dominated nationalist historiography.

As well as her powerful and important investigations of memory and history, Djebar has also been a pioneering and highly influential figure among African women writers. As increasing numbers of African women have gained access to education, the number of women writers has grown considerably. Two texts from the late 1970s/early 1980s illustrate the exploration by women writers of sexuality and gender in postcolonial Africa, expressing the desires and concerns of women and charting the 'crisis of masculinity' (ideas also explored in the work of male authors such as Sembene and Farah). Buchi Emecheta's *The Joys of Motherhood* (1979) is an ironic but deeply compassionate portrayal of a 'traditional' Igbo Nigerian wife who devotes her life to her husband and her children, only to discover that the family structure she values so highly is disintegrating under the pressures of life in Lagos. The influential novel, *Une si longue lettre* (1981, trans. So *Long a Letter*), by the Senegalese author Mariama Bâ represents the expression of female concerns as inextricably linked to writing and education. However, despite the challenges to male authority in African fiction, it is significant that many female authors are based in the west – Calixthe Beyala (Cameroon/France), Véronique Tadjo (Ivory Coast/UK), Buchi Emecheta (Nigeria/UK), Chimamanda Ngozi Adichie (Nigeria/USA), Ahdaf Soueif (Egypt/UK) – where they have more liberty from the social constraints that continue to mark many women's lives in Africa. Indeed, the ambivalence of African women's journeys to Europe has become an important theme in the work of African women writers; the Franco-Cameroonian author Calixthe Beyala explores the liberating and alienating effects of emigration to Europe for African women in her novels *Le Petit Prince de Belleville* (1992) and its sequel *Maman a un amant* (1995).

The post-independence period ushered in the era of mass migration from the former colonies to the former colonial centres, and writing about the experience of migration has become central to much African fiction. Driss Chraïbi's novel *Les Boucs* (1956, trans. *The Butts*) constitutes a groundbreaking work in its representation of the gulf between the educated immigrant author and the largely uneducated immigrant masses. The author seeks to 'represent' his fellow immigrants both politically and in literary terms but is forced to accept that any such move will necessarily be flawed due to his social and cultural distance from them. Some African authors fled their countries as political exiles – Ngugi wa Thiong'o, Wole Soyinka, Ahmadou Kourouma, Nuruddin Farah – while others have gone abroad to seek greater personal freedom – Assia Djebar, Driss Chraïbi, Calixthe Beyala. Other 'African' authors have largely grown up in Europe, taken there as children by their parents. Should their work be considered 'African' or 'European', or a hybrid product of both? For example, the 'Beur' (slang for people of North African origin) writers of France – Medhi

Charef, Azouz Begag, Faïza Guène – occupy an ambiguous position between France and Algeria, an ambiguity often dealt with both thematically and stylistically in their work.

In the era of globalization, there is now an important diaspora of African writers, chiefly but no longer exclusively living in the former colonial centres. Writing about francophone North African literature, Winifred Woodhull argues that this global movement of people, capital and information makes it necessary to view North African culture within a global framework, rather than as the expression of individual national identities (Woodhull 2003). The work of the Moroccan critic and author, Abdelkebir Khatibi is in this respect exemplary. His autobiographical text *Amour bilingue* (1990, trans. *Love in Two Languages*) views Maghrebian identity as highly fluid and steeped in the culture of the entire Mediterranean region. Equally, the work of the Algerian authors Assia Djebar and Leïla Sebbar consistently traverses national and cultural boundaries in its exploration of the intertwined histories of France and Algeria. Woodhull's argument might also be generalized to other parts of Africa: Ben Okri's Booker Prize-winning novel *The Famished Road* (1991) relates the independence of Nigeria within a complex narrative framework that blurs the boundaries between 'magic' and 'modernity'; the Anglo-Egyptian author Ahdaf Soueif deals with alienation and belonging in the short stories in *Sandpiper* (1996), which examine transcultural journeys between Europe and the Middle East.

The exploration of the transcultural and transnational nature of the contemporary world is thus at the heart of much African fiction. However, as has been argued throughout this chapter, we must beware excessively generalized definitions of African literature: many styles, approaches and themes exist, not all of which fit the latest postcolonial theoretical paradigms. In approaching African texts, we need to balance considerations of the global and the local: to what extent is the text embedded in the cultural context of its production and how does it engage with globally relevant issues of culture and identity? Postcolonial criticism has been particularly strong on the latter question; there is now a pressing need to develop understanding of 'local' issues in order to create a more informed comparative approach to postcolonial African literatures and cultures.

RECOMMENDED FURTHER READING

Achebe, Chinua, *Morning Yet on Creation Day* (London: Heinemann, 1975).

Gikandi, Simon (ed.) *Encyclopedia of African Literature* (London: Routledge, 2003).

Griffiths, Gareth, *African Literatures in English: east and west* (Harlow: Longman, 2000).

Julien, Eileen, *African Novels and the Question of Orality* (Bloomington, IN: Indiana University Press, 1992).

Ngugi wa Thiong'o, *Decolonising the Mind* (London: James Currey, 1986).

Oke, Ulusolo and Oje, Sam Ade (eds) *Introduction to Francophone African Literature* (Ibadan: Spectrum Books, 2000).

6

AUSTRALASIA

ALICE BRITTAN

TERRA NULLIUS

Long before the late-eighteenth century voyages of British explorer and cartographer Captain James Cook, the islands of the South Pacific shimmered like a tantalizing dream in the European imagination. Ancient Greek astronomers and mapmakers had posited the existence of a great Southern Continent, and in 1642 the Dutch sent an expedition in search of the rumoured Southern Land, where they hoped to find abundant wealth in the care of nonchalant natives. Unfortunately for Holland, the land that was found did not fulfil the glittering promises of fable. On the contrary. The expedition's leader, Abel Tasman, reached what appears on contemporary maps as New Zealand, as well as Tasmania, the large island southeast of mainland Australia that now bears his name, but he was unimpressed by the riches of the region and terrified by the indigenous inhabitants, particularly the Maori of New Zealand, who interpreted his greetings as a declaration of war and handily dispatched several members of his crew. Not until 1768, when the far more determined Captain Cook launched a vessel bearing the powerful British flag, did the quest to find, to map and to colonize the legendary continent of the South recommence in earnest.

By the late eighteenth century, when Captain Cook and his crew set sail in the *Endeavour* for the South Seas, Britain was master of the largest colonial empire in history. As the emissary of King George III, Cook did not hesitate to claim the territory he charted and named as the property of the British crown, including Tahiti, the north and south islands of New Zealand, and the land mass he called New South Wales: the ancient prophesy of a vast Southern Continent come true. The decision in 1787 of the British Parliament to turn Australia into a penal colony, a place of ignominious exile for British criminals and other undesirables, may be traced to the details of Cook's encounter with the region's aboriginal peoples, whose presence on the continent is usually reckoned by historians to be between forty and sixty thousand years. Like many explorers of the time, Cook was a prolific diarist, and his journals record a crucial difference between his encounters with the Australian Aborigines and the New Zealand Maori. Cook and his travelling companions repeatedly expressed amazement at the material minimalism of the Aborigines and at their cool indifference to exchanging goods with the British. As a consequence, Cook rapidly and mistakenly concluded that the people of Australia had 'no idea of traffic' (1852: 263), no acquaintance with or interest in the principles of trade, and that they were by extension without culture or coherent social structure. In a matter of a few sentences, Cook demoted all the aboriginal peoples of Australia to the status of 'animals' (212). By contrast, Cook and his crew found that the New Zealand Maori were eager to engage in trade, and while it was unthinkable that their civilization could be equal to that of the British, the Maori were quickly judged a formidable and intelligent people of considerable, if 'primitive', cultural accomplishment.

The historical consequences of Captain Cook and his crew's impressions of the Aborigines and the Maori were enormous. In the 1780s, the British Parliament was debating where to establish a large and remote penal colony that would be suitable for farming, capable of supporting a financially-independent settlement, and very difficult to escape. The newly-minted United States of America had refused to continue accepting shipments of British prisoners, and in this respect the timing of the American Revolution could not have been worse for Britain, where rapid industrialization had swelled the ranks of the urban poor and created more desperate, starving thieves than the nation's jails could possibly house. Australia was chosen as the new destination for Britain's convicts in part because it was judged to be *terra nullius*, a Latin term and legal ruling meaning 'land belonging to no one', and therefore available for seizure and settlement. The accounts of Captain Cook and the testimony of Sir Joseph Banks, the amateur botanist who also sailed aboard the *Endeavour*, helped to persuade Parliament that the Aborigines had no legal claim to any part of Australia: they did not appear to cultivate the land, which in the late seventeenth century had been established by the influential British political philosopher John Locke as the main criterion for land ownership, and their disinterest in trade suggested to the British that, unlike the Maori, they had no stable concept of property. Thus, in 1787, convict transportation to New South Wales began, and in 1788, after a voyage of eight months, the vessels of the First Fleet arrived on the other side of the globe and dropped anchor in the harbour that Sir Joseph Banks had dubbed Botany Bay. The system of convict transportation to Australia, meticulously researched and vividly reconstructed in *The Fatal Shore* (1988) by historian Robert Hughes, continued for over seventy years.

The judgement that Australia was *terra nullius* meant not only that the British could claim legal sovereignty over the entire continent, effectively declaring the Crown as the new and undisputed owner, but also that they did not need to negotiate any formal treaties with the Aborigines. Why would one make a deal with people who never held title to the land in the first place? By contrast, Britain would never seriously have considered that the Maori's presence in New Zealand should overrule its own desire to settle the islands and harvest the valuable resources of the region, including whale oil, flax and timber, but colonial administrators did feel compelled to recognize, at least nominally, the Maori's legal rights to land and property. Thus, in 1840, when British settlement of New Zealand was already well underway, the much-contested Treaty of Waitangi was signed by a gathering of British and Maori leaders. No such document has ever existed in Australian history. Historian James Belich, among many others, has studied the duplicities of the Treaty of Waitangi, which in the minds of the British signatories stripped the Maori of legal title to their ancestral lands, but in the minds of the Maori signatories did no such thing (Belich 1996). There are many reasons for the radical misunderstandings produced by the Treaty, and not the least of them is the fact that the British never intended to establish fully reciprocal political and economic relationships with the Maori, or with any other colonized people, and therefore declarations of fair dealing were necessarily disingenuous. However, the agreement signed at Waitangi is testament to more than the manipulative self-interest of the Crown. From between the lines of that document emerge some of the most complex, far-reaching and enduring cultural and legal problems produced by the encounter between the British and the indigenous peoples of the South Pacific.

The British spoke a different language from the Maori or the Australian Aborigines, and not only in the obvious sense. Captain Cook and his colonial successors valued, above all, the cultural power of the *written* rather than the spoken word, of texts rather than talking, and whether they wrote or conversed they used the vocabulary of capitalism, which means that they understood land, natural resources and material goods as commodities that could be bought and sold at prices determined by the conventions of the marketplace. The Aborigines and the Maori inhabited richly symbolic cultural worlds, but they did not write words as Europeans did, and although they operated sophisticated exchange systems, their economies were not governed by the principles of modern capitalism. The Aborigines, for example, found abhorrent and plainly incomprehensible the idea that land could be treated as private property, to be bought and sold, or even to be owned in the first place. Land was sacred, indivisibly connected to physical, imaginative and spiritual life, no more a commodity for sale than a parent or child. In the immensely complex and locally variable web of beliefs and customs that shaped Aboriginal relationships to land there was no place for the central and unquestioned premise of British colonists: that land was merchandise to be traded for money or goods, claimed with words written on paper, or simply taken by force.

The history of Aboriginal resistance to British settlement is as long as the history of settlement itself, but official restitution for – or even acknowledgement of – the colonial legacy of physical and cultural violence has been relatively recent and, in the minds of most, wholly inadequate. (The question of what economic or social forms restitution should take has been posed in many postcolonial settings and is not easily answered.) Not until 1992, when an Aboriginal man named Eddie Mabo sued the state of Queensland, did an Australian court formally rule that native title, or the legal right to land, was not dissolved by the British declaration of sovereignty over the entire continent in the late eighteenth century. The decision did not change the fabric of daily life in Australia, but it carried tremendous symbolic weight, precisely because it admitted that the system of British law is simply one among others: it recognized that as a form of representation writing does *not* automatically annul oral tradition, or text trump speech, and that the capitalist definitions of private property that undergirded British settlement are not the only viable definitions of ownership, and cannot simply annihilate their historical rivals, despite being backed by the wealth and weaponry of the empire.

THE FIFTH QUARTER

In 1824 a homesick British administrator who had been sent to New South Wales to audit the state's finances wrote an ill-tempered letter home to his wife in which he expressed a popular perception of the young colony. G. T. W. B. Boyes dismissed the continent as 'this fifth or pickpocket quarter' of the globe (Chapman 1985: 190), where nothing useful or valuable was contributed to the earth's riches because its inhabitants were all thieves. Robert Hughes makes the important point that 'about four-fifths of all transportation was for "offenses against property"' (1988: 163), including forgery, theft, counterfeiting and swindling, but Boyes's complaint, apart from being a vastly inaccurate characterization of early Australian productivity, was simply a reiteration of the common belief that the Southern Continent was a kind of monstrous non-place, and its citizens the members of a topsy-turvy non-society. Like the British poet Barron Field, who in 1819 unflatteringly called Australia 'this fifth part of the Earth' (quoted in Smith 1985: 227), Boyes excommunicates the antipodes from nature, morality and arithmetic reason: the fifth quarter is an accidental, deviant remainder in the mathematics of God's creation. It may well be the sly addition of an unsupervized demon. This devilish possibility was seriously entertained in the 1830s by none other than naturalist Charles Darwin, who, according to scholar Peter Conrad, described the flora and fauna of New South Wales as 'freaks [that] could not have been dreamed up by the same god who designed the northern hemisphere' (Conrad 2000: 18).

The pervasive colonial idea that Australia was a late and unholy afterthought derived not only from its startling antipodean geography – its reversal of the European seasons, its unfamiliar plants, animals and topography – but also from the unexpected consequences of the convict system, which produced forms of social and economic mobility that were unthinkable, even scandalous, in England. Boyes, like many other administrators and free British settlers, was appalled by the affluence of some former convicts, who served their sentences and then entered local society as resourceful businessmen. Legal historian David Neal writes that by the early nineteenth century, liberated convicts 'dominated the mercantile class in Sydney, and held more property than the free settlers' (1991: 6), a rousing triumph for those cast out of England as human waste, but a stinging humiliation for those who emigrated to Australia by choice and still valued the old hierarchies of home. Charles Dickens's classic novel *Great Expectations* (1861), about a British convict named Abel Magwitch who serves his time in New South Wales and then returns to England illegally with a fortune earned through honest enterprise, explores the deep moral outrage, the quivering social horror, attached to the very idea that wealth and power might be acquired by rehabilitated criminals. The British colonies of settlement were usually regarded as lands of opportunity for the intrepid and hardworking, but when former convicts prospered in Australia, their success was often seen as confirmation that the moral order of the place was as upside-down as its position on the world map.

If there were many who condemned Australia, in the poet A. D. Hope's memorable phrase, as a 'vast parasite robber-state' (quoted in Pana 1996: 32), there were also those who took a distinctly brighter view. Literary critics Coral Lansbury and Irina Grigorescu Pana have both argued that even in the nineteenth century, Australia was regarded by optimistic if somewhat naïve souls as an Arcadia, a kind of Edenic land-before-time, where a return to the ostensible simplicity of pre-industrial life was possible (Lansbury 1970; Pana 1996). Matthew Kneale's novel *English Passengers* (2000) wittily satirizes this very view, following a delusional band of Englishmen in their quest to find the garden of Eden in nineteenth-century Tasmania. Alas, their search ends in madness and death. On the other hand, Peter Carey's novel *Jack Maggs* (1997), which re-writes Dickens's *Great Expectations* from the perspective of the convict, draws implicitly on what Irina Pana calls the 'renovatio ethos' (1996: 30), the anti-nostalgic idea that Australia could be transformed from a place of banishment into a literal and imaginative home, even for those who suffered the physical and psychological tortures of penal servitude, and that the youth and provisionality of settler culture might be understood not as an obstacle but as the open door of opportunity. The novels of David Malouf, including *Harland's Half Acre* (1984) and *Remembering Babylon* (1993), also explore the experiences of settlers, who, even as they endure an agonizing desire for the life left behind, reach a new and more enlightened understanding of themselves, and gradually come to see Australia not as the Babylon of Biblical exile, but as the Jerusalem of home-coming.

If in Australia *renovatio*, or fruitful self-transformation, was seen by some as possible but hard won, during the same period New Zealand was presented to potential emigrants as the 'Britain of the South' (Belich 1996: 298–99). According to this view, little self-transformation would be required of settlers, and no homesickness would be produced by their move across the planet, because New Zealand was simply Britain relocated and improved by a mild climate and abundant farmland. This Arcadian vision, in which New Zealand was imagined as a younger, less populous and less polluted version of the British Isles, also influenced British perceptions of other islands in the region, but to quite different effect. If New Zealand was a promising but untutored child, places such as New Guinea were frankly wayward, culturally immature but not youthful, arrested in a state of permanent and incurable primitivism. Like the Aborigines of Australia, the inhabitants of the South Pacific islands were believed to represent humankind at an early stage of development: not as the growing child is heir to the parent, but as a fossil is a record of an eclipsed ancestor. As Australia itself was called an impossible fifth quarter of the earth, its indigenous people, and those of neighbouring islands, were seen as culturally fossilized, so out-of-time and so distant from the advances of European civilizations that they were like living museum pieces made redundant by the arrival of modern man. Even in the late nineteenth and early twentieth centuries, when some settlers began to view the 'savage' as more noble than ignoble, deserving of study and sympathy rather than extermination, the shift did not change the belief that indigenous people and their cultures were necessarily doomed to extinction as the anachronistic remains of human history.

THE DRUG OF ANALOGY

The British judgement of New Zealand as the 'Britain of the South' and of Australia as *terra nullius*, an illicit fifth quarter and a land either of dying primitives or of Edenic Arcadia, all depended on what novelist David Malouf characterizes as the drug of analogy (1993: 169). An analogy is an extended comparison between two seemingly dissimilar things, not an opiate or a hallucinogenic substance, so what exactly does Malouf mean? In his own study of settlement, critic Paul Carter writes that '[a]ny orientation to the new environment depends initially on finding resemblances between it and the home left behind', and that 'the very possibility of comparison implies a conceptual vocabulary that can be transported from one place to another' (1992: 2). For Carter, the comparison of the new with the familiar is like a bridge that allows humans to cross a chasm in space, to defy rather than accept the impasse. Analogies are perceptual bridges built from portable conceptual vocabularies, which are ways of seeing, understanding, representing and judging people, places and ideas. In Carter's view, an analogy is thus an inevitable and necessary response to the problem of the unknown. Inevitable or not, many writers and scholars share Malouf's intuition that to see, describe and evaluate a new place only or even primarily in imported terms may prevent people from actually understanding the world around them. To analogize is thus to become intoxicated by visions. As Reverend Frazer observes in Malouf's novel *Remembering Babylon*, *'the very habit and faculty that makes apprehensible to us what is known and expected dulls our sensitivity to other forms, even the most obvious. We must rub our eyes and look again, clear our minds of what we are looking for to see what is there'* (1993: 130 – italics in original). For Malouf, analogy does not allow us to make contact with the new; it simply disguises the unknown as the familiar.

The consequences of what David Malouf calls the drug of analogy and Irina Pana 'the way of elsewhere' (1996: 32), namely the historical habit of seeing through the lens of Britain, are both political and aesthetic. Captain Cook decided that the Aborigines were animals because what he glimpsed of them did not match the meanings of the words 'humanity', 'civilization' and 'culture' that he carried in his mind on his voyage to the South Pacific. The dire repercussions of his judgement have already been sketched above, which remind us that comparisons are very often evaluations: they assume one set of definitions as the fixed standard by which all others will be measured, and probably found wanting. In the 1930s, a group of Australian poets calling themselves Jindyworobaks, an Aboriginal word understood as meaning 'to annex, to join' (Ingamells 1969: 249), produced a manifesto outlining the flaws in another kind of comparative vocabulary: the metaphors and similes of poetry. To develop an authentic and relevant Australian literary culture, argued the Jindyworobaks, writers must give up their reliance on an imported English tradition in order to see the natural 'spirit of the place' (Ingamells 1969: 250) with clear eyes. 'It has been a piteous custom', declaimed Rex Ingamells, the leader of the Jindyworobaks, 'to write of Australian things with the English idiom, an idiom which can achieve exactness in England but not here' (252). The result was not just inept poetry, but what critic A. A. Phillips would later call the 'cultural cringe', which he defined as the widespread 'assumption that the domestic cultural product will be worse than the imported article' (quoted in Pana 1996: 74).

In different ways, Rex Ingamells and A. A. Phillips both argued that imported British culture stifled and shamed Australians. But how exactly does a nation stop comparing and cringing? In hindsight, the philosophy of the Jindyworobak poets, rooted in a romantic belief in the spirit of nature and history, seems simplistic and even racist. The Jindyworobaks took their name from an Aboriginal language, and urged poets to draw inspiration from Aboriginal legends, songs, and rites; but they also believed that '[t]he blacks that remain are a degenerate, puppet people' (Ingamells 1969: 262) without a future, capable of providing no more than the fertilizing ashes from which settler culture might arise. Aboriginal history was conceived as the wreckage from which an authentically indigenous, a uniquely Australian, representational vocabulary might be salvaged for the use of the anxious conqueror. Not surprisingly, contemporary Aboriginal writers and activists such as Mudrooroo and Roberta Sykes contest the idea that they were ever a 'degenerate, puppet people' as well as the suggestion that their cultures should be annexed to solve the historical problem of the newcomers' cultural cringe. Although Mudrooroo commended the initiative of the Council for Aboriginal Reconciliation, formed in 1992, to bring 'the Indigenous people of Australia into the mainstream, not only physically but culturally' by making 'Indigenous motifs and myths [. . .] the well-springs of a vibrant Australian culture' (1997: 1, 2), his approval depends on the inclusion of Aborigines as active *partners*, and on the understanding of their 'motifs and myths' as a living and changing tradition.

In 1935 one critic explained the literary challenges that faced Australian writers by observing that 'Australia [. . .] is not yet in the centre of the map and has no London' (Ingamells 1969: 259). The statement is an excellent example of compare-and-cringe. Writers cannot literally rearrange the position of the continents on the globe, but in their work many have sworn off the drug of analogy, which defines the antipodes primarily by the fact that it has '*no* London' and is '*not yet* in the centre of the map'. Beginning in the 1940s, the novelist Patrick White undertook to tell epic stories about Australian history and life that would demonstrate that the makings of rich, complex literature were not only to be found in London, but in his own unprestigious corner of the world. He was awarded the Nobel Prize in 1973. As Graham Huggan argues, contemporary Australian fiction has questioned even the 'supposed impartiality of the map' (1994: 11), examining it not as an indisputable representation of geographical reality but as a 'geopolitical claim' (9) that 'focus[es] the mapreader's attention on the centre, thereby promoting or proclaiming the supremacy of a particular worldview' (11). By turning images and descriptions of maps into contestable claims rather than immutable facts, writers have suggested that a position on the bottom rather than the top of the earth depends on the perspective from which names are bestowed and maps drawn. When Captain Cook claimed New South Wales as British territory he did so by charting and comparative christening: the region was *New* to European eyes; it lay to the *South* of the Northern hemisphere; and it commemorated *Wales*, on Britain's west coast. The Dutch mapmaker who named Nieuw Zeeland, or *New* Zealand (Sea-land), followed a similarly relational logic. Thus when Maori refer to their country as Aotearoa (land of the long white cloud), they are not only insisting upon the priority of their own names, but refusing to be positioned on the world map as a secondary term in a European analogy.

IDENTITY CRISES

If analogies helped some settlers understand who and where they were, others wanted nothing more than to burn their perceptual bridges. The Fifth Quarter section above briefly described one of the unforeseen and shocking results of the convict system, which was that many former criminals, most from the very bottom of the British class system, rose to positions of considerable economic and social power within the colony of New South Wales and in New Zealand. When we recall that transportation was a substitute for execution in England, we can state the case more colourfully: condemned men and women arose from the dead to claim stature among the living. All of Britain's settler colonies offered newcomers the opportunity to reinvent and improve themselves, but Australia's great distance from England, coupled with the unique history of convict transportation, made it a fertile place for remarkable social metamorphoses. As Patrick Morgan writes, in the nineteenth century the 'antipodes is not just the other, but the opposite, the overthrowing of the old moral order' (1997: 174). In such a land people could become the opposite of their former selves, and more than one seized the opportunity with almost theatrical flair.

Partly because in early settlement the roles of aristocrat and outlaw were frequently reversible, contemporary Australian literary culture has become very sensitively attuned to what is now called identity imposture. Debates about the meaning of multiculturalism and about the relationship between Anglo-Celtic settlers – people originally from the British Isles – and visible minorities, including Aboriginal peoples, have made the idea of personal authenticity paramount, and slippery identities suspicious indeed.

In an article that gives historical context for David Malouf's novel *The Conversations at Curlow Creek* (1996), in which an Anglo-Irish gentleman moves to Australia in the early nineteenth century and becomes a hunted rebel outlaw, Patrick Morgan argues that the novel's premise is 'one of the great organising principles of the Australian colonial novel' (1997: 178). Nineteenth-century writers and readers, he maintains, were fascinated by stories about those who fell, rose or were pretenders to new social positions. The real legal case of the Tichborne claimant, an uneducated Australian butcher who in the 1870s sailed to England and identified himself as a missing British aristocrat named Sir Roger Tichborne, immediately influenced several novels, including Marcus Clarke's classic, *His Natural Life* (1874), and continues to resonate in contemporary Australian fiction. Peter Carey's *My Life as A Fake* (2003) draws on a more recent case of fraudulence, the Ern Malley Hoax, which was concocted in the early 1940s by two young poets from Sydney who set out to ridicule modern poetry and ended up impressing the literati of the English-speaking world. The tongue-in-cheek poems they wrote under the name of Ern Malley were not only published in Australia to great acclaim, but were taken seriously by international luminaries such as British poet T. S. Eliot.

The Ern Malley Hoax embarrassed readers and publishers of poetry, but it was not nearly as politically flammable as the contemporary cases of literary imposture examined by Graham Huggan in *The Postcolonial Exotic* (2001) and in many of the essays collected in Maggie Nolan and Carrie Dawson's edited collection, *Who's Who? hoaxes, imposture and identity crises in Australian literature* (2004). How did the nineteenth-century 'renovatio ethos', or self-transformation, come to be condemned as cynical trickery? In the 1950s, the Australian government began to abandon the White Australia Policy, which for over fifty years had restricted immigration to citizens of the British Isles. In the 1970s, the government began to replace its longstanding philosophy that immigrants and Aborigines should assimilate to the dominant culture with policies that encouraged multiculturalism or the preservation of ethnic identity. These changes have made many Australians think about the nature and significance of racial and cultural identity in new ways. Some white Australians fear that their way of life is threatened and undermined by non-white newcomers. Many immigrants and Aborigines, on the other hand, feel that government programmes and festivals that encourage public displays of diversity – crafts, clothes and cuisine – are no more than insubstantial charades of political correctness. As critic Sneja Gunew writes, multiculturalism often masks the unwillingness of the historically dominant group, in this case white citizens, to think or behave differently, while reducing immigrants to performers in shows of 'folkloric exotica and nostalgia firmly oriented toward the past' and without 'relevance in the present' (1990: 112). If government policies designed to foster diversity are superficial and misguided, they have also steeply raised the stakes of racial and cultural identity. Who you are – your race, name, history, religion – has monetary as well as personal value. Your identity may help you to qualify for a government programme, receive a grant, sell a piece of art or secure a publishing contract and an audience eager to read an insider's account of a particular life experience. In the eyes of some, faking your name is nothing less than theft.

Scholars including James Clifford and Graham Huggan argue that while multiculturalism and globalization have made human identities more fluid – it is now possible, for example, to look Asian but call oneself a New Zealander, just as it is possible to buy Nike clothing or watch Hollywood movies almost anywhere in the world – these same forces have heightened our desire for examples of untainted, authentic or pure embodiments of local culture (Clifford 1988, 1997; Huggan 2001). The reader who learns that despite the name on the cover of a book the author is not racially Maori, or fully Aboriginal, or truly a refugee from the former Communist bloc, rarely takes pleasure in the discovery, or is moved to philosophize about the conflicting ways in which we define identity. Instead, like a tourist who finds that the boomerang he just bought was made in China, the reader feels cheated. The exposed author is therefore likely to be attacked and ridiculed, as has happened more than once in Australia in recent years – perhaps most famously to Helen Demidenko, whose elaborate pretence to Ukrainian descent was exposed shortly after her novel *The Hand That Signed the Paper* (1994) was published to great acclaim (Mycak 2004; Goldie 2004). Is it not criminally fraudulent, asked the press, for a writer to fabricate Ukrainian ancestry in order to promote a book about Ukrainian–Nazi collaboration? Around the same time, similarly outraged questions were asked of a white man named Leon Carmen after he revealed himself as the true author of an award-winning book presented to the public as the 'autobiography' of an Aboriginal woman named Wanda Koolmatrie (Nolan 2004). The paradoxes and complexities contained in these highly-publicized cases of what many have called fraud – multiculturalism that demands racial and cultural purity, and globalization that values the local product – reflect the broader challenges faced by Australia and New Zealand as they work to connect their colonial histories, as predominantly white settler societies with enduring cultural loyalties to Britain and the West, with the uncertainties and opportunities of postcolonial nationhood.

RECOMMENDED FURTHER READING

Callahan, David (ed.) *Contemporary Issues in Australian Literature* (London: Frank Cass, 2001).

Carter, Paul, *Living in a New Country: history, travelling and language* (London: Faber and Faber, 1992).

Hodge, Bob and Mishra, Vija, *Dark Side of the Dream: Australian literature and the postcolonial mind* (North Sydney, NSW: Allen and Unwin, 1991).

Huggan, Graham, *Territorial Disputes: maps and mapping strategies in contemporary Canadian and Australian Fiction* (Toronto: University of Toronto Press, 1994).

Hughes, Robert, *The Fatal Shore: the epic of Australia's founding* (New York: Random House, 1988).

Keown, Michelle, *Postcolonial Pacific Writing: representations of the body* (London: Routledge, 2005).

Mudrooroo, *Indigenous Literature of Australia: milli milli wangka* (Melbourne: Hyland House Publishing, 1997).

Nile, Richard, *The Making of the Australian Literary Imagination* (St Lucia, Qld.: University of Queensland Press, 2002).

Smith, Bernard, *European Vision and the South Pacific* (New Haven, CT: Yale University Press, 1985).

Williams, Mark and Leggott, Michele, *Opening the Book: new essays on New Zealand writing* (Auckland: Auckland University Press, 1995).

7

CANADA

MARK SHACKLETON

HISTORICAL CONTEXTS

On 9 June 1990 the Cree politician and band chief Elijah Harper held an eagle feather in his hand and said the single word 'no'. His refusal of what was known as the Meech Lake Accord – a series of proposed amendments to the Constitution of Canada that on the one hand attempted to recognize the province of Quebec as a 'distinct society', and on the other hand failed to guarantee the same for Canada's Aboriginal peoples – can be regarded as a symbolic 'post-colonial moment' in Canadian history. In effect it challenged the view that France and Great Britain are Canada's 'founding nations', for from a First Nations (Native Canadian) perspective the country has fifty-eight founding nations, not just two (see Dickason 2002: x).

Inhabited originally by Aboriginal peoples, the first permanent European settlements in Canada were established in the early seventeenth century: by the French at Port Royal in 1605 and Quebec City in 1608, and by the English in Newfoundland around 1610. Initially, the two colonies developed separately, the French settling around the St Lawrence River valley, whereas the British occupied the so-called Thirteen Colonies to the South. However, competition over territory and goods such as fish and furs led to the protracted French and Indian Wars (1689–1763), culminating in victory for the British.

The classic aspects of colonialism are in evidence in Canada, namely the settlement of territory, the exploitation of resources and the urge to control the indigenous peoples, but immediately qualifications need to be made. First, there evolved different degrees of identification with the mother country among the European settlers. Britain's imperial history goes back to the colonization of Ireland in the early twelfth century, whereas France's first colony was Canada. In New France, as it was known, the French showed a stronger desire for full constitutional assimilation with the mother country than the British. Second, in certain cases the distinction between colonizers and colonized becomes blurred, as the case of the Acadians demonstrates. Acadia was a region of eastern Canada settled by about one hundred French families in the early 1600s. These Acadians developed friendly relations with the aboriginal Mi'kmaq and wished to maintain a position of neutrality between the French and the British. In 1754, after refusing to take an oath of allegiance to the British monarch, more than 12,000 Acadians were expelled. Their homes were burned, their lands confiscated and families were split up and dispersed throughout British North

America; some were deported back to France. Many were shipped down to Louisiana, where 'les Acadiens' became 'the Cajuns'. Third, the relationship between settlers and indigenous peoples in Canada shows that relations between the colonizers and the colonized need to be studied in specific contexts. In the French and Indian wars of the seventeenth and eighteenth centuries (known as the Intercolonial Wars or the War of the Conquest by the French) the Iroquois allied themselves with the British and the Algonquin and Huron with the French, in part to settle old scores. The Wars resulted in the decimation and pacification of Native peoples, a depressingly familiar feature of colonization throughout the world; but the actual conflicts between the colonizer and the indigene took different forms in seventeenth-century Canada from those found later in, for example, eighteenth-century Australia or nineteenth-century USA.

Depending on one's perspective, Canada's history can either be seen as the extension of European colonization or as a stage in the decolonization of the British empire. Taking the latter view, Canada's constitutional moves towards decolonization can be seen as a form of non-violent resistance to direct colonial rule, a step taken typically by white settler communities. In 1867 Canada was the first of the settler nations (Canada, Australia, New Zealand, South Africa) to become a 'Dominion', in other words an overseas territory of the British Crown which has achieved political autonomy. Canadian history has also seen other more violent forms of resistance, however, the most famous being the 'rebellions' of the Métis leader Louis Riel. Riel is, even today, a controversial figure who can be regarded as a litmus test to one's political perspective, and to changing perceptions of Canadian history. The Red River Rebellion (1869–70) led directly to the province of Manitoba entering the Canadian Confederation, allowing some to see Riel as 'a father of Confederation', and he was an icon of the extreme Front de Libération du Québec in the 1960s. Following the military skirmishes of 1885 known as the North-West Rebellion the Cree chiefs Poundmaker and Big Bear were imprisoned, and eight other native leaders were hanged. Riel himself was tried and hanged, intensifying discord between the province of Quebec and English-speaking Canada. This crucial period of Métis and Cree resistance has been painstakingly reconstructed in two novels by Rudy Wiebe (a non-Native Canadian whose parents were German-speaking Mennonites, who had emigrated from Russia): *The Temptations of Big Bear* (1973), which focuses on the life of the Plains Cree leader, and *The Scorched-Wood People* (1977), which portrays Riel and the Métis revolts. The Métis writer Beatrice Culleton Mosionier provides in passing a picture of the demonization of Louis Riel in official histories of the 1950s in her novel *In Search of April Raintree* (1983). Since the 1990s there have been repeated calls for Riel's conviction to be officially revoked by the Canadian Parliament.

This brief historical overview is in no way comprehensive, but is intended to raise the issues of perspective in historical accounts. Put simply, we need in any historical account to ask the question: 'whose history?'. The following sections outline literary production in Canada since the 1960s, particularly the impact of

Native Canadian and so-called 'minority' writing. The intention is to focus on writing which offers a postcolonial perspective on Canada, involving a reconfiguration of what it means to be Canadian.

FIRST NATIONS LITERATURE WRITTEN IN ENGLISH

Native and Métis writers are today demanding a voice [. . .] theirs should be considered the resisting, post-colonial voice of Canada.

(Hutcheon 1989: 156)

Orature, the rich tradition of Aboriginal oral literature in Canada in the form of epics, legends and tales, goes back thousands of years, but with the exception of isolated examples like the Mohawk writer Emily Pauline Johnson (1861–1913), there are very few works by Native Canadian writers published before the 1960s. Such texts that did appear were usually heavily edited by non-Natives, as was the case with the Okanagan writer Mourning Dove (1888–1936), whose novel *Cogewea* (1927) clearly shows the stylistic influence of her editor Lucullus McWhorter. Editorial paternalism was matched by the attitude of the Canadian government towards Native peoples. The Indian Act of Canada (1876) effectively made status (i.e. registered) Indians wards of the state, and it was not until the astonishingly late date of 1960 that Canadian Natives received the right to vote.

The late 1960s to the mid-1970s saw the publication of crucial works in which Native Canadian writers expressed their unmediated views. *The Unjust Society* (1969), the first book by Harold Cardinal (Cree), was a direct challenge to Prime Minister Pierre Trudeau's presentation of Canada as 'the just society'. Maria Campbell (Métis) wrote in the introduction to her autobiography, *Half-Breed* (1973): 'I write this for all of you, to tell you what it is like to be a Halfbreed woman in our country. I want to tell you about the joys and sorrows, the oppressing poverty, the frustrations and the dreams' (2). Howard Adams's (Métis) *Prison of Grass*, first published in 1975, has now become a classic revisionist history of the three-hundred-year history of settlement on the western plains of Canada, seen from a historically researched and documented Native/Métis perspective.

Representation and language issues are central to emerging First Nation writings of the late twentieth century. Lee Maracle's *Bobbi Lee: Indian rebel* (1975), an as-told-to autobiography published initially under the name of the editor Don Barnett, raised the question of Eurocentric framing and appropriation of Aboriginal oral life narratives. The failure to overcome class, ethnic and cultural divisions in Native/non-Native collaborations was later explored in Maria Campbell's and Linda Griffiths's *The Book of Jessica* (1989). Language as a basic marker of colonial authority, imposed on colonial subjects in order to control them, is also the experience of a generation of Native writers who went through the residential school system. These schools were part of the official governmental policy of compulsory assimilation in which Native children, particularly in the 1950s and 1960s, were sent to distant residential (i.e. boarding) schools. Here they were prohibited from speaking their Aboriginal language and forced to speak English or French. Two outstanding accounts of this painful experience are given in Basil Johnston's autobiographical *Indian School Days* (1988) and Tomson Highway's semi-autobiographical novel *Kiss of the Fur Queen* (1998).

A particular feature of Native Canadian writing is the strength of its women writers. In the USA, by contrast, the Native American literary renaissance which took off from the publication of N. Scott Momaday's Pulitzer prize-winning *House Made of Dawn* (1968) was dominated in its early stages by male writers. In the 1980s, however, Canada saw the publication of Beatrice Culleton Mosionier's *In Search of April Raintree* (1983), Jeannette Armstrong's *Slash* (1987) and Ruby Slipperjack's *Honour the Sun* (1987). These novels have been both praised (and patronized) by what has been seen as their directly-presented 'naïve' realism and autobiographical 'authenticity'. Critics such as Helen Hoy, however, have pointed out that Native literature may well require different aesthetic approaches than those usually applied by the Eurocentric critic (Hoy 1999). In addition, there is a greater understanding today that attention needs to be paid to what Native writers say about their own work and cultures (see Lutz 1991: 6–8).

Edward Said has argued in *Culture and Imperialism* that slogans, pamphlets, newspapers, folktales, heroes, epic poetry, novels and drama are all means by which national cultures can be reasserted and the effects of colonization resisted (1993: 260). The Trickster figure, part of Native oral narrative traditions, has been consciously used as a symbol of cultural resistance in particular by a wide range of First Nations dramatists. The Toronto-based Native Earth Performing Arts Incorporated has been a leading force in Native Canadian drama since 1982, and under the artistic directorship of Tomson Highway began in 1988 an annual script festival for Native writers known as 'Weesageechak Begins to Dance', honouring in its name the Cree trickster. Under Native Earth's auspices a number of plays which foreground the Trickster figure have been work-shopped or performed, including Highway's *The Rez Sisters* (1986) and *Dry Lips Oughta Move to Kapuskasing* (1989); Daniel David Moses's *Coyote City* (1988); Monique Mojica's *Princess Pocahontas and the Blue Spots* (1989) and Beatrice Culleton Mosionier's *Night of the Trickster* (1992). The role of the Trickster figure as an emblem of cultural survival is summed up by Highway's 'A Note on the Trickster', which prefaces all his earlier published work. It concludes 'Without the continued presence of this extraordinary figure, the core of Indian culture would be gone forever' (1998: np).

In this brief survey of First Nations literature there is, of course, the danger of homogenizing and generalizing, and to counter this it should be said that a wide variety of positions, from traditionalist to postmodern, have been taken up by First Nations writers. Many, if not all, defy simple classification. For example,

Highway's emphasis on the Trickster figure is from one perspective a traditional Native element, but his plays are in fact a hybrid of Native and western elements, including classical Greek drama, grand opera, the sonata, country and western, blues and so on. His early mentors are equally eclectic, including the anglophone poet and playwright James Reaney and the Québécois novelist and playwright Michel Tremblay.

Warnings about viewing Native literature through a postcolonial lens have been made by a number of Native Canadians, among them Lee Maracle, Jeannette Armstrong and Thomas King. In 'Godzilla vs. Post-Colonial' (1990), King introduces four 'vantage points' – tribal, polemical, interfusional and associational – which avoid seeing Native literature solely in terms of a reaction to the arrival of European settlers. 'Tribal' literature is presented in the Native language and is directed towards the tribe or community itself. 'Polemical' literature (King includes Mosionier's *In Search of April Raintree*, Campbell's *Halfbreed* and Adams's *Prison of Grass*) is concerned with the clash of Native and non-Native cultures. 'Interfusional' literature blends oral and written literature. Finally, 'associational' literature refers to contemporary Native writers who focus on the daily activities of Native life, organizing the plots of their works along 'flat' narrative lines without the climaxes and denouements typical of non-Native writing. King's scheme should be regarded as suggestive rather than definitive, and is particularly useful in that it questions Eurocentric assumptions about literary criteria. His landmark novel *Green Grass, Running Water* (1993), has elements of all four types, arguably the most significant being the 'polemical' and the 'interfusional'. In the novel, Coyote and four ancient trickster Indians continuously disrupt the narrative and through their dialogues and stories decentre ethnocentric ideologies of land, religion and literature. *Green Grass* is among other things a series of trickster tales that educate through laughter, a comedic challenge to ecological imperialism, a satire on stereotypes of Native peoples, and a brilliant series of counter-discursive skirmishes with a wide range of mainstream texts including the Bible, Fenimore Cooper and John Wayne movies.

Other works which challenge fixed literary and historical frames and assumptions include Daniel David Moses's play *Almighty Voice and His Wife* (1991), which reclaims the history and life of Almighty Voice, a Cree Indian, hounded and killed by the Mounties in 1897 for the initial misdemeanour of illegally slaughtering a cow; Margot Kane's deconstruction of popular stereotypes of Indian women in her one-woman play *Moonlodge* (1990); and Monique Mojica's two-woman play *Princess Pocahontas and the Blue Spots*, which in a series of 'transformations' foregrounds the constructed nature of Native female stereotypes.

First Nations literature has been established over the past forty years through Native and Métis publishing houses (such as Theytus Books, Pemmican Publications Inc., Kegedonce Press, Gabriel Dumont Institute Press), as well as through Canadian publishers active in First Nations publishing (e.g. Fifth

House, Talonbooks, University of Manitoba Press) and there is an increasing interest in Native North American writing among international publishing houses – Oxford University Press's 1998 *An Anthology of Canadian Native Literature in English*, second edition, edited by Daniel David Moses and Terry Goldie, is a case in point. Mention should also be made to the work of Jeannette Armstrong as Director of the En'owkin International School of Writing in Penticton, British Columbia, in encouraging a generation of First Nations writers. That said, Thomas King has warned against myths of progress and improvement which might be implied by the terms 'pre-colonial', 'colonial' and 'post-colonial' (1990: 11), and neo-imperial inequalities are still in place. There would, however, appear to be greater attention paid to listening and learning from Native writers by non-Native scholars, and an increasing confidence among Native writers in the use of English as a 'weapon', seeing themselves in Paula Gunn Allen's term as 'word warriors' (1986: 51–183). Although writers like Jeannette Armstrong in her essay 'Keepers of the Earth' have said that they feel expressive limitations in a second language (English) which 'does not contain the words I require' (1995: 317), there is also a keen awareness that English (or, in Quebec, French) remains the language of power. Scholar and poet Emma LaRocque (Plains-Cree Métis) sums this up when she writes 'I have sought to master this language so that it would no longer master me' (1993: xxvi).

ANGLOPHONE CARIBBEAN AND ASIAN WRITERS IN CANADA

The land we now call Canada was already multicultural, and multilingual, before the arrival of the first Europeans.

(Kamboureli 1996: 11).

Smaro Kamboureli draws attention to the fact that Canadian multiculturalism is not a recent phenomenon, as witnessed by the diverse cultures of pre-contact Aboriginals on the North American continent. Moreover, early colonial settlement included diverse ethnic groups, including approximately two thousand Black Loyalists, former slaves and free men from the American colonies, who came to Nova Scotia in 1783. Chinese immigration began with the British Columbia gold rush (1858) and later in the 1880s the Canadian Pacific Railway hired about fifteen thousand Chinese labourers, one-third of whom stayed on after their contract ended. Immigration from South Asia began in the 1890s. Although the Black and Asian presence in Canada has a relatively long history, it was not until the 1970s that Canadian-Caribbean and Canadian-Asian writers began to be published in any numbers. This section focuses on two groups of so-called 'minority' writers who have had a significant impact on Canadian literature. A survey of this writing not only reveals the diversity of this writing, but also the complexity and ambivalence of Canadian multiculturalism.

Government commitment to multiculturalism began with Prime Minister Pierre Trudeau's 1971 White Paper, and culminated in the Canadian Multiculturalism Act (1988). The professed intention of this legislation was to respect the cultural and racial diversity of Canadian society, but critics have pointed to a longer history of discriminatory laws and practices particularly directed towards Asians, such as the Chinese Exclusion Act (1923–47) and the internment of Canadian-Japanese in the Second World War (1939–45). Others have critiqued the tokenism of official multiculturalism – 'one day set aside to eat yams and get dressed up', in the words of Himani Bannerji (quoted in Kamboureli 1996: 183) – while prevailing racist attitudes remain unchanged. Smaro Kamboureli has argued that historically the prevailing (but not uncontested) ideology has been to define Canada as a cohesive and homogenous nation, identity being asserted by what it excludes: Aboriginals and later the new immigrants (Kamboureli 1996). In the field of literary studies, Arun P. Mukherjee has critiqued Northrop Frye and Margaret Atwood as nationalist critics perpetuating an essentialized (white) Canadian character (1995: 428). Frye wrote of a 'garrison mentality' in the Canadian psyche, a throwback to the threatened and isolated garrisons of colonial times, and Atwood in *Survival* (1972) refigured this theme in terms of victims and survival.

Diversity and complexity are immediately apparent when investigating individual writers. Within the anglophone Caribbean population itself there are marked political, historical and linguistic differences, and between individuals there are widely ranging ethnic, class and gender perspectives. There is certainly no consensus on identification with the 'homeland'. Neil Bissoondath, born in Trinidad, presents one extreme when he acknowledges that 'I am no longer Trinidadian [. . .] I do not share the hopes, fears, joys and views of Trinidadians' (quoted in Kamboureli 1996: 427). The other extreme is presented by the novelist and poet Arnold Itwaru, born in Guyana and resident in Toronto since 1969, who says 'ethnic identity cannot exist in severance from [. . .] its members' history, their social memory, their fundamental historical consciousness' (quoted in Kamboureli 1996: 196).

One way of organizing such diversity is to take a diasporic perspective in order to focus on such themes as displacement, acculturation, generational differences, past histories and the notion of 'home', themes which may or may not occur in the works themselves. Barbados-born Austin Clarke's 'Toronto trilogy' – *The Meeting Point* (1967), *Storm of Fortune* (1973) and *The Bigger Light* (1975) – which depicts the lives of Barbados immigrants in Canada, can be studied in this light. Diaspora studies also places the dispersal of individuals around the world within actual political and historical contexts. In addition to a strong Jamaican presence in which women writers predominate (Louise Bennett, Olive Senior, Lorna Goodison, Pamela Mordecai, Lillian Allen, Honor Ford-Smith, Makeda Silvera, Rachel Manley, Afua Cooper, Nalo Hopkinson) many well-known Canadian writers of Caribbean extraction have roots in either Trinidad or Guyana, countries which have large Asian populations, the result of the indenture system which brought Indian workers to the colonies of various European powers in the mid-nineteenth century. Life on a plantation in colonial

Guyana is the subject of Arnold Itwaru's first novel *Shanti* (1990). Other Indo-Guyanese of note who have lived in Canada most of their working lives include the poets and novelists Cyril Dabydeen and Sasenarine Persaud.

Trinidad has been the home of significant Indo-Caribbean and Afro-Caribbean writers who have come to Canada. The Indo-Caribbeans include Harold Sonny Ladoo, Neil Bissoondath and Ramabai Espinet, all descended from Indian indentured labourers, who in very different ways address life in Trinidad and Canada. Born in 1945, Ladoo lived in Toronto with his son and wife from 1968, but met a brutal and untimely death, probably murdered, in 1973 on a return visit to his home country. His first book *No Pain Like This Body* (1972), set in 1905 in an imaginary Carib Island, but clearly a portrait of Trinidad, addresses for the first time in literary form the desperate struggle for survival of first- and second-generation Trinidadian East Indians practising subsistence farming. His second novel, *Yesterdays*, published posthumously in 1974, is a scatological comedy that casts a critical but compassionate eye on present-day Trinidad, but also satirizes colonizing Christianity in the West Indies. Thus, the son of the family, Poonwa, seeks to initiate a Hindu mission to Canada to do to Canadians what their missionaries did to Trinidad's Hindus. Neil Bissoondath arrived in Toronto in 1973 at the age of eighteen. In his first novel *A Casual Brutality* (1988), the protagonist, a Toronto doctor, Raj Ramsingh, returns to his homeland Casaquemada (a thinly-disguised Trinidad) to find the post-independence island prey to dictatorship and violence, a violence that takes the life of his wife and son. Ladoo's and Bissoondath's work can be interestingly compared from the point of view of voice. The vitality of Ladoo's work derives in large part from his use of Indo-Caribbean dialect, whereas Bissoondath employs formal standard English. The effect of dialect in encouraging an identification with both the speaker and the setting can be contrasted with the distancing effect of standard English. In addition to Ladoo and Bissoondath, mention should be made of poet and novelist Ramabai Espinet, whose novel *The Swinging Bridge* (2003) is an important account of indenture history and memory from the woman's point of view.

Two notable Afro-Caribbean women writers have both been critics of multiculturalism: poet, short-story writer and film director Dionne Brand from Trinidad; and poet, novelist, playwright, essayist and short-story writer Marlene Nourbese Philip from the sister island of Tobago. Brand, who moved to Toronto in 1970, has critiqued multiculturalism for compartmentalizing ethnic minorities into cultural groups without addressing fundamental inequalities of power. Philip, who came to Canada in 1968, has argued that a policy of multiculturalism is mere window-dressing unless it is combined with a clearly articulated policy of anti-racism. Works like Philip's *Frontiers: essays and writings on racism and culture 1984–1992* (1992), or Brand's documentary film *Sisters in the Struggle* (1991), represent the effort made by minorities during the 1980s and 1990s to challenge the widespread assumption that Canada somehow transcended racism. Ormond McKague's edited collection *Racism in Canada* (1991) to which

Emma LaRocque, Arun Mukherjee and Nourbese Philip, among others, all contributed, is still essential reading today.

South Asian writers in Canada are both numerous and diverse, and a brief comment on two of the best-known names, Michael Ondaatje and Rohinton Mistry, shows how dangerous it would be to overgeneralize about so-called diaspora writing. Mistry grew up in Bombay (Mumbai) and immigrated to Canada in 1975. He has articulately challenged the assumption that immigrant writers must *per se* write about the meeting of two (or more) cultures, or that he must write about racism. In works like *A Fine Balance* (1995) and most recently *Family Matters* (2002) Mistry's focus has been life in Bombay and in particular the life, customs and religion of the Parsi minority to which he belongs. Ondaatje, born in Sri Lanka in 1943, also comes from a minority group, the Burghers, of Dutch-Tamil-Sinhalese-Portuguese origin. Unlike Mistry, Ondaatje set his early novel, *In the Skin of a Lion* (1987), in Canada, evoking both Canadian logging camps, urban Toronto in the late 1920s and 1930s, and that city's Macedonian community. His most celebrated novel, *The English Patient* (1992), however, is set in Italy at the end of the Second World War, and interrogates all artificially imposed political boundaries and the construction of nation states, which cause wars. His next novel, *Anil's Ghost* (2000) returns us to contemporary civil war in Sri Lanka. Ondaatje has seen himself as part of that early generation of diaspora writers, including Salman Rushdie, Kazuo Ishiguro, Ben Okri, and Rohinton Mistry, who left and did not come back, but who took their country of origin with them to a new place (see Kamboureli 1996: 241).

Both Mistry and Ondaatje came to Canada for the cultural and educational opportunities it could offer – the so-called 'pull' factor. Other writers came as refugees, in effect 'pushed' out of their country of birth or origin. Such writers are instanced by Bahadur Tejani, a poet, novelist and short-story writer with Gujarati roots, who was forced to leave Uganda after Idi Amin expelled Asians in 1972, and he lived for several years in Vancouver. Better known is M.G. Vassanji, who was born in Kenya of parents who were second- and third-generation Indians in Africa, and who came via Tanzania and the USA to Canada in 1978. Vassanji's own family history as well as the life of his protagonists in such novels as *The Gunny Sack* (1989) and *The In-Between World of Vikram Lall* (2003) show how the diasporic experience can involve multiple displacements. In 1982 Vassanji co-founded the influential *The Toronto South Asian Review* (TSAR – later renamed *The Toronto Review of Contemporary Writing Abroad*). The journal branched into publishing, and since 1985 TSAR publications have become increasingly important in publishing fiction and criticism particularly pertaining to Asia and Africa.

Asian writing in Canada also includes Japanese-Canadian and Chinese-Canadian writing. The collective experience of internment and dispersal in the aftermath of the bombing of Pearl Harbor on 7 December 1941 is a theme that unites the writing of many significant Japanese-Canadian writers. Joy Kogawa's *Obasan* (1981), records in painful detail the daily-increasing xenophobia that underlay the removal of all Japanese-Canadian citizens away from the west coast during the Second World War. This forced relocation in squalid camps mainly in the prairies led, not infrequently, to family rupture and deaths. *Obasan* has become a canonized text in Canadian literature, and has played a similar pedagogical role to Mosionier's *In Search of April Raintree* in informing a wide Canadian readership of the shameful treatment towards minorities that had previously been kept hidden. Both novels have also been adapted for younger readers, appearing as *Naomi's Road* (1986) and *April Raintree* (1984), and a translation of *Naomi's Road* has been adopted as a textbook for Japanese junior high schools. *Obasan* relies heavily on Muriel Kitagawa's *Letters to Wes and Other Writings on Japanese Canadians, 1941–1948*, edited by Japanese-Canadian scholar and poet Roy Miki. Miki and Kogawa have been key figures in the redress movement – that is, the initiative to gain from the Canadian government an acknowledgement of historical guilt and financial reparation to Japanese Canadians, which was finally achieved in 1988. Kerri Sakamoto's *The Electrical Field* (1998), set in an Ontario suburb in the 1970s, shows how contemporary Japanese-Canadians still live under the shadow of the internment camps, a theme that unites *nisei* (second generation) and *sansei* (third generation) Japanese-Canadian writers.

An important figure in Chinese-Canadian writing, particularly on the West Coast, is short-story writer, poet and editor Jim Wong-Chu. With Bennett Lee he co-edited *Many-Mouthed Birds: contemporary writing by Chinese Canadians* (1991), containing short fiction and poetry by twenty Chinese Canadians, among them Sky Lee, Paul Yee and Fred Wah. Sky Lee's *Disappearing Moon Café* (1990) conforms to the pattern of many immigrant novels in chronicling the lives of four generations of Chinese-Canadians as they gradually become part of Canada. The feminist perspective of the protagonist's need to understand the secrets of her own family as well as discovering her own needs as a young mother recall Maxine Hong Kingston's *The Woman Warrior* (1976). Evelyn Lau represents a younger generation of writers and has, by contrast, a resistance both to being seen as Chinese-Canadian and to political and feminist stances. Her autobiographical *Runaway: diary of a street kid* (1989), which deals with juvenile prostitution and drug addiction, can be compared to a number of other 'skid row' autobiographies by minority writers including Ronald Lee's *Goddam Gypsy* (1972), Maria Campbell's *Half-Breed* (1973), Lee Maracle's *Bobbi Lee: Indian rebel* (1975), Anthony Apakark Thrasher's *Thrasher: skid row Eskimo* (1976), and James Tyman's *Inside Out: an autobiography of a Native Canadian* (1989).

CONCLUSIONS, REAPPRAISALS AND ABSENCES

Any survey of a nation's literature leaves out more than it includes. Well-known Canadian writers like Robertson Davies, Margaret Atwood and Alice Munro have been avoided deliberately, partly because they have already received a great deal of critical attention, but also because the focus of this chapter has been on writing which has challenged and questioned the anglocentric domination in Canadian literature. A more serious omission is the absence – for reasons of space – of a discussion of francophone writing, which can with some justice claim that it is often overlooked in postcolonial studies of Canada, which is regrettably dominated by speakers of English. The recommended further reading section below should prove helpful in partially offsetting this gap.

Another lacuna is the absence of a regional approach to Canadian literature, although regionalism has often been seen as a defining feature of Canadian culture. Racial minority writers have typically been excluded from standard anthologies of 'Prairie fiction', 'Maritime fiction', 'West coast writing' and so on, because the notion of region has implicitly been linked to European notions of nationhood and a national literature. Indigenous and ethnic writing frequently constructs alternative Canadas and challenges regionalist hegemonies. Indeed to induct, say, Maria Campbell's *Half-Breed* and Joy Kogawa's *Obasan* into the canon of 'Prairie fiction' would be salutary, as it would inevitably explode myths of settler triumphalism over the land. First Nations writers like Jeannette Armstrong, too, require from the reader a reappraisal of Eurocentric notions of land and identity.

This chapter's focus on First Nations, Caribbean and Asian writing also excludes other so-called 'minority' writing, such as Italian-Canadian literature and a strong tradition of Ukrainian-Canadian literature, for which *The Oxford Companion to Canadian Literature* (second edition, 1997) provides a useful survey. It should also be noted that First Nations and other racial minority writings are not mutually exclusive categories. Collections of essays and interviews like Makeda Silvera's *The Other Woman: women of colour in contemporary Canadian literature* (1995), or anthologies such as Smaro Kamboureli's *Making a Difference: Canadian multicultural literature* (1996), which bring together Native and immigrant writers, have recognized this.

Finally, it is possible to look beyond national boundaries and view Canada from a more global perspective. Canada as a settler culture has most frequently been contrasted with Australia (and to a lesser extent New Zealand) as shown by Terry Goldie's *Fear and Temptation: the image of the Indigene in Canadian, Australian, and New Zealand literature* (1989) and Graham Huggan's *Territorial Disputes: maps and mapping strategies in contemporary Canadian and Australian fiction* (1994). Moreover, recent work by Diana Brydon, George Elliott Clarke and Rinaldo Walcott have sought to extend Paul Gilroy's seminal *The Black Atlantic: modernity and double consciousness* (1993) to include not only the transnational connections between the black cultures of Africa, America, the Caribbean and Britain, but also of Black Canada (Brydon 2001a; Brydon 2001b; Clarke 1996, Walcott 2003).

RECOMMENDED FURTHER READING

Black, Ayanna (ed.) *Fiery Spirits and Voices: Canadian writers of African descent* (Toronto: HarperCollins, 2000).

Boudreau, Diane, *Histoire de la littérature amérindienne au Québec: Oralité et écriture* (Montréal: L'Hexagone, 1993).

Clarke, George Elliott, *Odysseys Home: mapping African-Canadian literature.* Toronto: University of Toronto Press, 2002.

Kamboureli, Smaro (ed.) *Making a Difference: Canadian multicultural literature* (Toronto: Oxford University Press, 1996).

Kröller, Eva-Marie, *The Cambridge Companion to Canadian Literature* (Cambridge: Cambridge University Press, 2004).

Maurizio, Gatti. *Être écrivain amérindien au Quebec: Indianité et creation littéraire* (Montréal: Hurtubise HMH, 2006).

New, W. H., *A History of Canadian Literature*, second edition (Montréal: McGill-Queen's University Press, 2003).

Shek, Ben-Zion. *French-Canadian and Québécois Novels* (Toronto: Oxford University Press, 1991).

8
THE CARIBBEAN

MELANIE OTTO

'BEYOND THE HORIZON': THE LOCATION OF THE CARIBBEAN

Defining the Caribbean geographically also determines what is included in the term Caribbean literature. In his introduction to *La isla que se repite* (1989, trans. *The Repeating Island*), the Cuban novelist and critic Antonio Benítez-Rojo offers the following definition:

> In recent decades we have begun to see a clearer outline to the profile of a group of American nations whose colonial experiences and languages have been different, but which share certain undeniable features. I mean the countries usually called 'Caribbean' or 'of the Caribbean basin'.
>
> (1996: 1)

For the definition of Caribbean literature, Benítez-Rojo's phrase 'of the Caribbean basin' suggests an interesting geographical range and has the potential to transform the way we think about Caribbean cultures. Geographically, the Caribbean basin is regarded as an entity, comprising the Caribbean islands as well as the coastal areas of the USA, South and Central America. However, literary and cultural studies has tended to segment the region into anglophone, francophone and hispanic units, etc., and comparative studies of the literatures and cultures of the Caribbean Basin are relatively rare.

However, the Caribbean is not just confined to the geographical region of the Caribbean basin. In her introduction to *The Penguin Book of Caribbean Verse in English* (1986), Paula Burnett writes:

> Caribbean literature is, of course, first of all by and for Caribbean people. Like any culture, it gives expression to a particular people's experience. But Caribbean literature is also international in a special sense, both because it is a unique cultural hybrid, and because the Caribbean experience is being lived and explored artistically in Europe and North America as well as in the Caribbean region itself.
>
> (1986: xxiii)

These remarks remind us that Caribbean literature is not just literature produced in the Caribbean itself but also in other parts of the world, such as Britain, France, Spain, the USA and Canada, where many people from the Caribbean live today. In a similar sense, 'Caribbeanness will always remain beyond the horizon' (Benítez-Rojo 1996: xi); its parameters will always remain fluid.

In *The People Who Came* (1986), a three-volume history of the Americas for Caribbean secondary schools edited by Kamau Brathwaite, Alma Norman writes:

> We who live in the Caribbean might be called 'people on the move'. Our people have always migrated from the Caribbean to other regions. In the past, people also migrated in great numbers *to* the Caribbean. They came from Africa, from Asia, and from Europe.
>
> (1986: 6)

Norman adds that even the first Americans, who inhabited the hemisphere before the arrival of Christopher Columbus in 1492 and the other 'people who came' after him, had migrated there from elsewhere. The Caribbean experience, therefore, implies a double diaspora: a migration to the Caribbean from elsewhere between the sixteenth and nineteenth centuries, and from the Caribbean to other parts of the globe, beginning in the middle of the twentieth century. This experience has had a great impact on the development of the region's languages and literatures.

Many of the Caribbean nations gained independence from Europe in the 1960s, although some of the territories of the francophone Caribbean, such as Guadeloupe, Martinique and Guyane (French Guyana), are still colonies of France (each is formally a *département d'outre-mer*). Especially in the anglophone Caribbean, independence was followed by a wave of emigration to the British 'motherland' in the hope of partaking in an economic prosperity that was lacking at home. The first generation of Caribbean emigrants, who came to Britain in the 1950s and 1960s, is known as the 'Windrush Generation' after the name of the first boat that took Jamaicans to London in 1948, the *SS Empire Windrush*. Today there are also large diaspora communities in the USA, especially from the hispanic and francophone Caribbean, such as Puerto Rico and Haiti, and in Canada mainly from the anglophone and francophone Caribbean.

LANGUAGE IN THE CARIBBEAN: MOTHER TONGUE OR FOREIGN ANGUISH?

> *a foreign anguish*
> *is english –*
> *another tongue*
> *my mother*
>   (Philip 1993: 32)

These lines from the Trinidadian poet Marlene Nourbese Philip's 'Discourse on the Logic of Language' point to the important role of language in the literatures and cultures of the Caribbean, which has its roots in the region's historical and economic reality. Unlike in other parts of the postcolonial world, very few aboriginal languages survive in the Caribbean due to the decimation of the

Amerindians in the early centuries of colonization, and although the slaves brought their indigenous languages with them from Africa, they lost the memory of those languages relatively quickly (some critics suggest through a deliberate policy of language suppression in order to prevent the possibility of slave rebellions). Consequently, 'the transplanted Africans found that psychic survival depended on their facility for a kind of *double entendre*' (Ashcroft, Griffiths and Tiffin 1989: 146) with regard to the language of the slave master: 'They were forced to develop the skill of being able to say one thing in front of "massa" and have it interpreted differently by their fellow slaves' (146). Out of this 'radical subversion of the meanings of the master's tongue' (146) has evolved a new language, which, although different from that of the former slave master and indigenous to the Caribbean, still retains a European base. The region's 'quest for decolonisation', therefore, often takes place at a cultural level first and foremost in the 'battle for language' (Torres-Saillant 1997: 7).

Caribbean forms of language are usually referred to as creole or patois in the franco- and anglophone parts of the region. However, some writers, such as the Barbadian poet and critic Kamau Brathwaite and the Jamaican poet Mutabaruka prefer the term 'nation language' (see Brathwaite 1984 and 1993) to patois, as the latter term is sometimes perceived as derogatory and the language it designates as merely derivative of the standard language. Moreover, whereas creole is spoken by white, mixed-race and black West Indians alike, 'nation language' most often designates only Afro-creole, focusing on the African heritage of the Caribbean. Since the grammar of creole or patois can be very different to that of the standard European languages, these new forms are now recognized as languages in their own right rather than as 'dialects'. Creole is, in this sense, no longer a 'foreign anguish' but a mother tongue. The fact that there are various forms of creole indicates that it is not one monolithic language but a conglomerate of lects or speech patterns, ranging from standard English to forms that use European words but have grammar structures similar to those found in West Africa. This range of speech patterns is often called the 'creole continuum'.

CULTURAL MODELS OF CREOLIZATION

In the development of creole languages the act of moving beyond mere imitation of the former colonial powers is a vital step towards the formation of independent Caribbean identities. But the notion of what it means to be 'creole' goes far beyond issues of language. It affects every aspect of Caribbean life. Creolization as a cultural model, in fact, traverses linguistic borders in the Caribbean. The word 'creole' also means Caribbean-born, as opposed to aboriginal or European-born. It is not a racially specific term in the region but applies to people of all races whose place of origin is the Caribbean. (In the USA, however, it is applied only to the descendants of the early French settlers in

Louisiana.) The cultural processes of creolization have become a central preoccupation of several Caribbean thinkers, for a number of reasons.

Before writers began to focus on creolization as a particular way of thinking about identity in the Caribbean beyond European categorization, there was a movement that propagated the reorientation specifically towards the region's African heritage: Négritude. (Brathwaite's and Mutabaruka's notion of 'nation language', for example, is influenced by this reorientation.) Négritude sought to define Caribbean cultural identity in historical and racial affiliations to the so-called 'mother' continent of Africa. Its main thinkers in the Caribbean (it also had an African counterpart) were Léon Damas (French Guyana) and Aimé Césaire (Martinique), whose main works in this movement were, respectively, *Pigments* (1937) and *Cahier d'un retour au pays natal* (1939, trans. *Notebook of a Return to my Native Land*). Négritude advocated a rejection and even defiance of anything European, and an identification with everything African, turning erstwhile 'negative' terms applied to people of African descent (such as 'Negro' and 'savage') into signifiers of black pride. Although a very powerful expression of cultural identity in the early decades of the twentieth century, its tenets were later rejected as too simplistic and restrictive, and not representative of the mixed-race and multicultural reality of Caribbean life. A complementary movement to the mainly francophone Négritude writers was the Latin American Negrismo, which began to develop in the 1920s. Also focusing on the African element in Caribbean and Latin American culture, Negrismo's main exponent was the Cuban poet Nicolás Guillén. The movement had close ties with the Harlem Renaissance and its central figure, Langston Hughes, who met Guillén in Cuba.

In spite of his own dedication to the African roots of Caribbean culture, Kamau Brathwaite's definition of 'creolization' is much more inclusive than that of the Négritude writers. In *The Development of the Creole Society in Jamaica* (1971) Brathwaite says of the creole society of Jamaica between 1770 and 1820: 'The single most important factor in the development of Jamaican society was [. . .] a cultural action [. . .] based upon the stimulus/response of individuals within the society to their environment and – as white/black, culturally discrete groups – to each other' (2005: 296). What links the Jamaican creole society of the late eighteenth and early nineteenth centuries to the creole societies of the twentieth and twenty-first centuries is the interaction of two or more distinct cultural and racial units in order to form 'a "new" construct, made up of newcomers to the landscape and cultural strangers each to the other' (296). Creolization is, therefore, a distinctly Caribbean form of hybridity.

Brathwaite's definition of 'creolization' follows very closely Fernando Ortiz's idea of 'transculturation' (for more on this idea, see Chapter 10: Latin America). Ortiz is a Cuban critic who is a generation older than Brathwaite, and his main work on transculturation is *Contrapunteo cubano del tabaco y el azucar* (1940, trans. *Cuban Counterpoint: Tobacco and Sugar*). Ortiz lists five stages within the process of transculturation: antagonism (white domination and black resistance); compromise (the races begin to mix); adjustment (imitation of Europe by mixed-race creoles); self-assertion (creoles recover their self-respect and dignity); and integration, which Ortiz regards to be still in the future.

Ortiz's influence can also be felt in the work of the fellow Cuban thinker Antonio Benítez-Rojo. His most influential book, *The Repeating Island*, is dedicated to Ortiz but departs significantly in scope and approach from the author of *Contrapunteo*. Benítez-Rojo reads the Caribbean from a postmodernist perspective, using Chaos theory to create a cultural metaphor for the Caribbean, the island that repeats itself:

> Which one, then, would be the repeating island, Jamaica, Aruba, Puerto Rico, Miami, Haiti, Recife? Certainly none of the ones that we know. That original, that island at the center, is as impossible to reach as the hypothetical Antillas that reappeared time and again, always fleetingly, in the cosmographers' charts.
>
> (1996: 3–4)

The emphasis on repetition breaks down the hierarchy between the original (presumably European culture) and the derivative (Caribbean cultures). Nothing is fixed. There is only a flux of signifiers with no beginning and no end. Benítez-Rojo approaches the idea of creolization in a similar way. He argues that for the (descendants of) slaves the new Caribbean environment demanded new ways of relating. Some aspects of the ancestral African cultures became obsolete in this new environment. Only fragments of them could be meaningfully used and had to be adjusted to a new way of life. He argues that other cultures coming to the Caribbean – from India, China and elsewhere – also underwent such a process of fragmentation. Moreover, creolization never produces a fixed cultural unit but fragments that are always in a state of flux – that 'come together in an instant to form a dance step, a linguistic trope, the line of a poem, and afterwards they repel each other to re-form and pull apart once more, and so on' (2002: 202).

What is often called 'creolization' in the anglophone Caribbean appears as *antillanité* and *creolité* in the francophone Caribbean. For Édouard Glissant, who coined the term *antillanité* (Caribbeanness) in *Le Discours Antillais* (1981, trans. *Caribbean Discourse*) and developed it further in *Poétique de la relation* (1990, trans. *Poetics of Relation*), Caribbean reality contains the potential to link cultures across language barriers. Being Martinican himself, his work engages with that of Césaire. Glissant, however, rejects the older writer's emphasis on Africa and conceives of his own concept of Caribbeanness as something that goes beyond identification with one race and one place: 'We are the roots of a cross-cultural relationship' (1992: 67). For Glissant, Caribbeanness is multiracial and multilingual. He also sees the region as part of the Americas, so his focus is more hemispheric than that found in other cultural models of creolization.

Thinkers who use Glissant's work as a starting point are Patrick Chamoiseau,

Raphaël Confiant and Jean Bernabé, from Martinique. In their seminal work *Eloge de la Créolité* (1989, trans. *In Praise of Creoleness*, 1990) they present their own movement of *créolité* or 'creoleness'. Whereas for Glissant race is just one among many issues, Chamoiseau, Confiant and Bernabé specifically promote the racial diversity of the Caribbean and the literary value of the creole language. Rejecting Glissant's hemispheric view as too vast, the authors focus on small countries like Martinique and describe creoleness as the result of a process of interaction and transaction between the different cultures of the Caribbean. They differ from other thinkers in their argument that creolization is not just limited to the Caribbean but also occurs in the Seychelles, Mauritius and Reunion (an argument also made by Glissant). Moreover, Chamoiseau, Confiant and Bernabé also claim that creolization is not a pan-Caribbean phenomenon, as it did not occur, allegedly, in northern Cuba, which has a strong Andalusian influence, and in the Hindu-dominated parts of Trinidad.

Creolization, then, might be thought of as one of the defining features of Caribbean life. The following sections will deal with specific instances of creolization in literary and cultural production.

CREATING CARIBBEAN PARADIGMS: CALIBAN AND ERZULIE

> *ogrady says*
> . . .
> *say*
>
> *i*
> *am your world*
> *you must not break*
>
> *it*
> (Brathwaite 2001: 88)

Many Caribbean writers reject the uncritical use of 'Western' intellectual paradigms – postmodernism, feminism and even postcolonialism – in the reading of their work. Instead they have negotiated their own paradigms to more accurately reflect their ways of experiencing the world.

One of the most powerful metaphors of Caribbeanness is the figure of Caliban from Shakespeare's play *The Tempest* (1611). Many writers from the region challenge Shakespeare's depiction of Caliban as bestial and brutal, and reclaim the image as an icon of Caribbean self-assertion. Although Shakespeare does not explicitly state that the setting of *The Tempest* is the Caribbean, the tropical island environment together with the power relations between Prospero and Caliban are suggestive of the master–slave relationship found on the plantation. In this context, the Caliban–Prospero dyad returns us to the issue of language. Caliban is Prospero's slave. Prospero also claims that Caliban did not know the use of language until Prospero taught him to speak, so the only way

Caliban can express himself is within the parameters of his 'master's' tongue. In his collection of essays *The Pleasures of Exile* (1960), the Barbadian novelist George Lamming argues that for this reason Caliban is imprisoned in Prospero's language: 'There is no escape from the prison of Prospero's gift. [. . .] This is the first important achievement of the colonising process' (1992: 109). He is defined by Prospero but cannot define or speak for himself. Lamming is one of the first anglophone Caribbean writers to claim Caliban as a metaphor for the enslaved.

However, most writers are quick to point out the subversive element in the Caliban–Prospero relationship. This is a reading of Caliban put forward by Kamau Brathwaite. In 'Nam(e)track', the poem from which the opening lines to this section are taken, Brathwaite depicts a war of words between O'Grady, a plantation owner, and an unnamed enslaved mother, who calls O'Grady 'the man who possesses us all'. At the centre of their struggle is a child, the slave mother's son. Implied in these characters are the personae of Prospero, Sycorax (Caliban's supposedly African mother), and Caliban himself. O'Grady's/Prospero's insistence on Caliban's repetition of his words is symbolic of the erasure of Caliban's African heritage, resulting in an enforced identification with the slave-master's culture. But Sycorax acts as a counterforce to Prospero, reminding Caliban of his African origins – evidence that he, and by extension the slaves, did in fact have a 'mother tongue' (a culture) before the arrival of Prospero. It is this alternative culture that gives him the power to resist and subvert Prospero's power. By the end of 'Nam(e)tracks' Caliban talks back to Prospero in 'nation language', stating 'but e nevva maim what me mudda me name' (2001: 94).

The most influential work on Caliban in the Spanish Caribbean is the Cuban critic Roberto Fernández Retamar's essay 'Calibán: apuntes sobre la cultura de nuestra América' (1971, trans. 'Caliban: Notes Toward a Discussion of Culture in Our America). Fernández Retamar's essay is particularly valuable in that it provides an encyclopaedic and cross-cultural approach that chronicles the changing perceptions on Caliban within the American hemisphere. He begins with an etymology of Caliban, arguing that Shakespeare used an anagram of 'cannibal'. Cannibal itself is traced back to the navigation logbooks of Christopher Columbus, where the word appears as one of the forms of the ethnic name *Carib* or *Caribes*, a fierce nation of the West Indies, who are recorded to have been *anthropophagi* (eaters of human flesh). Caliban is depicted as monstrous because of this association with 'cannibal', which also gives Prospero the 'permission' to enslave him. From there Fernández Retamar provides a history of the reception of the Caliban image within 'our America' (i.e. south of the Rio Grande) that ranges from the nineteenth century to late 1960s (see also Chapter 10: Latin America).

It was not until the late 1960s that Caliban was taken up as a symbol of pride by Caribbean writers. Kamau Brathwaite was among the first to do so, together with Aimé Césaire, who wrote his own version of *The Tempest*, *Une tempête* (1968). In Césaire's play Caliban is a black slave and Ariel a mulatto (mixed-race) slave. Both Caliban and Ariel attempt to gain their freedom from their 'master' Prospero. Caliban's approach to freedom is through rebellion while Ariel tries to appeal to Prospero morally and intellectually. Thus we see Ariel being aligned with the Caribbean intellectual and Caliban as the descendant of slaves. Caliban's rebellion fails. In his final speech, he accuses Prospero of lying to him and holding him inferior, and the speech has become a classic example of the oppressed and colonized rejecting the oppressor and colonizer.

Feminist writers in the Caribbean are beginning to reject the figure of Caliban as failing to reflect the female perspective of Caribbean history (see Torres-Saillant 1997). Joan Dayan, for example, proposes Erzulie, a goddess from the Haitian Voodoo pantheon, as a female counterpart to Caliban, arguing that 'Erzulie [. . .] tells the history of women's lives that has not been told' (1996: 43). In Voodoo iconography, which often uses Catholic imagery as Voodoo was outlawed for a long time, Erzulie is sometimes depicted as Our Lady of Czestochowa. The icon of Czestochowa shows a black Madonna with a child in her arms, and in one of her many aspects this manifestation of Erzulie is the patron spirit of single mothers, lesbians and women who experience domestic violence. The child in her arms is said to be her daughter Anaïse – a detail that points not only to the subversive potential of Voodoo with regard to the dominant culture but also to the strong mother–daughter bond found in many Caribbean societies.

According to Voodoo tradition, Erzulie fought in the Haitian slave rebellion in the late eighteenth century, which resulted in Haiti's independence from France in 1804. Some writers perceive a distinct link between the rebellion and some rites of the Haitian Voodoo cult. The scars that appear on the icon of Czestochowa/Erzulie's face are believed to be injuries received on the battlefield. She embodies the spirit of rebellion, the desire to throw off the yoke of enslavement. But those are not her only wounds. It is said that she had her tongue cut out by her own people, forced into silence by those closest to her, who feared she would betray their secrets should she be captured by the French (see Brown 2001). As the story goes, the dark, rebellious Erzulie refuses marriage with any of the other Voodoo gods who are regarded as her sexual partners, and she raises her daughter on her own. However, she frequently participates in ritual marriages with the living, and some of these marriages are with women. Thus she emerges as an independent childbearing woman, who defies conventional sexuality and the authority of the patriarchal family, and offers the possibility of having a child without a man. In doing so she also offers an alternative family structure – one which reflects the all-female households characteristic of many Caribbean societies, where women are often forced to rely on their own resources. Hand in hand with this economic situation goes the fact that many traditions and customs are handed down through the female line, from mother to daughter.

One writer who engages at length with this strong mother–daughter bond and its potentially subversive subtext is Jamaica Kincaid. She revisits this theme in a number of her books, most notably in *At the Bottom of the River* (1983), *Annie*

John (1985), *Lucy* (1990) and *The Autobiography of My Mother* (1996). A recurring issue in all of these pieces is the separation of the mother from the daughter within the process of growing from girlhood into womanhood. In keeping with Erzulie's association with all-female communities, Kincaid frequently eroticizes the mother–daughter bond to emphasize the intensity of emotions between women. Theirs is a homoerotic Eden without Adam. The image of the Eden of childhood, the period of same-sex love and friendship, suggests that its destruction is brought about by a heterosexual male entity. But the most prominent masculine presence in many of Kincaid's works is the mother (figure) herself. As the phallic mother she enacts the role usually ascribed to the father, who represents that part of the family that stands in for society as a whole. His task is to break up the asocial symbiosis of mother and child in order to enable the child to become an independent social entity. In Kincaid's texts the mother herself assumes this role.

The mother figures in Kincaid's work are depicted as ambivalent entities, both loved and hated, conforming to the dominant culture (patriarchal and colonial) and subversive at the same time. In the story 'Girl' (from *At the Bottom of the River*), the mother's instructions about how to become a model of English womanhood are interspersed with instructions in Caribbean herbal lore and magic, telling the girl how to perform an abortion or cast a love spell. These instructions speak of female independence and subversion. As a consequence, the mother acts out the role of Erzulie teaching her daughter Anaïse how to survive in a colonial world dominated by men, both black and white.

Although Kincaid works within the parameters of woman-centred networks, her work never mentions Erzulie explicitly, although the rebellious aspect of the Haitian spirit is there both in her mother and her girl characters. Writers who explicitly construct a narrative around Erzulie are the Guyanese writer Pauline Melville in her story 'Erzulie' (from *The Migration of Ghosts*, 1998) and the Haitian-American novelist Edwidge Danticat in *Breath, Eyes, Memory* (1994). The following section of this chapter concentrates on Melville, as her story is less well known than Danticat's novel, in which Erzulie emerges as a transcultural metaphor, straddling the divide between people of European, African, East Indian and Amerindian descent (see also Pyne-Timothy 2001).

In the story Erzulie is a convicted murderess, known by the name of Shallow-Grave because of the way she buries her victims. These victims are invariably male and are all connected, in one way or another, to the pollution of Guyana's rivers. Shallow-Grave herself reacts physically to the pollution by developing sores and ulcers on her skin. In this sense, she is a metaphor for Guyana itself, a country ravaged not only by the legacy of colonialism but also by neo-colonial exploitation. Margot, the story's other main character, serves Erzulie in the traditional Voodoo sense. Like Shallow-Grave herself, Margot embodies the nation of Guyana crippled by neo-colonial dependence. Like Erzulie she is mute and thus isolated from those around her. Although Shallow-Grave does not heal Margot's muteness, she does give healing and happiness in other forms as a return for Margot's service. In this sense, the story proposes a different kind of servitude to that of the plantation, one that enriches rather than oppresses.

The utterance of the name 'Erzulie', which happens only once in the entire story, not only lends depth to the text but broadens its geographical scope. Guyana becomes linked to Haiti, and the island in turn to Brazil, where we see Erzulie for the last time before we leave the story. Erzulie unites the Americas by bringing into consciousness their submerged African heritage. In this sense, the Haitian spirit fulfils a similar function to Caliban. However, Erzulie is not a metaphor that is claimed across the Caribbean in the same way as Caliban. Erzulie is also a lot 'younger' than Caliban in terms of being claimed as a cultural icon that encapsulates a particularly female perspective of Caribbean reality. Other female writers from the anglophone Caribbean use the image of the Jamaican maroon queen Nanny instead of Erzulie, such as Michelle Cliff in both her novels *Abeng* (1984) and *No Telephone to Heaven* (1987). But Nanny is a less potent metaphor than Erzulie in terms of cross-culturality as the maroon warrior remains largely a Jamaican icon rather than a pan-Caribbean one.

SOME KEY FORMS, THEMES AND FIGURES IN THE CARIBBEAN

Caribbean literature has a long oral tradition, which is heavily influenced by African forms of storytelling and song brought to the Caribbean by the slaves. Musical forms such as reggae and calypso are direct descendants of these early African oral traditions. Reggae, especially Bob Marley's interpretation of it, is perhaps the most famous popular art form to come out of the Caribbean. A creation of the 1960s, it reflects the waning political optimism of the post-independence era, especially among the urban poor, and often represents an outcry against the poverty and dispossession of urban ghetto dwellers. It is also heavily influenced by the Rastafarian celebration of Africa as the promised land. Black people are seen as the chosen race exiled in 'Babylon' (the white West). The Trinidadian calypso had a similarly political appeal and is a direct descendant of an African form of satire, although it does not draw on Rastafarian belief. In the realm of popular theatre the Sistren Theatre Collective represents an outstanding achievement. Founded in 1977 by a group of white and black Jamaican women, the Collective began as a special employment programme, focusing on the ordinary lives of women, who would perform their stories on stage. Aided by Honor Ford-Smith, these stories were eventually transcribed and collected in the anthology *Lionheart Gal* (1986).

In the field of poetry many writers now straddle the divide between oral and written forms. This has not always been the case. Caribbean oral forms are often presented in patois or creole. Frequently referred to as 'bad talk' within the anglophone Caribbean, patois was not regarded as an appropriate medium for poetry, and children were discouraged from speaking it in school. In the anglophone Caribbean, the Jamaican Claude McKay was the first poet to bring patois or vernacular speech into the literary tradition in the early decades of the twentieth century. McKay soon emigrated to the USA, where he became part of the Harlem Renaissance and wrote almost exclusively in the standard language to further the wider cause of black people. It was not until Louise Bennett devised a system of transcribing patois into a written form, that the vernacular became a regular medium in the literary tradition. Born in Jamaica in 1919, Bennett captures the everyday speech of Jamaicans in her poetry. Although she often performed her work, it was also published – as is that of many other writers who straddle the divide between the oral and the written. Her most famous work is the collection *Jamaica Labrish* (1966), 'labrish' being a Jamaican creole term for 'gossip'.

Whereas the work of most Caribbean writers exhibits a degree of hybridization, the writings of the St Lucian poet Derek Walcott thematize the divided heritage of Caribbean life and letters. Walcott is of mixed black African, Dutch and English descent, a fact that pervades his poetry. 'A Far Cry from Africa' (1962) epitomizes his own inner division, which he sees as paradigmatic for many peoples of the Caribbean:

> I who am poisoned with the blood of both,
> Where shall I turn, divided to the vein?
> I who have cursed
> The drunken officer of British rule, how choose
> Between this Africa and the English tongue I love?
> Betray them both, or give back what they give?
> How can I face such slaughter and be cool?
> How can I turn from Africa and live?
>
> (1992: 18)

Consequently, Walcott rejects any clear affiliation to race or nation, but argues, in the words of one of his poetic characters Shabine, 'I had no nation now but the imagination' (350). Despite this, he feels deeply rooted in Caribbean society with its cultural fusion of African, Asiatic and European elements. Walcott's breakthrough as a poet came with the collection of poems, *In a Green Night* (1962), a book that had a great impact not only on the perception of Caribbean poetry abroad but also within the Caribbean itself. But Walcott is also known as a playwright. In 1959, he founded the Trinidad Theatre Workshop which produced many of his early plays.

One of the best-known novelists from the Caribbean is Jean Rhys. Her most famous book is *Wide Sargasso Sea* (1966), a rewriting of Charlotte Brontë's character of Bertha Mason in *Jane Eyre* (1847). Born in Dominica in 1890, Rhys is of white creole descent. In *Wide Sargasso Sea*, she confronts the possibility of another side to Brontë's novel. The story of Bertha, the first Mrs Rochester, gives a voice to a character that remains silent in *Jane Eyre*, thus offering an alternative narrative to that of bestial madness. Rhys allows us to reinterpret the fate of Antoinette/Bertha by leaving the ending open. In *Jane Eyre*, Bertha starts the fire and leaps to her death. *Wide Sargasso Sea*, on the other hand, ends with Antoinette's resolution to act rather than a description of her death. Rhys's novel can thus be said to extend the possibilities of the earlier text. The Guadeloupan writer Maryse Condé has undertaken a similar project in her novel *La migration des coeurs* (1995, trans. *Windward Heights*), a retelling of Emily Brontë's *Wuthering Heights* (1847) transposed to the island of Guadeloupe. It tells the story of the 'African' Razyé (a creole word for a type of heather that grows on Guadeloupan cliffs) and Cathy, the mulatto daughter of a man who takes the orphan Razyé in and raises him. Ultimately rejected (like Brontë's Heathcliff), Razyé flees to Cuba, where he makes his fortune. On his return he discovers that Cathy has married the son of a socially prominent creole family. Razyé takes revenge for the loss of his love, which, like *Wuthering Heights*, continues into the next generation.

The rewriting of the master narratives of English literature is a common practice among postcolonial writers – *The Tempest*, as we have seen, being another case in point. The telling of a story from another perspective can be seen as an attempt to explore the gaps and silences in a text. As an extension of language use, writing is one of the strongest forms of cultural hegemony and the rewriting of the colonial canon becomes a subversive and liberating act for the (formerly) colonized.

Caribbean writers whose work can be situated in the Latin American tradition of magic realism are the Cuban novelist Alejo Carpentier and Guyanese novelist and poet Wilson Harris. Both writers, but Harris more particularly so, thematize the myth of El Dorado (the kingdom of gold) in their writings. Harris's best-known novel is *The Palace of the Peacock* (1960), which recalls colonial expeditions into the heartland of Guyana in search of El Dorado. Donne, one of the main protagonists, leads a multiracial crew (symbolic of the multiracial make-up of Guyana) through the rainforest on a nameless river in pursuit of a group of Amerindian labourers who have escaped from his plantation. The journey in pursuit of the folk becomes a quest for personal and communal salvation, during which the atrocities of colonization are magically transformed and healed. Alejo Carpentier's novel *Los Pasos Perdidos* (1953, trans. *The Lost Steps*) deals with a similar theme of salvation. But whereas Harris's crew reaches and remains in a utopian El Dorado, Carpentier's main protagonist loses access to this Edenic existence once he decides to return to his everyday world.

Many writers from the Caribbean now live in other parts of the world, be that in the old colonial centres such as France and Britain or in other parts of the Americas, such as the USA and Canada. These writers often thematize the experience of exile and diaspora and of adapting their Caribbean heritage to a new environment. Among the most prominent of these writers are the Trinidadian V. S. Naipaul, who is of East Indian descent, and the St Kitts-born, British-raised novelist Caryl Phillips. Their work, although different in many respects, is characterized by a refusal to belong to any nation or racial community, and stresses the migratory, transnational character of their personal history which they see reflected in the history of the Caribbean itself.

Much of contemporary criticism on Caribbean literature and culture not only relocates the region within the context of the Americas at large but also foregrounds the situation of the Caribbean in an increasingly globalized world. Phenomena such as creolization, which was formerly regarded as uniquely Caribbean, are today frequently read, most notably by Glissant in *Poetics of Relation*, as occurring globally. In this context, the Caribbean serves as a model for transcending linguistic borders and colonialist divisions. Moreover, many Caribbean writers now live in the USA, Canada and Europe. The works they produce there, as transnational and hybrid as their migrant authors, challenge existing definitions of American Studies and English Literature and even redefine the parameters of postcolonial studies itself.

RECOMMENDED FURTHER READING

Benítez-Rojo, Antonio, *The Repeating Island: the Caribbean and the postmodern perspective*, second edition, trans. James Maraniss (Durham, NC: Duke University Press, 1996).

Breiner, Laurence, *An Introduction to West Indian Poetry* (Cambridge: Cambridge University Press, 1998).

Dash, J. Michael, *The Other America: Caribbean literature in a New World context* (Charlottesville, VA: University Press of Virginia, 1998).

Davies, Carole Boyce and Fido, Elaine Savory (eds) *Out of the Kumbla: Caribbean women and literature* (Trenton, NJ: Africa World Press, 1990).

Donnell Alison, and Welsh, Sarah Lawson (eds) *The Routledge Reader in Caribbean Literature* (London: Routledge, 1996).

Fernández Retamar, Roberto, *Caliban and Other Essays*, trans. Edward Baker (Minneapolis, MN: University of Minnesota Press, 1989).

Glissant, Édouard, *Caribbean Discourse: selected essays*, trans. J. Michael Dash (Charlottesville, VA: University Press of Virginia, 1992).

James, Louis, *Caribbean Literature in English* (London: Longman, 1999).

Mardorossian, Carine M. (2005), *Reclaiming Difference: Caribbean women rewrite postcolonialism* (Charlotteville, VA: University of Virginia Press, 2005).

9

IRELAND

LUZ MAR GONZÁLEZ ARIAS

IRISH LITERATURE: PROBLEMS OF DEFINITION

Approaching Irish literature involves facing the uneasy task of finding out exactly what results from the sum of the two terms which form this phrase. As is only to be expected from a country that has undergone several waves of cultural and political colonization throughout its history, in Ireland identity has remained one of the central concerns of academics, writers and politicians. Received notions of Irishness – as imagined in colonial and canonical nationalist discourses – have been persistently challenged by the changing realities of the country, as have assumptions about what constitutes Irish writing.

The literary output of Ireland includes works that use the Irish language as a creative medium, together with those written in Hiberno-English: the particular form of English spoken in Ireland. Irish literature is also inclusive of texts written in more standardized, less vernacular, forms of English by the diasporic subjects living and working beyond the physical frontiers of Ireland. In addition, writing from Northern Ireland – created via an act of Partition after Ireland achieved independence in 1921 – is also an important part of what we today term Irish literature, while it is also differentiated by the province's specific cultures and vexed history. Students interested in present-day Ireland will furthermore encounter the myriad of multicultural voices that flood contemporary, Post-Celtic-Tiger Ireland – originally from areas as diverse as Asia, Africa, Latin America and Eastern Europe. In their own right, any writings produced inside the many communities currently sharing the imaginary and real landscapes of Ireland may be analysed under the rubric of Irish literature.

The debate on exactly what makes a literary text Irish has been kindled by the traditional inclusion of Irish authors in university syllabuses, anthologies and literary histories devoted to English literature. Although writers like William Butler Yeats and James Joyce engage in the Irish geographical, social and political universe in their work, they have been skilfully – or clumsily – adopted as part of the English cultural mainstream. In order to do so, the criteria of origins and date of birth have sometimes been privileged over theme or vernacular uses of the English language. It has been sometimes considered that Irish writers born before the coming of the Irish Free State are British, as are those born in Northern Ireland. These contestable if convenient chronological and spatial divisions have justified the participation of Jonathan Swift, George Bernard

Shaw, Oscar Wilde and Samuel Beckett – to name but a few – in the construction of the English literary canon. Although Seamus Heaney has long been a citizen of the Republic of Ireland and has overtly expressed his disagreement with the inclusion of his work in anthologies that contain the label 'British literature' in their title, he has also been appropriated by English literary courses on account of his place of birth being Northern Ireland. Michael Alexander's recent *A History of English Literature* (2000), for instance, makes use of the national criterion in the selection of representative authors, and thinks of Swift, Berkeley, Sterne, Goldsmith, Burke, Edgeworth, Yeats, Joyce, Beckett and Heaney as 'eligible' (5). *The Norton Anthology of English Literature*, arguably one of the anthologies most frequently consulted by readers wanting to get a fairly representative panorama of English literature of all times, includes in its last edition (Abrams and Greenblatt 2000) not only the work of Irish writers born in Northern Ireland (such as Seamus Heaney and Paul Muldoon) or before the Irish Free State, but also poems by Eavan Boland (Dublin-born, 1944) together with a choice of authors primarily associated with the former colonies of the empire, such as Anita Desai, Derek Walcott, Chinua Achebe and V. S. Naipaul. While this selection responds to the several ways in which the concept of English literature has changed over the past decades, partly due to the emergence of postcolonial writing in the English language and its interaction with the English literary tradition, it also illustrates the continuing awkward practice of canonizing Irish (and other) authors under English, or British, rubric.

The study of Irish literature has traditionally suffered from such multiplicity of often culturally insensitive conceptualizations. Students interested in critical approaches to Irish authors may find that, depending on editorial, institutional and university policies, Yeats, Joyce, Boland and Heaney can be read as part of courses on Anglo-Irish, English or postcolonial literatures. The apparent contradictions that such a phenomenon may involve for the definition of Irish literature can be perceived as one more consequence of the uneasy political and cultural relationships that have endured between Britain and Ireland for generations.

Approaching Irish Studies, then, involves being aware that Irish literature may include, at least, all of the different kinds of cultural endeavours mentioned above. Given the current moment of multicultural exchange in today's Ireland, its literature keeps challenging received conceptions of what an Irish text is or should be, so that origins, geography and even imaginary communities are enlarged and utterly transformed. This essay stems from the belief that Ireland is the first and the last colony of the British empire and that its historical legacy has underpinned much of the literary production of the country. For obvious reasons of space, it would be impossible to cover the authors and the main critical approaches developed in the different areas which Irish literature encompasses. Hence, using selected examples, the ensuing sections will focus exclusively on the Republic of Ireland and the implications that its literature has raised for postcolonial reading and writing practices.

POSTCOLONIAL THEORIZATIONS OF IRELAND

In recent years Irish Studies has significantly enlarged its scope through a long-expected participation in postcolonial theory. For the Irish poet Paula Meehan the postcolonial dimension of the country is self-evident since, as she remarks, '[j]ust because we declared ourselves an Independent Republic [. . .] doesn't mean that psychically we suddenly wake up as citizens of a Republic. Decolonising the mind takes generations' (in González Arias 2000: 299). Meehan's words immediately bring to mind the expression associated with Ngugi wa Thiong'o regarding the cultural aftermath of colonialism in Africa, and draw an appropriate parallel between Ireland and other former colonies of the British empire in their struggle for cultural and political self-determination. However, the position of Ireland within postcolonial studies has been peripheral until recently, when an invigorating and growing body of texts has began to readdress the terms of the relationship between Irish Studies and postcolonial thinking.

Ireland has historically been the object of different waves of occupation, which include the Vikings, the Anglo-Normans and the British. The British colonization of Ireland ended in 1921, following military hostilities, with the signing of the Anglo-Irish Treaty, which endorsed the Partition of the territory into the Irish Free State and Northern Ireland – the latter remains under British sovereignty. In 1948 the Irish Free State was reconstituted as the Republic of Ireland, and it formally left the British Commonwealth of Nations. Although the years since 1921 are often considered by many to mark the country's post-independence period, for others Ireland's status as a postcolonial location remains questionable. Some point to the Act of Union of 1800 (which merged the kingdoms of Britain and Ireland) as beginning a long history of Irish participation in British colonial expansion. Hence, Ireland has emerged as something of an anomaly in the history of British colonialism and, consequently, in the past it has been disqualified from being admitted into the orbit of postcolonial studies.

This latter view is clearly stated in an early survey of postcolonial studies by Bill Ashcroft, Gareth Griffiths and Helen Tiffin, *The Empire Writes Back* (1989), which excludes Ireland from the postcolonial project on the basis that

> [w]hile it is possible to argue that these societies [Ireland, Scotland and Wales] were the first victims of English expansion, their subsequent complicity in the British imperial enterprise makes it difficult for colonized peoples outside Britain to accept their identity as post-colonial.

> (1989: 33)

The most active objection to the application of postcolonial thought to the Irish situation has been articulated by the neo-colonial 'revisionist historians', who consider that the objectivity of Irish historiography is endangered by the simplifications and idealizations inherent in Irish nationalist discourses. In its attempts to offer what its practitioners insist on calling 'objective' accounts of the Irish past, the revisionist project underestimates the colonial legacy and consciously silences traumatic episodes such as The Great Famine (1845–49) or the death of anti-colonial revolutionary heroes. Their strategy of editing out of the historical text any events complicit with anti-colonial Irish nationalism has triggered the antagonism of the other side of this dichotomous debate, the so-called 'nationalist historians'. Peter Berresford Ellis's attack on historical revisionism, summarized in his 1989 Desmond Greaves Memorial Lecture, rejects the praxis of such distortions of Irish history and warns his colleagues against what he considers a neo-colonial cultural practice that 'in its mildest form apologizes for English imperialism [. . .] or in its strongest form supports that imperialism' (1989; np).

In the midst of such polarized debates, the Field Day Theatre Company, created in Derry in 1980, came to offer a more comprehensive analysis of the complexities of the Irish past and present. The Field Day project started as an artistic collaboration between playwright Brian Friel and actor Stephen Rea with the formation of a theatre company that would transcend the political and religious factions that divided the country, creating a new imaginary space – that has been referred to as the 'fifth province' – from which to offer a discourse of unity. The first production staged by the company was Friel's *Translations* (1980). The play is set in 1833 in an English-speaking community of county Donegal, where a detachment of the Royal Engineers has arrived in order to carry out the controversial task of rendering into English the Gaelic place names of the Irish map. Friel makes his Irish characters trilingual – speaking Irish, Latin and Greek – and separates the cultural and historical traditions they belong to from that of their English neighbours. With an intelligent weaving of personal relations at a time of political and cultural strife, *Translations* denotes as well as contests ancient divisions, and concentrates on what would become the main preoccupations of the Field Day Group: language, place, memory and history.

Field Day soon turned into an ambitious response to the apparently irresolvable dichotomies that had dominated debates on Irish identity – Unionist versus Nationalist, Northern Ireland versus the Republic of Ireland, Protestants versus Catholics. Authors as prominent as Seamus Heaney, Tom Paulin and Seamus Deane facilitated its growth and influential role within the field of Irish Studies. The Group initiated the publication of pamphlets mostly addressed to an academic audience wishing to explore Irish culture and the myths associated with the construction of the Irish nation. Edward Said's pamphlet on 'Yeats and Decolonisation' (Deane 1990), for instance, triggered the growing interest of Irish academics in postcolonial theory as an appropriate framework from which to account for the specificities of the Irish situation. The valuable contribution of the Field Day pamphlets to the debates opened by historians placed the Group in an antagonistic relationship with the revisionists and, as opposed to the latter's agenda, determined that discourses on Irish identity would be in part worked out against ideas of Britain and British participation in Irish history.

The most lasting effect of the Field Day project has been *The Field Day Anthology of Irish Writing* (1991), a three-volume work edited by Seamus Deane and conceived as a representation of the plurality of voices encompassed by the label 'Irish Literature'. Consciously working against the English appropriation of Irish authors, the anthology functions as an instrument for the 'decolonization of the mind' and for the creation of a specific Irish artistic tradition. Despite its merits, the anthology was the object of harsh criticism for its paucity of female names. Two extra volumes have been recently published (Bourke *et al.* 2002) focusing exclusively on the role of women in the creation of Irish literature. The debates on the marginalization of women from the systems of representation in Ireland remain open, and the new volumes are seen by many feminist critics as an appendix, an appropriate metaphor for women's subaltern position in a patriarchal literary establishment.

Although Ireland has previously been regarded as a marginal or peripheral case within postcolonial studies, in the 1990s there commenced a tendency of 'writing back' not only to colonial discursive practices but also, and foremost, to the postcolonial theorizations that had excluded the country from their agendas. David Lloyd's *Anomalous States: Irish writing and the post-colonial moment* (1993) contributes to putting Ireland firmly in the purview of postcolonial studies. In the words of Gerry Smyth, the book 'not only allows for alternative interventions in existing critical debates, but also for the inauguration of newly imagined ones' (1994: 44). The 'anomalous' in Lloyd's title has come to represent that ambiguous relationship between Ireland and Britain that inspired the contradictory responses to the Irish situation outlined above. Lloyd interrogates decontextualized applications of theory and contends that for Ireland to be part of the postcolonial project its colonial and nationalist histories must be taken into account. Ten years after the publication of the book, Lloyd summarized his postcolonial project in his editorial for a special issue of *Interventions*:

> The distinctiveness of Ireland's history of colonial domination precludes any so direct an application of generalizing or 'transferable' theories. As at once one of the earliest colonies caught up in Europe's westward expansion and a society intimately bound to the cultural and, especially, the religious context of Western Europe, Ireland has always been both a template and an anomaly.
>
> (2003: 318)

In the five essays that make *Anomalous States* Lloyd sets out to dismantle the strong reliance the Irish have traditionally had on the construction of an idea of nation as the sole means to achieve self-definition. His study searches for an alternative discourse from which to understand Irish identity, after too much recalcitrance in both colonial and official nationalist imaginings. Lloyd's argument denounces the various ways in which the political situation of Northern Ireland has determined existing debates on Irish identity and, hence, has hindered alternative analyses. Through his critical approach to W. B. Yeats, James Joyce, Samuel Beckett and Seamus Heaney, Lloyd highlights the transformation of counter-hegemonic discourses of nationalism into hegemonic discourses within the framework of the nation-state. Lloyd's study is ground-breaking in its portrayal of the Irish specificities within the postcolonial agenda but the book sometimes fails to offer definite solutions to the complex questions it poses.

In *Inventing Ireland: the literature of the modern nation* (1995) Declan Kiberd also alludes to the 'anomalous' state of Ireland and denounces the traditional exclusion of Irish literature and history from canonical postcolonial discourses. Kiberd contends that it is precisely the mixed experience of the Irish as both victims and exponents of British expansionism which 'makes them so representative of the underlying process' (5). For Kiberd, the postcolonial condition exists beyond strict chronological and/or political divisions, so that whenever a native writer 'formulates a text committed to cultural resistance' (6) s/he immediately becomes postcolonial. This is illustrated by William Butler Yeats, who articulates his poetic discourse from the margins of the same mainstream that had appropriated his work by flooding his pages with signs of an unquestionable difference. Kiberd defends the paradigm of subject-matter as a valid indication of a postcolonial or anti-colonial attitude, and counteracts the dynamics of systematically including Irish writers born before Partition in anthologies of English literature. His readable style and his use of the work of Edward Said and Frantz Fanon have turned *Inventing Ireland* into a major achievement in the postcolonial theorization of the country's literature. Kiberd's statement that it is 'less easy to decolonize the mind than the territory' at the onset of the book (6) has strong implications for the contemporary world, where processes of nation-formation and the influence of the former mother country have not yet lost their power over Irish culture.

In *Deconstructing Ireland: identity, theory, culture* (2001) Colin Graham acknowledges that Irish criticism is still tied to 'a narrative which celebrates the entity of the nation as the logical and correct outcome of the process of anti-colonial struggle' (82). However, the growing critique of the ideology and praxis of nationalism in the postcolonial world demands a serious interrogation of the Irish nation as an ethically valid construction. For Graham even post-nationalism evolves rather than rejects the national, while postcolonialism perceives the nation as an ideological product of a colonial regime that should not be totally trusted. One of Graham's merits in his contributions to the postcolonial theorizations of Ireland lies in his analysis of the myths of authenticity on which his interrogated idea of the nation was constructed. Especially relevant at moments of identity crisis, discourses of authenticity are nostalgic of the past and authorize themselves through myths of origins, stereotypical representations of landscape and vernacular uses of the language. Graham points at the self-legitimating referentiality of the 'authentic' and the mystification of the past it involves to further query the ways in which the national can distort any approach to Irish culture.

Whereas Ireland has previously occupied a liminal space within postcolonial studies, Irish criticism is gradually leaving the margins in favour of a strong discourse of the country's particularities as a former colonized area. Even the authors of *The Empire Writes Back* would surely struggle to exclude Ireland from their definition of postcolonial literatures as having emerged

> in their present form out of the experience of colonization and asserted themselves by foregrounding the tension with the imperial power, and by emphasizing their differences from the assumptions of the imperial centre. It is this which makes them distinctively post-colonial.
>
> (1989: 2)

As Lloyd, Kiberd and others have shown, Irish literature reclaims both its difference from and its similarities with the other artistic discourses of the postcolonial world. The term postcolonial always runs the risk of homogenizing under its rubric the diversity of the experiences it encompasses. Nonetheless, the anomalous specificity of Irish history and culture prevents any general application of postcolonial thought to its literature and makes possible, instead, an approach *adapted* to its colonial and postcolonial realities. As we will see in the next section, the thematic weight of Irish writing often falls strongly on the historical context of its occupation, independence and subsequent national debates.

CONTEMPORARY LITERATURE: 1980–2006

Colonial experiences place writers in the midst of a difficult dilemma: how to engage in the wrongs against their community by means of an artistic articulation devoid of propagandistic flavour. At the time of Partition, Irish authors often engendered in their writing an overt or covert anti-colonial stance that sometimes endangered, sometimes enriched, their literary value. Irish writing at the end of the twentieth century is not blind to its colonial legacy – namely the political debates characteristic of a divided territory – and the literary text frequently becomes an agent in the reconstruction and critique of evolving models of national identity. The referenda on abortion and divorce in Ireland, and the reawakening of political conflicts (or 'Troubles') in Northern Ireland between Unionists and Republicans from the late 1960s, turned the 1980s into a particularly rich terrain for artistic creations.

In 1981 the Irish territories were shaken by the hunger strike initiated by members of the Irish Republican movement in Northern Ireland, who demanded from the British government the status of political prisoners after being labelled terrorists and criminals for their anti-British campaigns. Bobby Sands, dead after sixty-six days of strike, became the symbol for national liberation, his emaciated body reminiscent of the martyrdom of a Christ ready to die for his fellow men. This political climate inspired a number of literary responses that portrayed the Troubles in the North in strongly polarized terms, and that exposed the wounds of a nation for which few could envisage a hopeful future.

Brendan Kennelly's 1982 poem 'The House That Jack Didn't Build' (1990: 150–52) takes a metaphorical approach to the dichotomous occupation of Ireland. The poem opens with a biblical reference to the creation of the world by God, here identified with Jack, the personification of British imperialism. Sanctioned by his divine power, Jack decides to take 'this little house / Nicely situated on the side of a hill / Within walking distance of the sea' (150), and evicts the former occupant, a disempowered Irishman. From his discourse, Jack, in possession of the speaking voice, constructs the Irish as his archetypical other. '[A] perfect expression / Of the civilized mind', Jack utterly transforms the invaded landscape '[n]ot exactly, to be fair, in a spirit of love / But with a genuine desire to improve / Others, particularly' (151). In using the opposed dichotomies of light versus darkness, and civilization versus brutality, to metaphorize the colonial predicament, the poem exposes the discursive nature of irreconcilable colonial definitions inherited by subsequent Irish generations. 'Statement of the Former Occupant' (Kennelly 1990: 152–54) offers a native response to such deprivation and abuse. A 'smiling', 'civilising', 'mannerly' and 'language-changing' Jack is warned of the dreams of vengeance that haunt the wounded Irishman. Now occupying the position of speaker, the evicted man makes a counter-narrative from which to achieve self-definition after being relegated to the systemic margins for too long.

Other, less polarizing ways of figuring the situation in Ireland have been used in Irish literature, such as classical Greek tragedies. Fifth-century BC Athens, perceived as the epitome of civilization and justice, has for example provided the resources for a literature of resistance against British oppression, while offering a comfortable distance, both in terms of time and in terms of space, through which the tensions in present-day Ireland can be artistically approached. Seamus Heaney's *The Burial at Thebes: Sophocles'* Antigone (2004) maintains the original setting of the Greek tragedy but consciously attempts to 'hibernize' the plot. Sophocles' eponymous heroine finds herself under Creon's rule, who has decreed that no burial rites will be offered to Polyneices, Antigone's brother and a political enemy of the King. Antigone's desire to honour the soul of her brother leads to her transgression of Creon's law and is ultimately responsible for the tragic ending. Heaney found in the Greek myth an appropriate analogue for the authority which the British Prime Minister Margaret Thatcher and her Government had enjoyed over the corpses of the hunger strikers in 1981. The new title given to the tragedy reflects its intertextual connection with the events following the death of Francis Hughes, on strike for fifty-nine days, and the treatment of his body as state property. For a good part of the journey towards Hughes's final destination his body had been in the charge of security forces, perceived as an insulting act of defiance by his political comrades, family and friends, for whom the individual rights of the deceased had been violated. As Heaney remarked, '[p]utting "burial" in the title signals to a new audience what the central concern of the play is going to be' (2005: 14). This political subtext determines that Heaney's translation will abound in words strongly connoted in

Ireland, such as 'patriot', 'terrorize' or 'troubles', and participates in the strategy of recovering classical theatre as an adequate space for ethical debates in principle very different from those of ancient Athens.

The 1980s were also marked by an increasing engagement with the politics of gender. Not only did the referenda on abortion and divorce contribute to the destabilization of the traditional pillar of Irish society, the Catholic Church, but also the idea of nation, as sanctioned by the political establishment of the country, was seriously interrogated in the work particularly of women writers. As Nira Yuval-Davis has theorized, in processes of nation-formation women systematically play the roles of biological and symbolic reproducers of their imaginary communities, resulting in their subsequent marginalization in the systems of representation (Yuval-Davis 1997). The mythical figures of Dark Rosaleen and Cathleen Ní Houlihan became the emblems of the national cause, personifications of a territory sometimes victimized, sometimes victorious, but unquestionably worth dying for. The strong nexus formed by nationalism and Catholicism further feminized the land under the figure of Mother Ireland, reminiscent of Mother Mary, the asexual icon of sacred motherhood offered as the model of perfection to which women should aspire. Irish Woman (singular and capitalized) and the Land (also capitalized) became metaphors for each other and were thus oversimplified in iconic and idealized images remote from the realities of Irish women's lives.

After centuries of reification, from the 1980s Irish women writers start leaving the uncomfortable position of the powerless national muse and explored instead the multiple possibilities that the sexualized female body offered. In her influential essay 'A Kind of Scar: The Woman Poet in a National Tradition' (1994), Eavan Boland denounces the praxis of using women as icons and figments at the service of the nation and reclaims visibility for the women writers in her country. The difficult journey from being the disembodied object of a poem to becoming the poem's subject and speaker has been undertaken and explored by writers and critics alike (Mills 1995; Warner 1996) and has triggered the publication of anthologies entirely devoted to this hidden part of the Irish literary tradition (Smyth 1990; Donovan *et al*. 1994, to mention only a couple of examples). Eavan Boland's 1980 collection *In Her Own Image* inaugurates the decade with poems on the specificities of inhabiting a female body. In one poem, 'Tirade for the Mimic Muse', the speaker despises the national icon for falsifying '[t]he kitchen screw and the rack of labour' and for becoming a slut ready to pay homage to patriarchal politics: 'You are the Muse of all our mirrors./ Look in them and weep' (1995: 55–56), declares the rebellious voice. Part of this striking collection is 'Anorexic', a poem about a starved Eve that has internalized religious teachings about her sinful female forms. Boland's protagonist perceives her body and her soul as two dichotomous terms impossible to reconcile and identifies with her non-corporeal side. Eve desires to disappear from the physical level, going back to Adam's rib again, as if she had never been away, to 'grow / angular and holy' (59). Eve's eating disorders do not stem from the requirement of the beauty myth but from cultural, religious and political problems that have stigmatized female physicality as a hindrance in a male-oriented spirituality.

The normative definition of the Irish nation is also interrogated by means of a transversal approach that recovers other areas of the systemic margins. Paula Meehan deals not only with female agency in her poetry, but also with the unmapped territories of Dublin, a city associated with Joyce's writing in the collective psyche of Ireland. The dispossessed, the underclass and the poor also find a space of their own in the changing literary canon of the present. Meehan's poem 'Molly Malone', part of the sequence 'The Lost Children of the Inner City' in *Dharmakaya* (2000), addresses the need to recover 'out of the debris of history' (25) the real story of the seventeenth-century prostitute that time turned into a Dublin anthem but kept away from the official records of Irish history.

The status of the Irish language in the construction of national identity also acquires thematic weight in contemporary writing. Louis de Paor calls the shift from Irish to English in the nineteenth century 'the ultimate translation' that degraded the native tongue (in Pierce 2000: 1140). For many writers, the choice of Irish as a creative medium is a political statement against cultural colonization. Biddy Jenkinson, for instance, reacts against the imbalance between the two languages by forbidding any translations of her work into English. As is the case in other postcolonial areas, translation is perceived as both an aid to Irish writers working with the Irish language – since it provides a wider readership and international recognition – and a hindrance to the creative force of a suppressed tongue. Many Irish writers are aware that English is their 'step-mother tongue' – the language of empire in which every word comes loaded with a power relationship – but also acknowledge the inevitability of using English if that was the language of the home.

The Irish-language poet Nuala Ní Dhomhnaill establishes a parallel between the roles traditionally assigned to women and the perpetuation of the marginal status of the Irish language in Ireland (see Somerville-Arjat and Wilson 1990: 154), where it is still associated with an essentialist Arcadia unpolluted by civilization but unable to account for the requirements of the contemporary world. As well as these postcolonial and feminist reasons, Ní Dhomhnaill importantly declares that in choosing her creative medium she is not simply asserting a specific political agenda: 'I have no choice. I can write prose in English no bother, and even jingles and verse, but *never* poetry' (1992: 18). Ní Dhomhnaill also links her pre-colonial language with the Celtic tradition of folk tales and myth. Her revisions of the story of Queen Medb and Cú Chulainn, translated into English by Michael Hartnett (Ní Dhomhnaill 1993: 110–25), dismiss derogatory perceptions of Gaelic as the language of farmers and poverty by infusing into the legends strong political vindications. In Ní Dhomhnaill's text Queen Medb is no longer the *femme fatale* of the traditional saga, but an empowered female that overshadows the heroic character of Cú Chulainn by exposing his complicity with recalcitrant patriarchal thought.

Race and ethnicity have also become significant preoccupations in recent years. The unprecedented economic expansion of the country, known as the 'Celtic Tiger', precipitated the arrival of massive numbers of immigrants in Ireland, a traditional exporter rather than recipient of exiles. In colonial discourses, colour had stood not just for racial difference but also for a supposed cultural inferiority, radically opposed to Anglo-Saxon whiteness. Ethnically different but racially white, the Irish were nonetheless constructed as black to highlight their subaltern position. This tendency to racialize ethnicity has left important traces in contemporary Irish literature, where the paradigm of colour reappears in debates about Irish identity. In Roddy Doyle's celebrated urban novel, *The Commitments* (1987), a group of young Dubliners form a band that plays soul music – one character remarks that the Irish are the blacks of Europe. Similarly, the Irish musician and campaigner Bono has identified the 'Irishness' attributed to his band U2 with that of soul music in North America. In 'Bono: The White Nigger' the singer states that '[t]he Irish, like the blacks, felt like outsiders. There's a feeling of being homeless, migrant, but I suppose that's what all art is – a search for identity' (in Pierce 2000: 936). Such transcultural engagements between Irish and black American contexts have opened up new ways of thinking about Irish identity and creativity.

However, the arrival of unprecedented numbers of immigrants in Ireland in the past decades has also triggered a dangerous reawakening of illiberal nationalist sentiments, which threaten to result in the racial 'whitening' of the Irish as a means of differentiating from newcomers. The economic comfort of the Celtic Tiger is not paralleled by a similar level of social satisfaction, and the sociologist Ronit Lentin has invoked the past of the Irish as racialized others to counteract the tendencies towards racial prejudice in the country (1999). In a similar vein, Lia Mills's recent novel, *Nothing Simple* (2005), centres on the difficulties that an Irish family encounter on their arrival in the USA. The discriminatory treatment and the legal problems they face in the land of promise echo current political debates on citizenship and identity in Ireland, perhaps paving the ground for new definitions of Irishness where an inclusive multiculturalism outwits racial and cultural exclusion.

Irish writing is dealing with unmapped territory at the beginning of the third millennium. The danger is that myths of an essential Ireland, of an 'authentic' version of the culture, will be recovered from the national archives to avoid the uncertainties of the present. Marina Carr's play *Ariel* (2002) – a revision of Euripides' *Iphigenia at Aulis* – presents us with a crumbling world in which the bases of the old country – the Church, the Family and the State – can no longer account for the realities of an utterly changed island. Carr consciously uses the symbols most commonly associated with Irish authenticity as a means for her characters to achieve some security. However, the playwright seriously interrogates the very symbols she uses and warns the readers against their self-destructive powers. It is a warning which, as the third millennium begins, may help secure a hopeful future for Ireland – its literature, its politics, its people.

RECOMMENDED FURTHER READING

Bourke, Angela, Kilfeather, Siobhán, Luddy, Maria, MacCurtain, Margaret, Meaney, Gerardine, Ní Dhonnchadha, Máirín, O'Dowd, Mary and Wills, Clair (eds) *The Field Day Anthology of Irish Writing: Irish Women's Writing and Traditions, Volumes IV & V* (Cork: Cork University Press, 2002).

Deane, Seamus (Gen. Ed.) *The Field Day Anthology of Irish Writing*, three volumes (Derry: Field Day, 1991).

Eagleton, Terry, *Heathcliffe and the Great Hunger: studies in Irish culture* (London: Verso, 1995).

Graham, Colin, *Deconstructing Ireland: identity, theory, culture* (Edinburgh: Edinburgh University Press, 2001).

Kiberd, Declan, *Inventing Ireland: the literature of the modern nation* (London: Jonathan Cape, 1995).

Lloyd, David, *Anomalous States: Irish writing and the post-colonial moment* (Dublin: The Lilliput Press, 1993).

10
LATIN AMERICA

CLAIRE TAYLOR

PROBLEMS WITH A 'POSTCOLONIAL LATIN AMERICA'

The countries emerging from the former Spanish and Portuguese colonies in the early nineteenth century (with, to a lesser extent, those from the former French colonies) have come to be known as 'Latin American', the term deriving from the fact that their language had Latinate roots. However, this term has raised debate in some circles: opponents of the term note that 'Latin America' is itself a Europeanizing nomenclature, being coined as it was by the French as a counterpart to US expansionism. Nevertheless, 'Latin America' remains the most useful of the available terms to describe those nations in the Americas which were formerly Iberian colonies.

After the decline of the Spanish and Portuguese empires in the nineteenth century, the region of Latin America entered into a period that in strictly chronological terms might be called postcolonial, as the former colonies broke away from colonial rule. Yet 'postcolonial' means something clearly more value-laden than this, and has provoked intense debate in Latin American studies, with several eminent scholars disputing the relevance of the term to describe Latin American experiences and cultural practices. While, on the one hand, Latin American theorists such as Sara Castro-Klarén have lamented the lack of attention given to Latin America by postcolonial theory, pointing out that the 'subject of English-speaking Post-Coloniality writes the world and itself without awareness of a previous, major, if not modular, colonial period and Post-Colonial experience' (1995: 45), others, such as anthropologist J. Jorge Klor de Alva have inveighed against the use of the term. Klor de Alva, one of the foremost opponents of the use of postcolonial theory, has protested that 'Mexico is not another version of India, Brazil is not one more type of Indonesia' (1995: 247), and asks, 'is an error being committed when scholars apply tools and categories of analysis developed in the twentieth century for understanding British colonialism, especially in India and Africa, to make sense of the experiences of sixteenth to eighteenth-century Latin America?' (264). Klor de Alva's assertion that Latin American experience has been '"colonized" after the fact' (246) reveals his concern that a theoretical discourse developed principally in an anglophone context should not be applied indiscriminately to Latin American experiences.

The differences between Latin America's experience of colonization and independence, and that of the former British colonies which formed the basis for much postcolonial theory, have been carefully indicated by many. Joseba

Gabilondo, for instance, has reminded us of the 'chronological difficulties of applying the condition of "postcoloniality" to an area that, historically speaking, has been postcolonial since the nineteenth century' (2001: np). Walter Mignolo, meanwhile, highlights the crucial differences in terms of language, since Spanish in itself was already losing its hold against the growing influence of English, and, to a lesser extent, French and German, by the eighteenth century (Mignolo 1995). Thus, the new Latin American nations were already speaking what Mignolo has termed the 'lesser languages' of Spanish or Portuguese, and within this the native American languages, which had already been suppressed during the colonial period, were further marginalized. For others such as Mark I. Millington, it is less the specificities of a particular Latin American nation that make the notion of the postcolonial problematic, than the fact that the nation itself exists in tension with global forces, to the extent that, 'the concern of post-colonial studies is that local specificity ceases to have any significance. It has become harder and harder to tell where one culture ends and another begins, not just within the metropolis but globally' (2000: 37).

However, while the crucial differences between Latin America's experience of empire and independence, and the experiences of former British or French colonies, are clear, for many writers these differences do not negate the usefulness of postcolonial theory. A series of prominent writers and thinkers have engaged directly with the term (see for instance, Kadir 1993; Mignolo 1995; Fiddian 2000; Davies 2000; Millington 2000; and Thurner and Guerrero 2003) and have suggested some fruitful interconnections between postcolonial theories and Latin American experiences. Moreover, there are many more such writers who, while not explicitly responding to anglophone postcolonial theory, do indeed engage in a process of, to borrow Tomás Rivera's term, 'decolonizing the mind' (1982: 10) in their formulations of difference, otherness and marginalized voices. Thus, while the legitimacy of the term itself is disputed, a variety of important figures in Latin American thought, literature, art and popular culture can be understood in relation to broader definitions of the postcolonial. Indeed, in Latin America there has been a longstanding tradition of intellectuals challenging the lingering social and cultural legacies of Iberian colonialism, and attempting to forge local, national or pan-Latin American identities which do not conform to European models imposed by the imperial powers.

FIRST GENERATION: CIVILIZATION AND BARBARISM

With the overthrow of Spanish and Portuguese rule and the forming of the various Latin American nations, much writing in the region from the nineteenth century narrated the nation in Homi K. Bhabha's terms (Bhabha 1990), yet not all of this escaped the European frames of reference which had defined Latin America in the colonial era. As has been noted by Mignolo among others, much nineteenth-century Latin American thought tended to reproduce European conceptualizations, even if these were directed to Latin American ends, thus forming part of what Mignolo has termed 'first generation' postcolonial intellectuals (1995: 183). A case in point is Domingo Sarmiento, whose famous *Facundo: Civilización y barbarie* (trans. *Facundo, or, Civilization and Barbarism*) of 1848 presented his native Argentina – and, by extension, Latin America as a whole – as being characterized by the binary of civilization and barbarism. Tellingly, Sarmiento's analysis located the barbarous in the wild pampas, the areas where the nomadic indigenous populations still lived, and championed greater European immigration – preferably, for Sarmiento, northern European immigration – as the solution to his country's problems. Sarmiento's arguments, while largely discredited nowadays, are nevertheless important for the resonance they came to have in Latin American thought, as successive generations of writers have returned to his founding binary, whether to modify or directly challenge it.

A key work which maintains resonances of Sarmiento's civilization–barbarism binary is the important essay written by Uruguayan writer José Enrique Rodó in 1900, *Ariel*. While setting up a now familiar conflict between reason and instinct as represented by the Shakespearean figures of Ariel and Caliban respectively, Rodó chose to focus his attention on Latin America's relationship with the USA. Seeing the USA as utilitarian and based on greed, Rodó proposed for Latin America an ideal based on intellect and noble aspirations. Yet Rodó's thesis, exhorting Latin Americans to take up the civilizing role in the face of North American greed, still maintained the founding binary of civilization–barbarism – albeit with Latin Americans representing the face of civilization – and, significantly, continued Sarmiento's project of favouring the civilization side of this binary. As will be discussed below, Rodó's thesis was to be challenged considerably later in the twentieth century by Roberto Fernández Retamar, whose radical reversal of the Ariel–Caliban binary proposed a new conceptualization of Latin Americanness.

TRANSCULTURATION, CALIBAN AND THE SPACE-IN-BETWEEN

After the first generation of postcolonial Latin American thinkers comes a series of intellectuals who, in the twentieth century and beyond, have argued for a Latin American identity not restricted to imitation of European models. One of the most important developments in this mode of thinking was Cuban Fernando Ortiz's groundbreaking notion of transculturation, which he made public in 1940 (see Davies 2000 for further details of Ortiz's development of this notion, as well as Chapter 8: The Caribbean). Transculturation could well be viewed as a postcolonial theory before postcolonial theory itself was fully formulated in a francophone and anglophone context: note that, for instance, what is considered one of the founding texts of postcolonial theory, Frantz Fanon's *Peau noir, masques blancs* (1952, trans. *Black Skin, White Masks*), was published more than a decade *after* Ortiz had developed his theories. The term 'transculturation' was coined by Ortiz in response to what he saw as the inadequacies of the term 'acculturation' used in anthropology at the time. Ortiz proposed that:

> We understand the term *transculturation* better expresses the different phases of the process of transition from one culture to another, because this process does not consist solely of acquiring a foreign culture, which is what the Anglo-American term *acculturation* means, but it implies [. . .] a partial *disacculturation*, and moreover, the subsequent creation of new cultural phenomena, which could be called *neoculturation*.
>
> (1978: 96 – current author's translation)

Ortiz saw this state of transculturation as accurately defining his own country's status, and argued that Latin American identity lies not on either side of a given binary – as Sarmiento and his contemporaries would have it – but instead in a constant process of negotiation between different sets of codes. Transculturation, therefore, offered an understanding of national and Latin American identity which would take into account mutual transferences through the cultures in contact, and which paved the way for a non-essentializing concept of identity. An indication of the lasting impact of Ortiz's theory can be seen in the fact that it has travelled back to the metropolis in a variety of formats, with disciplines as diverse as translation studies and studies in travel writing making fruitful use of Ortiz's terms of analysis (see for instance Shaw 1988; Pratt 1992).

Another such 'second generation' Latin American thinker is Roberto Fernández Retamar, whose 1971 essay 'Calibán: apuntes sobre la cultura de nuestra América' (trans. 'Caliban: Notes Toward a Discussion of Culture in Our America') engages with postcolonial issues and concerns (see also Chapter 8: The Caribbean). Fernández Retamar, replying to Rodó's essay discussed above, argues that the Latin American symbol should not be the idealized Ariel as Rodó saw it, but the troubled Caliban. For Fernández Retamar:

> Our symbol then is not Ariel, as Rodó thought, but rather Caliban. [. . .] Prospero invaded the islands, killed our ancestors, enslaved Caliban, and taught him his language to make himself understood. What else could Caliban do but use that same language – today he has no other – to curse him, to wish that the 'red plague' would fall on him? I know no other metaphor more expressive of our cultural situation, our reality. [. . .] What is our history, what is our culture, if not the history and culture of Caliban?
>
> (1989: 14)

Caliban stands as a useful emblem of the Latin American in that he can only use borrowed terms with which to express himself; that is, there is no 'essential' Latin American identity which can be expressed free from the constraints of an imposed, colonial language. A point which is significant in Fernández Retamar's formulation, and which shares common ground with Ortiz's notion of transculturation, is that he does not reject the terms of the colonial powers, but rather argues that the strategic exploitation and manipulation of these terms must be the form of expression for Latin Americans. Again, such a concept would seem to pre-empt concepts of sly civility, mimicry and hybridity expounded by Bhabha some years later (see Bhabha 1994). Moreover, the neatness of Fernández Retamar's argument lies in the fact that the textual strategy he employs is in itself an example of what he describes: taking up the paradigm of Caliban, from European literary tradition, to describe the Latin American condition, Fernández Retamar is using borrowed terms.

Within the Portuguese-speaking world, the Brazilian critic Silviano Santiago was also instrumental in the development of Latin American theory which challenged the metropolis. Santiago developed the notion of the 'discourse in-between' which emphasized the hybrid character of any colonial process. In an influential essay of 1971, Santiago argued that 'Latin America establishes its place on the map of Western civilization by actively and destructively diverting the European norm and resignifying preestablished and immutable elements that were exported to the New World by the Europeans' (2001: 30). For Santiago, therefore, Latin America's relationship to the former colonizing powers of Europe is an active one; Latin America does not merely repeat pre-existing European paradigms, but reworks them and contaminates them, producing its own Latin American identity through the subversion of colonial norms.

THE SUBALTERN, TESTIMONIO AND CULTURAL STUDIES

While the majority of the thinkers mentioned above were working in contexts not overtly theorized as postcolonial, there have been in recent decades instances of close alliances between Latin American scholarship and postcolonial theory. One direct intersection between anglophone postcolonial theory and Latin American studies can be seen in the founding of the US-based Latin American Subaltern Studies Group in the 1990s, a project inspired by the work of the Subaltern Studies Group of South Asian scholars (see Latin American Subaltern Studies Group 1995: 135–36). In common with subaltern studies groups elsewhere in the globe, the Latin American Subaltern Studies Group aims to recover voices not registered by historical discourse, subjects silenced by political and social systems, and communities excluded from the ruling elites. One of the areas of focus of this group is a growing area within Latin American studies as a whole: the narrative form known as *testimonio*. *Testimonio* is a form of writing (or, in some cases, sound and visual recording) that transcribes a first-person, usually oral account, and attempts to give voice to those traditionally excluded from literacy. For the Group, the testimonial text 'leads to a new emphasis on the concrete, the personal, the "small history", writing (or video work) by women, political prisoners, lumpen, and gays' (140). *Testimonio* has been the subject of great interest recently, in that, unlike elite literature, it is seen as inextricably linked to the social conditions in which is it produced, and arguably forms a part of social practice in itself.

Probably the most famous of *testimonios* is Guatemalan Rigoberta Menchú's 1983 work, *Me llamo Rigoberta Menchú y así me nació la conciencia* (trans. *I, Rigoberta Menchú: An Indian Woman in Guatemala*). In this work, Menchú's voice not only conveys her personal experiences of oppression, but is overtly formulated as representative of collective experiences, as she states that, 'it's not only my life, it's also the testimony of my people. [. . .] My story is the story of all poor Guatemalans' (1984: 1). As such, *testimonio* has been seen as a voice for the marginalized subaltern, and has been described by Elzbieta Sklodowska as a type of '"solidarity pact" forged between intellectuals and the common people' (2003: 103). However, since a *testimonio*, in its written form at least, functions through the transcription of an oral account by a literate editor or compiler, this relationship between the narrator and the compiler has engendered considerable debate, as regards the tensions involved in the conveying of the experience of an illiterate, rural, usually indigenous subject through an educated, frequently metropolitan, and white, compiler.

While *testimonio* has frequently been the cultural product of choice for those searching to uncover the voice of the subaltern within Latin American studies, no less important is culture in a wider sense. As several Latin American/ist scholars have indicated, the recent expansion of focus to diverse varieties of cultural practices in Latin American studies represents a move away from the elitist field of literature to a consideration of more truly popular forms of expression (see Latin American Subaltern Studies Group 1995; Millington 2000). Thus, while writers may be the first point of departure in the forging of a postcolonial identity, no less important are the many figures in art, film and popular culture whose works convey a sense of otherness to their publics. Indeed, the visual arts are often uniquely placed to convey an overturning of colonial concepts in striking images. Examples such as Joaquín Torres-García's ink drawing, *Inverted Map of South America* (1936), which reverses the conventional representation of the American continent, excluding the USA from the map and locating Chile and Argentina at the top, suggest a rejection of (neo-) colonial powers. Torres-García's work represents just one example in the vast field of Latin American cultural production that functions to contest dominant systems of power, and there remains much fruitful work to be done on this area in the twenty-first century.

Chicano/a identities

While the writers and artists outlined above focus on Latin American experiences and identities as lived in the Latin American nations, an additional and undeniable Latin American presence – called by some a nation – lies in the Chicano/a population resident within the USA. Estimated in a recent census at some 32.8 million, the Hispanic population within the USA is growing, with

Chicanos – those of Mexican origin – forming one of the largest and most vocal groups, 66 per cent of the total Hispanic population (Therrien and Ramirez 2000). The pioneering developments of Chicano/a writers and artists from the late 1970s onwards have offered new conceptualizations of the postcolonial subject. For many, the efforts of Chicano/a writers were not only directed at expressing the Chicano community, but had a more profound impact; in the words of Tomás Rivera, Chicano/a writing functions to 'decolonize the mind' (1982: 10), suggesting that the overthrowing of colonial power must be undertaken in systems of thought, as much as in instances of direct economic or military domination.

While for Latin American writers of earlier generations the imperial power was still Spain, for Chicanos the principal imperial power is the USA, and their efforts in articulating an independent identity focus on challenging this power. One of the key concepts developed by Chicano/a thinkers from the late 1960s and throughout the 1970s was that of Aztlán, or the mythical homeland of Chicanos which formed a symbolic, if not actual, homeland that united Mexican Americans and provided them with a common sense of identity (see Anaya and Lomelí 1989 for a collection of key essays on the concept of Aztlán). In addition to the written word, Chicano/a artists have also been influential in developing a space of expression for Chicanos, in particular the Chicano/a muralist movement that emerged in the late 1960s. The murals, often involving the help of members of the local community in which the mural was painted, covered issues relevant to Chicanos such as poverty, racism and bilingual education, and helped to foster a sense of common identity for Chicanos. As Thea Pitman has explained it, 'Chicano muralists often sought to express the Chicano spirit formally through an eclectic mixture of visual idioms taken from fine art and from popular culture, thus representing the hybrid nature of the Mexican-American' (Pitman 2005: 335), and hence providing a visual contestation to the dominant US culture.

One particularly important development within Chicano/a culture has been the focus on gender afforded by Chicana writers since, for Naomi H. Quiñonez and others, marginalization for Chicanas comes not only from the discourse of the USA as a neo-imperial power, but also from within masculine Chicano discourse itself (2002: 141). The most notable figure among Chicana writers is Gloria Anzaldúa, whose groundbreaking 1987 work *Borderlands/La frontera* offered a series of essays and poetry which deal with a queer Chicana consciousness. Anzaldúa's highly original work examines the function of language in the process of colonization, proposing a strategy of code-switching, 'from English to Castillian Spanish to the North American dialect to Tex-Mex to a sprinkling of Nahuatl to a mixture of all these' which represents for Anzaldúa 'the language of the Borderlands' (1999: 20). These borderlands, while referring in one sense to the US-Mexican border, take on a wider meaning in Anzaldúa's definition, covering the 'psychological borderlands, the sexual borderlands and the spiritual borderlands [. . .] the Borderlands are physically present whenever two or more cultures are physically present, wherever two or more cultures edge each other' (19). Thus, the borderlands represent the multiple heritages and identities which make up Chicano/a subjects, offering a non-essentializing formulation of Chicano/a identity.

Chicana writers have also been influential in challenging stereotypes of colonial discourse in their revision of Mexican iconic figures. Cordelia Candelaria reviews the figure of La Malinche (discussed in Chapter 4: The Spanish and Portuguese empires), and reads her 'as an account of the prototypical Chicana feminist. [. . .] By adapting to the historical circumstances thrust upon her, she defied traditional social expectations of a woman's role' (1980: 6). Significantly, Candelaria's formulation refuses to participate in the perpetuation of the derogatory depiction of La Malinche as 'La Chingada' ('the violated woman') and thus source of shame, but instead revalues her as a positive role model for the Chicana writer. Moreover, La Malinche has been viewed as a specifically postcolonial figure, since, according to Quiñonez, she is emblematic of the Chicana writer in her status as postcolonial interpreter:

> The role of first wave Chicana writers may be compared to that of La Malinche, who, as interpreter during the conquest, possessed the skill of adaptation during a time of intense cultural upheaval. Hence the often ambiguous role of the interpreter becomes part of postcolonial discourse.
>
> (Quiñonez 2002: 138)

In this way, the revisiting and revaluation of previously denigrated figures such as La Malinche forms a postcolonial praxis, both in terms of the recuperation of an indigenous heritage, and in terms of the continuing process of interpreting and code-switching which embodies the postcolonial subject.

CONCLUSION: LATIN AMERICA TALKS BACK

The range of Latin American writers and artists whose works challenge enduring colonial perspectives reveals fruitful intersections with postcolonial discourses that are being formulated elsewhere around the globe. Indeed, as was the case with Ortiz, it could well be argued that Latin American literary and cultural theorization has always been postcolonial *avant-la-lettre*; writings of and about Latin America have engaged for more than a century with notions of otherness, difference and the forging of an independent identity. Moreover, the strength and innovation of Latin America's contribution to the postcolonial debate may arguably lie in its stance of talking back to the metropolis. The fact that theories such as transculturation or the strategy of Caliban which were formulated in the 'third world' of Latin America are now informing first world scholarship is evidence of the reversal of the flow of theory as conventionally perceived. Latin America can no longer be conceived of as a site of 'raw material' – to take up Ketu H. Katrak's provocative phrase (2006: 239) – on which Anglo-European discourses impose their terms. Instead, Latin America must be acknowledged as another diverse locus of the enunciation of postcolonial theory and cultural practice, actively creating discourses and promoting identities which challenge old and new imperial powers.

RECOMMENDED FURTHER READING

Anzaldúa, Gloria, *Borderlands/La frontera: the new Mestiza*, second edition (San Francisco, CA: Aunt Lute Books, 1999).

Fernández Retamar, Roberto, *Caliban and Other Essays*, trans. Edward Baker (Minneapolis, MN: University of Minnesota Press, 1989).

Fiddian, R. (ed.), *Postcolonial Perspectives on the Cultures of Latin America and Lusophone Africa* (Liverpool: Liverpool University Press, 2000).

Kadir, Djelal, *The Other Writing: postcolonial essays in Latin America's writing culture* (West Lafayette, IN: Purdue University Press, 1993).

Ortiz, Fernando, *Contrapunteo cubano del tabaco y el azúcar: advertencia de sus contrastes agrarios, económicos, históricos y sociales, su etnografía y su transculturación* (Caracas: Bilioteca Ayacucho, 1978 [1943]).

Santiago, Silviano, *The Space In-Between: essays on Latin American culture*, trans. Tom Burns, Ana Lucía Gazzola and Gareth Williams (Durham, NC: Duke University Press, 2001).

11
SOUTHERN AFRICA

KAI EASTON

CONSTRUCTING 'SOUTHERN AFRICA'

If regions are social constructs, how might we decide what constitutes 'Southern Africa'? Why justify a separate chapter for this region when the literary output of West Africa, for example, is so prolific? How distinct is Southern Africa's colonial history, and what criteria do we use to choose which countries fall into this dynamic region?

There is, in fact, a range of configurations for the region we call 'Southern Africa', depending on our point of reference. In South Africa, it generally refers just to those countries south of the Cunene and Zambezi rivers: South Africa, Lesotho, Swaziland, Namibia, Botswana, Zimbabwe, and the southern half of Mozambique. Other demarcations often additionally include Angola, Zambia and Malawi, and this is the geographical scope of Michael Chapman's encyclopaedic *Southern African Literatures* (2003) – readers looking for a comprehensive survey of the region's literatures will find an excellent guide here. The United Nations designates only five countries, while the scholarly *Journal of Southern African Studies* is geographically expansive, with occasional forays into the Democratic Republic of the Congo, Tanzania and the Indian Ocean islands of Madagascar and Mauritius.

There are similar problems of inclusion and exclusion when mapping the region in literary and cultural terms. International publishing ventures, book reviewing, and teaching practices tend to canonize select texts from African writing in metropolitan, European-derived languages. Many African writers live overseas, and so questions of writing *on* and writing *from* a place continue to provoke debates about nationality and authenticity. For example, in Alexandra Fuller's autobiographical *Don't Let's Go to the Dogs Tonight: an African childhood* (2001) and *Scribbling the Cat: travels with an African soldier* (2004), she claims an 'African' identity rather than a national Zimbabwean identity. Yet she constantly has to qualify this claim: she was born in Britain to British parents, grew up in Rhodesia, and her family now live in Zambia while Fuller is married to an American and lives in the USA. Then there is the multiplicity *within* a nation. In South Africa, which today has eleven official languages, it is difficult, as Leon de Kock (2005) and Lewis Nkosi (2006b) have both argued, to speak of 'South African Literature' in the singular. Clearly, the plural form is needed, which begs the question of whether there is a truly 'national' literature in any of the countries in the region – as well as underlining the fact that no uniform sense of a 'regional' identity (social, political or cultural) exists in the area as a whole.

This chapter does not escape these problems: rather, it contends that the very attempt to write about 'postcolonial' Southern African studies requires the incorporation of issues of identity and representation into the discussion. This chapter focuses briefly on those countries and texts most *visible* in postcolonial studies now: both classic texts and new titles. This necessarily makes for limitations and might replicate unfairly the marginality of literatures that neighbour South Africa and Zimbabwe, the two most productive nations in terms of fiction, and both former British colonies which have only quite recently become independent from white settler rule (Zimbabwe in 1980; South Africa in 1994). On the other hand, writing from these two countries has been prolific despite decades of armed struggle – for many years the African National Congress (ANC) opposed the apartheid Afrikaner Nationalist Government; while Zimbabwe African National Union (ZANU) and Zimbabwe African People's Union (ZAPU) guerrilla fighters battled against Ian Smith's regime in Rhodesia (now Zimbabwe). There has been *relatively* less literary output from Angola and Mozambique, especially in English translation, which have suffered civil wars since independence from Portugal in 1975; or from South African-controlled South West Africa, now Namibia, which only became independent in 1990; or from Botswana, which made a successful transition to independence so much earlier in 1966.

Reasons of space necessitate a focus on some important landmark texts in contemporary fiction and autobiography. One aim in this introductory chapter is to consider what is 'Southern Africa' postcolonially; in other words, from the perspective of the twenty-first century, how do the recurring themes of colonialism, apartheid, war, nationalism and independence now appear in the writing of this particular region? How long does it take for recent events or great dramatic political shifts to be written into the cultural landscape? Thinking locally and globally, how might Southern African cultures disrupt the claims of certain postcolonial theories? What conversations can we identify between texts across geographies and generations?

WRITING SOUTHERN AFRICA: COLONIAL SETTLEMENT TO CULTURAL DIFFERENCE

The first topic to be addressed is the ambitious and groundbreaking *Women Writing Africa* project created by the Feminist Press at the City University of New York. This project provides a counterpoint to the canonization of selected literary texts that we see in most overviews, since it consists of six varied and wide-ranging anthologies, supplemented by a substantial introduction. Many of the writings collected in *Volume 1: Southern region* (2003) are archival, and diversity of representation across race, place, genre and language are negotiated carefully. The texts range across court records, songs, speeches, stories, letters and memoirs. In terms of territory, the editors pragmatically focus on Botswana, Lesotho and Swaziland (all three of which were protectorates of the British

Crown), and the white settler colonies of Namibia, South Africa and Zimbabwe (xxiv). Importantly, as the co-editors argue in their Introduction, '[t]his anthology challenges colonial habits of mapping (for European colonization arbitrarily mapped identities under territories), in that many of our texts cross borders or thematize border-crossing' (Driver *et al.* 2003: 4).

Such 'colonial habits of mapping' have left an impression which remains powerful today. From the fifteenth century, when the Portuguese began circumnavigating the globe, the corpus of European travel writing on Africa has steadily grown. The Portuguese navigator Bartolomeu Dias rounded the Cape of Good Hope in 1488, and was followed in 1497 by his compatriot Vasco da Gama, the first European to discover the sea route to India. Centuries later, in 1820, British settlers arrived on the shores of Algoa Bay – where Dias and da Gama had both dropped anchor – to begin a new life on the eastern Cape frontier. To the west of the region, on the Atlantic side, and before the British finally won control of the Cape in 1806, the Dutch had made their mark on the southern tip of the continent, establishing what was initially a refreshment station for trade to the East Indies in 1652. This very brief version of European exploration and settlement has been seen, until recently, as foundational in South Africa, marking an 'originary' moment in history and literature. Much of the early colonial writing was preoccupied with naming and claiming the newly-colonized landscape, as explored in J. M. Coetzee's seminal book of essays, *White Writing: on the culture of letters in South Africa* (1988). But colonialism was inevitably a two-way encounter. The diaries and journals of colonial officials reveal how dependent they were on native guides for their discoveries; and they acknowledge indigenous names even while claiming ownership of 'virgin' territory. Even in early attempts to map and describe the region, we find evidence of indigenous perspectives and practices which inflected the business of colonial settlement. The nineteenth-century British naturalist, William Burchell, provides one such example. While he advocated further colonial settlement at the Cape, he was also sympathetic to the native Khoi inhabitants, and went to great lengths to map the Colony accurately, placing indigenous names on his map alongside British ones. Significantly, Burchell was not inclined to include Dutch names – for this was just at the point that Great Britain had wrested the Cape from the Netherlands.

The emergence of a distinctly South African sense of national identity that cleaves from European jurisdiction can be traced to the early twentieth century, and the beginnings of colonial and South African nationalism can be detected in some important literary texts. One is Sir Percy FitzPatrick's classic children's book, *Jock of the Bushveld* (1907), an adventure story about a transport rider and his faithful bull-terrier in the Transvaal. Of Irish and English ancestry FitzPatrick has been singled out by historians for his early self-identification as 'South African' (see Dubow 1997). But in terms of South African *fiction*, literary critics usually place Olive Schreiner's earlier 'feminist settler' (Boehmer 1995: 88) work, *The Story of an African Farm* (1883) as marking the beginning of the

South African novel. Alan Paton's *Cry, the Beloved Country*, published in 1948, just as the Afrikaner Nationalists came to power, is, next to Schreiner's, perhaps the best-known novel from South Africa. Although Paton has been criticized for his liberal humanist position, the novel and its film adaptation have consistently appeared on syllabi around the world.

This chapter may initially seem to be constructing a genealogy of writing that is racially divided, where 'white writing' (Coetzee 1988: 11), to *mis*use Coetzee's phrase, seemingly takes precedence. This, of course, would be a mistake, since indigenous oral cultures have long been producing their own cultural representations in abundance: in their own languages, through praise poetry, storytelling, song and today through other media, such as radio and film (see, for example, Brown 1998, 1999; Coplan 1994; Fardon and Furniss 2000; Gunner 2000, 2006; Gunner and Gwala 1991). This is a risk we inevitably take when focusing exclusively on print culture, however, since the conditions for literary production in Southern Africa have historically been racially segregated.

Perhaps the most important writer in this context is Sol T. Plaatje, author of the epic romance, *Mhudi* (1930), which was written in England between 1917–20. Plaatje was a cosmopolitan, educated writer. He worked often in the language of Tswana, and he was also a formidable translator, but he chose to write *Mhudi* in English. A founding member and Secretary of the South African Native National Congress (now the African National Congress or ANC), he travelled with a delegation to England to appeal to the British Government after the legislation of the 1913 Natives' Land Act, which disenfranchised the majority indigenous African population from most of the arable land in South Africa. About this Act, he wrote *Native Life in South Africa* (1916), one of the most important works of the time (in the light of current land reform programmes in South Africa and Zimbabwe, Plaatje's writing remains pertinent). Equally, his novel, a hybrid text in its use of English (it is influenced by Shakespeare and the adventure tradition of writers such as Rider Haggard), is also integrated with Tswana oral tradition. Like many postcolonial texts, then, *Mhudi* can be read as a counter-narrative to colonial writings on Africa. Significantly, it challenged official versions of South African history while also envisioning national unity between black and white, Afrikaner and English. Moreover, it is an early nationalist text that is strikingly attentive to gender, giving most of its narrative space over to a woman, the eponymous heroine. This novel is highlighted here also because it has never been as canonical globally as the Nigerian writer Chinua Achebe's wonderful but ubiquitous *Things Fall Apart* (1958), which it precedes by decades (see Chapter 5: Africa: North and sub-Saharan).

THE QUESTION OF HISTORY

Revising and revisiting history, then, are not new to writing in Southern Africa, although the metafictional strategies used to *question* history are much more recent. We can discover such strategies in Nobel Prize-winner J. M. Coetzee's

South African-based fiction, from *Dusklands* (1974) to the Booker Prize-winning *Disgrace* (1999). His publishers hailed *Dusklands* as South Africa's 'first modern novel'. It is a two-part novella, and experimental in terms of its narrative complexity. The first narrative is set in 1970s North America during the Vietnam War, while the second is set on the eighteenth-century Southern African frontier – from the Cape into present-day Namibia – and constitutes a rewriting of an explorer's narrative by his remote ancestor, Jacobus Coetzee. *Dusklands* clearly made a break with the dominant school of social realism, influencing fellow writers, such as André Brink, one of the original Sestigers (an Afrikaans literary movement), whose own novels after the more realist *A Dry White Season* (1979) have become increasingly self-reflexive, questioning the boundaries between fiction and history, and delving into the archives (see, for example, his 1993 novel *On the Contrary* about the eighteenth-century adventurer Estienne Barbier).

This kind of history-playing is not really the territory of the doyenne of South African letters, the 1991 Nobel Prize-winner Nadine Gordimer, in whose work one discovers a more socially-concrete, lived sense of history, such as we find in her *tour de force*, *Burger's Daughter* (1979). Yet it is fascinating to note three 'new' South African texts by contemporary women writers, Elleke Boehmer, Zoë Wicomb and Ann Harries – all South Africans who have based themselves in Britain – which also play seriously with the matter of history. Boehmer's elegant third novel *Bloodlines* (2000), weaves together a transnational story of W. B. Yeats, Irish nationalism and the Anglo-Boer War with a contemporary narrative set in the last days of apartheid. The drama that opens her novel is ostensibly based on the story of Robert McBride, the ANC activist responsible for the Magoo's Bar bombing in Durban in 1986. As the title *Bloodlines* implies, Boehmer's novel also inserts itself into a genre of postcolonial literature about the colonial obsession with miscegenation. Like Wicomb's innovative *David's Story* (2000), it follows in the tradition of Doris Lessing's *The Grass is Singing* (1950), Daphne Rooke's *Mittee* (1951, a bestseller in the USA in its day), and Lewis Nkosi's *The Mating Birds* (1986), and is a reply to the scientific racism of Sarah Gertrude Millin's earlier *God's Step-children* (1924), about which Coetzee has written an important essay, 'Blood, Taint, Flaw, Degeneration' in *White Writing*.

Wicomb's *David's Story* is a family and political history that dances between past and present Griqua identity (the Griqua are descended from South Africa's multiracial 'coloured' population). It engages with the stories of the iconic historical figures of Saartje Baartman, who was exhibited in nineteenth-century Paris and London as 'The Hottentot Venus' (her remains were only returned to South Africa from Paris's Musée de l'homme in 2002), and Krotoä-Eva, the seventeenth-century translator for the first Cape governor Jan van Riebeeck. Krotoä-Eva married Pieter van Meerhof, a Danish surgeon – the first interracial marriage at the Cape of Good Hope, before such things were prohibited – but when he died her children were sent to live with a Dutch family and, alcoholic and destitute, she was banished to Robben Island (see Nuttall and Coetzee 1998). Ann Harries's impressive and witty debut novel, *Manly Pursuits* (1999), subverts prevailing ideas of masculinity and empire, and features a cast of imperial historical personages – from Alfred Milner and Cecil Rhodes to Leander Starr Jameson, Rudyard Kipling, Oscar Wilde and Olive Schreiner.

THE 'NEW' SOUTH AFRICA

In the late 1980s, before the announced release of Nelson Mandela, the ANC member Albie Sachs, now a Constitutional Court judge in South Africa, made the controversial statement that the famous slogan, 'Culture is a weapon of the struggle', should be banned (see Sachs 1998). This sentiment had also been expressed by the novelists and critics Lewis Nkosi and Njabulo Ndebele, who argued that black South African writing during apartheid was little different from journalism (Nkosi 2006a), or was too concerned with 'spectacle' (Ndebele 2006). While 'struggle' literature dominated the South African literary scene, a great many texts have contributed to a crucial archive of apartheid: the theatre of Athol Fugard, John Kani and Winston Ntshona; the photographs and stories of dispossession and forced removals in Durban's Cato Manor, Johannesburg's Sophiatown and Cape Town's District Six; life stories such as Elsa Joubert's novelistic transcription of Poppie Nongena (1978); Ruth First's diary of detention, *117 days* (1965); and autobiographies such as Ezekiel Mphahlele's *Down Second Avenue* (1959), Bloke Modisane's *Blame Me On History* (1963) and Ellen Kuzwayo's *Call Me Woman* (1985). However, no autobiography in the history of South Africa could be more significant than Nelson Mandela's international bestseller *Long Walk to Freedom* (1994), published just as he was elected President.

In an address on 'The Republic of Letters After the Mandela Republic', Lewis Nkosi writes:

> In the postcolonial state of South Africa, two elements demand our attention: the politics of instant, enforced reconciliation, of which the Truth and Reconciliation Commission (TRC) is a notable example, and the continuing and vexed land question which seems unresolvable through the ministrations of the bourgeois nationalist state.
>
> (2006b: 328)

These two elements – reconciliation and the land question – are part of a number of significant concerns in the cultural activities of the 'new' South Africa (the quotation marks are often used to question the extent to which contemporary South Africa has become new, and to warn that newness perhaps remains more of a goal than a gain). The recent and prodigious literary cultural output of the region includes Wicomb's second novel, *Playing in the Light* (2006), Nadia Davids's play, *At Her Feet* (2006 [2003]), Ronnie Govender's debut novel *Song of the Atman* (2006), Phaswane Mpe's debut novel *Welcome to Our Hillbrow* (2001),

Ivan Vladislavić's *Portrait with Keys* (2006), Rayda Jacobs's novel *Confessions of a Gambler* (2003), J. M. Coetzee's novel *Disgrace* (1999), Antjie Krog's account of the Truth and Reconciliation Commission in *Country of My Skull* (1998), the films *Yesterday* (2004) and *Forgiveness* (2004), Njabulo S. Ndebele's *The Cry of Winnie Mandela* (2003), and Lewis Nkosi's novel *Mandela's Ego* (2006). Their concerns range across the topics of racial categorization in the 1950s and 'playing white', gender and religion (the local and the global), a generational and political history of the descendants of indentured Indian labourers in Natal, stories of the city, migrancy and AIDS, Truth and Reconciliation, and the fictionalization of South Africa's iconic couple by two established critics who have each written – as it happens – novels that feature Nelson and Winnie Mandela. The following section will focus in detail on the first of those novels listed above.

Wicomb's *David's Story*, a novel which explores narrative unreliability, nation-building and myths of 'totalizing colouredness' (Wicomb 1998: 105) has already been mentioned. Her recent work, *Playing in the Light*, is one of six titles launched by Umuzi, a new South African imprint of Random House. In its title, the novel casts its net beyond and within South Africa's borders: echoing Toni Morrison's *Playing in the Dark: whiteness and the literary imagination* (1992) and Zakes Mda's 1995 novel *She Plays with the Darkness* (set in Lesotho) as well as a book on cultural theory, *Hiding in the Light: on images and things* (1988) by Dick Hebdige. It is set in Cape Town in the mid–late 1990s during the TRC hearings, and explores its primary location in both the past and the present. From the outset, the iconic images of Table Mountain and Robben Island raise questions about travel and tourism, and about the Cape as a historical and contemporary commodity. Linked to these images of travel and tourism in the Cape, however, is a story of strategic racial categorization. The novel explores what Sarah Nuttall calls the 'mutual entanglements' (2004: 737) of racial identities: in particular, the historical and contemporary ways of fixing, acquiring, celebrating or (conversely) illicitly hiding coloured identity.

Intertextually, there is a surprising moment towards the end of *Playing in the Light*, when the main character, Marion Campbell, on a brief holiday to Europe, refers to two purchases she has made at the famous Clarke's bookshop in Cape Town. She is advised to read Nadine Gordimer's *The Conservationist* (1974) and J. M. Coetzee's *In the Heart of the Country* (1977). These novels are known in South Africa only by a small literary reading public. Both are books about the South African landscape, and both are about white characters on their farms, trying to belong. Significantly, each was written in the dark days of apartheid: 1977 was the year of Black Consciousness leader Steve Biko's death in detention. Despite owning a travel agency, Marion is averse to travel and yet finds herself on a train to Scotland, reading two challenging novels from South Africa which revise her engagement with South African history. While *Playing in the Light*, on the surface, is about a conservative white woman in her late thirties who voted Nationalist, her genealogy, as she discovers on her travels, is more complex. Her parents 'crossed over' at a time of increasing legislation, racialization and categorization, just at the moment of the establishment of South Africa's Population Registration Act of 1950. As *Playing in the Light* suggests, the need to engage critically and openly with South Africa's past is one way of moving forward to a 'new' South Africa, and both reading and writing have an important role to play in forging these engagements.

TRAVERSING BORDERS, BREAKING FRAMES

In her essay, 'Shame and Identity: the Case of the Coloured in South Africa' (1998), Wicomb takes issue with Homi K. Bhabha's account of the 'history of postcolonial migration, the narratives of cultural and political diaspora' (Bhabha 1994: 5). Wicomb argues that Bhabha's thinking is 'inadequate for a group who in the *suppression* of their slave origins have adopted an excessively proprietorial attitude towards the Cape' (1998: 105 – emphasis added). Wicomb's novel discussed above and her essay also allow us to think again of ways of looking at travel and diaspora that have become familiar in postcolonial studies. The cultural and historical realities of the Cape, situated at the intersection of the Atlantic and Indian Oceans, cannot be understood via Paul Gilroy's oft-cited conception of the 'Black Atlantic' (Gilroy 1993; see also Nuttall 2004). Gilroy's model simply does not fit the history of slavery in South Africa which *imported* rather than exported slaves, from other colonies in the Southern African region – Angola, Mozambique and Madagascar – and further east from India, Ceylon and Indonesia.

These historical stories of forced migration and slavery are just as essential to understanding 'Southern Africa' as a region as the narratives of war and apartheid that have dominated the contemporary landscape. To get a sense of different fictional borders consider, for example, the Angolan novelist José Eduardo Agualusa's enchanting epistolary novel *Nação crioula* (1997, trans. *Creole*) – about the travels of a Portuguese aristocrat in the mid-nineteenth century, from Portugal to Brazil to Angola – and also the stunning magical realism of Mozambique's Mia Couto. The South African novelist in exile, Bessie Head, traversed many of the racial, national and cultural borders of Southern Africa, as well as writing powerfully of Botswana. The daughter of an upper-class white mother and a black stable-hand, Head was raised by a coloured family in what was then Natal (far from the dominant coloured community in the Cape that Wicomb writes about). She was a teacher and a journalist for the legendary *Drum* magazine in Johannesburg before she went into exile in Botswana to escape the oppressive legislation of apartheid. Her novels include *When Rain Clouds Gather* (1968), *Maru* (1971) and *A Question of Power* (1973); other important works are *The Collector of Treasures and other Botswana Village Tales* (1977) and *Serowe: village of the rain-wind* (1981). These books have made her one of Southern Africa's most truly regional (as opposed to national) writers. As Rob Nixon explains:

If Head's regional perspective began as a symptom of her viciously administered life, one of her singular achievements was to transform that regionalism into a groundbreaking literary vision. Almost all her writings are set in a Botswanan village and accumulatively they convey a powerful sense of the ceaseless border crossings of imperialists, missionaries, refugees, migrant workers, prostitutes, school children, teachers, and armies that score Southern Africa as a region.

(1994: 113)

Botswana's first High Court female judge, Unity Dow, has followed in Head's footsteps, having recently published her fourth novel, *The Heavens May Fall* (2006). As a human rights lawyer, her fiction takes on the problems around her – of poverty, abuse and the pandemic of AIDS that is sweeping the country. Botswana has the most progressive AIDS policy in the region, supported by the Bill and Melinda Gates Foundation, at a time when South Africa is suffering long delays in the administration of treatment due to President Mbeki's years of AIDS denialism, and Zimbabwe is facing the consequences of President Mugabe's stand-off with western donors.

Despite the increasing censorship under Mugabe's current regime, which has caused many artists to cross its borders, Zimbabwe has a prodigious record of cultural production, from the music of Thomas Mapfumo and Oliver Mtukudzi, to the novels of Tsitsi Dangarembga, Chenjerai Hove, Shimmer Chinodya, Dambudzo Marechera and Alexander Kanengoni. Dangarembga's widely-acclaimed novel *Nervous Conditions* (1988) – its title taken from an introduction to Frantz Fanon's *Les Damnés de la Terre* (1961, trans. *The Wretched of the Earth*) – purposefully neglects the issue of war, the staple theme of much male writing from Zimbabwe, although the war of liberation features in its long-awaited sequel, *The Book of Not* (2006). Her focus on the plight and pain of women has prompted her fellow novelist Yvonne Vera to write, 'Dangarembga does not apologize for the taboo in her mouth. For being a witness. If speaking is still difficult to negotiate, then writing has created a free space for most women much freer than speech' (1999: 3). Neither does Vera apologize in her collection of short stories or in any of her five novels for the taboo topics in her fiction: rape, incest, abortion and infanticide. Indeed, her last novel was *The Stone Virgins* (2002), a brave book about Mugabe's persecutions in Matabeleland in the early 1980s. Vera was writing a further novel, *Obedience*, before her untimely death from AIDS, aged only forty, on 7 April 2005 in her husband's home in Toronto.

Southern Africa lost three great talents within months of each other: Yvonne Vera, Phaswane Mpe and K. Sello Duiker. If the twentieth century brought the challenges of colonialism and wars for independence, civil wars and new nation-hood, the twenty-first century is bringing home the challenges of globalization, terrorism and AIDS. This is what the great Mtukudzi is singing in *Todii*, but so are the local *isicathamiya* groups in KwaZulu-Natal. These are the things which Ishtiyaq Shukri tells us in his debut novel *The Silent Minaret* (2005); and what

Yesterday, the first Zulu feature-film to be nominated for an Academy Award, shows us in Leleti Khumalo's outstanding performance. In Southern Africa, the future awaits.

RECOMMENDED FURTHER READING

Attridge, Derek and Jolly, Rosemary (eds) *Writing South Africa: literature, Apartheid and democracy, 1970–1995* (Cambridge: Cambridge University Press, 1998).

Attwell, David, *Rewriting Modernity: studies in black South African literary history* (Pietermaritzburg: University of KwaZulu-Natal Press, 2005).

Barnard, Rita, *Apartheid and Beyond: South African writers and the politics of place* (Oxford: Oxford University Press, 2006).

Beinart, William, *Twentieth-Century South Africa*, second revised edition, (Oxford: Oxford University Press, 2001).

Brown, Duncan, *To Speak of this Land: identity and belonging in South Africa and beyond* (Pietermaritzburg: University of KwaZulu-Natal Press, 2006).

Chapman, Michael, *Southern African Literatures*, second revised edition (Pietermaritzburg: University of Natal Press, 2003).

Gray, Stephen, *Southern African Literature: an introduction* (Cape Town: David Philip, 1979).

Gumede, William Mervin, *Thabo Mbeki and the Battle for the Soul of the ANC* (Cape Town: Zebra Press, 2005).

Muponde, Robert and Primorac, Ranka (eds) *Versions of Zimbabwe: new approaches to literature and culture* (Avondale, Harare: Weaver Press, 2005).

Ngara, Emmanuel (ed.) *New Writing from Southern Africa: authors who have become prominent since 1980* (Oxford: James Currey, 1996).

Nuttall, Sarah and Michael, Cheryl-Ann (eds) *Senses of Culture: South African Culture Studies* (Oxford: Oxford University Press, 2000).

Rasebotsa, Nobantu, Samuelson, Meg and Thomas, Kylie (eds) *Nobody Ever Said AIDS: poems and stories from Southern Africa* (Cape Town: Kwela, 2004).

van Wyk Smith, Malvern, *Grounds of Contest: a survey of South African English literature* (Cape Town: Juta, 1990).

12

SOUTH AND EAST ASIA

ANSHUMAN MONDAL

COLONIALISM AND DECOLONIZATION IN ASIA

Asia has been the theatre of competition, conflict and even, on occasion, collaboration between five European colonial empires. Beginning with the establishment of Portuguese colonial outposts in western India following a decisive naval victory at the Battle of Diu in 1509, which introduced a system of armed trading (and gunboat diplomacy) into the shipping routes of the Indian Ocean (Chaudhuri 1985), Asia's fabled riches – its spices, textiles, minerals and precious metals – attracted first the attention of Europe's merchants and then its monarchs as trade subsequently led, in turn, to conquest. Soon after, the Spanish established a colony in the Philippines, while the Dutch acquired the Indonesian archipelago and Malacca on the Malay peninsula. The British established themselves first in the Indian subcontinent and then expanded eastwards, taking Burma, the Straits Settlements (Malacca, Singapore and Penang), the Malay Peninsula and Borneo. The French conquered Indochina, a region comprising modern Vietnam, Cambodia and Laos. Following the Sino-Japanese War of 1894–95, and with the collapse of the Qing dynasty imminent, the European powers scrambled for leases on Chinese territories and obtained trading concessions which brought China into the orbit of European hegemony (Cotterell 2002). In 1898, following the Spanish-American War, the USA also became an imperial presence in Asia, taking over the Philippines from the Spanish.

Only Siam and Japan avoided direct colonial subjugation and, in due course, the latter would enter the imperial race in Asia. Alarmed at the encroachments of the European colonial powers in China and scarred by its recent encounter with the USA in 1854, the Meiji emperor's court embarked on a period of rapid reform and modernization which developed into the first fully modern state in Asia by 1900. The Sino-Japanese War of 1894–95 constituted the first of its overseas imperial adventures, and in 1905 it successfully challenged European supremacy by defeating Russia. In hindsight, this first major victory of an Asian state over a European power prefigured the beginning of the end for European colonialism in Asia. As European territories gradually fell to the Japanese imperial advance – so that by May 1942 Japan briefly became the only imperial power in East and South-East Asia – there arose increasing and intensifying demands for independence from nationalists emboldened by Japan's dismantling of the aura of European invincibility.

As a result, at the end of the Second World War (1939–45), circumstances 'were not propitious for the restoration of colonial systems' (Stockwell 1992:

12). However, despite losing their prestige and authority in the face of Japanese advances, and in spite (or perhaps even because) of the psychological blows that these reversals delivered – the British, it is said, never fully recovered from the trauma of surrendering the supposedly 'impregnable' fort of Singapore – the first instinct of the European colonial powers was indeed to attempt to restore their colonial status in Asia. The immediate postwar years were therefore marked by what one historian has termed a 'new imperialism' (Stockwell 1992: 20) in East and South-East Asia. Nevertheless, the fate of this 'new imperialism' was decisively shaped by the independence and Partition of India and Pakistan in 1947 on the one hand, and the victory of Mao Zedong's Chinese Communist Party in 1949 on the other. These two seismic historical events quickly limited the scope for manoeuvre of the three main European colonial powers in the region and they experienced contrasting fortunes during the protracted period of decolonization.

Concluding that the loss of India meant an accommodation with nationalist forces in their other colonies, the British Government pursued a strategy of yielding independence within the framework of the Commonwealth of Nations (successful with respect to Malaysia, not so with Burma). In contrast, the French and the Dutch 'refused to acknowledge the reality of post-war politics' (Cotterell 2002: 247) and attempted to fully restore their colonial authority using a combination of negotiation, military force and reliance on the support of the United States. The USA, however, was equivocal; President Roosevelt's anti-imperialism (and the USA's own neo-imperial interests in the region) had to be carefully balanced by the need to keep 'implacable imperialists' such as the French leader Charles De Gaulle and the British Prime Minister Winston Churchill onside within the emergent context of Cold War *realpolitik*, both in Europe and in Asia. Accordingly, it supported the French in Indochina but not the Dutch in Indonesia. As a result, the process of decolonization in Asia was uneven: sometimes swift and relatively peaceful (the Indian subcontinent, Malaysia and, to a lesser extent, Burma), sometimes relatively swift and violent (Indonesia), but also protracted and incredibly violent (Indochina). Asian anti-colonial movements were also heterogeneous, ranging from elite-collaborationist (as in Malaysia), elite-led but mass-based (as in the Indian subcontinent and Indonesia) and the popular insurrectionary movements, usually communist, of Indochina.

Given this history of colonialism and decolonization, it is not surprising that Asia has received substantial attention from scholars working within postcolonial studies. However, the bulk of this attention has been directed to one particular region, namely South Asia (comprising the modern states of India, Pakistan, Sri Lanka and Bangladesh). Why has South Asia – and India in particular – acquired such a dominant presence in postcolonial studies? One response concerns the fact that two of the most highly influential postcolonial theorists, Homi K. Bhabha and Gayatri Chakravorty Spivak, are Indian, and have throughout their careers helped to direct the agendas of postcolonial studies through their development of critical theories that address South Asian preoccupations and concerns, with largely South Asian contexts and situations in mind (Young 2001: 339–40). There is, however, another side to this question: why have East and South-East Asia been relatively inconspicuous in postcolonial studies? The two questions are related and together they help to illuminate the privileging of certain locations operating within postcolonial studies with respect to Asia. The following section will attempt to move beyond the privileging of South Asia in postcolonial discourses, for two reasons: as a way of illuminating the wider historical and cultural changes that have been often neglected, and in order to expose recent developments in South and East Asian studies in the postcolonial field.

CULTURE, IDENTITY AND THE COLD WAR

In his monumental *Postcolonialism: an historical introduction* (2001), Robert J. C. Young argues that there is a continuity between anti-colonial politics and postcolonialism, and that the latter has emerged out of the development of what he calls 'tricontinental' Marxism – that is, a Marxism directed towards the specific concerns and contexts of the three colonized continents of Asia, Africa and Latin America. 'The triumph of tricontinental theorists', he suggests, 'was to mediate the translatability of Marxist revolutionary theory with the untranslatable features of specific non-European historical and cultural contexts' (6). In other words, anti-colonial politics largely drew on the resources of one of the most incisive critiques of modern colonialism and imperialism, namely Marxism, but adapted its concepts and theoretical paradigms in order to suit their own circumstances (see also Chapter 16: Materialist formulations).

Tricontinental Marxism was therefore a 'transculturation of Marxism' (169) and, in charting its genealogical impact on postcolonialism, Young restores Mao Zedong's fundamental role in the history of the struggle for decolonization. Inspired by Mao's mobilization of the peasantry, anti-colonial liberation movements were 'increasingly inclined to identify with the peasantry rather than the urban proletariat and to present themselves as peasant revolutions. The communist commitment to the urban proletariat as the only vanguard revolutionary force had been a constant impediment to its political success in the predominantly rural tricontinental societies' (183). In spite of his insights, Mao was dismissed as Director of the Chinese Communist Party's Peasants' Department by the Comintern (an organization established by Lenin following the Russian Revolution to help direct the course and practice of communist revolutions across the world) which remained committed to the policy of a 'United Front' with bourgeois nationalists in their struggle against European and Japanese imperial interests. This policy was based on an orthodox Marxist appraisal of China's socio-economic conditions which precluded the recognition of the peasantry as a viable revolutionary force.

While Mao's flexibility enabled the Chinese Communist Party (CCP) to mount the first successful communist revolution outside the West, by the same token Young argues that it was precisely the Communist Party of India's (CPI) unremitting orthodoxy which prevented it from acquiring any political momentum during decolonization and left the various communist factions politically marginalized for decades after independence. As Young describes it, Indian communism failed to challenge for the leadership of the national liberation movement, which was occupied first by Gandhians and then by Congress Socialists whose leader, Jawaharlal Nehru, became India's first prime minister, and whose 'model of cosmopolitan secularism [. . .] until recently formed the dominant pattern for Indian intellectuals' (339). Ironically, this may be one of the factors which has contributed to India's prominence in postcolonial studies because India's broad, elite-led mass movement mobilized anti-colonial forces by concentrating on culture and identity, and by wrestling with the ideological problems posed by religious, ethnic, regional and linguistic differences within India itself. The emphasis was on cultural politics rather than social revolution, and this has been attractive to postcolonial scholars interested in the 'subjective effects' as well as 'objective material conditions' of colonized peoples.

The CPI's political marginality also enabled India to remain relatively distant from and non-aligned to the global geopolitics of the Cold War. In this context, the contrast between Young's recovery of Mao's importance in the history of decolonization and his own glossing over of Ho Chi Minh's contribution in Vietnam is instructive as to the reasons why South-East Asia has been largely overlooked within postcolonial studies. If, as Young claims, postcolonialism has developed out of tricontinental Marxism, then Vietnam's struggle against decolonization is as much a part of this narrative as Mao's success in China. Indeed, Ho Chi Minh's acknowledgment of Mao's influence is recorded but the struggle against the French in Indochina (and Ho Chi Minh's contribution to tricontinental Marxism) is mentioned by Young only in passing, as opposed to the struggle of the Algerians and Frantz Fanon, which warrants two chapters. This emphasis corresponds to the prevalent imbalance of interest between Algeria and Vietnam within postcolonial studies, even though the French determination to restore its colonial authority in Indochina is indicative of the region's importance within the French empire. What lies behind this imbalance?

First, it was Indochina's tragedy that all three of the struggles for national liberation from French colonial rule – in Vietnam, Cambodia and Laos – were eventually engulfed by the Cold War. Although Cold War dynamics shaped the denouement of decolonization in Malaya and Indonesia as well, it was only Indochina, and Vietnam in particular, which suffered the misfortune of becoming a 'front line' in what the USA believed to be a global struggle between communism and the 'free world'. The French, dependent as they were on US support, quickly learned to align their interests with US anti-communism, emphasizing the VietMinh's communism over its nationalist credentials (Tarling 2001). In contrast, Sukarno's suppression of a communist insurgency in Indonesia earned him US approval, doomed the Dutch and kept Indonesia out of the fray. However, alarmed by the Chinese Revolution in 1949 and the subsequent Sino-Soviet treaty in 1950, nervous about communist encirclement on two fronts, and reliant on the French to help contain the Soviet threat in Europe, in Indochina the USA supported the war against the VietMinh, bearing 'nearly 80 per cent of the war's cost' (Cotterell 2002).

Subsumed within the dynamics of the Cold War, the anti-colonial war in Vietnam has been displaced from the history of decolonization and resituated primarily as an arena for the ideological struggle between capitalism and communism. Thus, it has fallen victim to the Eurocentrism which postcolonialism often struggles against. Indeed, some postcolonial scholars, subject to the disciplinary mechanisms which reproduce such boundaries and divisions within the Anglo-American academy, have largely maintained this excision. It could also be argued that since postcolonial studies emerges from the convergence of tricontinental Marxism and post-Marxist intellectual currents within Europe, exemplified most vividly by the influence of Michel Foucault's work on Edward W. Said's *Orientalism* (1978), and of Jacques Derrida's work on the postcolonial scholarship of Spivak and Bhabha (see Chapter 14: Poststructuralist formulations), the consequent emphasis on culture, language, discourse, textuality and identity may have precluded attention to locations such as Vietnam where such issues were submerged by more immediate and pressing concerns attendant on large-scale military conflict, as Arthur Cotterell vividly outlines:

> Although it singularly failed to crush the Viet Minh, the US war machine did succeed in devastating much of Vietnam and killing and maiming many of its people. In contrast with American casualties – 58,000 dead and 150,000 wounded – the Vietnamese losses were colossal: at least 2 million died and twice that number were wounded. Probably the full extent of the suffering will never be known. Just as damaged as its inhabitants was the land itself. Apart from the record tonnage of bombs dropped during the American intervention, more than 100,000 tonnes of toxic chemicals was sprayed on jungle, forest, swamp, plantation and orchard. As a result of the spraying of defoliants food production was put in jeopardy for several years, and Vietnam did not become an exporter of rice again till 1989. More worrying are the unseen effects of dioxin, the highly toxic constituent of notorious Agent Orange.
>
> (2002: 286)

While acknowledging – and accepting – Young's insistence that postcolonial *cultural* critique has nothing to apologize for since cultural politics has frequently played a vital role in anti-colonial resistance (Young 2001: 8), the sheer scale of the damage inflicted on people, property, infrastructure and environment during the almost thirty years of war in Vietnam (and which engulfed neighbouring Cambodia and Laos too, resulting in 600,000 Cambodian deaths alone) marks this tragic history as particularly indigestible to the interests and methodologies of cultural critique.

THE ANGLOSPHERE

In contrast, postcolonial studies has found, in the relatively more peaceful decolonization of South Asia, a suitable environment for the exploration and theorization of its preoccupation with the politics of representation, the operations of colonial discourse, its effects on the psychology of the colonized and the psychology of resistance, the staging of the colonial encounter as a contrapuntal negotiation between discrepant knowledge-systems, and the limits and possibilities of hybridity – although this has often involved the elision of historical tragedies in the region, such as Partition and its genocidal consequences. Such issues were not unique to South Asia, however, and the problems of refashioning culture and identity as a response to the upheavals and dislocations of colonialism were also experienced by many of the other regions in Asia. For example, the tensions generated by the attempt to construct a singular national identity from of a multiplicity of regional, ethnic and religious differences – not to mention the complication of geographical separation in the case of the island archipelagos – were germane to what are now Malaysia, Indonesia, the Philippines and Burma. All these nations shared with the Indian subcontinent a common postcolonial problem: their respective national movements were trying to create a single nation-state encompassing regions which had hitherto never been unified other than by the colonial states they were trying to supplant.

In Malaysia, for instance, communalism had become so entrenched that when the British proposed a postwar political settlement in which common citizenship would be available for Malays, Indians and Chinese within a unitary state encompassing all the Straits Settlements and Malay Sultanates (but not Singapore), the largest political organization of the time, the United Malay National Organization (UMNO), was formed in protest at the very idea of political equality between Malays and the minority Chinese and Indians. As a result, political rights and citizenship were restricted to Malays, which in turn triggered an insurrection by the Malaya Communist Party (MCP), an organization dominated by ethnic Chinese angered by their political disenfranchisement. This resulted in an Emergency which lasted until 1960, beyond the granting of independence in 1957. The communal issue was partly addressed by the establishment of a federal framework for independent Malaysia, marking the very structure of the state from its inception.

In contrast, Indonesia attempted to come to terms with its inherent diversity by abolishing its initial federal arrangements and replacing them with a highly centralized unitary state. Indonesia contains the largest Muslim population in the world; however, the geography of an island archipelago comprised of hundreds of islands ensures that even its Muslim population is far from culturally homogeneous. Furthermore, at the eastern end of Indonesia Bali remains steadfast to its Hindu traditions, and large Christian communities can be found on Amboina, the southern Celebes and Sumatra. Unsurprisingly, Indonesian leaders – very much like their counterparts in India – felt compelled to stress unity-in-diversity, adopting secularism and playing down its Islamic image.

Burma also followed the trajectory from federalism to a centralized unitary state – as in Indonesia, this path led eventually to the transfer from democracy to military dictatorship – but in this case it was not the outcome of a deliberate policy but rather of the failure of the federal arrangements agreed between Aung San's Anti-Fascist People's Freedom League (AFPFL) and the departing British. Designed to accommodate the political interests of the minorities in Burma – the Karen, the Shan and the Mon peoples – federalism did not long survive the assassination, in 1947, of Aung San and six other leaders of the AFPFL 'at the very moment political skills were required to secure national unity' (Cotterell 2002: 311). Civil war broke out soon after as the Karen rose in rebellion in 1948, and this drew in several other minorities and political factions. The Karen rebellion continues to this day in the northern hills of Burma (Ghosh 1998). International pressure demanding the restoration of civilian and democratic government has focused on the movement led by the Nobel Peace Prize winner, Aung San's daughter, Aung San Suu Kyi, and has largely overlooked the issue of ethnic conflict. But it is clear that one of the main priorities of any restored democracy would have to be the political integration of the country's minorities, comprising as they do almost one-third of its population.

For the Philippines, in contrast, the problem of unity is marked, on the one hand, by religious tensions between the Roman Catholic majority and the Muslim population of the southern island of Mindanao, and on the other by regional antagonisms between the islands. Unlike the other archipelagos in this region, the Philippines never had a historical equivalent to Java, which operated as a political and cultural 'anchor' during medieval times. The establishment by the Spaniards of Manila as the capital has, to some extent, provided a point of focus for the Philippines, but it is clear that the centripetal unifying force that this provides is offset by the persistent disruptive centrifugal forces of separatism.

Of these regions, only Malaysia and Burma shared with South Asia its experience of British colonialism, and given the institutional context of postcolonial studies' emergence within the Anglo-American academy it is perhaps unsurprising that it should be the British territories in Asia that have provided the principal resources for enquiries into the formation of colonial discourses and the resistance to them. This is reinforced by the strong ties that continue to bind the postcolonial South Asian nations to the 'Anglosphere', aided by the prevalence and historical provenance of English as a linguistic medium in the region. In particular, the strong institutional links between the Indian academy and its counterparts in Britain and the USA, with its well-worn trails from Calcutta, Delhi and Bombay to Oxford, Cambridge, Harvard, Columbia and so on, have enabled scholars from South Asia to make a deep impact on the formation and development of postcolonial studies in the West. In contrast, such avenues of entry were not so readily available for Burmese and Malaysian scholars. Burma's isolationism has largely rendered it somewhat marginal to postcolonial concerns notwithstanding its role as a *cause célebre*; Malaysia, for its part, has oriented itself more firmly towards its South-East Asian and Australasian neighbours in the region, as exemplified by its prominence in the Association of South-East Asian Nations (ASEAN). Moreover, English as a medium of linguistic communication and instruction never sank its roots in Malaysia as deeply as it has in South Asia, although in the era of US-led globalization this is rapidly changing.

Furthermore, what also distinguishes South Asia from these other former British territories is the existence of a vigorous anglophone literary tradition that has been strongly and warmly received in Britain and the USA. This, perhaps as much as anything else, has bound South Asia to the Anglosphere in ways not available to Burmese and Malaysian literary traditions, the inequities and imbalances of translation and the global literary market being what they are. The emergence of postcolonial studies from within literary departments in British and US universities has undoubtedly enabled this anglophone tradition to occupy a principal position in its discourses, encompassing as it does much more than recent blockbuster novels and prize-winning contemporary authors. From the early nineteenth century, South Asians have employed English to articulate their tortuous relationship to colonial modernity and their own place within it. Using English, nationalists and social reformers such as Rammohun Roy, M. G. Ranade, Pherozeshah Mehta, B. G. Tilak, G. K. Gokhale, M. A. Jinnah, M. K. Gandhi, Jawaharlal Nehru and Subhas Chandra Bose have debated how, why and if they should 'modernize' their culture. As lawyers they have both enforced and contested the laws established by the colonial state; as politicians they have deployed its rhetorical flexibility in debating chambers, legislative councils and on the streets and *maidans*, critiquing the finer points of legislation on the one hand, fashioning a discourse capable of mobilizing increasing numbers of supporters on the other. Writers, artists and journalists – the novelists R. K. Narayan, Mulk Raj Anand, Kamala Markandaya, Anita Desai, Salman Rushdie, Amitav Ghosh and Arundhati Roy, for example; poets like Michael Madhusudan Dutt, Henry Derozio, Sarojini Naidu, A. K. Ramanujan and Nissim Ezekiel; and journalists such as Bipinchandra Pal, Khushwant Singh and Ved Mehta – have created a body of work that has documented in precise, meticulous detail the evolving relationships between colonizers and colonized on the one hand, and between South Asians on the other, providing insights into the operations of colonialism and the processes of resistance adjacent to and sometimes contesting those discourses that may have been more directly related to the field of political struggle. Above all, English has been domesticated in South Asia such that, as Raja Rao put it in the famous preface to his groundbreaking novel *Kanthapura* (1967):

> English is not really an alien language to us. [. . .] We are all instinctively bilingual, many of us writing in our own language and in English. We cannot write like the English. We should not. We cannot write only as Indians. [. . .] Our method of

expression therefore has to be a dialect which will someday prove to be as distinctive and colourful as the Irish or the American. Time alone will justify it.

(1967: vii)

Time, indeed, has justified it, and the day to which Rao looked forward has long since passed as several generations of Indians have grown accustomed to using English both formally and informally, in public and in private.

Furthermore, South Asia is the location of Britain's longest, most intimate and involved colonial encounter. It has exerted a profound influence on the British imagination, an influence that has been intimately absorbed into British culture; being the 'jewel in the crown' of the British empire, its hitherto most valuable and prized colonial asset, it has provided Britain with its most durable and embedded models of Asiatic cultural and civilizational difference. Since the relationship extends back so far, South Asia is also the site – in both physical and discursive senses – of the largest *archive* documenting it (Richards 1993). In British minds, the Raj was something *more* than just a colony: it represented Britain's imperial destiny, a mirror in which the British could see a reflection of themselves not as mere planter-settlers but as an imperial race, and the natural heirs to the great Mughals. As such, it is in India that the British colonial experience was at its most intense, and the historical record in South Asia provides ample testimony to the strengths and weaknesses, convictions and contradictions of British colonial rule. The scope of the archive that remains provides a resource for postcolonial scholars that is unparalleled in Asia and unsurprisingly is the principal focus of attention for postcolonial research in that region.

POSTCOLONIALISM IN SOUTH ASIA

Robert J. C. Young's account of postcolonial theory's indebtedness to India inhabits his wider narrative about the development of postcolonialism out of tricontinental Marxism. In this regard, he identifies the period of Emergency rule by Indira Gandhi's Congress Government (1975–77) as a pivotal moment in the dissolution of Indian Marxism's rigorous attachment to Marxist orthodoxy. The Emergency crystallized the 'developing prestige of tricontinental, particularly Maoist, Marxism in the 1960s and 1970s, partly inspired by the successful peasant revolt at Naxalbari in West Bengal in 1967' in a search for 'left, and alternative left, alternatives' (Young 2001: 349). He concludes that '[t]he dominance of India in postcolonial theory is *in part* the result of this theoretical deferred action in which Marxism has been rewritten and transformed according to a trajectory indebted to the work of twentieth-century tricontinental political-activist theorists' (351, emphasis added).

It is important to acknowledge that Young's is a necessarily partial account, a consequence of the narrowness of his focus on the Marxist lineage. While that dimension was indeed crucial to the development of postcolonial theory in India, and goes a long way to explaining the dynamics behind the important theoretical contributions of Bhabha, Spivak and the *Subaltern Studies* group (see Chapter 14: Poststructuralist formulations), it nevertheless overlooks some broader developments in post-independence India that revolutionized not just *theory* but also other cultural fields, in particular literature. These developments also came to a head during the Emergency, which was a symptom of a deep crisis in Indian national life. The lineages of this crisis are crucial not only in determining the exact context of the theoretical developments in India during the late 1970s and 1980s but also in establishing why they paralleled transformations in the cultural sphere, and why both of these followed a broadly post- or anti-nationalist trajectory. In other words, the increasing convergence between Marxism and poststructuralism in theory, and the escalating recurrence of post-modernist features in anglophone Indian literature, both share a common historical genealogy that reached crisis point during the Emergency, and both are responses to it.

The origins of that crisis can be traced back to the pressures incumbent on the newly independent Indian nation-state, pressures that it shared with its colonial predecessor. The historians Sugata Bose and Ayesha Jalal have pithily described them as 'the overlapping dialectics of centralism and regionalism [and] nationalism and religious assertion' (1998: 201). In other words, from its inception the Indian state was marked by a tension between central government and regional autonomy on the one hand, and by tensions between its constituent religious communities, on the other, that continually picked away at the national fabric. Both of these dimensions were only partially resolved by independence – through the federalism enshrined in the Constitution and by the self-mutilation of the national body represented by the Partition of 1947 – a deferral which meant that these tensions continued to develop throughout the subsequent decades.

The 'steady pilferage by the Centre of powers that constitutionally belonged to the regions' (Khilnani 1997: 51) paradoxically provoked regional assertion. With all effective power being increasingly routed through New Delhi, local grievances and problems were invariably channelled *against* the federal centre; while, at the same time, the frustrations of having no proper autonomy to speak of also encouraged greater radicalism, resulting in a number of secessionist movements in regions such as Assam, Punjab and Nagaland, as well as Kashmir. The central authorities responded by flexing their political muscles to even greater extent, dispatching the army to these regions and effectively imposing martial law. The increasing authoritarianism this heralded was sealed by the declaration of a state of Emergency in 1975 by the Prime Minister, Indira Gandhi. It was at this point that the centre–region dialectic combined most significantly with the dynamics of religious communalism that had always been present on the flip-side of the Indian nationalist imagination. After ending the Emergency in 1977 by calling surprise elections, Indira Gandhi was perhaps equally surprised to find herself at the wrong end of the result. The resulting coalition government soon fell; meanwhile, Indira Gandhi had begun to salvage some of her popularity by subtly changing the discourse of 'national' identity, altering her rhetoric to appeal to a core 'Hindu' constituency that could act as an electoral bulwark against the increasing appeal of regional secessionists.

The impact of this turbulence on the Indian cultural imagination and its national self-image was profound. The old models of Indian nationalism, derived from Nehru and Mahatma Gandhi, that had animated the struggle against colonial rule lost their credibility. The crisis of the state thus resulted in a corresponding crisis of representation in both its political and discursive senses. The ideational structures that had upheld the ideology of a secular, democratic nation – structures derived from the political legacy of the Enlightenment – had buckled under the pressure, and splintered India's sense of itself. It is unsurprising, then, that postmodernism begins to emerge at this time among English-speaking intellectuals and artists as a cultural vocabulary through which the superseded discourses of Indian nationalism might be subjected to interrogation, for its basis is in critiques of the very concept of 'representation' itself, which in turn is correlated ideologically to a suspicion of grand narratives and the state.

This convergence between disavowal of Indian nationalism's grand narratives, suspicion of the state and postmodern theory has been most forcibly articulated by the *Subaltern Studies* historians, their revisionist Marxism usefully and strategically (and increasingly) deploying concepts derived from poststructuralism (see Chapter 14: Poststructuralist formulations). Their emergence at precisely that moment in Indian history when the crisis of nationhood was at its most intense is no coincidence, for their challenge to the dominance of elite or state-centred perspectives on Indian colonial and postcolonial history was one of the most creative responses to, as well as devastating critiques of, the formation of the postcolonial nation-state. Their focus on the histories of subaltern peoples which had previously escaped the notice of nationalist and colonial historians was both an affirmation of the role of subalterns in the historic formation of the modern Indian nation – in ways usually at odds with the narratives of elite historians – and a critique of the nation's self-representation, which had systematically silenced or excised their contributions.

The intervention of Gayatri Chakravorty Spivak in the fourth volume of *Subaltern Studies* and her subsequent collaboration with Ranajit Guha – the leading figure and inspirational mentor of the collective – has internationalized their influence. The methodological and theoretical concerns of the group have now been extended to histories of South America, Africa and other parts of Asia. Their impact on academic historiography is particularly noteworthy since that discipline has long been suspicious of postcolonialism's literary and culturalist orientation. In that respect, their contributions to the development of postcolonial histories are as important as Said's, Bhabha's and Spivak's have been to literary scholars.

SOUTH AND EAST ASIAN FUTURES

While South Asia, of all the Asian regions, occupies a dominant position within postcolonial studies, it is clear that this is not solely due to the prominence of Homi K. Bhabha and Gayatri Chakaravorty Spivak, nor indeed of the *Subaltern Studies* collective. Rather, their work's provenance is due to the particular conditions of receptivity that have, throughout its development, oriented the field of postcolonial studies towards the Indian subcontinent. Besides their abilities as theorists of impressive scope and flexibility, and the intrinsic merits of their work, which are considerable, their prominence – and that of South Asia in general – represents a particular confluence of historical, intellectual, cultural and political forces that have shaped the history of Asia on the one hand, and the Anglo-American academy on the other. These same forces have determined the relative inconspicuousness of East and South-East Asia in postcolonial studies. As the field develops, it is hoped that the boundaries – conceptual, disciplinary, linguistic – that have hitherto excluded these regions will be dismantled and the rich complexity of Asian history during the colonial and postcolonial periods will be yet further enriched.

RECOMMENDED FURTHER READING

Anderson, Benedict, *Spectres of Comparison: nationalism, Southeast Asia and the world* (London: Verso, 1998).

Bose, Sugata and Jalal, Ayesha, *Modern South Asia: history, culture, political economy* (London: Routledge, 1998).

Chakrabarty, Dipesh, *Provincializing Europe: postcolonial thought and historical difference* (Princeton, NJ: Princeton University Press, 2000).

Cotterell, Arthur, *East Asia: from Chinese predominance to the rise of the Pacific Rim* (London: Pimlico, 2002).

Guha, Ranajit and Spivak, Gayatri Chakravorty (eds) *Selected Subaltern Studies* (New York: Oxford University Press, 1998).

Mehrotra, Arvind Krishna (ed.) *A History of Indian Literature in English* (London: Hurst and Company, 2003).

Stockwell, A. J., 'Southeast Asia in War and Peace: The End of European Colonial Empires' in Nicholas Tarling (ed.) *The Cambridge History of South-East Asia: volume 4: from World War II to the present* (Cambridge: Cambridge University Press, 1992), pp. 1–57.

Tarling, Nicholas, *Southeast Asia: A Modern History* (Oxford: Oxford University Press, 2001).

Young, Robert J. C., *Postcolonialism: an historical introduction* (Oxford: Blackwell, 2001).

13

DIASPORA

JAMES PROCTER

Unlike the preceding chapters, which focus in the main on specific geographical and national terrains, diasporas are more commonly associated with movements through and between locations, and even with dislocation. In fact, the concept of diaspora has been developed by many postcolonial critics to challenge the supremacy of national paradigms. In postcolonial studies, 'diaspora' can appear both as naming a *geographical* phenomenon – the traversal of physical terrain by an individual or a group – as well as a *theoretical* concept: a way of thinking, or of representing the world.

Etymologically, diaspora derives from the Greek (*dia* meaning over; *sperien* meaning to sow or scatter) and 'invokes images of multiple journeys' (Brah 1996: 181). While it was originally used to refer specifically to the exile of the Jews from Palestine, more recently the term has been adopted and adapted by postcolonial scholars and artists to refer to the forced and voluntary migrations set in motion by empire. As Edward Said notes in the concluding section of *Culture and Imperialism* (1993), 'Movements and Migrations': 'Imperialism consolidated the mixture of cultures and identities on a global scale' (407). Moreover, as Bill Ashcroft, Gareth Griffiths and Helen Tiffin remind us, 'Colonialism itself was a radically diasporic movement, involving the temporary or permanent dispersion and settlement of millions of Europeans over the entire world' (1998: 69).

However, diaspora is not something that simply happens in the colonies. Europe and the USA (the focus of this chapter) are also *home* to significant postcolonial settler communities from Africa, the Caribbean, South Asia and elsewhere. While 1492 has taken on a foundational significance in postcolonial studies as the year in which the Spanish explorer Christopher Columbus arrived in the Americas, it is often forgotten that this was also the year in which the North African Moors, who had occupied Spain for some 700 years, were ousted from Granada. Such prolonged *internal* diasporic presences mean that, as Paul Gilroy puts it, 'the figure of the migrant must be made part of Europe's history' (2004b: xxi). Gilroy's remark appears in the foreword to *Blackening Europe* (2004), a collection of essays edited by Heike Raphael-Hernandez that demonstrates how European cultural forms, from Spanish Flamenco to contemporary hip hop in France and Germany, have been accented by African American music in a way that questions the comforting boundaries between Europe and its others, and between Europe and the USA.

Rather than treating Europe and the USA as discrete national communities

151

across which diasporas move, this chapter will consider how diasporas pose a challenge to the naturalized boundaries conventionally separating these locations. Focusing specifically on the black diaspora, it will explore the possibilities of what Paul Gilroy has elsewhere termed 'non-place based' (1997: 328) forms of community. In *The Black Atlantic* (1993), Paul Gilroy rejects the nation as an organizing category by seeking 'to produce an explicitly transnational and intercultural perspective' (15). Rather than focusing on, say, 'black British' or 'African American' culture, *The Black Atlantic*

> settle[s] on the image of ships in motion across the spaces between Europe, America, Africa, and the Caribbean as a central organising symbol [. . .]. Ships immediately focus attention on the middle passage, on the various projects for redemptive return to an African homeland, on the circulation of ideas and activists as well as the movement of key cultural and political artefacts: tracts, books, gramophone records, and choirs.
>
> (1993: 4)

Circulation, movement, passage and journeying are Gilroy's preferred metaphors here, allowing him to move beyond what he takes to be the narrow, sclerotic confines of the nation. Such metaphors allow Gilroy to demonstrate the extent to which the black presence has critically contributed to, and drawn on, the supposedly discrete development of Western modernity. As John McLeod notes, 'This makes a nonsense *both* of a sense of the West as ethnically and racially homogeneous, and of ideas concerning an essentialized, common "black" community separated from Western influence' (2000: 229). For Gilroy, the Atlantic's significance is more than symbolic (a metaphor for movement and migration), or geographical (as a space that divides and connects Europe, the USA, Africa and the Caribbean). As the setting for the 'triangular' slave journeys that marked the beginning of a black diaspora in the sixteenth century, the Atlantic's significance is also historical.

For almost four hundred years, ships loaded with commercial goods set sail from Europe to the west coast of Africa, where cargo was exchanged for slaves. From here, waves of African slaves were forcibly shipped across the so-called 'middle passage' to the Americas and the plantation settlements of the Caribbean islands and to South and North America. The slave ships then returned to Europe loaded with sugar and other commodities from the colonies. By the time slavery and the slave trade were abolished in the nineteenth century by the European empires and the USA, it is estimated that over ten million West Africans had been transported to the New World.

As well as being sites of misery, death and oppression, the slave ships facilitated the passage and exchange of new ideas and cultural formations. The triangular trade routes did not simply circulate human cargo and other precious commodities of empire, they also stimulated a diasporic black imagination and calls for the abolition of slavery. The slave trade brought significant numbers of African slaves into the heart of the metropolitan centres of Europe and the

USA, cities like New York, Boston, London and Liverpool. Often working as domestic servants, it was within the metropolis that exceptional figures such as Ignatius Sancho (1729–80), Phillis Wheatley (1753–84) and Olaudah Equiano (1745–97) first learned to read and write, and where they found a ready outlet and audience for their work.

For example, Phillis Wheatley was taken from Senegal as a child and shipped to the USA. Arriving in Boston in 1761, she worked in the home of John and Susannah Wheatley who recognized her ability and had her educated. Phillis Wheatley's poems were published in England and North America and she made several journeys across the Atlantic, on one occasion to oversee the publication of her 1773 volume, *Poems on Various Subjects, Religious and Moral*. Phillis Wheatley's transatlantic travels and publications were followed by those of other slaves and former slaves such as Olaudah Equiano. *The Interesting Narrative of the Life of Olaudah Equiano* (1789) records Equiano's Atlantic adventures and his experiences of travelling at sea and in England and the Americas.

As C. L. Innes notes, many of these eighteenth-century writers and writings 'complicate and subvert assumptions about genre, authenticity, and the boundaries between oral and literary composition' (2002: 3). For example, both Wheatley and Equiano draw on African, American and European cultural traditions in their work. Equiano's autobiography documents Igbo customs in Africa, but it does so in a manner that adapts the anthropological perspectives of early European travel writing. Wheatley's 'On Being Brought from Africa to America' (1768) images her journey through biblical metaphors of transformation – 'Remember, *Christians*, *Negros*, black as *Cain*, / May be refin'd and join th' angelic train' (Gates and McKay 1997: 171) – while more generally her poetry adopts the neoclassical forms and tropes associated with classical Greek and high European literature.

It is within this context that Paul Gilroy argues that the works of Equiano and Wheatley 'ask to be evaluated on their own terms as complex, *compound* formations. [. . .] Their legacy is most valuable as a mix, a hybrid, recombinant form, that is indebted to its "parent" culture, but remains assertively and insubordinately a bastard' (1997: 323). The mass movements of African slaves and of individuals like Wheatley and Equiano suggest a black Atlantic network which has nodal points in Africa, the USA and Europe, but which highlights movement (literal *and* imaginative) both beyond and between them.

The emergence of a black Atlantic imagination in the 1700s and 1800s was consolidated in the twentieth century with the emergence of Pan-Africanism. The Pan-African Congress, which moved back and forth between the USA and Europe, represented a more organized political attempt to exploit the transnational connections first established within eighteenth-century slave writing. While Pan-Africanism's investment in a unifying black African consciousness was in part a rejection of the compound formations Gilroy associates with earlier slave narratives, the movement sought to connect blacks internationally, across the USA and Europe, by holding conferences in New York, Lisbon, Brussels, Paris and London.

A key figure in the Pan-African movement was W. E. B. Du Bois (1868–1963). Born in Massachusetts, Du Bois went on to study for his PhD at the University of Berlin, and spent much of the 1920s travelling between Europe and the USA to organize the Pan-African Congress. Many of his writings articulate what Du Bois termed 'double consciousness', a term which refers specifically to the dilemma of being black and American, and which led Du Bois to knit together national and transnational perspectives in his work. Many see Du Bois's most famous text, *The Souls of Black Folk* (1903) as the embodiment of the spirit of double consciousness. The book combines a bewildering range of genres and discourses – music, autobiography, sociology, poetry, history, fiction – in a manner that is reminiscent of the recombinant forms of Wheatley and Equiano. Each section opens with a piece of conventional poetry that is typically attributed to a canonical European writer (Lord Byron, Friedrich Schiller, Elizabeth Barrett Browning, Alfred Tennyson), but which also includes white American poets such as James Lowell and Edward Fitzgerald's translation of the Persian poet, Omar Khayyám. These poems are followed by the bars from a 'sorrow song': a communally composed and therefore anonymous piece of music sung by African American slaves. One of the effects of this juxtaposition of European and African, oral and scribal, literary and musical, high and popular intertexts, is the opening up of a series of transatlantic crossings, or dialogues, which draw into question the presumed integrity and unity of African, American and European forms.

The work of Du Bois had a profound influence on what is sometimes regarded as the francophone counterpart of Pan-Africanism: Negritude (see also Chapter 5: Africa: North and sub-Saharan and Chapter 8: The Caribbean). Negritude emerged in Paris before and after the Second World War and is primarily associated with the African and Caribbean diasporic intellectuals Léopold Sédar Senghor (Senegal) and Aimé Césaire (Martinique). Involving the development of a distinctively African aesthetic, Negritude was frequently articulated in explicit opposition to European cultural values. Nevertheless, it also emerged out of a sustained critical dialogue with African American writers like Du Bois, European thinkers such as Jean-Paul Sartre and canonical texts like William Shakespeare's play *The Tempest* (1611). Such diasporic intertexts, connections and conversations have come to characterize black Atlantic thinking since the Second World War.

By the early 1950s, Paris had become home to a number of black American writers (including Chester Himes, Richard Wright and James Baldwin) keen to escape the growing racial divisions in the USA. Until relatively recently, African American scholars dismissed the 'European' work of these otherwise canonical black writers. Indeed, even the relatively recent first edition of the *Norton Anthology of African American Literature* (1997) provides the following gloss on

Richard Wright (who, along with Senghor and Césaire, founded the journal *Présence Africaine* in 1947):

> Despite [his] prodigious output during the 1950s critics generally agree that Wright's career as a serious literary artist ended in 1946, when he left the United States. They argue that while France liberated Wright as a person, it shackled his creative expression, dulling the vivid memories of his childhood and early life, deadening his ear to the rhythms and cadences of black American speech, all of which he had captured so compellingly in such works as [. . .] *Black Boy*. The result was contrived and artificial work, full of windy abstractions.
>
> (Gates and McKay 1997: 1379)

Ultimately concurring with this view of the European Wright as shackled, dull, deadening, contrived and artificial, the *Norton Anthology* (which plays a powerful role in canon formation on both sides of the Atlantic) endorses an evaluation of his work within a purely national paradigm. Not only does such a reading neglect the significant African *diasporic* tradition out of which Wright writes, it also neglects what Gilroy calls the intercultural 'value of [Wright's] critical perceptions that could only have been gained through [. . .] restlessness, even homelessness' (1993: 150) in Europe.

Partly as a result of Gilroy's work, the intercultural perspectives of postcolonial and black Atlantic literature have been paid much closer attention within the academy in recent years. Indeed, the *Norton*'s gloss on Richard Wright might be said to represent something of an anomaly in the 1990s, when, as Elleke Boehmer has put it, 'definitions of postcolonial literature [were] almost necessarily cosmopolitan, transplanted, multilingual, and conversant with the cultural codes of the West' (1995: 237). If diasporic cultural production like Wright's was critically neglected until relatively recently then, Boehmer suggests, if anything it has been granted too much attention since the 1990s. While Gilroy's notion of the black Atlantic offers no easy vision of cosmopolitanism and is notably alert to the pain and suffering that transatlantic travel historically denotes, it is arguably caught up in more recent tendencies in postcolonial studies outlined by Boehmer.

Furthermore, in her essay 'Journeying to Death: Paul Gilroy's *The Black Atlantic*', Laura Chrisman argues that Gilroy's version of diaspora is uncritically utopian and that it is too quick to delegitimize nationalism, which she insists has positive, or progressive elements. She goes on to argue that Gilroy's recovery of Europe as a valuable site of African American cultural production (in, for example, the work of Du Bois and Wright) neglects Europe 'as historically, and structurally, oppressive for blacks from the colonies' (2003: 79). In support of her argument Chrisman refers to the Senegalese artist Sembène Ousmane, whose novel *Le docker noir* (1956, trans. *Black Docker*) focuses on the exploitation of a black migrant in Marseille. She also footnotes Ama Ata Aidoo's *Our Sister Killjoy* (1977) and Caryl Phillips' *The European Tribe* (1987) as instances of 'less-than-positive' (88) representations of Europe.

This chapter will conclude by reflecting on Caryl Phillips' *The European Tribe*, a text which brings our account of both European and US diasporas up to the present and which exemplifies the contemporary diasporic links between Europe and the USA. Born in St Kitts in 1958 before moving to England as a baby, Phillips currently divides his time between Europe and the USA. His writing is self-consciously immersed within a diasporic European and US literary 'tradition' that includes African Americans like Du Bois, Wright and Baldwin, European/American modernists such as T. S. Eliot, Joseph Conrad and Virginia Woolf, and black Britons from Equiano and Sancho to Linton Kwesi Johnson. Such eclectic literary roots/routes are often self-consciously evoked in Phillips' fiction and non-fiction to challenge or elude the presumed integrity of national paradigms and to forge new transatlantic connections.

In his *The European Tribe*, Caryl Phillips offers a definition of Europe as 'a continent extending from Asia to the Atlantic Ocean' (1987: vii). This is a definition that seems to disturb the common-sense boundaries of Europe as a self-contained location, inviting us to think of Asia and the Atlantic as spaces that delimit and define Europe rather than as beyond its limits. It is a definition that puts into operation a quite specific tension in the text, posed as it is against what Phillips regards as the increasingly 'tribal' character of Europe: 'the rise of nationalistic fervour, which leads people to close ranks into groups' (xi).

Phillips begins his European journey in the Moroccan city of Casablanca. The effect of this unlikely outset is to further stretch the imaginative boundaries of Europe, which appears now, in North Africa, as a ghostly colonial legacy and as the *France Soir* newspaper on which English tourists wipe their derrières. Phillips then travels to Gibraltar and on to more familiar European ground. Yet even Gibraltar, Phillips reminds us, is 'a corruption of the Arabic words *Jebel Tariq*, meaning Tariq's mountain' (21), an etymology that registers earlier Moorish conquests, migrations and settlements. In moving between Casablanca and Gibraltar, then, we do not simply move from Africa to Europe, but from Europe to Africa. As Phillips continues through Spain, France, Venice, Amsterdam, Ireland, Germany, Poland, Norway and the Soviet Union, he explores the character of European racism and the various ways it interpellates him as outsider. At the same time his narrative simultaneously unsettles the familiar boundaries between inside and outside, belonging and unbelonging, familiarity and unfamiliarity, local and stranger, which often underpin racism. Phillips' itinerary is typically 'diasporic' in this sense. Indeed, it is through his appropriation of the genre of the travel narrative in *The European Tribe* that Phillips is able to rework the familiar tropes of 'wandering' (xi), disorientation and unbelonging within a diasporic context.

The black Atlantic is never far from Phillips' Europe, and the USA is surprisingly central to his text. Phillips mentions television coverage of a hijacking in Columbia by the Gibraltar Broadcasting Corporation, Casablanca as Hollywood film set, the travels of Chester Himes and Hemingway in Spain, and lunch in the South of France with James Baldwin. Moreover, Phillips opens *The European*

Tribe by acknowledging the formative role that the USA has played in terms of his chosen career as a writer, particularly the impact of his reading Richard Wright for the first time in Los Angeles. At the same time, he records his alienating encounters with racism in New York and Salt Lake City as well as his sense of dismay at the Americanization of Europe. It is perhaps Phillips' restless sense of dis-ease with both Europe and the USA that has led him more recently to describe the Atlantic as both his 'home' and his preferred resting place: 'I wish my ashes to be scattered in the middle of the Atlantic Ocean at a point equidistant between Britain, Africa and North America' (2001: 304).

It remains to be seen whether such recent, if relatively established, articulations of diasporic identity will be unsettled or extended by the *new* diasporic subjects that have come to preoccupy the European and North American imagination since 9/11. What Paul Gilroy calls the 'war against asylum seekers, refugees, and economic migrants' (2004b: xii) is a warning against complacency where the notable success of contemporary diasporic writing in Britain – from Zadie Smith to Monica Ali – is concerned. How do we square the mainstream success of Ali's *Brick Lane* (2003) with the current rise of Islamophobia in Britain? Can refugees find a productive alignment within existing diasporic discourses, as the thematic concern with asylum in recent novels by Caryl Phillips (*A Distant Shore*, 2003) and Abdulrazak Gurnah (*By the Sea*, 2001) suggests? Or is there a danger that '[t]he figure of the immigrant is part of the very intellectual mechanism that holds us – postcolonial Europeans, black and white – hostage' (Gilroy 2004: xxi)?

RECOMMENDED FURTHER READING

Brah, Avtar, *Cartographies of Diaspora: contesting identities* (London: Routledge, 1997).

Braziel, Jana Evans and Mannur, Anita (eds) *Theorizing Diaspora: a reader* (Oxford: Blackwell, 2003).

Chow, Rey, *Writing Diaspora: tactics of intervention in contemporary cultural studies* (Bloomington, IN: Indiana University Press, 1993).

Gilroy, Paul, *The Black Atlantic: modernity and double-consciousness* (London: Verso, 1993).

Innes, C. L., *A History of Black and Asian Writing in Britain, 1700–2000* (Cambridge: Cambridge University Press, 2002)

Kalra, V., Kahlon, R. K. and Hutnyk, J. (eds) *Diaspora and Hybridity* (London: Sage, 2005).

McLeod, John, *Postcolonial London: rewriting the metropolis* (London: Routledge, 2004).

Nasta, Susheila, *Home Truths: fictions about the South Asian diaspora in Britain* (Basingstoke: Palgrave, 2001).

Procter, James, *Dwelling Places: postwar black British writing* (Manchester: Manchester University Press, 2003).

Part III
POSTCOLONIAL FORMULATIONS

14
POSTSTRUCTURALIST FORMULATIONS

STEPHEN MORTON

POSTCOLONIAL THEORY AND THE QUEST FOR CRITIQUE

The impact and influence of so-called poststructuralist thought on the development of postcolonial studies have been widely acknowledged by critics who are both sympathetic to and critical of poststructuralism. For some critics, such as Homi K. Bhabha, Gayatri Chakravorty Spivak, Robert J. C. Young and Dipesh Chakrabarty, poststructuralism is part of a broader questioning of the values of the European enlightenment, and its claims to universalism. For others, such as Benita Parry, Neil Lazarus, Aijaz Ahmad, Arif Dirlik and Pal Ahluwalia, the development of postcolonial theoretical formulations through a critical engagement with the vocabularies of poststructuralist theory provided by the psychoanalyst Jacques Lacan, and the philosophers Jacques Derrida and Gilles Deleuze, signifies the depoliticization of a postcolonial studies that has its origins in left-oriented national liberation movements. By framing political resistance in the abstract terms of signs, codes and discursive strategies, in other words, materialist critics of a postcolonial theory informed by the work of Jacques Derrida and Michel Foucault argue that postcolonial theory – either wittingly or unwittingly – denies the agency and voice of the colonized.

A case in point is the reception of the work of Edward W. Said. Said's *Orientalism* (1978) is often credited as being the foundational text of postcolonial theory, and colonial discourse studies; one of the reasons for this is Said's engagement with the work of the French poststructuralist historian and philosopher Michel Foucault. As Said puts it in his introduction to *Orientalism*:

> I have found it useful [. . .] to employ Michel Foucault's notion of a discourse, as described by him in *The Archaeology of Knowledge* and in *Discipline and Punish*, to identify Orientalism. My contention is that without examining Orientalism as a discourse one cannot possibly understand the enormously systematic discipline by which European culture was able to manage – and even produce – the Orient politically, sociologically, ideologically, scientifically, and imaginatively during the post-Enlightenment period.
>
> (1978: 3)

However, as Said goes on to assert, his work importantly departs from that of Foucault in its belief in 'the determining imprint of individual writers upon the otherwise anonymous collective body of texts constituting a discursive formation like Orientalism' (23). For some of Said's recent commentators, the influence of Foucault's argument that discourse mediates the exercise of dominant systems of power and knowledge on Said's thought has been greatly exaggerated. In a powerful reassessment of Said's work, Timothy Brennan has argued that Said's intellectual formation was shaped more by Eric Auerbach's modernization of philology and Giambattisto Vico's science of history than by Foucault's discursive formations (2006: 93–125). In a similar vein, Abdirahman A. Hussein has argued that 'Said's criticism, in *Orientalism* and elsewhere, is rooted (unlike Foucault's and very much like Gramsci's) in a dialectical tradition which affords considerable latitude to individual agency' (2002: 14). While Said's engagement with Foucault in *Orientalism* is often invoked as one of the pivotal moments in the poststructuralist formulation of postcolonial studies, this claim clearly misrepresents Said's intellectual position. Yet, even if his intellectual position is more dialectical than Foucauldian in orientation, Said's engagement with the dialectical thought of Marxist intellectuals such as Antonio Gramsci, Theodor W. Adorno and Lucien Goldman is nevertheless analogous to the search of postcolonial theorists such as Bhabha and Spivak for an appropriate conceptual form to critique the social, cultural, economic and political impact of colonialism.

THE CRITIQUE OF DIALECTICAL THOUGHT

Moreover, what 'materialist' criticisms of a postcolonial theory informed by poststructuralism tend to overlook is the way in which *both* a postcolonial theory informed by materialist thought *and* a postcolonial theory informed by poststructuralism are influenced by the ghost of the nineteenth-century German philosopher Georg Wilhelm Friedrich Hegel and his idea of the dialectic. As a philosophical concept, the dialectic is constituted of a dichotomy between two antithetical terms, such as the master and the slave, or the state and civil society, which are resolved through a process of negation and sublation. In Hegel's philosophical logic, every term in a dialectical series is preserved as an element in a coherent structure of totality. In the struggle between the master and the slave, for example, the negation of the dialectical antagonism between these two categories does not simply involve the negation of the master or the slave. Rather, negation for Hegel involves the overcoming of a dialectical opposition, while preserving the term which has been overcome. Hegel used the term 'sublation' to describe this simultaneous overcoming and preservation in a movement towards a totality.

Hegel's dialectical thought has provided thinkers from Karl Marx, Friedrich Engels and Vladimir Lenin through to Jean-Paul Sartre, Frantz Fanon and Adorno with a method that has allowed them to account for systems of historical injustice or oppression, such as capitalism, slavery or colonialism. One of the problems with this use of Hegel's dialectical method for a postcolonial theory informed by the activism of national liberation movements is that Hegel's writing is itself hampered by the racist and Eurocentric determinants of his geographical view of world history. In the appendix to his introduction to *Vorlesungen über Philosophie der Geschichte* (1830, trans *Lectures on the Philosophy of World History*), for example, Hegel asserted that '*Africa proper* [. . .] has no historical interest of its own, for we find its inhabitants living in barbarism and savagery' (1975: 172). In Hegel's dialectical view of history, 'the African' lives in an 'undifferentiated and concentrated unity'; 'their consciousness has not yet reached an awareness of any substantial objectivity'; and, as a consequence, the African 'has not yet succeeded in making this distinction between himself as an individual and his essential universality, so that he knows nothing of an absolute being which is other and higher than his own self' (177). By defining Africa and Africans in the terms of a racist and Eurocentric model of historical progress, Hegel concludes that Africa is 'an unhistorical continent, with no movement or development of its own' (190).

It is partly the racism and Eurocentrism that underpins Hegel's dialectical thinking that has prompted philosophers and theorists from Sartre and Fanon to Derrida and Bhabha to question and rethink the categories of Hegelian thought. In volume one of his *Critique de la raison dialectique* (1960, trans. *Critique of Dialectical Reason*), Sartre diagnosed the violence of colonialism and argued that the economic disempowerment of the colonized – which he called 'pauperisation' – was not simply a necessary result of contact between an underdeveloped and a developed society, but was rather motivated by the economic exigencies of colonialism. In the case of French colonialism in Algeria during the nineteenth century, for example, Sartre argued that 'the colonial goal was to produce and sell food to the metropolitan power at less than world rates and that the *means* of achieving this goal was the creation of a sub-proletariat of the desolate and the chronically unemployed' (1976: 717). Against the French colonialists' attempt to negate the lives of the Algerians through a process of economic superexploitation, in which Algerians were forced to subsist on poverty-wage labour, Sartre argued that the

> only possible way out was to confront total negation with total negation, violence with equal violence [. . .]. Thus the Algerian rebellion, through being desperate violence, was simply an adoption of the despair in which the colonialists maintained the natives; its violence was simply a negation of the impossible, and the impossibility of life was the immediate result of oppression.
>
> (1976: 733)

Following Marx's claim to have inverted the Hegelian dialectic in his preface to volume one of *Capital* (1867), Sartre proceeded to offer a dialectical reading of the use of violence during the Algerian liberation struggle:

> The violence of the rebel *was* the violence of the colonialist; there was never any other. The struggle between the oppressed and the oppressors ultimately became the reciprocal interiorisation of a single oppression: the prime object of oppression, interiorizing it and finding it to be the negative source of its unity, appalled

the oppressor, who recognized in *violent rebellion*, his own oppressive violence as a hostile force taking him in turn as its object.

(1976: 733)

Against Hegel's racism and Eurocentrism, Sartre thus offered a critique of dialectical thinking that clearly located the source of violent anti-colonial struggle in Algeria during the 1950s in the violence of French colonial occupation and oppression for over a century.

In a similar vein, the Martinique-born psychiatrist and intellectual spokesman for the Front de libération nationale d'Algerie (FLN) Frantz Fanon questions the validity of Hegelian thought in the colonial context. In *Peau noire, masques blancs* (1952, trans. *Black Skin, White Masks*), Fanon argued that 'Ontology [. . .] does not permit us to understand the being of the black man' (1986: 110) precisely because western philosophers such as Hegel have defined black people as savage, inferior and sub-human. In response to this negative definition of black people in western thought, Fanon, along with writers such as Léopold Senghor, attempted to define an idea of Negritude that was separate from the 'racial epidermal schema' underpinning western thought and representation (112). However, as he proceeds to explain with reference to Sartre's *Orphée Noir* (1948, trans. *Black Orpheus*), an essay that formed the preface to an anthology of African poetry, Fanon's 'effort' to 'reclaim [his] negritude' was 'only a term in the dialectic' (132). In Fanon's account, Sartre's critique of Negritude in 'Black Orpheus' ultimately rehearsed some of the problems of racism and Eurocentrism in Hegelian thought. In Sartre's words, Negritude functioned as a 'transition and not a conclusion, a means and not an ultimate end' in his broader dialectical model of history (Sartre cited in Fanon 1986: 133).

Against this dialectical model of history, Fanon offered an existentialist riposte to Sartre's dissolution of Negritude in the Hegelian dialectic:

> The dialectic that brings necessity into the foundation of my freedom drives me out of myself. It shatters my unreflected position. Still in terms of consciousness, black consciousness is immanent in its own eyes. I am not a potentiality of something, I am wholly what I am. I do not have to look for the universal. [. . .] My Negro consciousness does not hold itself out as a lack. It is. It is its own follower.
>
> (1986: 135)

By asserting his social and historical experience as a black man against Sartre's attempt to negate this experience via Hegelian dialectics, Fanon used the tools of Sartre's existential thought to counter his argument.

Significantly, Fanon developed this critique of the dialectic further in 'The Negro and Hegel', the second section of chapter seven of *Black Skin, White Masks*. In this chapter, Fanon observes that 'absolute reciprocity' is at 'the foundation of [the] Hegelian dialectic' (217). Crucial to the Hegelian notion of consciousness of self, Fanon claims, is the 'concept of recognition' (217); and when the (white) other withholds this reciprocal recognition from the (black) self, the (black) self must struggle to re-establish this: 'I demand that notice be taken of my negating activity insofar as I pursue something other than life; insofar as I do battle for the creation of a human world – that is, of a world of reciprocal recognitions' (218).

If *Black Skin, White Masks* combines Fanon's insights as a psychiatrist into the damaging effects of colonialism and racism on the psychological constitution of the colonizer and the colonized with his critical engagement with Sartre's post-Hegelian existential philosophy, his posthumously published essay collection *Les Damnés de la Terre* (1961, trans. *The Wretched of the Earth*) may appear to offer an analysis of the violent liberation struggle in French-occupied Algeria during the 1950s. This collection includes essays on the violence of colonialism and anti-colonial resistance, spontaneity, national culture and the pitfalls of national consciousness, as well as an account of the relationship between colonial war and mental disorders. Yet, in 'Concerning Violence', the essay that forms the opening chapter of *The Wretched of the Earth*, Fanon also develops his critique of Hegelian thought and the struggle for recognition in *Black Skin, White Masks*. In an account of the geographical structure of the colonial world, for example, Fanon argued that the colonial world is 'a world cut in two'; it is a world 'without reciprocal exclusivity' in which no 'conciliation is possible' between the settler and the native (1967: 31–32). Furthermore, it is precisely because the Manichean logic of the colonial world forecloses the recognition of 'the native' as a human, argues Fanon, that 'the native' turns to violence: 'For he ["the native"] knows that he is not an animal; and it is precisely at the moment he realizes his humanity that he begins to sharpen the weapons with which he will secure his victory' (35). In this way, Fanon describes decolonization as part of 'the native's' struggle for recognition as a sovereign human subject as well as a struggle for national liberation.

DECONSTRUCTING THE HUMAN

If Fanon sought to 'refashion the human in the wake of racialising systems of power and violence' (Silverman 2005: 124), poststructuralist thinkers such as Derrida, Foucault, Bhabha and Spivak have questioned the possibility of recuperating the category of the human from its provenance in Eurocentric systems of thought. As Robert J. C. Young explains, it was the recognition that European humanism was founded on a system of exclusion that defined Jews and the colonized as non-human Others which prompted many French intellectuals of the post-war generation to develop a sustained critique of 'Man' (1990: 121–23). Certainly, Young is right to emphasize that '"anti-humanism" was not merely a philosophical project' (123), but part of a broader political critique of the ideologies of racism and anti-Semitism that underpinned western humanism. Yet the theoretical arguments of the poststructuralist thinkers who became associated with anti-humanism did not simply oppose the conceptual terms of western humanism, for to do so would be to remain trapped in the terms of that philosophical system, and the political ideologies that it supported. As the Jewish Franco-Maghrebian philosopher Jacques Derrida explained in a 1972 account of how the deconstruction of Hegelian dialectics involves the reversal and displacement of the violent hierarchies that structure classical philosophical oppositions:

> [I]n a classical philosophical opposition we are not dealing with a peaceful coexistence of a *vis-à-vis*, but rather with a violent hierarchy. [. . .] To deconstruct the opposition, first of all, is to overturn the hierarchy at a given moment. To overlook this moment of overturning is to forget the conflictual and subordinating structure of opposition. Therefore one might proceed too quickly to a neutralization that in practice would leave the previous field untouched, leaving one no hold on the previous opposition, thereby preventing any means of intervening in the field effectively.
>
> (2004: 39)

Derrida here describes, in a vocabulary that recalls Fanon in 'Concerning Violence', how classical philosophical oppositions, such as the struggle for recognition between the master and the slave in Hegel's *Phänomenologie des Geistes* (1807, trans. *Phenomenology of Spirit*), are founded on a violent hierarchy. Moreover, by emphasizing the 'conflictual and subordinating structure of opposition', Derrida's deconstruction of western metaphysics could be seen to parallel Fanon's critique of the violence of colonialism in *The Wretched of the Earth*. Indeed, it is Derrida's theoretical challenge to western metaphysics and its false claims to universality that have made him such an attractive figure to postcolonial theorists such as Spivak and Bhabha.

For example, in *The Postcolonial Critic* (1990) Spivak explains how Derrida's deconstruction of western metaphysics did not merely challenge the arguments of European philosophers from Plato to Heidegger, but also called into question the way in which western reason has been imposed on the rest of world as part of colonialism's civilizing mission:

> Where I was brought up – when I first read Derrida I didn't know who he was, I was very interested to see that he was actually dismantling the philosophical tradition from *inside* rather than *outside*, because of course we were brought up in an education system in India where the name of the hero of that philosophical system was the universal human being, and we were taught that if we could begin to approach an internalisation of that human being, then we would be human. When I saw in France someone was actually trying to dismantle the tradition which had told us what would make us human, that seemed interesting too.
>
> (1990: 7)

For Spivak, Derrida's deconstruction of western humanism was not merely philosophical in its emphasis, but also provided the conceptual tools to dismantle the cultural and political foundations on which western imperialism had been built. Such an approach is exemplified in Spivak's magnum opus, *A Critique of*

Postcolonial Reason (1999), in which she argues that the philosophy of Kant, Hegel and Marx has provided western imperialism with a philosophical ratio-nale, while at the same time providing the conceptual tools for criticizing impe-rialism: 'our sense of critique is too thoroughly determined by Kant, Hegel, and Marx for us to be able to reject them as "motivated imperialists", although this is too often the vain gesture performed by critics of imperialism' (6–7). For Spivak, the task of postcolonial critique is to develop the ethical insights of deconstruc-tion in order to 'discover a constructive rather than disabling complicity between our own position and theirs [Kant, Hegel and Marx]' (3–4). Like Fanon in *Black Skin, White Masks* and *The Wretched of the Earth*, Spivak recognizes how the western systems of knowledge that were used to support western colonialism can also be used to question and critique that system. Yet, where Fanon uses Sartrean existentialism to challenge the racism and Eurocentrism of Hegelian dialectics, Spivak draws on the conceptual tools of deconstruction. As she explains in *A Critique of Postcolonial Reason*, 'A deconstructive politics of reading would acknowledge the determination as well as the imperialism and see if the magisterial texts [of western philosophy] can now be our servants' (7).

THE SUPPLEMENT AND THE SUBALTERN

In a similar vein, the postcolonial theorist Homi K. Bhabha has re-constellated Derrida's deconstructive concept of the supplement to account for Fanon's anti-colonial humanism. If Fanon's thought is constituted by a splitting between 'a Hegelian–Marxist dialectic, a phenomenological affirmation of Self and Other and the psychoanalytic ambivalence of the Unconscious' (Bhabha 1994: 41), Bhabha argues that this splitting is not a sign of incoherence on Fanon's part; rather it is a symptom of 'a restless urgency in Fanon's search for a conceptual form appropriate to the social antagonism of the colonial relation' (41).

For Bhabha, Fanon's search for an appropriate conceptual form to describe the 'social antagonism of the colonial relation' in the 1950s prefigures Derrida's formulation of the supplement in the later 1960s: a concept that is itself defined by its restlessness and resistance to conceptual representation. As Derrida explains in *De la grammatologie* (1967, trans. *Of Grammatology*) 'compensatory and vicarious, the supplement is an adjunct, a subaltern instance which takes-(the)-place' (1976: 145). For Derrida the supplement is a pre-ontological entity, which cannot be grasped as a positive concept in the terms of philosophical discourse. The supplement thus stands as a constantly shifting limit, or a condi-tion of possibility, which defines the coherence of western philosophical truth, but cannot be grasped as a concept in itself. In his re-reading of Derrida, Bhabha argues that the supplement's resistance to representation is analogous to the social category of the subaltern, or those subordinate social groups who are not represented within the terms of a dominant political system, such as a constitu-tional democracy or a military dictatorship.

The term 'subaltern', as it has been developed by theorists such as Bhabha and Spivak in postcolonial studies, has its origins in a particular reading of the Italian social theorist Antonio Gramsci. In his 'Notes on Italian History' in *Quaderni del carcere* (1948–51, trans. *Prison Notebooks*) Gramsci defined 'the subaltern classes' by contrasting them to 'the historical unity of the ruling classes [which] is realized in the State':

> The subaltern classes, by definition, are not unified and cannot unite until they are able to become a 'State': their history, therefore, is intertwined with that of civil society and thereby with the history of States and groups of states.
>
> (1971: 52)

In Gramsci's definition, the history of the subaltern classes in nineteenth-century Italy was subordinated to the political will of the ruling class. While Gramsci does not explicitly define the social composition of the subaltern in his 'Notes on Italian History', his earlier account of the historical conditions in Southern Italy (which maintained the subordination of the Italian peasantry and prevented an alliance between the rural peasantry in Southern Italy and the industrial bourgeoisie in Northern Italy) in 'Some Aspects of the Southern Question' (1926), offers a concrete example of what Gramsci meant by the term subaltern. As Gramsci puts it, 'The Northern bourgeoisie has subjugated the South of Italy and the Islands, and reduced them to exploitable colonies' (1957: 28).

The term subaltern was subsequently adopted by South Asian historians such as Ranajit Guha, Gyanendra Pandey, Dipesh Chakrabarty and David Arnold in the 1980s to describe 'the general attribute of subordination in South Asian society whether this is expressed in terms of class, caste, age, gender and office or in any other way' (Guha 1982: vii). The *Subaltern Studies* historians sought to recover the political will, consciousness and agency of different subaltern social groups from the historical archives of the colonial state, and focused on documents such as criminal records, newspapers and reports of court trials (see also Chapter 12: South and East Asia). The problem with this approach to subaltern insurgency was that it assumed that the way in which acts of subaltern insurgency were represented by the colonial state was an accurate reflection of the ways in which the subaltern understood their own reasons for participating in a political uprising, such as a riot, a strike or a protest. Indeed, for many of the *Subaltern Studies* historians, as Spivak argues in 'Deconstructing Historiography' (1987), the political will, consciousness and agency of the subaltern is a theoretical fiction rather than a positive fact that can be recovered from the historical archives.

Like Gramsci in 'Some Aspects of the Southern Question' (1926), Spivak emphasizes the important role that the intellectual plays in representing the subaltern. In her highly influential essay 'Can the Subaltern Speak?' (1988), Spivak cites the example of a conversation between the French poststructuralist thinkers Gilles Deleuze and Michel Foucault, in which they claim that the oppressed can speak and know their own conditions, to caution against the posi-

tivist imperative to recover the political will, consciousness and agency of the
subaltern from the colonial archives that characterizes some of the work of the
Subaltern Studies historians. As Spivak suggests, Deleuze and Foucault's argument is problematic because it surreptitiously establishes them as absent intellectual proxies who efface their own position in representing the subaltern.
Whereas Gramsci stressed that 'It is [. . .] important and useful for the proletariat that one or more intellectuals, individually, adhere to its programme and
its doctrine; merge themselves with the proletariat, and become and feel themselves an integral part of it' (1957: 50), Spivak raises questions about how such
an alliance between the intellectual and the subaltern could come about in a way
that is not detrimental to the subaltern.

In Bhabha's use of the term subaltern, however, the concept of subalternity
would seem to contain more radical significance. If the subaltern is taken to
mean both the colonized (in Fanon's definition) and one who takes (the) place,
then this may seem to suggest that the subaltern would become part of an independent nation once decolonization is achieved, and *ipso facto* cease to be a
subaltern. Yet, as many theorists and writers have argued, the emergence of a
decolonized nation-state was often not accompanied by a transformation in the
social structure of that nation state (Guha 1982; Spivak 1987; Mbembe 2001;
Young 2001). As a consequence, the subaltern remained in many cases subaltern (in the Gramscian sense), and did not take the place of anything or anyone.
For this reason, Bhabha's complex conflation of the subaltern (in the Gramscian
sense) with the supplement (in the Derridian sense) and the native or the colonized (in the Fanonian sense) would appear to be both untenable and out of
synch with the material reality of decolonization.

If the subaltern is read as a situated category of subordination, however, it is
possible to read Bhabha's argument as both a critical and an ethical development of Fanon's account of decolonization. Such a development would specify
the ways in which decolonization had failed to emancipate subaltern groups,
such as the rural peasantry or indigenous peoples. Yet rather than simply
continuing Fanon's political injunction for revolutionary violence to complete
the unfinished project of decolonization for subaltern constituencies who regard
decolonization as a bourgeois revolution which benefited the educated middle-
class elite, postcolonial theorists such as Bhabha and Spivak interrupt Fanon's
political injunction to replace the dominant group by an act of physical violence
with an ethical injunction to the supplement. Rather than falling prey to the
violent logic of the dialectical struggle between the native and the settler,
Bhabha suggests that the supplement as subaltern instance is precisely anti-
dialectical, and interrupts the cycle of violence described by Fanon in
'Concerning Violence': 'The anti-dialectical movement of the subaltern instance
subverts any binary or sublatory ordering of power and sign' (Bhabha 1994: 55).

It is precisely this anti-dialectical thought of the supplement that underpins
Spivak's discussion of an ethical encounter with the other in her commentaries
on the Bengali writer Mahasweta Devi. In the 'Translator's Preface' to *Imaginary*

Maps (1995), for example, Spivak suggests that an experience of the impossibility of an ethical engagement with the singularity of the other occupies a
supplementary relationship to rational political programmes: 'For a collective
struggle *supplemented* by the impossibility of full ethical engagement [. . .] the
future is always around the corner, there is no victory, but only victories that are
also warnings' (Devi 1995: xxv). Such an argument is not merely theoretical. For
in the context of a recently-decolonized nation-state, such as India, the collective struggle for national liberation did not lead to the empowerment of all
sectors of Indian society. For this reason, Spivak's emphasis on ethical singularity is motivated in part by an awareness that decolonization did not bring
about a social transformation.

POSTSTRUCTURALISM, POLITICS AND THE POSTCOLONY

For the philosopher Peter Hallward, the postcolonial thought of Spivak and
Bhabha exemplifies 'the singular orientation of postcolonial criticism [. . .] in its
torturously evasive clarity' (2001: 24). But, as he also suggests, one problem with
their work is that despite their calls for specificity, their commitment to difference and their refusal to represent disenfranchised, subaltern constituencies,
they ultimately lack the political and moral urgency of Fanon's writing in *The
Wretched of the Earth*. As a consequence, Hallward suggests, the poststructuralist thought of both Bhabha and Spivak disavows the achievements of decolonization, and thereby divests postcolonial criticism of the political tools necessary
to identify and criticize contemporary forms of imperialism.

Such a criticism of a postcolonial theory centred on discourse and textuality
may seem compelling in its gesture to the real, material politics and collective
political resistance associated with decolonization. But such arguments can also
simplify what is meant by the political in both colonial and postcolonial spaces.
Indeed, for the postcolonial theorist Achille Mbembe in his study *On the
Postcolony* (2001), the forms of governance established in many sub-Saharan
African countries by European colonial powers did not simply lay the foundations for a form of political sovereignty and civil society modelled on modern
European nation states such as France, Germany or Britain. Instead, 'the colony
is primarily a place where an experience of violence and upheaval is lived, where
violence is built into structures and institutions' (174). Consequently, colonial
governmentality undermined rather than enabled the possibility of political and
economic sovereignty in the postcolony. It is for this reason that Mbembe questions the optimism that is sometimes associated with decolonization:

> Is there any difference – and, if so, of what sort – between what happened during
> the colony and 'what comes after?' Is everything really called into question, is
> everything suspended, does everything truly begin all over again, to the point
> where it can be said that the formerly colonized recovers existence, distances
> himself or herself from his/her previous state?
>
> (2001: 196–97)

Since the sovereign power of European colonial government was established through a system of violence instituted through the structures and institutions of the barracks and the police station, Mbembe questions whether political sovereignty in the postcolony transforms the violent political foundations of the colony. Mbembe develops these questions further in his essay 'Necropolitics' (2003). Drawing on the work of Giorgio Agamben and Michel Foucault, Mbembe contends that the regime of biopolitical control operating in European bourgeois civil society does not hold in the European colony; instead biopolitical control is replaced with necropolitical control, or the threat of violence and ultimately death by the colonial ruler:

> the sovereign right to kill is not subject to any rule in the colonies. In the colonies, the sovereign might kill at any time or in any manner. Colonial warfare is not subject to legal and institutional rules. It is not a legally codified activity.
>
> (2003: 25)

Following Foucault's argument in *Society Must Be Defended* (published posthumously in 1997) that the function of racism is to regulate the distribution of death, Mbembe argues that it is the right to violence and killing that defines relations of power in the European colony. In the light of this argument, Mbembe's claim that death is a form of agency for people who live under colonial occupation helps to clarify the significance of violent, anti-colonial insurgency as an assertion of political sovereignty in the context of a colonial regime that defines politics in terms of the right to injure, torture and kill its subjects with impunity.

Moreover, Mbembe's recourse to European thinkers such as Georges Bataille, Martin Heidegger, and Agamben to formulate his argument that death and violence constitute the political in the postcolony complicates those materialist critiques of postcolonial theory, which contend that poststructuralist thought disavows the achievements of decolonization and the economic impact of globalization. On the contrary, it is precisely Mbembe's rethinking of political and economic sovereignty via the thought of Bataille, Heidegger and Agamben that enables him to analyse the various ways in which the political, social and economic institutions of the postcolony after national liberation in many sub-Saharan African countries failed to provide a foundation for meaningful political sovereignty, and to posit a link between the privatization of state sovereignty and the creation of private military and paramilitary organizations, or armies of business (Mbembe 2001: 78–79). Such an argument may seem to challenge the political claims of a Marxist-oriented postcolonial theory, which often seeks to recover the emancipatory spirit of decolonization. Yet in raising questions about the meaning of political and economic sovereignty after colonialism via the theoretical work of Bataille, Heidegger, Foucault and Agamben, Mbembe demonstrates the continuing importance of poststructuralist thought for contemporary postcolonial studies.

Conclusions

The poststructuralist critique of the humanist subject and philosophical concepts such as the dialectic have certainly contributed to the formulation of a critical and political vocabulary that is appropriate to critique the systems of knowledge that underpin western imperialism. While poststructuralism was never explicitly aligned with the anti-colonial liberation thought of Frantz Fanon, the formulation of poststructuralism was nonetheless a product of decolonization in post-war France, and has provided some of the most influential postcolonial theorists, such as Homi K. Bhabha and Gayatri Spivak, with a set of conceptual tools to challenge the cultural and philosophical legacies of colonialism. As Kristin Ross has argued, the formulation of a new humanism in the thought of Aimé Césaire and Frantz Fanon parallels the poststructuralist declaration of the death of the subject (Ross 1995: 157–96). The problem with a postcolonial theory that is too centred on the critique of the sovereign subject, the deconstruction of western metaphysics and the claim that all collective political resistance to imperialism is recuperated within a dominant system of power and knowledge – as many critics have argued – is that it runs the risk of denying the efficacy of collective political action, and the persistence of imperialism under the guise of neo-liberal globalization. Yet, as the recent work of postcolonial scholars such as Achille Mbembe and Dipesh Chakrabarty demonstrates, the poststructuralist thought of Agamben, Foucault, Heidegger, Bataille and Derrida continues to provide what Bhabha calls 'a conceptual form appropriate to the social antagonism of the colonial relation' (1994: 41).

Recommended further reading

Bhabha, Homi K., *The Location of Culture* (London: Routledge, 1994).

Gandhi, Leela, *Postcolonial Theory: a critical introduction* (New York: Columbia University Press, 1998).

Moore-Gilbert, Bart, *Postcolonial Theory: contexts, practices, politics* (London: Verso, 1997).

Said, Edward W., *Orientalism* (Harmondsworth: Penguin, 1978).

Spivak, Gayatri Chakravorty, *The Postcolonial Critic: interviews, strategies, dialogues*, Sarah Harasym (ed.) (New York: Routledge, 1990).

——*The Spivak Reader*, Donna Landry and Gerald Maclean (eds) (New York: Routledge, 1996).

——*A Critique of Postcolonial Reason: towards a history of the vanishing present* (Cambridge, MA: Harvard University Press, 1999).

Varadharajan, A., *Exotic Parodies: subjectivity in Adorno, Said, and Spivak* (Minneapolis, MN: University of Minnesota Press, 1995).

Young, Robert J. C, *White Mythologies: writing history and the west* (New York: Routledge, 1990).

——*Postcolonialism: an historical introduction* (Oxford: Blackwell, 2001).

15

CULTURALIST FORMULATIONS

JAMES PROCTER

Culturalism is not a school of thought, an intellectual movement, or a theory. Nor is it (like Marxism, poststructuralism and New Historicism), an '-ism' with which postcolonial critics self-consciously identify. Rather, it is best thought of as the tendency to foreground and explore the central role of culture in maintenance of (neo-)colonial power and postcolonial dissidence. Such an awareness of culture as a crucially determining factor in the ways we see and act upon the world, and not simply (or innocently) a passive reflection of social reality, can be found in the work of critics who, as we shall see, take different attitudes to the centrality of culture in many postcolonial studies.

Coined in 1979 by Richard Johnson, the term was first used in order to link some of the underlying assumptions of the 'founding fathers' of cultural studies: Richard Hoggart, E. P. Thompson and Raymond Williams. Specifically, it was adopted to problematize the perceived emphasis of these three critics on human agency (on the ability of 'the people' to bring about cultural change in society) in a way that underestimated culture's structuring role. The influence of structuralism, especially the work of Roland Barthes and Louis Althusser, on cultural studies in the 1970s led to the emergence of the view that cultural formations (language, texts, advertisements, music, etc.) actually *determine* what it means to be human in the first place. In postcolonial studies, the term is more frequently invoked to describe the privileging of cultural over, and at the expense of, economic concerns in the study of colonial and postcolonial formations. Such invocations have become increasingly commonplace of late as postcolonial studies experiences something of a materialist 'turn' (see Chapter 16: Materialist formulations). While the earliest accounts of postcolonialism in foundational texts like Bill Ashcroft, Gareth Griffiths and Helen Tiffin's *The Empire Writes Back* (1989), and journals such as *Kunapipi*, *The Journal of Commonwealth Literature* and *ARIEL*, took literary culture as their primary focus, recent studies such as Robert J. C. Young's *Postcolonialism: an historical introduction* (2001) and new journals such as *Interventions* assign literature a relatively minor role in order to recover materialist formations that some consider to have been neglected in early postcolonial studies. Hence, for some critics, culturalism describes a trend in postcolonial studies which emphasizes the cultural *above and beyond* economic and materialist factors – and so the term is used as an unfavourable, and sometimes derogatory, label by some postcolonial intellectuals to describe the perceived problematic assumptions of others. It is to such critiques of culturalism that this chapter turns first.

One of the effects of the materialist turn in postcolonial studies has been the downsizing and delegitimation of the key assumptions of culturalism: for example, the common-sense view, implicit in a text like *The Empire Writes Back*, that literary texts should form the starting point of a critique of colonialism. Marxist-influenced critics such as Laura Chrisman, Neil Lazarus, Arif Dirlik, Benita Parry, Aijaz Ahmad, Crystal Bartolovitch and Ella Shohat have all written against the prevailing culturalist climate of the 1980s and 1990s in order to realign postcolonial studies within what might now be broadly characterized as a materialist paradigm. For example, in *Postcolonialism* Robert Young points to Edward Said's culturalist 'misreading' of Foucault's praxis-led notion of discourse in *Orientalism*, a misreading he believes has reduced colonial discourse analysis to 'just a form of literary criticism' (2001: 394). In *Nationalism and Cultural Practice in the Postcolonial World* (1999), Neil Lazarus similarly complains that postcolonial studies is 'constitutively informed' (9) by the textualist, antifoundationalist thrust of postmodernist and poststructuralist thought, claiming that, as a consequence, prominent Marxists like Terry Eagleton, Fredric Jameson and Raymond Williams have been 'severely *deprivileged* in the field' (12). Meanwhile, in a series of essays collected in *Postcolonial Contraventions* (2003), Laura Chrisman bases her critique of Paul Gilroy's *The Black Atlantic* (a highly influential text in the canon of postcolonial studies) on what she regards as its symptomatic culturalism:

> Gilroy's formulations mesh neatly with the 1990s metropolitan academic climate [. . .] in which postmodernist intellectual concerns with language and subjectivity infused both academia and 'new left' politics to create a dominant paradigm of 'culturalism' for the analysis of social relations. This development risked abandoning the tenets and resources of socio-economic analysis. Aesthetics and aestheticism were made to function both as explanation of and solution to social and political processes.
>
> (2003: 73)

By placing culturalism within quotation marks above, Chrisman appears to indicate that the term's meaning is equivocal, or at least difficult to determine precisely. However, like most postcolonial critics of culturalism she does not elaborate on what she means by the term. There is a danger, here and in others' work, that culturalism becomes a convenient way of dismissing the vexed relationship between aesthetics and politics. While Chrisman is surely right to question the view that aestheticism is an end in itself, it is difficult to imagine any postcolonial critic who would claim such a view. Perhaps, in contending with culturalist formulations in postcolonial studies, we must remain healthily sceptical to critiques of culturalism while acknowledging that culture alone will always be inadequate as an absolute explanation or solution.

There are at least two problems with the materialist–culturalist divide which has arguably come to shape several key debates in postcolonial studies today. First, it implies a neat distinction between material and cultural realms and critical practices. In her introduction to *Postcolonial Contraventions*, Chrisman argues that postcolonial studies is 'the provenance of materialist, historicist critics as much as it is of textualist and culturalist critics' (1) in a way that implies two mutually exclusive schools of thought. However, many of the essays that follow, including her opening chapter on the significance of labour, corporate power and consumption in Joseph Conrad's novella *Heart of Darkness* (1899), combine culturalist and materialist approaches in exemplary and illuminating ways. For example, and via a sustained and sensitive close reading that we would normally associate with culturalism, Chrisman 'connects the existential with the economic, the internal with external disciplinary regimes' (36). In fact, many postcolonial critics would argue that the economic and the cultural are two sides of the same coin and that it is impossible to separate one from the other. Indeed, in her famous essay 'Can the Subaltern Speak?', Gayatri Chakravorty Spivak insists on the analytic value of the 'subaltern' as a term to describe historic rela- tions between India's subordinate and elite *classes*. At the same time, she high- lights the need to put the economic 'under erasure' in order to attend to the *discursive and cultural* constitution of the subaltern subject. For Spivak, materi- alism and culturalism are not incompatible approaches: placed in dialogue with one another, they can work productively in important ways which contest the sense, or the propriety, of a divide between them (see Spivak 1999).

A second problem with the materialist–culturalist divide, as it has been repre- sented by certain thinkers, is the implication that there has been a wholesale shift from culturalist to materialist modes of analysis in recent postcolonial criti- cism. But this is ultimately misleading. Materialist approaches have always been central to postcolonial studies (an understanding of Said's *Orientalism* (1978) that ignored the centrality of the Marxist thinker Antonio Gramsci would be inadequate), while recent postcolonial studies have *not* abandoned culture as a primary object of inquiry. On the contrary, conceptions of culture within postco- lonialism have, if anything, expanded, moving well beyond the traditional domain of literature to include the analysis of film, music, art, theatre, televi- sion, cultural identity, style and so on.

Moreover, critics like Robert Young have questioned the assumption that culturalism amounts to the abandonment of political and material concerns in the first place. Noting the importance of cultural politics to revolutionary leaders like James Connolly, Frantz Fanon and Amílcar Cabral, he says:

> For those on the left, particularly those working predominantly from an academic context, it may seem that culturalism involves a move away from more direct kinds of political action, but there are many positive theoretical arguments to be made for it: the culturalization of academic knowledges marks a shift towards a consider- ation of the subjective experiences of individuals, and socialized aspirations of groups and communities that complements the traditional modes of analysis of the political and economic systems of which they are a part. The culturalization of knowledge and politics also involves a recognition of transnational and often

gendered cultural differences and the significance of different forms of knowledge for different communities.

(2001: 8)

In other words, culturalist approaches enable the critique of supposedly indisputable truths or facts – such as scientific 'proof' in the nineteenth century that Africans were more primitive than Europeans – that present themselves as self-evident, common-sensical or natural at particular moments. What is apparently 'true' might better be thought of as discursive in this context: as resulting from cultural prejudice or problematic, provisional ways of representing the world. If we accept Young's point here, culturalism represents more than a retreat from politics; contrariwise, it might offer a vital political approach in demystifying and challenging (neo-)colonial 'truths'. A questioning of biological racism that exposes its *cultural* provenance provides an important basis for *denaturalizing* racist assumptions. There is nothing intrinsically apolitical about culturalism when seen in this way.

Arif Dirlik explores culturalism's contradictory potential more fully in his 1990 essay entitled 'Culturalism as Hegemonic Ideology and Liberating Practice'. He begins counter-intuitively by arguing that, while economic needs and political crises in postcolonial countries would seem to call for the abandonment of cultural questions in favour of urgent action, it is 'the realm of culture [. . .] that [. . .] demands priority of attention' (394):

> To avoid the question of culture is to avoid questions concerning the ways in which we see the world; it is to remain imprisoned, therefore, in a cultural consciousness controlled by conditioned ways of seeing [. . .] without the self-consciousness that must be the point of departure for all critical understanding and, by implication, for all radical activity.
>
> (1990: 395)

Having said this, Dirlik goes on to stress that he does not wish to support uncritically the notion of culturalism. As the title of his essay suggests, Dirlik regards culturalism as a *conflicted* concept, capable of participating in both cultural domination *and* liberation. As an 'ideology' that is uncritically adopted by western intellectuals, Dirlik sees culturalism as problematic because it reduces everything to culture in a way that allows the West to establish and maintain hegemony over the non-West. According to Dirlik, hegemonic culturalism

> identifies for us entire [postcolonial] peoples and eras in terms of the ways in which we think they see or saw the world. It helps us place them *vis-à-vis* one another, usually with ourselves at the center of the world and at the end of time.
>
> (1990: 395)

Culturalism's worrying hegemonic role has, Dirlik notes, led to radical intellectuals rejecting culturalism in favour of economism. Like Robert Young's views cited earlier, not only does Dirlik argue that this rejection neglects the significance of '*cultural* revolution' as a goal of postcolonial societies, it also risks complicity with bourgeois ideology, which identifies the economic as the key to social change.

Rather than embracing economics at the expense of culture, Dirlik calls for an alternative version of culturalism that is *Marxist* rather than hegemonic. If hegemonic culturalism sees culture in isolation as an autonomous abstraction, Marxist culturalism regards culture as having 'some autonomy' (425). By suggesting that culture is relatively autonomous rather than absolutely determined by economics, Dirlik is able to emphasize the importance of *agency* and experience in conceptions of culture. (Here Dirlik uses the work of E. P. Thompson and Arab intellectual Abdallah Laroui as examples of Marxist culturalism.) It is by restoring culture's 'double meaning, both as a "way of seeing" and as a way of making the world' (430) that Marxist culturalism makes available a 'liberating practice'.

Dirlik wrote his account of culturalism in the mid-1980s, before postcolonial studies had made its mark on the academy (his references in this essay are to the Third World intellectual rather than the postcolonial critic.) In more recent work of the 1990s, Dirlik has controversially come to dismiss postcolonialism outright as 'a culturalism' (by which he presumably means 'hegemonic culturalism') that is complicit with global capitalism. First published in an influential article entitled 'The Postcolonial Aura' (1994), this thesis did much to generate the materialist turn of the 1990s. However, his conclusions remain unsatisfactory to many of a more culturalist persuasion. For example, in his essay 'When was the Post-Colonial: Thinking at the Limit' (1996b) Stuart Hall has responded with indignation to Dirlik's wholesale dismissal of culturalism. Hall remains committed to the idea that culture is a key site where social realities are constituted and contested, rather than passively reflected. It is unlikely that Hall would accept Dirlik's earlier distinction between 'bad' hegemonic culturalism and 'good' Marxist culturalism. This is because he regards hegemonic struggle as involving an *ongoing negotiation* between dominant and subordinate groups, rather than as a binaristic showdown between oppressors and oppressed. In summarizing Dirlik's critique of culturalist postcolonialism alongside similar ones by Anne McClintock (1993) and Ella Shohat (1992) Hall detects a 'certain nostalgia' in their call for 'a clear-cut politics of binary oppositions, where clear "lines can be drawn in the sand" between goodies and baddies' (244):

> These 'lines' may have been simple once (were they?), but they certainly are so no longer. [. . .] This does not mean that there are no 'right' or 'wrong' sides, no play of power, no hard political choices to be made. But isn't the ubiquitous, the soul-searing, lesson of our times the fact that political binaries do not (do not any longer? did they ever?) either stabilize the field of political antagonism in any permanent way or render it transparently intelligible? 'Frontier effects' are not 'given' but constructed; consequently, political positionalities are not fixed and do not repeat themselves from one theatre of antagonism to another [. . .].
>
> (1996b: 244)

For Hall, political realities are never 'transparently intelligible' because their meanings are always already mediated or constructed through culture. This is not to argue that there is nothing but cultural indeterminacy: as Hall insists, there are always 'hard political choices to be made'. Rather, it is to acknowledge the important stake culture has in determining politics, however contradictory and unstable that determination might be.

Hall's materially-minded culturalism has been particularly influential in post-colonial debates on (cultural) identity since the 1980s. Central to his essays such as 'New Ethnicities' (1988) is the position that 'black' should be regarded as a cultural rather than a biological term of identification with 'no guarantees' in nature. The motivating force behind this argument is *not* a postmodern logic of subjectivity as endlessly discursive, where social and material factors disappear in a world regarded primarily as the sum of representations one might make about it. Although Hall borrows from poststructuralists like Jacques Derrida in 'New Ethnicities', any Derridean anti-foundationalism is tempered by a (Gramscian) socialist logic seeking to articulate new forms of collective identification at a critical moment in the 1980s when traditional class, gender and race alliances were breaking down (see Hall 1996a).

Hall's critique of Dirlik's economic determinism does not entail a wholesale rejection of material realities, but advocates the supple articulation (or linkage) of cultural and economic forces. Nevertheless, some critics feel that Hall's artic-ulation is too loose and call for more rigorous discussions of cultural–economic relations in future postcolonial studies (see, for example, Lazarus 1999). Meanwhile, others warn that the drift from postcolonial literary studies to post-colonial cultural studies during the 1990s (in terms of which Hall's work is best seen as a catalyst, rather than an example) does violence to the specificity, or *singularity* of postcolonial culture (Hallward 2001).

Peter Hallward's *Absolutely Postcolonial: writing between the singular and the specific* (2001) represents one of the most sophisticated and convincing cultur-alist defences of what Aijaz Ahmad (1996) has dismissively referred to as *literary* postcolonial studies in recent years. In his conclusion to *Absolutely Postcolonial*, Hallward responds to the call for a 'return' in postcolonial studies to focusing on material conditions, by arguing that Ahmad and other Marxist critics neglect the specificity of literary discourse and the theories it has given rise to:

> If literature did not offer some degree of creative disengagement from material circumstances [. . .] it would have been buried long before its materialist critics began arranging the funeral. The more forceful Marxist critics sometimes seem to forget that the post-colonial criticism they attack is primarily *literary* criticism, i.e. a practice of reading designed first and foremost to account for certain particular literary phenomena. It is not enough, then, simply to condemn the theory for its inadequate attention to other disciplines like 'political economy'.
>
> (2001: 334)

Hallward goes on to suggest that the scramble for interdisciplinarity within the

field has left many postcolonial critics with virtually nothing to say about literature itself.

A notable exception here is Deepika Bahri's *Native Intelligence: aesthetics, politics, and postcolonial literature* (2003). In her introductory essay on 'The End of Literature', Bahri puts it bluntly:

> This book is about the crisis of postcolonial literature, manifested in anxiety over its relevance, uncertainty about its value, and suspicions of the death of literature as a significant social form. At a stage in the development of capital when all that is solid seems predictably to be melting into the air on a worldwide scale, and artistic expression is increasingly regulated by technological expansion and market consid-erations, the value of the aesthetic sphere as a distinctive activity threatens to dissolve pari passu.
>
> (2003: 1)

Through detailed literary analysis of three Indian writers – Rohinton Mistry, Salman Rushdie and Arundhati Roy – Bahri makes a compelling case for attending to what Herbert Marcuse calls the 'aesthetic dimension' of postcolo-nial writing. While speaking critically of the way in which a certain brand of post-colonial literature has been reduced to information, politics and 'native informancy' (4), Bahri avoids the tendency, outlined above, to separate cultural and material realms. Through a careful, critical adoption of Frankfurt-School Marxism, Bahri insists that 'attention to the aesthetic innovations, plural origins, and "formal" commitments of postcolonial works uncovers their complex and uneven relationship to ideology, revivifying their potential to make novel contri-butions to the large project of social liberation' (6). According to the logic of Bahri's argument, to dwell on the cultural issue of aesthetics is not to relinquish political responsibilities in the material world. On the contrary, to analyse mate-rialism without paying attention to the aesthetic dimension is politically irre-sponsible in that it means neglecting a potential site of social transformation.

Certainly, it would be a mistake to imagine that it is possible, or even desir-able, to return to an unsullied culturalism that is unfettered from the material world. Nevertheless, Bahri's and Hallward's calls for greater cultural specificity – like Young's, Dirlik's and Hall's calls – need to be taken seriously. In different ways, these critics have challenged the view that culture is merely a barometer of the material world. As they suggest, it is culture's ability to contradict, question, defamiliarize and intervene in that world that makes the assumptions of cultur-alism valuable for postcolonial studies.

FURTHER RECOMMENDED READING

Bahri, Deepika, *Native Intelligence: aesthetics, politics, and postcolonial literature* (Minneapolis, MN: University of Minnesota Press, 2003).
Chrisman, Laura, *Postcolonial Contraventions: cultural readings of race, imperialism and transnationalism* (Manchester: Manchester University Press, 2003).

Dirlik, Arif, 'Culturalism as Hegemonic Ideology and Liberating Practice' in A. JanMohamed and D. Lloyd (eds) *The Nature and Context of Minority Discourse* (Oxford: Oxford University Press, 1990).

Hallward, Peter, *Absolutely Postcolonial: writing between the singular and the specific* (Manchester: Manchester University Press, 2001).

Harrison, Nicholas, *Postcolonial Criticism: history, theory and the work of fiction* (Cambridge: Polity Press, 2003).

Morley, David and Chen, Kuan-Hsing (eds) *Stuart Hall: critical dialogues in cultural studies* (London: Routledge, 1996).

Procter, James, *Stuart Hall* (London: Routledge, 2004).

16
MATERIALIST FORMULATIONS

DAVID MURPHY

Materialist critics have often enjoyed an antagonistic relationship to postcolonial studies. However, they have not uniformly rejected postcolonial studies; nor has postcolonial studies been as hostile to materialist criticism as has often been suggested. This chapter will thus attempt to trace the various ways in which materialist formulations have been deployed in relation to postcolonial studies. It is important first, though, to examine what exactly is meant by materialist criticism.

WHAT IS MATERIALIST CRITICISM?

Essentially, materialist criticism is concerned with analysing the cultural text within its historical context. In its most enlightening and complex forms, materialist criticism highlights the social, cultural, political, economic and gender issues – that is, the 'material' realities – with which the text engages and which in turn have shaped the text. However, in its less sophisticated forms, materialist criticism has been (rightly) accused of an oversimplified determinism; of using political and economic factors ultimately to decide – hence 'determine' – the meaning of a cultural text. Unsubtle materialist approaches do not take into account the complexity of the text's structure and status as a 'representation' – texts are *not*, we must remember, direct, unmediated reflections of the world.

When discussing materialist criticism it is necessary to consider the thought of Karl Marx, the hugely influential nineteenth-century German political and economic theorist, and founder of communism. While not all materialist critics are Marxists (i.e. people who believe in the overthrow of capitalist structures as a necessary step in creating more egalitarian societies), their work is informed by Marx's conceptual framework for the analysis of power relations within society. Materialist critics who engage primarily with literature and other cultural forms are often deemed cultural materialists (while those primarily addressing social, political and economic issues are called historical materialists). A key Marxist concept, one which has been widely circulated in literary and cultural studies, is that of the relationship between *base* and *superstructure*; the *base* is the economic structure underpinning a society (e.g. capitalism) while the *superstructure* consists of the culture and institutions that depend on this economic system. The text forms part of the superstructure of society, and it is the role of the critic to trace the relationship between the individual text and the wider social, political and economic base.

Throughout much of the twentieth century, Marxism was a hugely influential mode of analysis in various academic disciplines. However, the rise of postcolonial studies has coincided with the decline of Marxist analysis following the collapse of the Soviet Union and its client states, as well as the rise of postmodernist thought in universities. Essentially, postmodernism is suspicious of all 'meta-narratives', that is, of any attempt to explain the world using a single grand theory, and materialist/Marxist thinking has thus been subjected to sustained attack, especially within the field of postcolonialism, for what has been perceived as its imposition of an overarching western conceptual framework on non-western societies. Within literary and cultural studies, the dominant models for analysis are now often poststructuralism and deconstruction – modes of reading informed by postmodernist principles – which emphasize the fundamental ambiguity of all discourses and representations. In their turn, however, materialist critics have been keen to highlight the shortcomings of what they perceive as a primarily poststructuralist-inflected postcolonial studies.

MATERIALIST CRITIQUES OF POSTCOLONIAL STUDIES

It is often noted that the emergence of postcolonial studies helped to bring about the demise of the field of Commonwealth literature, which was deemed to view its object of study as a minor offshoot of 'metropolitan' literature. However, postcolonial studies also displaced the field of 'Third World Literature', which analysed the literatures of the emerging nations of the formerly colonized world, often focusing on the political critique of colonialism and neocolonialism in such works. For most materialist critics, the shift from 'Third World Literature' to 'Postcolonial Literature' constituted a movement away from a political consideration of culture to a postmodern/poststructuralist view of texts as the site of semantic ambiguity and textual play (Shohat 1992; McClintock 1993). For instance, the agenda for postcolonial studies that was announced by Ashcroft, Griffiths and Tiffin in their landmark text, *The Empire Writes Back* (1989) focuses primarily on hybridity, ambiguity, the in-between and the textual process of 'writing back' to the centre. This shift in emphasis – from the political/contextual to the cultural/textual – has often been described as a movement away from the binary oppositions of anti-colonial resistance to a consideration of the ambiguities of the postcolonial legacy. Many of the debates opposing materialists and poststructuralists have focused on competing visions of the postcolonial text either as a site of political resistance or as a site of the ambiguity of representation.

As postcolonial studies became more established, there developed a postcolonial 'critical orthodoxy', centred on the increasingly canonized theoretical thinking of the triumvirate of Homi K. Bhabha, Gayatri Chakravorty Spivak and Edward W. Said whose work has generally (although not exclusively, as we shall see below) been read as exemplifying several problems with poststructuralist formulations of the postcolonial. As the leading Marxist critic, Neil Lazarus, has recently noted in relation to the work of Bhabha: '"Postcolonialism criticism", as [Bhabha] understands and champions it, is constitutively anti-Marxist' (2004: 4); effectively, materialist criticism came to be seen by many as existing outside of, and in opposition to, the postcolonial field.

Three major criticisms levelled at postcolonial studies by materialist critics might be summarized as follows. First, it is argued that poststructuralist analysis focuses on textual issues at the expense of historical issues; essentially, this means that such criticism explores the *representation* of colonial or postcolonial contexts but refuses any direct connection between the text and the 'real' world (Parry 2002). The second criticism is closely linked to the first: whereas many poststructuralist critics, such as Bhabha, view hybridity, ambiguity and in-betweenness as notions central to postcolonialism, and have focused on the migrant as the archetype of a postcolonial identity, this generalized postcolonial hybridity is increasingly seen by materialist critics as the condition of a specific, cosmopolitan postcolonial elite, which has little to say about the experience of the vast majority of economic migrants (Brennan 1997). Finally, materialist critics have consistently questioned the ambiguity of postcolonial studies' temporal framework, which is viewed as prematurely celebratory in its positing of a postcolonial world, a world that materialists argue might better be classified as neocolonial; equally, the positing of a single 'postcolonial condition' means that settler colonies such as Canada and Australia are dealt with under the same heading as African and Asian colonies of domination (Mishra and Hodge 1993).

In order to illustrate better the conflict that underlies these criticisms, let us take briefly as an example one key debate that has opposed materialists and poststructuralists. Central to the materialist understanding of the process of decolonization has been the work of Frantz Fanon, the Martiniquan psychia-trist, and later spokesperson for the FLN, the Algerian nationalist movement in its war of independence against France. (The work of his fellow Martiniquan, Aimé Césaire, and the Tunisian, Albert Memmi, who both, like Fanon, wrote within a francophone context – a context too easily ignored by many critics in their desire to forge 'general' postcolonial theories – has also been influential.) In his hugely influential text, *Les Damnés de la Terre* (1961, trans. *The Wretched of the Earth*), Fanon assesses the social and cultural impact of colonization and outlines what he considers to be the necessary measures for creating truly inde-pendent and egalitarian postcolonial states. Fanon describes the need to create a national culture that would replace the repressive structures of the colonial era, and he warns against the dangers of corrupt leaders hijacking the national movement on behalf of a privileged elite who would seek to maintain the old colonial hierarchies. However, the materialist reading of Fanon is contested by poststructuralist readings of his work. Most influential has been Bhabha's inter-pretation of Fanon, which focuses on his early psychological work, *Peau noire, masques blancs* (1952, trans. *Black Skin, White Masks*); in his foreword to the English translation of Fanon's text, Bhabha presents the Martiniquan as the archetypal critic of a postcolonial identity, with its complex weave of mimicry and hybridity (see Fanon 1986: vii–xxvi). However, Neil Lazarus (1999) criticizes Bhabha for reading Fanon 'backwards', and thus neglecting Fanon's later work on the Algerian War of Independence. Bhabha's approach to Fanon's work is deemed to strip it of its political, contextual and historical elements – which is intellectually unacceptable to materialist critics. Effectively for Lazarus, then, Bhabha reads Fanon ahistorically in order to support his own view of the post-colonial project as centred on notions of hybrid, individual identities and the exemplary figure of the migrant.

Having explored some of the key debates opposing materialists and post-structuralists, it is clear that many materialist approaches to postcolonial studies are concerned with the lack of attention allegedly given in postcolonial studies to the political contexts and agency of postcolonial cultural texts, which are considered to be quickly divorced from their material moorings. With this in mind, the following sections will examine more closely the different materialist forms of engagement with postcolonial studies.

MATERIALIST REJECTIONS OF POSTCOLONIAL STUDIES

Two of the fiercest critics of postcolonial studies are Aijaz Ahmad and Arif Dirlik. It is worth noting that neither is a literary critic, both having made their intellectual reputations as political economists, and their critiques do not really engage in literary analysis; rather they are concerned with the theoretical assumptions underpinning postcolonial criticism. They denounce postcolo-nialism as a mere offshoot of postmodernism and argue that postcolonial critics who celebrate their own migrant hybridity – i.e. scholars from formerly colo-nized countries who work in top western universities – are unaware of their rela-tively privileged position within the global economy. Dirlik goes even further in his 1994 essay 'The Postcolonial Aura: Third World Criticism in the Age of Global Capitalism', where he presents postcolonialism as a conspiracy of silence about the inequalities of the neocolonial world order. Both critics are particu-larly scathing about the temporal vagueness of postcolonialism's framework, and Ahmad's is perhaps the best-known critique on this topic:

> In periodising our history in the triadic terms of precolonial, colonial and postcolo-nial, the conceptual apparatus of 'postcolonial criticism' privileges as primary the role of colonialism as the principle of structuration in that history, so that all that came before colonialism becomes its own prehistory and whatever comes after can only be lived as infinite aftermath.
>
> (1996: 280–81)

Such critiques of postcolonial studies are welcome additions to the debate, high-lighting the problems of theoretical over-generalization. However, it is ironic that Ahmad and Dirlik often treat all postcolonial critics as inherently simplistic in their thinking, and at times fall foul of the type of sweeping generalization that they themselves denounce. Furthermore, in choosing to place themselves *outside* of postcolonial studies, they effectively deny the possibility of furthering a materialist agenda *within* the field. As we shall see in the next section, this critique of Ahmad is echoed in the work of Marxists such as Neil Lazarus, Crystal Bartolovich and Benita Parry, who explicitly position themselves within the field of postcolonial studies. Equally, in their blanket dismissals of postcolonialism, Ahmad and Dirlik ignore the materialist concerns underpinning several major postcolonial critics. For example, the prominent Palestinian-born critic, Edward Said, is often aligned with poststructuralism for his borrowing of ideas on the relationship between knowledge and power from the French theorist, Michel Foucault. However, Said explicitly rejects Foucault's pessimism about the ability to resist discourses of power. Moreover, Said also borrows from the work of the Italian Marxist, Antonio Gramsci, using his ideas on 'hegemony' and 'domination' as a counterbalance to Foucault's all-encompassing view of power. Said's project might thus be described as an attempt to reconcile elements of both materialist and poststructuralist agendas. A similar project is at work, although expressed in a very different fashion, in the writing of the US-based Indian scholar, Gayatri Chakravorty Spivak, who deploys a complex mixture of deconstruction, feminism and Marxism in which issues of class and power occupy a central place alongside issues of gender and representation.

The examples of Said and Spivak suggest that their work might be most profitably conceived as 'post-Marxist', in that it takes on board certain Marxist ideas but ultimately seeks to go beyond and correct them. This stance is perhaps most evident in the work of the important British postcolonial scholar, Robert J. C. Young, who has been extremely critical of Marxism – especially in his *White Mythologies* (1990) – and has done so much to promote the poststructuralist agenda within postcolonial studies. In his hugely ambitious book *Postcolonialism: an historical introduction* (2001) Young argues that 'Postcolonial theory operates within the historical legacy of Marxist critique on which it continues to draw but which it simultaneously transforms' (6). For Young, postcolonialism is the attempt to marry (often Marxist-inspired) anti-colonial thought with poststructuralism. The western theories of Marxism are thus deemed to be 'corrected' by poststructuralism, which Young views as a fundamentally postcolonial project, designed to question the dominance of western knowledge. Writing of this 'working alliance' in postcolonial theory between Marxism and poststructuralism, Graham Huggan argues that the tension between the two approaches should be seen 'less as a sign of methodological incoherence than as further evidence of the field's unresolved attempt to reconcile political activism and cultural critique' (2001: 261). How can the discussion of often complex and ambiguous literary texts be combined with direct political critique? As the 1990s progressed, similar questions were echoed among materialist critics who wished to distance themselves from the wholesale dismissal of postcolonial studies as a field. What then did materialism have to offer?

MATERIALIST ENGAGEMENT WITH POSTCOLONIAL STUDIES

Even at the height of the poststructuralist 1990s, there was still space for materialist approaches within postcolonial studies. For instance, one of the first major postcolonial readers, edited by Patrick Williams and Laura Chrisman, spells out an explicit materialist agenda in its introduction, while refusing to neglect the major contribution of poststructuralism (1993: 1–20). In a more recent edited collection of essays encouraging Marxist engagement with postcolonial studies, Crystal Bartolovich criticizes Ahmad's 'repudiation' of the field: 'It seems to us that Marxist theorists can and should engage *with* postcolonial studies in mutual sites of concern, and concede to the field the authentic insights and advances that have been general within it' (2002: 10). As Bartolovich readily admits, concomitant with such a move is an acceptance of the errors and limitations of Marxism itself.

The British-based South African critics Benita Parry and Neil Lazarus are perhaps the most prominent Marxist critics who have chosen to engage fully with postcolonial studies as a field of inquiry. Despite their disagreements with poststructuralist orthodoxy, these critics have consistently striven to map out the materialist dimensions of the field. Both Parry and Lazarus are attentive readers of theoretical and fictional texts, and they are willing to acknowledge the value of key poststructuralist critical insights. For instance, Lazarus acknowledges Bhabha's notion of hybridity as a defining feature of certain postcolonial texts. However, for Lazarus (as for Parry), the promotion by Bhabha of hybridity as the archetypal postcolonial condition exclusively reflects the concerns of a cosmopolitan elite, which is taken as representative of the former colonies as a whole. This leads Lazarus to argue that

> Bhabha fails to address the material circumstances of the vast majority of migrants from the peripheries of the world system to the core capitalist nations. He fails to register in any plausible manner the political, economic, and social dimensions of the lives of these millions of people.
>
> (1999: 137)

However, Lazarus does not confine his critiques to the work of poststructuralist theorists. His book, *Nationalism and Cultural Practice in the Postcolonial World* (1999), features a meticulous problematization of Fanon's work on decolonization, identifying various errors and misjudgements, most notably Fanon's mistaken view that the 'native' culture of the colonized had effectively been wiped out by the colonizer. For Fanon, it is anti-colonial nationalist culture that fills the void left by empire, a move that poststructuralists have read as a heavy-handed dismissal of indigenous cultures in favour of a westernized norm. However, for Lazarus, the errors in Fanon's judgement on this issue must be balanced against the acuity of his judgement elsewhere, such as in his warnings about the 'pitfalls' of nationalism and the capacity for the 'national revolution' to become derailed by a bourgeois elite. Subsequent chapters in Lazarus's book go on to analyse sport and popular music as both 'popular' and 'global' cultural practices, thus moving beyond the binary oppositions between colonizer and colonized evoked in Fanon's work while continuing to analyse the economic and political dominance that governs these exchanges.

Benita Parry's essay 'Problems in Current Theories of Postcolonial Discourse' (originally published in 1987) from her book *Postcolonial Studies: a materialist critique* (2004) remains perhaps the most influential critique of poststructuralist ideas on the 'ambiguous' nature of colonial discourse. Parry provides a meticulous analysis of work by Bhabha and Spivak, not hesitating to praise the brilliance of certain aspects of their analysis, but decrying their depiction of all 'native' resistance to colonialism as 'essentialist' (i.e. presenting an inherently unified identity for the colonized – racial, national – which neglects real differences within colonized societies). In a later essay, Parry bemoans poststructuralism's focus on the literature of a Europhone, migrant (post)colonial elite, neglecting work in 'indigenous' languages as well as 'resistance literature': 'instead of attempting to compile a canon of Postcolonial Literature, we need to think about postcolonial literatures as a web of different strands, not all of which are woven out of "postmodern" materials' (2002: 72). In fact, in the past two decades, Parry has been a champion of 'resistance literature' and, in another influential essay, she provides a highly insightful reading of Césaire and other Negritude authors in order to redeem their ideas from the charge of essentialism (2004: 37–54).

Reflecting on the persistent quarrels between poststructuralists and materialists, Crystal Bartolovich argues that: 'In this longstanding dispute, a good deal of oversimplification, caricature, and trivialization has crept into the discourse on both sides' (2002: 1). As detailed above, recent moves by materialist scholars hint at a more productive future but, as will be discussed in the next section, there is also a more general sense that poststructuralism and materialism should become common, shared tools within postcolonial studies.

TEXTS AND CONTEXTS

Two important, recent interventions in the field have attempted to negotiate a path between the competing claims of 'text' and 'context'. Nicholas Harrison's book, *Postcolonial Criticism: history, theory and the work of fiction* (2003) is a finely-balanced analysis of the difficulties involved in determining the historical 'meaning' of the literary text. Using a series of case studies, Harrison analyses both the literary and the 'worldly' nature of all works of literature. For example, the analysis of Albert Camus's *L'Étranger* (1942, trans. *The Outsider*) assesses the claims of two starkly opposed critiques of the novel: Edward Said's influential 'postcolonial' reading in *Culture and Imperialism* (1993), which states that 'the facts of imperial actuality' are clearly visible in the text, and Roland Barthes's depiction of Camus's prose as an 'écriture blanche' or a blank style of writing, which is effectively 'neutral' in relation to the world it describes. For

Harrison, neither claim is ultimately sustainable: Said provides insufficient textual evidence for his claims, but nor is it possible to divorce the text from the social discourses of its time, as Barthes aims to do.

A similar approach is adopted in John McLeod's essay, 'Contesting Contexts' (2003), which traces how ideas have circulated and been taken 'out of context' within postcolonial studies, focusing on the borrowings from French-language theory in anglophone postcolonialism. Central to McLeod's argument is Said's notion of 'travelling theory', which highlights the capacity of ideas to migrate and take on new meanings in different contexts; what 'travelling theory' seeks to trace is not whether people get ideas 'right' – which is, of course, vital – but how ideas come to mean certain things and gain currency in specific contexts. For instance, Robert Young claims that Said himself 'gets Foucault wrong' when using his ideas in *Orientalism*, but McLeod defends Said against this charge, arguing in favour of the creative potential of 'travelling theory': 'Advocates of context-sensitive criticism must beware blinding themselves to the creative potential of "travelling theory" which, as Anglophone postcolonialism vividly demonstrates, can be enormously and urgently creative in breaking and making intellectual paradigms' (2003: 200). McLeod concludes that 'contexts are not simply to be ignored' (201) but paradoxically an attention to context can end up neglecting the material reality of the new situation to which the ideas have travelled. The basic point for McLeod is that if one of the main aims of postcolonial theory is to provide comparative analysis across former colonial boundaries, then it is vital at certain times to move beyond specific contexts, while nonetheless avoiding excessive generalization.

In presenting these two attempts at a synthesis, this chapter does not propose the reductive notion that the balanced approach between two opposing points of view is always the right one but rather that there exist un-nuanced versions of both materialist and poststructuralist approaches. Many of the examples contained in this chapter bear witness to the fruitful potential for dialogue between competing approaches within postcolonial studies; what then might be the future for a more materialist-inflected postcolonial studies?

NEW DIRECTIONS/NEW CHALLENGES

In two important recent interventions, the British-based scholar Graham Huggan adopts a largely materialist approach in his analysis of the structures of postcolonial studies as a field of research. Huggan's book *The Postcolonial Exotic* (2001) is a sociologically inspired analysis of the 'institutionalization' of postcolonial studies; that is, of the ways in which it has developed as a university subject. He distinguishes between the politics of 'postcolonialism', which he associates with anti-colonial discourse, and the commercialism of 'postcoloniality', by which he means that postcolonial studies' analysis of empire and discourse on race has itself become a commodity, another item for sale in a consumerized world. For Huggan, the recognition that postcolonial studies exists within the global market does not preclude dissent: 'for the postcolonial exotic is both a form of commodity fetishism *and* a revelation of the process by which "exotic" commodities are produced, exchanged, consumed' (264). It is the role of the postcolonial scholar to examine this process of commodification. In a later article, Huggan calls for the development of interdisciplinary approaches within postcolonial studies, which he views as teamwork-based projects, involving academics from various disciplines, addressing common sets of issues and problems (Huggan 2002). Postcolonial studies has always engaged with many disciplines – anthropology, history, cultural studies – but, for Huggan this has been at the abstract level of using language from other disciplines rather than adopting their specific techniques of analysis.

An interdisciplinary, teamwork-based approach would thus provide much-needed empirical analyses with which to reassess certain theoretical paradigms. Such a move would strengthen still further the materialist dimension of post-colonial studies. Taken together with the recent moves by Marxists such as Lazarus, Parry and Bartolovich, among others, it would appear that, for the moment at least, materialist formulations have begun to occupy a more central position within postcolonial studies; whether this is to be a short- or a long-term trend remains to be seen.

RECOMMENDED FURTHER READING

Ahmad, Aijaz, *In Theory: classes, nations, literatures* (London: Verso, 1992).

Bartolovich, Crystal and Lazarus, Neil (eds) *Marxism, Modernity and Postcolonial Studies* (Cambridge: Cambridge University Press, 2002).

Huggan, Graham, *The Postcolonial Exotic: marketing the margins* (London: Routledge, 2001).

Lazarus, Neil, *Nationalism and Cultural Practice in the Postcolonial World* (Cambridge: Cambridge University Press, 1999).

Parry, Benita, *Postcolonial Studies: a materialist critique* (London: Routledge, 2004).

San Juan jnr, E., *Beyond Postcolonial Theory* (New York: St. Martin's Press, 1998).

Young, Robert J. C., *Postcolonialism: an historical introduction* (Oxford: Blackwell, 2001).

17

PSYCHOLOGICAL FORMULATIONS

ABIGAIL WARD

Psychological theories have both been embraced and rejected by postcolonial writers and critics. This chapter briefly surveys some of the earlier psychological approaches to colonization offered by the writers Octave Mannoni and Frantz Fanon. It will then examine a group of writers most commonly termed 'trauma' theorists – Cathy Caruth, Dominick LaCapra and Marianne Hirsch – considering the important possibilities created by recent psychological formulations for the ever-shifting terrain of postcolonial studies.

DEFINITIONS AND DIFFICULTIES

Psychology is concerned with the study of mental processes and behaviour, both conscious and unconscious. A psychological approach to studying postcolonial cultures often establishes a way of reading which is attentive to the psychological effects of colonization and/or decolonization on formerly colonized and, frequently, colonizing peoples. Such effects may include, for example, inferiority or dependency complexes, the related internalization of racism, the traumatic legacies of colonization and the slave trade, and so on.

There is not, however, a straightforward, or unproblematic, relationship between psychology and postcolonialism, as Sam Durrant explains in his book *Postcolonial Narrative and the Work of Mourning: J. M. Coetzee, Wilson Harris, and Toni Morrison* (2004):

> Psychoanalysis, with its commitment to the well-being of the subject, encourages us to exorcise our ghosts, to come to terms with loss and move on. Deconstruction, with its commitment to the other, to that which 'unhinges' the subject, urges us to learn to live with ghosts. Postcolonial narrative, which addresses the individual reader both in his or her singularity and as a member of wider communities, is caught between these two commitments: its transformation of the past into a narrative is simultaneously an attempt to summon the dead and lay them to rest.
>
> (2004: 9)

In proposing that postcolonial works are poised between 'summon[ing] the dead' and 'lay[ing] them to rest', Durrant invites us to consider how postcolonial works often may be paradoxically caught between attempting to both remember and forget the traumatic past. In a similar fashion, the aims of postcolonial thought may sometimes share a conflictual relationship with the objectives of psychological discourses. It is worth maintaining this simultaneous sense of rapport and conflict between postcolonial and psychological aspirations as the chapter proceeds.

In addition, the tension between postcolonial narrative and Western psycho-analytic approaches is generated not only by the aim of psychology to exorcise the ghosts of the past, as Durrant suggests, but also by its alleged Eurocentrism. As Hussein Abdilahi Bulhan writes: '[t]he discipline of psychology did not of course emerge in a social vacuum unrelated to Europe's history of conquest and violence. From its beginning to the present, the discipline has been enmeshed in that history of conquest and violence' (1985: 37). However, psychology cannot be simply dismissed because of its complicity in colonialism, or its status as a 'Western' discourse. Bulhan also acknowledges that in order to understand the drive for, and effects of, colonization it is *imperative* to study this past from a psychological viewpoint. It is necessary to contend with psychology in order to discover new modes of postcolonial thought. For example, Leela Gandhi has suggested that postcolonial theory may be instrumental in countering what she calls a 'self-willed historical amnesia' concerning colonization: 'the colonial aftermath calls for an ameliorative and therapeutic theory which is responsive to the task of remembering and recalling the colonial past' (1998: 7–8). Rather than viewing decolonization as an absolute break from the colonial past, it would seem that it is important to remember (however difficult or traumatic) in order to enact a historical and psychological 'recovery', which may always contain 'gaps and fissures' but nevertheless is vital in understanding what has occurred (8). Postcolonial narratives often attempt such complex and difficult acts of remembering.

So that we may understand psychological approaches in postcolonial thought we need first to consider how early psychologists and psychiatrists wrote about colonialism. As Françoise Verges writes, colonial psychiatry descended from the *psychologie des peuples*, a discourse defining the relations between race, culture and psyche which arose in France in the latter half of the nineteenth century. Its scope had been restricted to the lower French classes; specifically, psychologists were interested in the 'vagabond', who was thought to be pathologically degen-erate, but theories about the insane and criminal were, however, soon applied to the colonized. As Verges notes: '[t]hough colonial psychologists wanted to base their conclusions on clinical observations, their biases led them to conclusions that ultimately argued a constitutional inferiority of the colonized' (2000: 89).

After the Second World War, a new approach towards studying the dynamics of colonization developed. In particular, several French-speaking theorists (often sympathetic to the plight of colonized peoples) began looking at the psychological effects of colonization on the colonized and colonizers, such as Octave Mannoni (France), Albert Memmi (Tunisia) and Frantz Fanon (Martinique). These separate francophone approaches sought, in different ways, to explore the psychological legacies of colonization. The work of Ashis Nandy in the early 1980s may also be included in this group, despite some signif-icant differences, and is worth mentioning here. Nandy's book *The Intimate*

Enemy: loss and recovery of self under colonialism (1983) was written thirty-three years after Mannoni's important text *Psychologie de la Colonisation* (1950, trans. *Prospero and Caliban: the psychology of colonisation*), and Nandy examines the relationship between India and Britain, rather than France and its former colonies. *The Intimate Enemy* also explores (from a late twentieth-century perspective) the effects of colonization on the colonized and colonizers – a central concern in the works of Mannoni, Memmi and Fanon.

In more recent years a body of research has emerged concerning 'trauma studies'. Sigmund Freud's early twentieth-century pronouncements on the reliving of traumatic experience have been influential for these later writers. In particular, Freud's essay 'Mourning and Melancholia' (1917) – in which melancholia is conceived of as an endlessly repeating remembering, and mourning, as a working through in order to forget – has proved highly fertile to those working in trauma studies. Some key examples are Cathy Caruth's influential work on trauma and Post-Traumatic Stress Disorder, and Dominick LaCapra's research into trauma associated with the Holocaust. Marianne Hirsch, who also writes predominantly about the psychological legacies of the Holocaust, poses the notion of 'postmemory' as a means of articulating trauma. Although these discussions do not primarily concern the effects of colonization or decolonization, they have proved helpful in thinking about how to talk about the traumatic legacies of this past.

The discussion which follows will be confined to these two influential conjunctures of psychological thinking: the early work of a group of francophone writers which dealt primarily with the psychological relationship between colonizer and colonized, and more recent anglophone criticism concerning trauma which, as shall be explained, may impact transformatively on contemporary postcolonial engagements with psychological matters.

EARLY PSYCHOLOGICAL APPROACHES

The French critic Octave Mannoni's *Prospero and Caliban* was one of the earliest texts in the abovementioned francophone psychological movement of the mid-twentieth century. *Prospero and Caliban* is arguably best known for being a subject of Frantz Fanon's attack in *Peau noire, masques blancs* (1952, trans. *Black Skin, White Masks*), but Mannoni's work should be examined first before moving on to explore Fanon's critique.

From the start of *Prospero and Caliban*, Mannoni makes very clear that his book does not aim to find a psychological solution to the problems engendered by colonization; rather, he desires to reveal the limitations of a psychological study of this recent past. Mannoni indicates that he wishes to move away from seeing the 'colonial situation' as the domination of the rich over the poor and weak; instead, he proposes, we need to think of colonialism as the meeting between 'two entirely different types of personality and their reactions to each other, in consequence of which the native becomes "colonized" and the

European becomes a colonial' (1993: 17). This 'meeting', he assures us, brings together two utterly different personality types, which are based on the assumption that 'the colonizing peoples are among the most advanced in the world, while those which undergo colonization are among the most backward' (26–27). It is, Mannoni tells us, crucial to look at the psychology of the colonizer as well as the colonized – we must explore both personality types in order to understand the psychology of colonization. This emphasis on examining the relationship between colonizer and colonized was also taken up by the Tunisian novelist and critic Albert Memmi in *Portrait du colonisé précédé du Portrait du Colonisateur* (1957, trans. *The Colonizer and the Colonized*), in which Memmi describes his aim as having been to 'reproduce, completely and authentically, the portraits of the two protagonists of the colonial drama and the relationship which binds them' (1990: 211). It is not sufficient to merely focus on the colonized; instead, we need to examine the psychological problems experienced by the colonized specifically *in the context of* their relationship with the colonizers.

Mannoni suggested that there were two main alternative psychological complexes which characterized the dynamics of colonialism: an inferiority complex and a dependency complex. The non-white European was more likely to suffer from the inferiority complex, while the black African suffered from the dependency complex. The inferiority complex 'springs from a physical difference taken to be a drawback – namely, the colour of the skin'; it therefore only occurs where a minority group finds themselves surrounded by those of a different colour (1993: 39). On the other hand, the dependency complex arises when the colonized receives an unasked-for favour from the colonizer. The colonized then asks for further items, or favours, and – though showing no gratitude – 'appears to feel he has some sort of claim upon the European who did him a kindness' (42). The dependency complex was aligned with a child's dependence on its parents; civilized people, Mannoni argued, break this dependency, but the formerly colonized is reluctant to do so. Mannoni bases many of his claims within the book on his study of the Malagasy people, which he then applies more generally to explore the effects of colonization. It would seem, however, that Mannoni's research was less than thorough; Maurice Bloch suggests in his introduction to the text that Mannoni's understanding of the Malagasy was at best limited, and adds that it would be 'very tiresome' to address all of the book's mistakes (in Mannoni 1993: xiv). Despite these perhaps obvious limitations of *Prospero and Caliban*, Mannoni's study remains important in seeking to comprehend the psychological effects of colonization, especially in his early attempt to understand the troubled history at the core of the relationship between colonizer and colonized.

By far the strongest early critical response to Mannoni's thinking came from Frantz Fanon, whose own work, without doubt, is the most well-known of psychological attempts to theorize the effects of colonialism. Writing during a turbulent period of decolonization in the French empire in the 1950s and early 1960s, Fanon's books *Black Skin, White Masks* and *Les Damnés de la Terre* (1961, trans. *The Wretched of the Earth*) – the latter of which was written as Fanon was dying from leukaemia – are two of the seminal works of postcolonial thought. A great number of studies have been devoted to Fanon, so this narrative shall only very briefly pause to reiterate some of the most important moments from his writing.

As mentioned above, Fanon devotes a chapter to criticizing Mannoni's work in making what Bloch has referred to as 'a very general but furious and largely deserved refutation' (in Mannoni 1993: vii). In particular, in *Black Skin, White Masks* Fanon is especially critical of Mannoni's notion of the inferiority and dependency complexes. Fanon argued that Mannoni had failed to comprehend the 'real coordinates' of the colonial situation (1986: 84), and also strongly objects to the suggestion in *Prospero and Caliban* that the inferiority complex may precede colonization; Mannoni refers to its *emergence* during this period, not its origin. Furthermore, Fanon suggests that the inferiority complex is over-simplified; Mannoni declares that it affects those of a racial minority but, as Fanon notes, '[a] white man in a colony has never felt inferior in any respect' (92). Fanon also refutes Mannoni's claim that some countries are inherently more racist than others and that there exist different 'types' of exploitation and racism. He is clear that racism remains unchanged, regardless of its target: he tells us that '[c]olonial racism is no different from any other racism' (88).

Like Mannoni, early on in *Black Skin, White Masks* Fanon reveals his interest in the effects of contact between the colonizer and the colonized, asserting that the juxtaposition of white and black people during colonization has created what he refers to as a 'massive psychoexistential complex' which he hopes, through analysis, to destroy (14). Possibly his most famous articulation of one of the elements of this complex, in his description of the way in which identity is constructed by one's contact with others, comes in the opening of his chapter of *Black Skin, White Masks* entitled 'The Fact of Blackness'. Fanon begins with the words: '"Dirty nigger!" Or simply, "Look, a Negro!"' (109). Through the racializing call of the other, the black person is stripped of subjectivity, and becomes conscious of himself as merely an object 'in the midst of other objects' (109). This awareness of self through calling is specifically generated by being 'recognised' as black by a white person: 'not only must the black man be black; he must be black *in relation to* the white man' (current author's emphasis) (110). Fanon therefore describes a traumatic split in the psyche, where a black person is not only reduced to an object by the white gaze but, as a consequence, behaves differently with white, as opposed to black, people. Fanon called this phenomenon 'two dimensions' (17); the American writer W. E. B. Du Bois had earlier referred to this condition in *The Souls of Black Folk* (1903) as 'double consciousness' (Du Bois 1969: 3). The double consciousness of the black American, Du Bois suggested, occurs precisely by 'looking at one's self through the eyes of others', and this is always negative (Du Bois 1969: 3). Both Du Bois and Fanon are hence emphatic that one of the greatest dangers facing the black man or woman is psychologically internalizing oppression and racism.

For Fanon, it would seem that it is impossible to disregard the roots of this Manichean dichotomy; he suggests that the unequal, and difficult, relationship between black and white people was generated by slavery. In his introduction to *The Wretched of the Earth*, Jean-Paul Sartre writes of colonization as a continuation of slavery: '[t]he European *élite* undertook to manufacture a native *élite*. They picked out promising adolescents; they branded them, as with a red-hot iron, with the principles of western culture' (in Fanon 1967: 7). Here, Sartre picks up on a theme dominant in Fanon's work, namely the continuation of mental enslavement under the guise of colonialism. The psychological relationship between colonized and colonizer is a continuation of that between slave and master. Albert Memmi had also written about colonization as a legacy of the slave past. The colonized has been uprooted from the past and denied a future; with the failure of assimilation, Memmi suggests the next possible option is to revolt against the colonizer: 'the colonial condition cannot be adjusted to; like an iron collar, it can only be broken' (1990: 194). In this phrase, which recalls again the enslavement of black people by white, we can see Memmi's conviction of the colonizer's 'ownership' of the colonized: a relationship that must be ended. Revolt and revolution are necessary for the colonizer to be rid of the 'disease' of colonization, and for the colonized to 'become a man' (217).

Ultimately, in rejecting Mannoni's reliance on superiority and inferiority complexes to explain a colonial mindset, Fanon calls for an understanding between races:

> Superiority? Inferiority?
> Why not the quite simple attempt to touch the other, to feel the other, to explain the other to myself?
>
> (1986: 231)

While many critics have explored Fanon's advocacy of political violence, this call for understanding is an equally important, though sometimes overlooked, aspect of his work: one which demands a psychological transformation every bit as far-reaching – and as necessary – as political revolution.

TRAUMA AND THE POSTCOLONIAL

So far three of the major mid-twentieth-century thinkers in colonial and postcolonial psychology have been discussed in order to highlight some of the pertinent issues involved in psychological approaches to postcolonialism. The remainder of this chapter will examine some later psychological approaches to the study of trauma which have proved very significant to postcolonial explorations of the belated, enduring effects of the traumatic colonial past.

The 1990s, in particular, saw a renewed interest in trauma studies, much of which was concerned with examining the late twentieth-century traumatic effects of the Jewish Holocaust on its survivors. Borrowing from a psychological method that is not specifically concerned with postcolonial contexts (such as the Atlantic slave trade, for example) necessitates a sensitive and cautious approach. In exploring books about trauma by Cathy Caruth and works by theorists primarily concerned with the psychological legacies of the Holocaust, such as Dominick LaCapra and Marianne Hirsch, we must be extremely careful not to minimise the considerable difference between Holocaust trauma and what we may term postcolonial trauma. However, these thinkers offer a critical vocabulary for, and ways of thinking about, trauma and memory which are highly valuable to a psychological exploration of the postcolonial. In *Writing History, Writing Trauma* (2001) Dominick LaCapra acknowledges the existence of important differences between the trauma of the Atlantic slave trade and that of the Holocaust, but also writes that '[s]lavery, like the Holocaust, nonetheless presents, for a people, problems of traumatization, severe oppression, a divided heritage, the question of a founding trauma, the forging of identities in the present, and so forth' (174). As LaCapra suggests in this quotation, a psychological approach to traumatic experience may prove helpful in seeking to understand the past and negotiate identities in the present: slavery, he reminds us, was also a traumatic past.

Cathy Caruth is one of the most well-known writers in the field of 'trauma studies'. In her edited collection of essays, *Unclaimed Experience: trauma, narrative, and history* (1996), Caruth defines trauma as an 'overwhelming experience of sudden or catastrophic events in which the response to the event occurs in the often delayed, uncontrolled repetitive appearance of hallucinations and other intrusive phenomena' (11). The overwhelming traumatic experience cannot be grasped during the moment of its occurrence, but only belatedly – through hallucinations, flashbacks and nightmares. In her works Caruth writes about Freud's contention that belatedness, or *Nachträglichkeit*, is a critical aspect of trauma, and argues that 'the history of trauma, in its inherent belatedness, can only take place through the listening of another' (11). This notion that trauma may only be understood as it is enunciated and, crucially, as it is heard by another is also suggested by the research of Shoshana Felman and Dori Laub. In *Testimony: crises of witnessing in literature, psychoanalysis, and history* (1992), Felman and Laub write that it is necessary for trauma to be heard in order for the victim to work through the traumatic experience. Unheard testimony does not enable healing to begin, but instead traps the survivor in a painful repetition of the event:

> Trauma survivors live not with memories of the past, but with an event that could not and did not proceed through to its completion, has no ending, attained no closure, and therefore, as far as its survivors are concerned, continues into the present and is current in every respect.
>
> (1992: 69)

Yet, expressing traumatic events is rarely a straightforward telling – the process is often difficult, painful and halted by the limits of language to articulate trauma. Ernst van Alphen writes of the unrepresentable nature of the Holocaust in his essay 'Symptoms of Discursivity: Experience, Memory, and Trauma' (1999). By positing the inexpressible nature of the Holocaust, van Alphen does not suggest the impropriety of the subject matter or, as Theodor W. Adorno famously proposed, the impossibility of acts of creation from the past of the Holocaust, but instead refers to 'the inability of Holocaust survivors to express or narrate their past experiences. The remembrance of Holocaust events is, then, technically impossible; this problem is fundamentally semiotic in nature' (26). This impossibility of enunciating trauma is also taken up by Lawrence L. Langer, who has argued in *Holocaust Testimonies: the ruins of memory* (1991) that words like 'killed' or 'died' are unsuitable when describing victims of the camps, as they cannot convey the magnitude of the horror. It would seem that sometimes language fails the survivor of trauma.

In *Le différend* (1983, trans. *The Differend: phrases in dispute*) the French philosopher Jean-François Lyotard posits that while there is a pressing need to articulate trauma, often it is impossible to do so:

> In the differend, something 'asks' to be put into phrases, and suffers from the wrong of not being able to be put into phrases right away. This is when the human beings who thought they could use language as an instrument of communication learn through the feeling of pain which accompanies silence [...] that what remains to be phrased exceeds what they can presently phrase, and that they must be allowed to institute idioms which do not yet exist.
>
> (1988: 13)

Lyotard identifies the need to voice experience but also cites the troubling realization that words can be incommensurate with traumatic encounters. He proposes that silence is painful – we might infer that it is absolutely necessary to talk about trauma – although he posits the existence of an immense chasm between what needs to be expressed and what can be comfortably accommodated within the existing limits of language. Phrases which exceed or transcend those limits necessitate the development of new modes of expression. Indeed, it may be useful to consider postcolonial creative acts in these terms: as attempts to discover new modes of expression which attend to, and seek to move beyond, the pain and trauma of the past (and in some cases the present).

As has been suggested, we need to make use of these thinkers' ideas both sensitively and creatively. Although Felman and Laub, Lyotard or Caruth are not explicitly dealing with trauma stemming from colonialism, as Caruth writes in *Trauma: explorations in memory* (1995):

> trauma itself may provide the very link between cultures: not as a simple understanding of the pasts of others but rather, within the traumas of contemporary history, as our ability to listen through the departures we have all taken from ourselves.
>
> (1995: 11)

Acting as a cross-cultural link, trauma may perhaps enable the process of listening and understanding that Fanon called for in *Black Skin, White Masks*. In *Representing the Holocaust* (1994), LaCapra similarly writes that he is interested in demonstrating why psychoanalysis is not merely concerned with the individual, but rather he argues that 'certain key psychoanalytic concepts (such as transference, denial, resistance, repression, acting-out, and working-through) are crucial in the attempt to elucidate the relation between cultures that come into contact' (9). This relation between cultures may, of course, include the contact between cultures during colonization – as previously indicated, the primary subject of study for the writers examined in the first part of this chapter. Yet, there is a danger in viewing trauma in a positive light, a caution that will be revisited below when exploring in further detail the work of LaCapra.

While trauma may provide, for Caruth, a means of linking to other cultures, in *Trauma* she articulates a common concern about the consequences of narrating trauma, which is that the telling of traumatic experience might also enact a forgetting: '[t]o cure oneself – whether by drugs or the telling of one's story or both – seems to many survivors to imply the giving-up of an important reality, or the dilution of a special truth into the reassuring terms of therapy' (vii). Working through the traumatic experience may, then, enact a kind of amnesia – yet, and seemingly paradoxically, due to the belatedness of trauma it is, of course, only through forgetting that the traumatic event can be grasped: '[t]he historical power of the trauma is not just that the experience is repeated after its forgetting, but that it is only in and through its inherent forgetting that it is first experienced at all' (8). It would seem that the apparent forgetting that accompanies the telling of trauma is one of the problems of trying to relieve trauma suffering. Nicola King also writes in *Memory, Narrative, Identity: remembering the self* (2000):

> Individual memories of personal histories are constantly reworked and re-translated in the present; so traumatic historical events seem to demand re-representation and re-reading, to resist the memorialisation which is also a kind of forgetting, the forgetting that assumes that remembering is finished.
>
> (2000: 180)

This is the paradox where remembering also enables a forgetting – or, to return to Durrant, the simultaneous 'attempt to summon the dead and lay them to rest'. In *Writing History, Writing Trauma* LaCapra also notes that working through may be resisted because of 'what might almost be termed a fidelity to trauma, a feeling that one must somehow keep faith with it' (2001: 22). In this way, trauma may act as a kind of shifting memorial to the dead: '[o]ne's bond with the dead [. . .] may invest trauma with value and make its reliving a painful but necessary commemoration or memorial to which one remains dedicated or at least bound' (22). LaCapra suggests it is not as simple as just wishing to forget; the victim also has a duty to the dead to remember past atrocities, and so trauma assumes a memorial function.

There can, it seems, be no straightforward experience of trauma; it is always belated or repeating and indirectly experienced. Caruth notes, in particular, that the image of the soldier who suffers nightmares has become a central image of trauma for the twentieth century (Caruth 1996: 11). But Post-Traumatic Stress Disorder, or the domination of the mind by an event beyond its control following a traumatic occurrence, is not only experienced by war veterans, but is applicable to a variety of other experiences – Caruth suggests rape, child abuse and auto and industrial accidents. (Caruth 1996: 58). Colonial trauma may, of course, be added to this list.

LaCapra suggests that the effects of trauma may extend beyond the immediate victims. He writes that, although the traumatic event has the greatest effect on the victim, it may affect – in varying ways – 'everyone who comes in contact with it: perpetrator, collaborator, bystander, resister, those born later' (1998: 9). LaCapra's phrase 'those born later' suggests an inheritance of traumatic experience that will be addressed in considering the work of Marianne Hirsch. Yet, although the after-effects of traumatic events affect everyone in differing ways, terms like 'victim' and 'survivor' must always be applied with caution. As LaCapra writes, 'the indiscriminate generalization of the category of survivor and the overall conflation of history or culture with trauma, as well as the near fixation on enacting or acting out post-traumatic symptoms, have the effect of obscuring crucial historical distinctions' (2001: xi). In other words, it is vital to avoid appropriating another's traumatic experience, but rather one should enact an 'empathic unsettlement' (41). This is a key term for LaCapra, and refers to the unsettling that precludes an easy, or inappropriate, identification with victims of trauma. It also ensures that the problematic attempt to view traumatic events in a positive way – for example, as life-affirming – is avoided.

One example of this desire to render traumatic experience as positive may be seen in the number of critics who suggest that there should be some kind of affirmative message that can be taken from the 'unspeakable horror' of slavery or, indeed, that a traumatic past might be interpreted into a hopeful fictional text. Writing of Toni Morrison's novel *Beloved* (1987), Cynthia S. Hamilton suggests that its central problem 'concerns the need to transform facts of unspeakable horror into a life-giving story, for the individual, for the black community, and for the nation' (1996: 429). Hamilton recognizes the seemingly commonplace expectation that a novel about the slave trade should contain some kind of reassuringly optimistic message for its reader. LaCapra suggests that empathic unsettlement creates a necessary 'barrier to closure in discourse and places in jeopardy harmonizing or spiritually uplifting accounts of extreme events from which we attempt to derive reassurance or a benefit (for example, unlearned confidence about the ability of the human spirit to endure any adversity with dignity and nobility)' (2001: 41–42). LaCapra posits an ethical, non-appropriative form of empathy which is necessary in order to understand the traumatic past, but this empathy does not transform trauma into either an easy identification, or bestow it with a positive message.

The concern with the ethics of empathy articulated by LaCapra can also be found in the work of Marianne Hirsch. In her many influential essays, Hirsch coins the term 'postmemory' as a way of explaining what she calls the belated 'memories' experienced by those who did not directly witness the traumatic events:

> Postmemory characterizes the experience of those who grow up dominated by narratives that preceded their birth, whose own belated stories are displaced by the stories of the previous generation, shaped by traumatic events that they can neither understand nor re-create.

> (1999: 8)

This passage may be reminiscent of LaCapra's phrase 'those born later'; we can see how Hirsch's term postmemory usefully distinguishes between 'actual' memories and those passed on to later generations. Hirsch writes that although she mainly explores postmemory in relation to the children of Holocaust survivors, she is clear about not wishing to limit the notion of postmemory to the remembrance of the Holocaust. Similarly, she writes in her essay 'Surviving Images: Holocaust Photographs and the Work of Postmemory' (2001) that 'although familial inheritance offers the clearest model for it, postmemory need not be *strictly* an identity position. Instead, I prefer to see it as an intersubjective transgenerational space of remembrance, linked specifically to cultural or collective trauma' (10). In writing about the possibility for postmemory as a potential space for cultural or collective trauma, Hirsch broadens the scope for empathy.

Postmemory is therefore especially useful in thinking about the how contemporary postcolonial writers can explore the remembrance of slavery, for example, in the absence of direct experience of this traumatic past. Postmemory may be helpful in conceptualizing the work of writers who do not claim to have experienced the trauma of slavery, but nonetheless feel an empathic remembrance of, or connection to, this past. In her essay 'Projected Memory: Holocaust Photographs in Personal and Public Fantasy' (1999) Hirsch writes that '[t]he term is meant to convey its temporal and qualitative difference from survivor memory, its secondary or second-generation memory quality, its basis in displacement, its belatedness' (8). The power of the experiences passed on to 'those born later', Hirsch contends, is sufficient to constitute 'memories', but crucially these are *post*memories: the temporal and qualitative distinction between the actual memories of survivors of trauma and those of later generations is central, as is postmemory's displacement, or 'belatedness' (signalled by the appendage 'post')'. Like LaCapra's notion of empathic unsettlement, Hirsch suggests that although postmemory is about adaptation of memory it is importantly mediated through an 'ethical relation' to the subject. This ethical empathy involves multiple connections: '[i]t is a question of conceiving oneself as multiply interconnected with others of the same, of previous, and of subsequent generations, of the same and of other – proximate or distant – cultures and subcultures' (9). Postmemory is not limited to those with the same background or culture, but can be extended across not only generations but also cultures: a temporal and spatial connection. This connection is at the core of postmemory: the past cannot be undone, or repaired, but postmemory suggests a means of connecting across temporalities and cultures that may enable the process of working through to at least commence.

CONCLUSION: SEEKING CONNECTIONS

Hirsch's emphasis on connections underlines the centrality of psychological matters to the study of the relationships between cultures, people, the past and the present. As Homi K. Bhabha writes in *The Location of Culture* (1994): '[r]emembering is never a quiet act of introspection or retrospection. It is a painful re-membering, a putting together of the dismembered past to make sense of the trauma of the present' (63). The kinds of psychological approaches to the postcolonial past considered above may enable the understanding of the traumatic present; yet, as Caruth, LaCapra and Hirsch would perhaps argue, the trauma of the present to which Bhabha refers may, in fact, be the belated experiencing of the traumatic events of the past. Psychological approaches to postcolonial locations seek to understand not only the relationship between different cultures, but also between past and present. We may not yet have seen all of the postponed effects of colonization; certainly many of today's racial anxieties in Britain may be traced back to Britain's colonial past and its historical relationships with its formerly colonized countries. However, as Hirsch writes: 'postmemory seeks connection. It creates where it cannot recover. It imagines where it cannot recall. It mourns a loss that cannot be repaired' (1998: 422). Postmemory calls for a creative and imaginative approach to what has occurred. The colonial past cannot be undone, but the notion of connection, it would seem, is central to beginning the process of mourning.

RECOMMENDED FURTHER READING

Caruth, Cathy, *Unclaimed Experience: trauma, narrative, and history* (Baltimore, MD: Johns Hopkins University Press, 1996).

Fanon, Frantz, *Black Skin, White Masks*, trans. Charles Lam Markmann (London: Pluto, 1986 [1952]).

LaCapra, Dominick, *Writing History, Writing Trauma* (Baltimore, MD: Johns Hopkins University Press, 2001).

Mannoni, O., *Prospero and Caliban: the psychology of colonization*, trans. Pamela Powesland (Ann Arbor, MI: University of Michigan Press, 1993 [1950]).

Memmi, Albert, *The Colonizer and the Colonized*, trans. H. Greenfield, introduced by Jean-Paul Sartre (London: Earthscan Publications, 1990 [1957]).

Part IV

A–Z: FORTY CONTEMPORARY POSTCOLONIAL WRITERS AND THINKERS

CHINUA ACHEBE (B. 1930) Born in Igboland, Nigeria, Albert Chinualumogu Achebe grew up amid the Igbo cultural practices of his people and the influence of Christianity and the Church. He began to write while a student at University College, Ibadan, fuelled by a passion for literature as well as a sense of dissatisfaction with the ways in which African locations were often represented in existing literature in English. His groundbreaking first novel *Things Fall Apart* (1958) contested many colonialist prejudices concerning African civilizations and peoples. It depicted life in an Ibo village at a period of transition, culminating in the arrival of British missionaries at the turn of the twentieth century, and explored the various responses of the villagers to the challenges of change. Achebe's subsequent writing extended and expanded his central themes, in works such as *No Longer at Ease* (1960), *Arrow of God* (1964) and *A Man of the People* (1966), while in 1987 he cast a critical eye over post-independence Nigeria in *Anthills of the Savannah*. In 1962 Achebe helped found Heinemman's influential *African Writers Series*, while his 1975 condemnation of Joseph Conrad's novel *Heart of Darkness* (1899) in an essay titled 'Conrad's Darkness' caused considerable debate and opened up important questions about the complicity of literary culture with political and racial politics. In 1990 Achebe was seriously injured in a car accident and has since been confined to a wheelchair. Since 1990 he has taught at Bard College, Upstate New York.

GLORIA ANZALDÚA (1942–2004) Born and raised in Texas, Gloria Anzaldúa spent most of her working life in California, supporting, editing and writing about the work of feminists, lesbian and gay people, women of colour, Chicano/a literature, and more besides. Her most influential and innovative work is *Borderlands/La Frontera: the new mestiza* (1987), in which she explores the possibilities of new forms of multiple, hybrid identities wrought from the cultural admixture of Chicanas and mestizas (women with native American and Spanish ancestry), influenced by her own experiences of the Chicana community and her lesbian sexuality. Mixing English and Spanish, and shifting constantly between different narrative genres, Anzaldúa sought a critical language which exemplified in its very form the myriad border crossings – national, cultural, racial, sexual

– and heteroglot condition of mestiza identity which, she suggested, offered new ways of reconceptualizing orthodox models of culture and identity. Her predominant metaphors are often bridges and borders, which she uses to figure and phrase the new, radical models of identity. She also co-edited *This Bridge Called My Back: writings by radical women of colour* (1981), an influential collection of Chicana, lesbian and feminist writings, and a number of books for children. She died, aged 61, from complications arising from diabetes.

MARGARET ATWOOD (B. 1939) Born in Ottawa, Canada, Margaret Atwood was educated at Victoria University in the University of Toronto, and also Radcliffe College, Harvard University, USA. She has emerged as one of Canada's most significant and internationally-renown writers, and is a skilled poet and novelist. Her novels include *The Edible Woman* (1969), *Surfacing* (1972), *Bodily Harm* (1981), *The Handmaid's Tale* (1986), *Cat's Eye* (1988), *Alias Grace* (1996), *The Blind Assassin* (2000) and *Oryx and Crake* (2003). Her fiction is generically diverse and ranges across a wealth of subject matter, although the issues of women, gender and survival are frequent preoccupations. For example, *The Handmaid's Tale* is set in a futuristic patriarchal dystopia, and concerns the attempts of the narrator, Offred, to endure and escape from the horrific incarcerating world in which she lives. *Cat's Eye*, perhaps Atwood's most autobiographical work, concerns the reflections of an artist, Elaine Risley, on her young life growing up in mid-twentieth-century Canada, and engages with the themes of female identity and relationships, the feminist movement and the role of art. Atwood's prolific work as a poet includes her collections *The Journals of Susanna Moodie* (1970), *True Stories* (1984) and *Interlunar* (1984), while she has also edited several important anthologies of Canadian literature, including *The New Oxford Book of Canadian Verse* (1982) and *The New Oxford Book of Canadian Short Stories in English* (1995).

B

ANTONIO BENÍTEZ-ROJO (1931–2005) Born in Panama and raised in Cuba, Antonio Benítez-Rojo was educated in the USA and Mexico, and established himself as a writer in 1960s Cuba with his prize-winning collection of short stories *Tute de reyes* (1967). In 1975 he the joined the Casa de las Américas, an organization created and based in Cuba which stimulates and forges links between cultural endeavours in Latin America and the Caribbean, and in 1979 was appointed Director of the Estudios de Caribe. In 1980 he defected from Cuba to the USA and worked as Thomas B. Walton, Jr., Memorial Professor of Spanish at Amherst College, Massachusetts. His works include a trilogy of books spanning three different genres: a novel, *El mar de las lentejas* (1979, trans. *The Sea of Lentils*); a collection of critical essays, *La Isla que se Repite* (1989, trans. *The Repeating Island*); and a book of short stories, *A View from the Mangove* (1998). *La Isla que se Repite* has become a highly influential book within postcolonial studies in both its Spanish and English versions. Drawing on Chaos theory, poststructuralist philosophy and Caribbean history, Benítez-Rojo offers a creolized vision of the Caribbean as simultaneously regional and global, and defined by the perpetual fractal and post-systemic cultural and historical shifts ranging across the archipelago of islands which link the Caribbean region to other times and places. His inspiring sense of the Caribbean as endlessly shape-shifting is reflected in the generic playfulness of his critical writings and his attempts to break down entrenched disciplinary divisions –

between literary criticism and mathematics, or creative writing and cultural critique.

HOMI K. BHABHA (B. 1949) One of the most influential thinkers in postcolonial studies, Homi K. Bhabha was born and raised in Bombay (now Mumbai) and came to England as a graduate student. Influenced by the writings of poststructuralist thinkers such as Jacques Lacan and Jacques Derrida, Bhabha's work often exposes the ambivalence and uncertainty at the heart of seemingly robust, powerful forms of knowledge. His critique of the discourses of colonialism uncovers a perpetual process of fracturing and splitting at their heart as they anxiously seek (but always fail) to secure knowledge about the colonized. His powerful analysis of nations and nationalism (both European and anti-colonial) has exposed their illiberal and coercive aspects, which are thrown into particular relief by the conceptual consequences of the transgressive border-crossings of migrants. Bhabha's sense of the postcolonial is driven by his theoretical commitment to challenging the stability and security of forms of knowledge which install totalizing models of cultural, racial and national purity and diversity, whether they be derived from colonizing nations or anti-colonial modes of resistance. In his major works – especially his edited volume *Nation and Narration* (1990) and his monograph *The Location of Culture* (1994) – he has turned to the liminal, interstitial location of the threshold, between and beyond borders, where the transformative conceptual possibilities of the postcolonial are emerging. Constantly criticized for the alleged obscurity of his written style, and condemned by some for his theoretical dismissal of Marxism and anti-colonial nationalism, Bhabha's writing purposefully confounds and contests the dominant languages of theory and criticism as part of his commitment to the emerging possibilities of postcolonial thought. He is currently Anne F. Rothenberg Professor of English and American Literature and Language at Harvard University, USA.

ERNA BRODBER (B. 1940) Born and raised in Jamaica, Erna May Brodber was educated at the University of the West Indies. She initially worked as a sociologist, and published a number of studies of Jamaican society which dealt with the cultures and circumstances of working-class communities, with particular focus on women and children: *Abandonment of Children in Jamaica* (1974), *A Study of Yards in Kingston* (1975), *Reggae and Cultural Identity in Jamaica* (1981), and *Perceptions of Caribbean Women: towards a documentation of stereotypes* (1982). Her literary works spring from her extensive knowledge of Jamaican culture and society, in both rural and urban environments, which influences the content and form of her creative writings. Her novels *Jane and Louisa Will Soon Come Home* (1980) and *Myal* (1988) draw extensively on Jamaican folklore, ritual, myth, orature and linguistic vernaculars, and can often seem difficult, cryptic or 'experimental' to those unfamiliar with Jamaican cultural norms. For example, *Myal* engages with complex notions of zombification and spirit thievery in its depiction of a rural Jamaican community, Grove Town, seeking to free itself from the confines of colonial education and a neo-colonial world. Brodber's creative commitment to cultural specifics is also evidenced in her novel *Louisiana* (1994), which draws on her collection and knowledge of Jamaican oral histories. Her recent books include *The Continent of Black Consciousness: on the history of the African diaspora from slavery to the present day* (2003) and *The Rainmaker's Mistake* (2007). Erna Brodber is currently Lecturer in Sociology at the University of the West Indies at Mona, Jamaica.

C

PETER CAREY (B. 1943) One of the Australia's most significant writers, Peter Carey was born in Victoria and studied science at Monash University. He has explored the historical and cultural legacies of Australia across a number of superbly written and imaginatively sustained novels, often engaging with several themes key to the region: settlement, identity, forgery, the convict past of European-descended Australians, myths of Australian heroism and criminality. Initially a short-story writer, Carey's early novels examined the expanse of Australian history, as in *Illywhacker* (1985) and *Oscar and Lucinda* (1988). His interest in mythic Australian figures is evidenced in his novels *Jack Maggs* (1997) and *True History of the Kelly Gang* (2001): the former rewrites the figure of Magwitch, the Australian convict figure from Charles Dickens's novel *Great Expectations* (1860–61), while the latter imagines the life of the outlaw Ned Kelly as told in a series of fictional letters. Perhaps due to his interest in how myths of Australia, and Australianness, have been forged from the histories of European settlement and penal servitude, Carey is especially interested in the themes of legitimacy, forgery and hoaxing. The one-hundred-year-old narrator of *Illywhacker* is a confidence trickster, while the novel *My Life as a Fake* (2003) explores the hoax surrounding the 1940s Australian 'poet' Ern Malley, who was in fact the fictional fabrication of two Sydney-based writers. In 1998 Carey was awarded the Commonwealth Writers Prize for *Jack Maggs*, but he provoked controversy by refusing to meet the UK's Queen – an invitation extended to all prize-winners – citing family reasons, although some critics thought his decision was perhaps politically motivated. Peter Carey lives in New York City, USA, and has taught Creative Writing at New York University (NYU).

AIMÉ CÉSAIRE (B. 1913) Born in Martinique, Aimé Césaire studied in 1930s Paris, where he met Léopold Sédar Senghor, a student from Senegal. Energized by the rich intellectual environment of Paris, and motivated by their contempt for the racism of colonial and metropolitan culture, they helped formulate the concept of Négritude. Négritude was an artistic and political project that valued and embraced the virtues of a shared black identity in direct contradistinction to the racist derogation of black cultures and peoples which each had experienced at close quarters. With Léon Damas they created the journal *L'Etudiant Noir* (trans. *The Black Student*), and their endeavours influenced a number of anti-racist movements in Europe and America. In contrast to Senghor, Césaire's understanding of Négritude was not so much indebted to a mystical sense of common black instincts and characteristics rooted in Africa, but rather looked to the experiences of suffering throughout the African diaspora which drew black peoples together. His greatest literary work, the long poem *Cahier d'un retour au pays natal* (trans. *Notebook of a Return to My Native Land*), first published in 1939, explored the sufferings of black peoples in Martinique and Africa, and urged these peoples to forge together and fight against racism and colonialism. Influenced by French surrealism, Césaire's poem was linguistically experimental and innovative, and suggested that a transformation of political fortunes must be matched by a transformation of consciousness and perspective. A major poet and dramatist, his later writings include his anti-colonial polemic *Discours sur le colonialisme* (1955, trans. *Discourse on Colonialism*) and an adaptation of William Shakespeare's play *The Tempest*, titled *Une Tempête* (1968). Césaire has spent much of his life as a political activist, first as a member of the French Communist party and later as the founder of the Parti Progressiste Martiniquais.

PATRICK CHAMOISEAU (B. 1953) Born in Fort-de-France, Martinique, Patrick Chamoiseau studied law at the University of Martinique and later in France. After returning to Martinique he established himself as an innovative and experimental writer, as well as a key figure in the Créolité movement (along with Jean Bernabé and Raphaël Confiant) which is influenced by, but also departs from, the work of Édouard Glissant. His co-authored essay 'Eloge de la créolité' (1989) attends to the linguistic transformation of language in everyday Martinique, and elsewhere, and points to the creative and artistic possibilities made possible by the vernacular histories and languages of such creolizing locations. Much of Chamoiseau's creative writing draws on such creolized cultural forms. His early books include *Chronique des sept misères* (1986) and *Solibo magnifique* (1998), but he came to international recognition with his novel *Texaco* (1992) which won the prestigious Prix Goncourt. Set in Martinique, the novel draws on a dazzling array of linguistic registers as well as local folktales in telling the magical history of a small shanty town near Fort-de-France that is threatened with extinction by the neighbouring oil company. In mixing oral history, myth, vernacular speech and the concerns of contemporary globalization, *Texaco* is, at one level, an attempt to discover a way of writing about Martinique which moves beyond the received cultural norms of France and French colonialism.

J. M. COETZEE (B. 1940) John Maxwell Coetzee was born in South Africa and educated at the University of Cape Town. He pursued his graduate studies in the USA at the University of Texas at Austin, where he wrote a doctoral thesis on the early work of Samuel Beckett. He returned to South Africa in 1972 and taught literature at the University of Cape Town, eventually becoming Professor of General Literature. His career as a novelist began with the publication of *Dusklands* (1974), and he has built a formidable reputation as a writer with novels such as *In the Heart of the Country* (1977), *Waiting for the Barbarians* (1980), *Foe* (1986) and *Disgrace* (1999). Coetzee's work engages with the history of South Africa and the realities of apartheid and its aftermath, but only obliquely so. Perhaps influenced by the experimental writing of Beckett and others, Coetzee's fiction is often formally playful or seemingly displaced from the contemporary world. *Waiting for the Barbarians* explores issues of colonial and cultural power germane to apartheid South Africa, yet the setting is an imaginary colonial outpost at the service of an unnamed empire. *Foe* rewrites Daniel Defoe's *Robinson Crusoe* (1719), often drawing on experimental and meta-fictional forms of storytelling as a way of endgendering postcolonial critique. Coetzee's novel *Disgrace* attracted a great deal of critical attention, in its sobering, controversial engagement with post-apartheid South Africa and the challenges of transition and change. Currently resident in Australia, Coeztee was awarded the Nobel Prize for Literature in 2003.

MARYSE CONDÉ (B. 1934) Maryse Condé was born in Pointe-à-Pitre, Guadeloupe. She was educated in Paris and went on to teach in Guinea, Ghana and Senegal, and later worked in France and the USA. She has described her journey from the Caribbean to Europe and then on to Africa as fundamental to the development of her thinking about race, culture and identity. As a student in France she encountered the realities of metropolitan racism which divided her from white French citizens, while in Africa her emerging sense of belonging to a pan-African black race was challenged by her encounter with the cultural differences of African peoples which contrasted with her Guadeloupean upbringing. Consequently, in her novels she explores the issues of slavery, history, race, colonialism, cultural identity and difference, in looking across the Caribbean, Africa and Europe. These include *Heremakhonon* (1976), a story of a young Caribbean woman who becomes involved with a corrupt African politician; *Ségou* (1984–85), a two-part innovative historical novel which explores the history of the Ségou region (now part of Mali) in the nineteenth century through the narrative of the royal Traore family; and *La migration des coeurs* (1995, trans. *Windward Heights*), a rewriting of Emily Brontë's novel *Wuthering Heights* (1847) set chiefly in Guadeloupe, which ranges across a number of Caribbean locations. One of the Caribbean's major contemporary writers, her work is gradually becoming better known in the English-speaking world through a number of translations. Condé is Emeritus Professor at Columbia University, USA, where she created the Department of Francophone Studies.

D

TSITSI DANGAREMBGA (B. 1959) Tsitsi Dangarembga was born in Mutoko, Rhodesia (now Zimbabwe), and educated in the UK and Rhodesia. Her early writing was for the theatre, but she came to critical attention with her groundbreaking and highly influential novel *Nervous Conditions* (1988). The first novel in English by a black Zimbabwean woman, *Nervous Conditions* takes its title from a phrase used in Jean-Paul Sartre's introduction to Frantz Fanon's *Les Damnés de la Terre* (1961, trans. *The Wretched of the Earth*). It explores retrospectively the efforts of a young girl, Tambudzai (Tambu) Sigauke, to attain education, self-determination and independence in the patriarchal realm of late-colonial Rhodesia, a country struggling to cope with the tensions created between tradition and transition. The novel also concerns the story of her cousin, Nyasha, whose anorexia comes to be linked in the novel to wider problems of identity, gender, tradition and patriarchy which particularly confront the lives of women. In 2006 Dangarembga published a sequel, *The Book of Not*, which follows Tambu's young life amid the Zimbabwean conflicts of the 1970s. In addition to her novels, Dangarembga is an accomplished filmmaker: she studied film in Berlin, Germany, where she lived throughout the 1990s. Her films include *Neria* (1993) *Everyone's Child* (1996) and *Kare Kare Zvako* (2004). Tsitsi Dangarembga lives in Zimababwe, where she runs a production company called Nyerai Films with her husband.

JACQUES DERRIDA (1930–2004) For much of his life, Jacques Derrida was considered perhaps the most important figure in French philosophy and critical theory, and often associated with the emergence of poststructuralism and its deconstructive modes of thought. In recent years, however, he has been reconsidered and understood as a specifically *postcolonial* thinker, whose paradigm-changing critique of western philosophy and modernity was fundamentally resourced by his particular cultural circumstances. He was born Jackie Derrida in El-Biar, Algeria, to a Jewish family. His education was interrupted in 1941 when he was expelled from his local school due to the anti-Semitic activities of the Vichy Government; yet he persevered with his studies and eventually entered Paris's École Normale Supérieure in 1952, where he met Louis Althusser and Michel Foucault. Derrida came to international prominence in the late 1960s with major works such as *De la grammatologie* (1967, trans. *Of Grammatology*) and *L'Ecriture et la différence* (1967, trans. *Writing And Difference*). In these works and others, Derrida explored the ways in which attempts to secure stable meaning and knowledge are inevitably undercut by the brigandly instability of language which renders all semantic hierarchies precarious and unsustainable. Such ideas have proved enormously influential for fellow postcolonial thinkers such as Homi K. Bhabha, Gayatri Chakravorty Spivak, and Edward W. Said, who have taken Derrida's deconstruction of western philosophy and metaphysics into the particular realms of colonial history, politics and discourse, and also the new critical languages and ethical aims of postcolonial critique. Among Derrida's later works are *Spectres de Marx* (1993, trans. *Spectres of Marx*), *De l'hospitalité* (1997, trans. *Of Hospitality*) and *Cosmopolites des tous les pays, encore un effort!* (1997, trans. *On Cosmopolitanism and Forgiveness*), within which he engages with a series of political and ethical issues – the reception and treatment of strangers, pain and its forgiveness, altruism and responsibility, the vision of ideology, refugees and asylum – which are proving highly influential in emerging work in postcolonial studies. Derrida died in Paris, aged 74, from pancreatic cancer.

ANITA DESAI (B. 1937) Born Anita Mazumdar in Mussoorie, India, to a German mother and Bengali father, Anita Desai was educated at Delhi University. Her first novel, *Cry, the Peacock*, was published in 1963, and her subsequent works include *Fire on the Mountain* (1977), *Clear Light of Day* (1980), *In Custody* (1984), *Baumgartner's Bombay* (1984), *Journey to Ithaca* (1995) and *Fasting,* *Feasting* (1999). Predominantly set in India, her writing explores the lives of women and their struggle for identity within the confines – both personal and political – of family, nation, history, and culture. One of her finest novels, *Clear Light of Day*, depicts two sisters forced to remember their earlier lives and the disintegration of their family in Delhi at the time of the communal troubles of India in 1947, as independence and Partition reshaped cultural and national relationships. Like most of her writing, the novel is formally complex and influenced by early twentieth-century writing in English in its intricate constellation of time, place and memory, and its complex symbolism. Desai has been considered by some as a writer of often sombre stories, but she has responded by arguing that her works eschew illusion and attempt to portray truth. She has recently contributed to the Program in Writing and Humanistic Studies at the Massachusetts Institute of Technology, USA.

F

FRANTZ FANON (1925–61) Born in Martinique, Frantz Fanon studied medicine and psychiatry in Lyon, France, and worked initially as a psychiatrist. His early writing brought together his experiences of colonialism with his psychiatric training, as he investigated the torturous psychological effects of colonization and racism on colonized peoples. In *Peau noire, masques blancs* (1952, trans. *Black Skin, White Masks*), Fanon powerfully exposes and critiques the invidious process whereby the colonized come to regard themselves as 'other', not fully human, and opens up the beginnings of a philosophical and existential critique of European humanism which would subsequently prove influential for a wealth of writers and thinkers. In 1953 Fanon joined the staff of Blida-Joinville Psychiatric Hospital in Algeria, and became involved in the Algerian struggle for independence from French rule. Expelled from Algeria in 1957 by the French, Fanon spent much of the rest of his life travelling across Africa and contributing to the anti-colonial and independence initiatives in Algeria, Tunis, Ghana and elsewhere. His collection of essays *Les Damnés de la Terre* (1961, trans. *The Wretched of the Earth*) stems from this period, and explores the operations of anti-colonial violence, the problems of Pan-Africanism, the pitfalls of national consciousness, and much besides. It was completed in the year that Fanon died from leukaemia in the USA where he was receiving treatment for his illness. His body was subsequently buried in Algeria. Fanon's influence remains profound across a range of contemporary contexts – from anti-colonial nationalism to theories of subjectivity – and his work is frequently cited, almost always approvingly, throughout the field of postcolonial studies. At times Fanon's significance as an intellectual and thinker has tended to obscure his political activism, and his work has often been cheerfully disconnected by some from the contexts of Algeria and the anti-colonial struggle, to the chagrin of certain critics.

ROBERTO FERNÁNDEZ RETAMAR (B. 1930) Born in Havana, Roberto Fernández Retamar is one of Cuba's leading intellectual figures, and has enjoyed a distinguished career as a poet, activist, critic and cultural worker. He studied in Havana, London and Paris, and has spent most of his life supporting the literary and cultural scene in Cuba. In 1964 he founded the National Writers and Artists Union of Cuba (UNEAC), and he is President of the Casa de las Américas, an organization created and based in Cuba which stimulates and forges links between cultural endeavours in Latin America and the Caribbean. His substantial body of poetry includes *Elegía como un himno* (1950), *Patrias* (1952), *Buena suerte viviendo* (1967), *Juana y otros temas personales* (1981), and *Aquí* (1995). His 1971 essay 'Calibán: apuntes sobre la cultura de nuestra América' (trans. 'Caliban: Notes Toward a Discussion of Culture in Our America') is an important exploration of the cultural predicament of Latin American and Caribbean peoples which has influenced a number of writers across the different nations and languages of the Americas.

BRIAN FRIEL (B. 1929) Born in Omagh, County Tyrone, in Northern Ireland, Brian Friel was initially a short-story writer but established himself in the 1960s as a playwright. In 1980 he co-founded the Field Day Theatre Company with the actor Stephen Rea, and later collaborated with the writers Seamus Deane, David Hammond, Seamus Heaney and Tom Paulin to form the Field Day Project. The primary aim of Field Day is the cultural critique of the divisions, armed hostilities and prejudices which have marred Northern Ireland's recent history, especially during the period known as the 'Troubles'. In 1980 the Field Day Theatre Company produced Friel's most famous and influential play, *Translations*. Set in 1833 in the Irish village of Baile Beag, County Donegal, the play explores the arrival of the first British Royal Ordnance Survey which is responsible for translating the local Gaelic place-names into English. The play charts the effect of the British presence, both socially and culturally, on the villagers – many of whom are studying at a local hedge school – while raising questions about language, identity, power, colonial control and anti-colonial resistance which are germane both to the play's early nineteenth-century setting and 1980s Ireland. His other major plays include *Making History* (1988), which concerns the infamous 'flight of the earls' from seventeenth-century Ireland that paved the way for the colonial plantation of Ulster, and *Dancing at Lughnasa* (1990), set in Baile Beag in the early twentieth century. Brian Friel lives in Donegal.

G

AMITAV GHOSH (B. 1956) Born in Calcutta, Amitav Ghosh was educated at Delhi University, India, and achieved a PhD in social anthropology from Oxford University, UK. His first novel, *The Circle of Reason*, was published in 1986, and was followed by *The Shadow Lines* (1988), *The Calcutta Chromosome* (1996), *The Glass Palace* (2000) and *The Hungry Tide* (2004). Ghosh's novels, both individually and as a body of work, range across South and East Asia – Bengal, Burma, India and elsewhere – and are often concerned with the endangered peoples, cultures and histories of the region who have suffered under European colonialism and its contemporary neocolonial antecedents. Yet his work is restlessly inventive and delightfully difficult to summarize collectively (*The Calcutta Chromosome* won the 1996 Arthur C. Clark award for Science Fiction). Ghosh is also a significant non-fictional writer. His book *In An Antique Land* (1992) draws on his doctoral studies as a social anthropologist and his experiences while living among local peoples in the Nile Delta in Egypt, while *Countdown* (1999) engages with the nuclear arms policies of India and Pakistan. In 2001 Ghosh controversially withdrew *The Glass Palace* from being considered as overall winner by the judges of the Commonwealth Writers Prize (it had already been declared winner of the Eurasian section of the prize) in protest against the legitimacy of the term 'Commonwealth Literature'. He currently lives in Brooklyn in the USA.

PAUL GILROY (B. 1956) The London-born son of the Guyanese writer Beryl Gilroy, Paul Gilroy's work ranges across black British cultural studies, the history of race, racism and resistance, black American culture, and more besides. An enduring critic of the protean, enduring operations of race in contemporary culture, he has written on the cultural significance of political advertisements, Snoop Dog music videos, the comedy of Sasha Baron Cohen, the art of LP sleeves, the creative wit of British rapper The Streets, the British boxer Frank Bruno and the intellectual legacies of W. E. B. Du Bois. His early work, *'There Ain't No Black in the Union Jack': the cultural politics of race and nation* (1987), explored the politics of race in postwar Britain while attempting to depart from some influential cultural materialist thinking which appeared ill-equipped to cope with the complexity and uniqueness of race, both socially and conceptually. His most influential book is *The Black Atlantic: modernity and double-consciousness* (1993), which explores the itinerant nature of the black diaspora in the Americas and Europe as a way of challenging the nationalist mode of much anti-colonial and anti-racist thought. Against the solidarities of race and nationalism, Gilroy turns to the itinerant journeys made by black people across the Atlantic over many centuries as suggesting new ways of thinking of black cultures as constantly in motion, shifting and changing, as ideas and resources in one location become rerouted in another. In his later work – such as *Between Camps: race, identity and nationalism at the end of the colour line* (2000) and *After Empire: melancholia or convivial culture?* (2004) – Gilroy has extended his formidable critique of the practices of nationalism, race, racism and racialization, while pointing out their worrying re-emergence since 9/11. Underwriting much of Gilroy's thinking is a faith in the progressive political and cultural possibilities of young people, and their convivial, informal and multicultural daily encounters which stubbornly oppose the activities of racism and nationalism. Gilroy is currently Anthony Giddens Professor in Social Theory at the London School of Economics, UK.

ÉDOUARD GLISSANT (B. 1928) Born in Sainte-Marie, Martinique, Édouard Glissant is a significant novelist, poet, essayist and philosopher whose work often takes as its inspiration the creolizing cultures of the francophone Caribbean as the means of reconceptualizing notions of pan-Caribbean art and identities. Glissant's work has sought new languages for, and conceptualizations of, the francophone Caribbean which move beyond the axioms of French colonial culture, the marginalized speech of French Creole and the nostalgic Afrocentrism of Négritude and other such movements. Rather than invest in unifying, singular and totalizing notions of a culture, or language, or homeland, Glissant sees in the creolizing and hybridizing realities of the Caribbean immense cultural and intellectual possibilities. In works such as *Poétique de la Relation* (1980, trans. *Poetics of Relation*), he has argued for relational models of language and identity which always recognize the diverse and multiple cultural fragments which make up the modern Caribbean; while the essays collected in *Le discours antillais* (1981, trans. *Caribbean Discourses*) repeatedly emphasize the variety, heterogeneity and protean instability of Martinique and the Caribbean as part of Glissant's attempt to set free new, radical ways of thinking. Glissant's advocacy of what has subsequently come to be known

as Creolité can also be traced in his works of poetry and fiction, which include *L'Intention poétique* (1969), *Mahagony* (1987) and *Ormérod* (2003). Glissant was recently Distinguished Professor of French at City University of New York, Graduate Center, USA.

NADINE GORDIMER (B. 1923) Born to an English mother and Lithuanian father near Johannesburg, South Africa, Nadine Gordimer studied briefly at the University of Witwatersrand and began writing at a young age. Her first collection of short stories, *Face to Face*, appeared in 1949, while her debut novel, *The Lying Days*, appeared in 1953. She has subsequently worked in these two genres, and has acquired a reputation as one of South Africa's most gifted and insightful writers. Her major works include the novels *The Conservationist* (1974), *July's People* (1981), *My Son's Story* (1990), *The House Gun* (1998) and *The Pickup* (2001). Gordimer has explored the racial and cultural challenges of South Africa from its apartheid days through to the period of transition to democracy, often through a series of probing portraits of intimate family life and relationships which are frequently intertwined with South Africa's political problems. In *July's People* a white South African family flees the political turmoil in Soweto and comes to live with their house-boy, July, in his village (the novel was initially banned in apartheid South Africa). *My Son's Story* concerns an affair between a black male activist school-teacher and a white female human rights worker, and the difficulties – both personal and political – it evokes. Gordimer's focus on such issues is mediated with an expert command of style and form, and she is particularly adept in creating unique and penetrating narrative voices. She was awarded the Nobel Prize for Literature in 1991.

PATRICIA GRACE (B. 1937) Patricia Grace was born and raised in Wellington, Aotearoa New Zealand, the daughter of a Pakeha (European-descended) mother and Maori father. She initially worked as a teacher while raising a family, and began to write in English about the experiences and lives of Maori peoples. She emerged in the 1970s as an important figure in a groundbreaking literary generation of Maori writers in English, which also included Witi Ihimaera and Hone Tuwhare. Grace's book of short stories, *Waiariki* (1976), was the first collection by a woman Maori writer, and was followed by the novels *Mutuwhenua* (1978) and *Potiki* (1986). Mixing English and Maori languages, and drawing on the cultural resources of Grace's Maori ancestry, *Potiki* explores the survival and fortunes of Maori peoples in Aotearoa New Zealand, especially regarding the vexed issue of land rights. Her other works include *The Sky People* (1984) and the novel *Baby No-Eyes* (1998). Grace's writing generally explores the recurring matters of land, genealogy and identity, the lives of women, the challenges of biculturalism, and the problems of abuse within the family. She is especially interested in the lives and perspectives of children, and she has also written specifically for children. A recipient of several prizes in Aotearoa New Zealand, Grace lives in Plimmerton on the ancestral land of Ngati Toa, Ngati Raukawa and Te Atiawa, near to her marae at Hongoeka Bay.

H

STUART HALL (B. 1932)   Born in Kingston, Jamaica, Stuart Hall migrated to the UK in 1952, and was educated at Merton College, Oxford University. With others such as E. P. Thompson and Raymond Williams, he helped to establish cultural studies as a field of academic enquiry in postwar Britain, and was active in the influential Centre for Contemporary Cultural Studies (CCCS) at Birmingham University, UK, which he joined in 1964. Much of Hall's work has drawn on developments in Marxist and leftist intellectual thinking in opening up ways of reading popular culture in relation to wider issues of power, hegemony and resistance. As Hall has argued, culture is always formative, rather than merely reflective, of social and political engagements and struggles; in both studying and practising culture, we acquire the agency to contest and transform the predominant, hegemonic structures of knowledge and feeling which seek to direct social and cultural life. Hall's significance extends across a range of fields; yet he is of particular interest to postcolonial studies for his work on race, resistance, diaspora and ethnicity. In essays such as 'New Ethnicities' (1988) he explores the politics of representation both of, and by, black writers and filmmakers, and the ways in which identity is being reconceptualized; while his essay 'Cultural Identity and Diaspora' (1990) mobilizes poststructuralist critical theories to fashion a way of reconceptualizing diaspora identities as perpetual processes of unfinished becoming. His essay 'When Was "the Post-Colonial"?: thinking at the limit' (1996) is perhaps one of the most readable and intelligent critiques of debates within postcolonial studies. A committed public intellectual, Stuart Hall worked for many years as Professor of Sociology at the Open University, UK, until his retirement in 1997.

SEAMUS HEANEY (B. 1939)   The eldest son of a rural Irish family, Seamus Heaney was raised in County Derry, Northern Ireland, and educated in Derry city and Belfast, where he studied literature, Irish, Latin and Old English languages. He began to write poetry in the 1960s and, on the strength of collections like *Death of a Naturalist* (1966), he was initially regarded as part of a new generation of 'Northern School' Irish poets. Heaney's poetry ranges across his rural Irish upbringing, the ancient myths and modern history of Ireland, and the 'Troubles' in Northern Ireland in the late twentieth century. His 1975 collection *North* contains his well-known 'bog poems' – such as 'Bog Queen', 'The Grauballe Man', 'Punishment' and 'Strange Fruit' – in which Heaney uses the discovery and exhumation in Jutland of the bodies of ritually-killed people to provoke images of, and questions about, terrorism and the paramilitary operations within contemporary Northern Ireland's divided communities. Although Heaney was raised in a Catholic, Nationalist family, his writing has sought to move beyond the bitter divisions between Nationalist and Unionist communities in Northern Ireland and, significantly, he joined the Field Day Project (founded in 1980 by the playwright Brian Friel and actor Stephen Rea) which attempted to proffer a cultural critique of the 'Troubles' which did not merely take sides. In Heaney's later collections, such as *Station Island* (1984) and *Seeing Things* (1991), we discover a deeply contemplative lyric consciousness, beloved of classical allusions, which is never far from figuring the ongoing political problems of the contemporary world – powerfully evidenced in his 2006 collection, *District and Circle*, which takes its title from London Underground's train lines, two of which (the Circle and Piccadilly lines) were bombed by terrorists on 7 July 2005. Heaney is also a significant translator, dramatist and essayist: his notable collections of essays include *The Government of the Tongue* (1988) and *The Redress of Poetry* (1995). In 1995 he was awarded the Nobel Prize for Literature.

K

JAMAICA KINCAID (B. 1949) Elaine Cynthia Potter Richardson was born and raised in Antigua. She migrated to New York City as a seventeen-year-old to work as an au pair (she changed her name to Jamaica Kincaid in 1973). She began to write for the *New Yorker* and published her first book of stories, *At the Bottom of the River*, in 1983. Short in length, often symbolically cryptic, and written in a seemingly unambiguous and unspectacular fashion, her early stories anticipated her later compelling fictional style. Her first novel, *Annie John* (1985), explores the life of a young girl growing up in Antigua and struggling with the tribulations of gender, family, education and impending adulthood, while *Lucy* (1990) depicts a young au pair in the USA struggling to fashion an identity for herself. The themes of family and motherhood rebound throughout her work, as in the novels *An Autobiography of My Mother* (1996) and *My Brother* (1997), while she is also the author of a non-fictional work about Antigua, *A Small Place* (1988), which is vituperative towards her anglophone colonial education, Antiguan political corruption, and the neo-colonial operations of contemporary global tourism. Kincaid teaches creative writing at Harvard University, USA, and cites among her passions gardening and the garden in literature (her book *My Garden* was published in 2001).

M

DAVID MALOUF (B. 1934) Born in Brisbane, Australia, to a Lebanese-descended father and English-Jewish mother of Portuguese ancestry, David Malouf was educated at the University of Queensland. He lived and worked in the UK during most of the 1960s and returned to Australia to settle in Sydney in 1968. He has written poetry, memoirs and short stories, and is best-known for his penetrating and finely-written novels. His writing takes the fortunes of Australia and its conflicts as its major themes, and often looks back across Australia's history. His first novel, *Johnno* (1975), is set in Brisbane during the 1940s against the backdrop of the Second World War, while *The Great World* (1990) tells of the imprisonment of two Australians by the Japanese during the Second World War. *Remembering Babylon* (1993) is set in the 1850s and explores a number of issues surrounding European settlement in its depiction of Gemmy Fairley, a thirteen-year-old English boy cast ashore in the far north of Australia and taken in by Aborigines, with whom he lives for sixteen years before attempting to re-enter colonial society. The novel won the inaugural International IMPAC Dublin Literary Award in 1996. His other works include *The Conversations at Curlow Creek* (1996) and *Fly Away Peter* (1999).

MUDROOROO (B. 1938) Born as Colin Johnson in Western Australia, Mudrooroo is an important if controversial figure in Australian literature, not least due to his association with the country's Aboriginal peoples. He spent several of his childhood years in welfare institutions, including an orphanage, and was later imprisoned for robbery and assault. His first novel, *Wild Cat Falling*, was published in 1965, after which he travelled in South East Asia (where he studied Buddhism) and Europe, before returning to settle in Australia. His subsequent novels include *Long Live Sandawarra* (1979), *Dr Wooreddy's Prescription for Enduring the Ending of the World* (1983), *The Kwinkan* (1993) and *Underground* (1998). Seen by many as a crucial figure in the emergence of Aboriginal literature in English – he changed his name to Mudrooroo in 1988 – his advocacy of Aboriginal arts and his self-declared Aboriginal identity are complicated by his ancestry, which some claim has nothing to do with Australia's Aboriginal peoples. In writing about and supporting Aboriginal peoples in opposition to the norms of Australian settler cultures, Mudrooroo's life and work raise difficult questions about Aboriginality as a genetic, racial, cultural, political or experiential form of identity, and the assumptions which underwrite these different models. His work has embraced (and is often shaped with recourse to) Aboriginal cultural forms, and has explored the genocidal practices of colonialism from something like an Aboriginal position, as evidenced by his remarkable novel *Dr Wooreddy* . . . which tells of the murderous colonization of Tasmania. In 2003 Mudrooroo left Australia and now lives in Nepal with his wife and son.

N

V. S. NAIPAUL (B. 1932) Born into a family of Indian descent, Vidiadhar Surajprasad Naipaul was raised in the village of Chaguanas, Trinidad, and later Port of Spain. In 1950 he won a scholarship to study at a British university and he elected to read English at University College, Oxford, UK. Naipaul settled in London after graduating and began to write about his early life in Trinidad. His early fiction depicted Trinidadian life from a satirical yet affectionate perspective, as epitomized by *A House for Mr Biswas* (1961), the novel which secured his reputation. In the 1960s Naipaul's satirical attitudes hardened somewhat, and in novels such as *The Mimic Men* (1967) and *Guerillas* (1975) he wrote in often unflattering, uncompromising terms about the inequities of life in the erstwhile British colonies, as well as the (as he saw it) despair and futility of the political and emotional lives of colonial peoples. In later years, Naipaul has come to reflect more self-consciously and sympathetically on his central themes of colonial dispossession and emotional and political bankruptcy, as evidenced by perhaps his finest novel, *The Enigma of Arrival* (1987), although his substantial body of travel writing remains unforgiving, as evidenced by his depictions of Arab and Islamic countries in *Among the Believers* (1981) and *Beyond Belief* (1998). Unsurprisingly, Naipaul is no stranger to criticism, especially from postcolonial writers and critics. But too few remember that he has written in depth and with remarkable sensitivity about the pain of growing up as a 'colonial', and of the challenge of trying to write about places such as Trinidad in a metropolitan literary tradition which never afforded the space or opportunity to think creatively about such locations. Among Naipaul's many awards are a Knighthood in 1990 and, in 2001, the Nobel Prize for Literature.

NGUGI WA THIONG'O (B. 1938) Born in Kamarithu, Kenya, and initially christened James Ngugi, the writer Ngugi wa Thiong'o was educated at Makarere University College, Uganda, and later at the University of Leeds, UK. He began writing fiction in English during the 1960s. In novels such as *The River Between* (1965) and *A Grain of Wheat* (1967) he explored life during the anti-colonial Mau Mau rebellion (1952–60) and examined critically the fortunes of Kenya since achieving independence in 1963. Perhaps his most important literary decision was to renounce his anglophone education, change his name and give up writing in English in favour of his native Gikuyu – a decision which provoked a famous debate with the Nigerian writer Chinua Achebe as to the possibilities and problems of writing fiction in the language of the British colonialists. In 1977 Ngugi was detained by the Kenyan authorities who did not take kindly to his play *Ngaahika Ndeenda* (trans. *I Will Marry When I Want*), and while in prison he wrote *Caitaani mūtharaba-Inī* (1980, trans. *Devil on the Cross*). He was released in 1978 but suffered intimidation for several years, and he eventually left Kenya for London in 1982, and later the USA. While in exile he produced a number of essays, plays and novels, including his important collection *Decolonising the*

Mind: the politics of language in African literature (1986) and his novel *Matigari* (1987). In 2004 Ngugi returned to Kenya for the first time in twenty-two years to a joyous welcome. A few days after his arrival he was brutally attacked in his apartment by intruders, and his wife was raped. Their attempts to bring the perpetrators to justice remain ongoing. Ngugi continues to live in the USA, and he is Professor of English and Comparative literature at the University of California at Irvine. His most recent novel is *Wizard of the Crow* (2006), which he translated from Gikuyu to English.

MICHAEL ONDAATJE (B. 1943) Born in Sri Lanka, Michael Ondaatje migrated to Canada (via England) where he established a career as a writer. He has written both poetry and fiction, although his work is characterized by its formally innovative style, and persistently challenges the generic boundaries of each. In books such as *The Collected Works of Billy the Kid: left handed poems* (1981) he combines creative writing, photographs, extracts from historical documents and other materials, in order to tell the story of Billy the Kid through a creative literary style – between and beyond fiction and poetry – which emphasizes melange, hybridity and collage. His novels *In the Skin of a Lion* (1987) and *The English Patient* (1992) also subvert linear narrative forms, in favour of a lyrical literary style which constellates a variety of different scenes and moments more redolent of poetry. For some, Ondaatje's frequently elegant and poignant literary voice reflects his life as a migrant and his experiences of itinerancy, displacement and dislocation. The focus of his work shifts restlessly back and forth across the history of Canada, war in Europe (notably in *The English Patient*) and the Sri Lanka of his birth – the latter is explored in his memoir *Running in the Family* (1983) and his novel *Anil's Ghost* (2000). Ondaatje has also done much to stimulate Canadian literary culture, chiefly through his editorial work for *Brick*, a journal of new writing.

P

CARYL PHILLIPS (B. 1958) Caryl Phillips came to the UK from St Kitts while only a few weeks old, and was raised in the northern English city of Leeds. After graduating from Queens College, Oxford, in 1979, he worked initially as a playwright. In 1985 he published his first novel, *The Final Passage*, and has since secured an international reputation as one of the world's leading novelists with his subsequent fiction: *A State of Independence* (1986), *Higher Ground* (1989), *Cambridge* (1991), *Crossing the River* (1993), *The Nature of Blood* (1997), *A Distant Shore* (2003) and *Dancing in Dark* (2005). Phillips's prose writing, notable for its innovative formal qualities and hauntingly still prose style, ranges across the cultural and racial legacies of colonialism in Africa, the Caribbean, Britain, America and beyond. In tracing the cat's cradle of connections which binds us all to the sordid histories of empire, Phillips explores the derogation of human life by racism and prejudice while constantly looking beyond these divisive encounters to a post-racial, ethically just future. In a similar vein, his non-fiction includes a meditation on the theme of home across several continents in *The Atlantic Sound* (2000), a collection of essays *A New World Order* (2001), and *Foreigners: three English lives* (2007). Previously Professor of Migration and Social Order at Barnard College, Columbia University, Phillips is currently Professor of English at Yale University, USA.

R

SALMAN RUSHDIE (B. 1947) Salman Rushdie was raised in Bombay (now Mumbai), India, and migrated to Britain in 1961. In 1968 he graduated from Kings College, Cambridge, where he read History, and he was initially employed as an advertising copywriter. His first novel, *Grimus* (1975), was a critical and commercial flop; his next, *Midnight's Children* (1981), earned him international admiration. His subsequent novels are *Shame* (1983), *The Satanic Verses* (1988), *Haroun and the Sea of Stories* (1990), *The Moor's Last Sigh* (1995), *The Ground Beneath Her Feet* (1999), *Fury* (2001) and *Shalimar the Clown* (2005). The publication of *The Satanic Verses* became a notorious international incident. Initially denounced by the Muslim community of Bradford, UK, as a work of blasphemy, the novel came to be banned in South Africa, India and Pakistan. On 14 February 1989, the Aya- tollah Khomeini, Iran's spiritual leader, decreed a *fatwa* which effectively sentenced Rushdie to death for blasphemy. Rushdie spent many years in hiding, and today lives in New York City. His work is characterized by an exhaustingly energetic, culturally kaleidoscopic and formally imaginative literary style, which expresses something of Rushdie's hybridizing experiences as a migrant writer who moves between cultures, continents and languages. A lover of cities, he has written dynamically about the Bombay of his birth, London and New York City; while he remains a staunch critic of the political failures of the South Asian subcontinent since decolonization and Partition, and (as in *Shalimar the Clown*) has written powerfully about the threat of global terrorism which has dogged his life since 1989 and has since come to define the new world order of the twenty-first century.

S

NAYANTARA SAHGAL (B. 1927) Nayantara Sahgal was born and raised in India. Throughout her life she has had close connections with India's anti-colonial elite: her mother, Vijaya Lakshmi Nehru Pandit, was the sister of the first Indian Prime Minister, Jawaharlal Nehru; her father was Ranjit Sitaram Pandit, a successful barrister and scholar, and supporter of India's pro-independence Congress Party (he died in prison in 1944). Sahgal's first cousin, Indira Gandhi, would become Prime Minister in 1966. Sahgal's writing has often taken the fortunes of India's politicians and social elite as its subject, in both non-fictional and literary modes, yet she has remained a firm critic of the corruption and hypocrisy of government and industry, often from a feminist perspective, and a supporter of civil liberties. Her non-fictional works – which include *Prison and Chocolate Cake* (1954), *From Fear Set Free* (1962), *Indira Gandhi's Emergence and Style* (1978), and *Indira Gandhi: her road to power* (1982) – range from memoir and autobiography to compelling political and historical critique. Her many novels include *Storm in Chandigarh* (1969), *Rich Like Us* (1985), *Plans For Departure* (1986), *Mistaken Identity* (1988) and *Lesser Breeds* (2003), and range across twentieth-century Indian history: *Plans for Departure* depicts the lives of a small European community in a Himalayan hill station in 1914, while *Rich Like Us* soberingly dissects the excesses and hypocrisy of the Indian elite during Indira Gandhi's 'Emergency', when democratic government was suspended between 1975–77. Sahgal lives in Dehadun, India.

EDWARD W. SAID (1935–2003) For many, the discipline of postcolonial studies begins with the publication of Edward W. Said's *Orientalism* (1978), although the range of his work is impossible to totalize under one convenient heading. Born in Jerusalem (which, in 1935, was part of the British Mandate of Palestine), Said spent his early years between Jerusalem and Cairo, and pursued his graduate studies in the USA. He spent much of his professional life as Professor of English and Comparative Literature at Columbia University, USA. A lifelong lover of literature and music, his initial work explored the relationship between culture and society, under the increasing influence of the poststructuralist thought of Jacques Derrida and Michel Foucault. In *Orientalism*, Said explored how the cultural endeavours of the European empires helped to project and secure 'the Orient', a fantastical Foucauldian figment of the colonizing imagination which bore little resemblance to any reality which existed (in this case) in the Middle East, but which nonetheless came to justify the European colonial conquest of such lands. In his later work *Culture and Imperialism* (1993), he explored how canonical European art was both complicit in and contested colonial attitudes, and he explored the resistance endeavours of the once-colonized world. Said maintained an enduring commitment to the fortunes of the Arab world and Palestinian freedom – although he could be highly critical of certain attitudes within Palestinian liberation organizations – and wrote powerfully about Palestine in *The Question of Palestine*

(1979) and *After the Last Sky: Palestinian lives* (1986). Unsurprisingly, Said's life was seldom free from controversy, and at times he was subject to hostility from Islamic and Jewish critics alike. That said, his powerful critique of the derogatory ways in which the West continues to represent Islam and Islamic cultures has acquired extra significance in the wake of 9/11. Said's valuable self-reflections on exile, and his love of music and literature, preoccupied his late works. He died from leukaemia in New York City, aged 67.

Ousmane Sembene (b. 1923) Born in 1923 in Casamance, southern Senegal, Ousmane Sembene is one of Africa's most important and admired writers and filmmakers. Expelled from school as young boy, he spent his early years in Dakar and worked as an apprentice mechanic and bricklayer. After seeing action in the Second World War, he moved to the French city of Marseilles (until 1960, when he returned to Senegal) and became active in workers' politics and the trade union movement, eventually joining the Communist party. His first novel, *Le docker noir* (1956, trans. *Black Docker*), drew on these experiences in its depiction of the lives of African workers in Marseilles. His subsequent important works engage with the fortunes of Senegal during and after independence from French colonialism, and include *Les bouts de bois de Dieu* (1960, trans. *God's Bits of Wood*), *Xala* (1973) and *Le dernier de l'Empire* (1981, trans. *The Last of the Empire*). Sembene's films also deal closely with the political and social fortunes of sub-Saharan Africa in the wake of empire, and have helped to establish postcolonial African cinema. *La noir de ...* (1966) concerns the difficult experiences of a Senegalese maid who is taken to work in France. *Xala* (1974), based on Sembene's novel of the same name, offers a satirical critique of the pitfalls of post-independence Senegal in its depiction of a cursed businessman seeking to cure his impotence. More recently, Sembene has critically explored the ritual practice of female circumcision in his film *Moolaade* (2004). In 2005 he received the Spirit of Saint-Louis Prize awarded by Washington-based Human Rights Watch Group.

Léopold Sédar Senghor (1906–2001) Born in the French colony of Senegal, Léopold Sédar Senghor was educated in 1930s France, where he joined with his friends Aimé Césaire and Léon Damas in setting up the journal *L'Etudiant Noir* (trans. *The Black Student*), an important instrument in the Négritude movement with which Senghor was centrally involved. A poet and politician, Senghor wrote against the racist and colonial imperatives of metropolitan France, often fuelled by his engagement with and commitment to socialism. During the Second World War he was interned by the German military as a member of the French army. In 1948 he published an influential anthology of poetry, *Anthologie de la nouvelle poésie nègre et malgache de langue français*, which included Jean-Paul Sartre's famous essay 'Orphée Noir' (trans. 'Black Orpheus') as its introduction. He became centrally involved in Senegalese politics, and in 1960 was elected the first President of Senegal when independence was achieved that year (he remained in office until 1980). He continued to write poetry throughout his life, and in 1978 was awarded the prestigious Prix mondial Cino Del Duca.

Vikram Seth (b. 1952) Vikram Seth was born in Calcutta and educated in the UK, the USA and China. He is a poet, travel writer and novelist, fluent in several languages, whose stylish books reflect his remarkable depth of knowledge regarding the cultures of Europe, and South and East Asia. His fictional career began with

The Golden Gate: a novel in verse (1986), set in California. Formally challenging and highly disciplined – the narrative proceeds through rhyming tetrameter sonnets – it suggests much of Seth's literary ambition and prodigious learning; indeed, most of his writing springs from his deep understanding and commitment to literary form. His next novel, *A Suitable Boy* (1993) engaged with the nineteenth-century English novel in both its scope and design. At a total of 1349 pages in length, it depicts the fortunes of four families during the immediate aftermath of independence and Partition in India, running up to the national election of 1952. Seth's fictional style echoes the elegant, patient writing of Nayantara Sahgal and Anita Desai, and deliberately draws on the work of George Eliot and Leo Tolstoy. In his third novel, *An Equal Music* (1999), he mobilizes his extensive knowledge of music in the story of two musicians; once again, the written style is disciplined and undemonstrative. Seth's non-fiction includes *From Heaven Lake: travels through Sinkiang and Tibet* (1983) and *Two Lives* (2005), a memoir of his great uncle and great aunt who met in Berlin in the 1930s. Seth lives in the UK and India.

WOLE SOYINKA (B. 1934) Akinwande Oluwole Soyinka was born in Abeokuta, in western Nigeria, and educated at the Government College in Ibadan and the University of Leeds, UK. A major figure in African theatre, Soyinka's dramatic works often reveal European and Yoruba cultural influences in depicting the fortunes and beliefs of the Yoruba peoples in Nigeria, in plays such as *A Dance of the Forests* (1960), *The Swamp Dwellers* (1961), *The Road* (1965), *Death and the King's Horsemen* (1976) and *The Beatification of Area Boy* (1995). Throughout his career he has remained engaged in the political and social conflicts in Nigeria, and has used his writing to comment on,

and often satirize, the workings of government and political leadership in the region – indeed, he was imprisoned between 1967–69 when Nigeria suffered a civil war, and subsequently recorded the experience in *The Man Died: the prison notes of Wole Soyinka* (1972). He is also a prose writer of significance: his challenging novel *The Interpreters* (1965) satirizes the middle-class intelligentsia of newly-independent Nigeria, while *Aké: the years of childhood* (1981) is an illuminating memoir of his early life. His book of essays *Myth, Literature and the African World* was published in 1976 and is well-known for its critique of the philosophy of Négritude expounded by the then President of Senegal, Léopold Sédar Senghor. Soyinka was awarded the Nobel Prize for Literature in 1986.

GAYATRI CHAKRAVORTY SPIVAK (B. 1942) Perhaps the most formidable of all post-colonial thinkers, Gayatri Chakravorty Spivak was born and educated in Calcutta, India, and pursued her graduate studies in the USA. A prolific and continuously brilliant critic, Spivak's work is influenced by and committed to the critical endeavours of deconstruction – she is the English translator of Jacques Derrida's *De la grammatologie* (1967) – and she has spent much of her career engaging in an interdisciplinary fashion with some of Europe's major philosophical and cultural works in order to effect a crisis within the forms of knowledge they propose, often by exposing the ways in which their conceptual schema installs or depends on invidious ways of thinking which are often at the service of colonialism. Her complex deconstructive reading of the work of G. W. F. Hegel, Julia Kristeva, Michel Foucault, and Gilles Deleuze can be found in her books *In Other Worlds: essays in cultural politics* (1987) and *A Critique of Postcolonial Reason: toward a history of the vanishing present* (1999). Spivak is just as committed to challenging some of the conceptual conveniences of feminist and postcolonial theory, as evidenced by her critique of the category of 'Third World women' and her fundamentally important essay 'Can the Subaltern Speak?' (1988) in which she casts doubt on the possibility, and propriety, of intellectuals retrieving the lost subaltern voices and agency of the colonized from the colonial archives (a preoccupation of the *Subaltern Studies* scholars of Indian history). Spivak's opponents frequently point to the alleged unreadability of her written style – Spivak's work is notoriously, and deliberately, hard to read – yet the profound intellectual challenges she poses frequently reward long, patient study. Spivak is currently Avalon Foundation Professor in Humanities at Columbia University, USA.

DEREK WALCOTT (B. 1930) Perhaps the finest English-language poet alive today, Derek Walcott was born in the Caribbean island of St Lucia. A child prodigy in painting and poetry, in 1950 he enrolled at the Jamaican campus of the fledgling University of West Indies, where he studied English Literature, French and Latin. Influenced as much by the art of classical European antiquity as by the vernacular lives and languages of ordinary Caribbean peoples, Walcott's poetry is often characterized by its compassionate response to the bloody past of Caribbean history, the eschewal of racial politics to solve the enduring inequalities of empire, and a pseudo-religious faith in the transformative and redemptive powers of art. These impulses can be detected through-out several collections of poetry, such as *In a Green Night* (1962), *The Castaway and other poems* (1965), *Another Life* (1973), *Midsummer* (1984), the epic *Omeros* (1990), *Tiepolo's Hound* (2000) and *The Prodigal* (2005). Walcott has also helped to nurture the development of drama in the Caribbean, and especially in Trinidad where he helped to found the Trinidad Theatre Workshop. His plays, such as *The Sea at Dauphin* (1954) and *Dream on Monkey Mountain* (1967), have been vital in contributing to the creation of a home-grown Caribbean theatre. In 1992 Walcott was awarded the Nobel Prize for Literature. He divides his time between St Lucia and the USA, where he teaches creative writing at Boston University.

BIBLIOGRAPHY OF WORKS CITED

Abrams, M. H. and Greenblatt, S. (eds) (2000) *The Norton Anthology of English Literature, Seventh Edition, Vols 1 & 2*, New York: Norton.

Achebe, C. (1975) *Morning Yet on Creation Day*, London: Heinemann.

Ahmad, A. (1996) 'The Politics of Literary Postcoloniality', in P. Mongia (ed.), *Contemporary Postcolonial Theory: a reader*, London: Arnold, 276–93.

Aldrich, R. (1996) *Greater France: a history of French overseas expansion*, Basingstoke: Palgrave.

—— (2005) *Vestiges of the Colonial Empire in France: monuments, museums, and colonial memories*, New York: Palgrave Macmillan.

Alexander, M. (2000) *A History of English Literature*, New York: Palgrave Macmillan.

Allen, P. G. (1986) *The Sacred Hoop: recovering the feminine in American Indian traditions*, Boston, MA: Beacon Press.

Allen, R. (1995) *The Arabic Novel: an historical and critical introduction*, second edition, Syracuse, NY: Syracuse University Press.

Al-Nowahi, M. M. (2000) 'The "Middle East"? Or . . . /Arabic Literature and the Postcolonial Predicament', in Henry Schwarz and Sangeeta Ray (eds) *A Companion to Postcolonial Studies*, Oxford: Blackwell, 282–303.

Alphen, E. van (1999) 'Symptoms of Discursivity: Experience, Memory, and Trauma', in Mieke Bal, Jonathan Crewe, and Leo Spitzer (eds), *Acts of Memory: cultural recall in the present*, Hanover, NH: University Press of New England, 24–38.

Anaya, R. A. and Lomelí, F. A. (eds) (1989) *Aztlán: essays on the Chicano homeland*, Albuquerque, N.Mex.: University of New Mexico Press.

Andrien, K. J. (ed.) (2002) *The Human Tradition in Colonial Latin America*, Wilmington, DE: Scholarly Resources Books.

Anzaldúa, G. (1999) *Borderlands/La frontera: the new Mestiza*, second edition, San Francisco, CA: Aunt Lute Books.

Appiah, K. A. (1992) *In My Father's House: Africa in the philosophy of culture*, London: Methuen.

Armstrong, J. (1995) 'Keepers of the Earth' in T. Roszak, M. E. Gomes and A. D. Kanner (eds) *Ecopsychology: restoring the earth, healing the mind*, San Francisco, CA: Sierra Club Books, 316–24.

Ashcroft, B. (2001) *Post-Colonial Transformation*, London: Routledge.

Ashcroft, B., Griffiths G. and Tiffin, H. (1989) *The Empire Writes Back: theory and practice in post-colonial literatures*, London: Routledge.

—— (1998) *Key Concepts in Post-Colonial Studies*, London: Routledge.

Attridge, D. and Jolly, R. (eds) (1998) *Writing South Africa: literature, Apartheid and democracy, 1970–1995*, Cambridge: Cambridge University Press.

Bahri, D. (2003) *Native Intelligence: aesthetics, politics, and postcolonial literature*, Minneapolis, MN: University of Minnesota Press.

Bartolovich, C. (2002) 'Introduction: Marxism, Modernity and Postcolonial Studies', in C. Bartolovich and N. Lazarus (eds) *Marxism, Modernity and Postcolonial Studies*, Cambridge: Cambridge University Press, 1–17.

Belich, J. (1996) *Making Peoples: a history of the New Zealanders from Polynesian settlement to the end of the nineteenth century*, Honolulu: University of Hawai'i Press.

Benítez-Rojo, A. (1996) *The Repeating Island: the Caribbean and the postmodern perspective* (*La Isla que se Repite: el Caribe y la perspectiva postmoderna*, 1989), second edition, trans. by James E. Maraniss, Durham, NC: Duke University Press.

—— (2002) 'Creolization and Nation Building in the Hispanic Caribbean', in T. Reiss (ed.) *Sisyphus and Eldorado: magical and other realisms in Caribbean literature*, Trenton, NJ: Africa World Press.

Berresford Ellis, P. (1989) 'Revisionism in Irish Historical Writing: The New Anti-Nationalist School of Historians', www.etext.org/Politics/INAC/historical.revisionism (accessed 8 January 2007).

Betts, R. (1991) *France and Decolonisation*, London: Macmillan.

—— (2005) *Assimilation and Association in French Colonial Theory, 1890–1914*, Lincoln, NE: University of Nebraska Press.

Bhabha, H. K. (ed.) (1990) *Nation and Narration*, London, Routledge.

—— (1994) *The Location of Culture*, London: Routledge.

Boehmer, E. (1995) *Colonial and Postcolonial Literature: migrant metaphors*, Oxford: Oxford University Press.

—— (2002) *Empire, the National, and the Postcolonial, 1890–1920: resistance in interaction*, Oxford: Oxford University Press.

Boilat, A. D. (1984) [1853] *Esquisses sénégalaises*, introduction by Abdoulaye Bara Diop, Paris: Karthala.

Boland, E. (1994) [1989] 'A Kind of Scar: The Woman Poet in a National Tradition' in *A Dozen Lips*, Dublin: Attic Press, 72–92.

—— (1995) *Collected Poems*, Manchester: Carcanet.

Bose, S. and Jalal, A. (1998) *Modern South Asia: history, culture, political economy*, London: Routledge.

Bourke, A., Kilfeather, S., Luddy, M., MacCurtain, M., Meaney, G., ní Dhonnchadha, M., O'Dowd, M. and Wills, C. (eds) (2002) *The Field Day Anthology of Irish Writing: Women's Writing and Traditions, Vol. IV & V*, Cork: Cork University Press.

Brah, A. (1996) *Cartographies of Diaspora: contesting identities*, London: Routledge.

Brathwaite, E. K. (1984) *History of the Voice: the development of nation language in Anglophone Caribbean poetry*, London: New Beacon.

—— (1993) *Roots*, Ann Arbor, MI: University of Michigan Press.

—— (2001) *Ancestors*, New York: New Directions.

—— (2005) [1971] *The Development of the Creole Society in Jamaica 1770–1820*, Oxford: Clarendon Press.

Brennan, T. (1997) *At Home in the World: cosmopolitanism now*, Cambridge, MA and London: Harvard University Press.

—— (2006) *Wars of Position: the cultural politics of left and right*, New York: Columbia University Press.

Brown, D. (1998) *Voicing the Text: South African oral poetry and performance*, Cape Town: Oxford University Press.

—— (ed.) (1999) *Oral Literature and Performance in Southern Africa*, Athens, OH: Ohio University Press.

Brown, K. M. (2001) *Mama Lola: a Vodou priestess in Brooklyn*, updated and expanded edition, Berkeley, CA: University of California Press.

Brydon, D. (2001a) 'Re-Routing the Black Atlantic', *Topia*, 5, 94–100.

—— (2001b) 'Black Canadas: Rethinking Canadian and Diasporic Cultural Studies', *Revista Canarias de Estudios Ingleses*, 43, 101–17.

Bulhan, H. A. (1985) *Frantz Fanon and the Psychology of Oppression*, New York: Plenum Press.

Burkholder, M. A. and Johnson, L. L. (2001) *Colonial Latin America*, second edition, New York: Oxford University Press.

Burnett, P. (1986) *The Penguin Book of Caribbean Verse in English*, London: Penguin.

Bushnell, D. and Macaulay, N. (1994) *The Emergence of Latin America in the Nineteenth Century*, second edition, New York: Oxford University Press.

Cabrita, J. M. (2001) *Mozambique: The Tortuous Road to Democracy*, Gordonsville: Palgrave Macmillan.

Campbell, M. (1973) *Half-Breed*, Halifax, NS: Goodread Biographies.

Candelaria, C. (1980) 'La Malinche, Feminist Prototype', *Frontiers: A Journal of Women Studies*, 5: 2, 1–6.

Canny, N. (1998) 'The Origins of Empire: An Introduction' in Nicholas Canny (ed.) *The Origins of Empire: British Overseas Enterprise to the Close of the Seventeenth Century*, Oxford: Oxford University Press.

Carey, P. (1997) *Jack Maggs*, London: Faber and Faber.

—— (2003) *My Life as a Fake*, New York: Knopf.

Carr, M. (2002) *Ariel*, Meath: The Gallery Press.

Carter, P. (1992) *Living in a New Country: history, travelling and language*, London: Faber and Faber.

Caruth, C. (ed.) (1995) *Trauma: explorations in memory*, Baltimore and London: Johns Hopkins University Press.

—— (1996) *Unclaimed Experience: trauma, narrative, and history*, Baltimore, MD: Johns Hopkins University Press.

Castro-Klarén, S. (1995) 'Writing Sub-Alterity: Guamán Poma and Garcilaso, Inca', in F. de Toro and A. de Toro (eds) *Borders and Margins: Post-Colonialism and Post-Modernism*, Frankfurt: Vervuert, 45–60.

Césaire, A. (1972) [1955] *Discourse on Colonialism*, trans. Joan Pinkham, New York: Monthly Review Press.

Chakrabarty, D. (2000) *Provincializing Europe: postcolonial thought and historical difference*, Princeton, NJ: Princeton University Press.

Chamoiseau, P., Confiant, R. and Bernabé, J. (1990), 'In Praise of Creoleness', trans Mohamed B. Taleb Khyar, *Callaloo*, 13, 891–92.

Chapman, P. (ed.) (1985) *The Diaries and Letters of G. T. W. B. Boyes. Vol. 1 1820–1832*, New York: Oxford University Press.

Chaudhuri, K. N. (1985) *Trade and Civilisation in the Indian Ocean: an economic history from the rise of Islam to 1750*, Cambridge: Cambridge University Press.

Childs, P. and Williams, P. (1997) *An Introduction to Post-Colonial Theory*, London: Prentice Hall/Harvester Wheatsheaf.

Chrisman, L. (2003) *Postcolonial Contraventions: cultural readings of race, imperialism and transnationalism*, Manchester: Manchester University Press.

Clarke, G. E. (1996) 'Must All Blackness Be American?': Locating Canada in Borden's

"Tightrope Time," or Nationalizing Gilroy's *The Black Atlantic*', *Canadian Ethnic Studies*, 28: 3, 56–71.

Clarke, M. (1874) *His Natural Life*, Melbourne: G. Robertson.

Clifford, J. (1988) *The Predicament of Culture: twentieth-century ethnography, literature, and art*, Cambridge, MA: Harvard University Press.

—— (1997) *Routes: travel and translation in the late twentieth century*, Cambridge, MA: Harvard University Press.

Coetzee, J. M. (1988) *White Writing: on the culture of letters in South Africa*, New Haven, CT: Yale University Press.

Cohn, B. S. (1987) *An Anthropologist Among the Historians and other Essays*, Delhi: Oxford University Press.

Conrad, P. (2000) 'New New World', *Granta*, 70, 12–37.

Cook, J. (1852) *The Voyages of Captain James Cook Round the World*, Vol. 1, London: John Tallis & Company.

Cooper, N. (2001) *France in Indochina: colonial encounters*, Oxford: Berg.

Coplan, D. B. (1994) *In the Time of Cannibals: the word music of South Africa's Basotho migrants*, Chicago, IL: Chicago University Press.

Cotterell, A. (2002) *East Asia: from Chinese predominance to the rise of the Pacific Rim*, London: Pimlico.

Davies, C. (2000) 'Fernando Ortiz's Transculturation: the Postcolonial Intellectual and the Politics of Cultural Representation' in R. Fiddian (ed.), *Postcolonial Perspectives on the Cultures of Latin America and Lusophone Africa*. Liverpool: Liverpool University Press, 141–68.

Dayan, J. (1996) 'Erzulie: A Women's History of Haiti?', in Mary Jean Green *et al*. (eds) *Postcolonial Subjects: Francophone Women Writers*, Minneapolis, MN: University of Minnesota Press, 1996, 42–60.

Deane, S. (ed.) (1990) *Nationalism, Colonialism and Literature: essays by Terry Eagleton, Fredric Jameson and Edward Said*, Minneapolis, MN: The University of Minnesota Press.

—— (Gen. Ed.) (1991) *The Field Day Anthology of Irish Writing*, 3 vols, Derry: Field Day Theatre Company.

de Kock, L. (2005) 'Does South African Literature Still Exist? Or: South African Literature is dead, long live literature in South Africa', *English in Africa*, 32: 2, 69–83.

De las Casas, B. (1992) [1552] *Short Account of the Destruction of the Indies*, ed. and trans. Nigel Griffin, London: Penguin.

Deming Lewis, M. (1962) 'One Hundred Million Frenchmen: The "Assimilation" Theory in French Colonial Policy', *Comparative Studies in Society and History*, 4, 129–53.

Derrida, J. (2004) [1981] *Positions*, trans. Alan Bass, London: Continuum.

—— (1976) [1967] *Of Grammatology*, trans. Gayatri Chakravorty Spivak, Baltimore, MD: Johns Hopkins University Press.

Devi, M. (1995) *Imaginary Maps*, trans. and ed. Gayatri Chakravorty Spivak, London: Routledge.

Dickason, O. P. (2002) *Canada's First Nations: a history of founding peoples from earliest times*, Don Mills Ont.: Oxford University Press.

Dickens, C. (1994) [1861] *Great Expectations*, ed. Margaret Cardwell, Oxford: Oxford University Press.

Dilke, C. W. (1880) [1868] *Greater Britain: a record of travel in English-speaking countries during 1866 and 1867*, seventh edition, London: Macmillan.

—— (1990) 'Culturalism as Hegemonic Ideology and Liberating Practice' in A. JanMohamed and D. Lloyd (eds) *The Nature and Context of Minority Discourse*, Oxford: Oxford University Press, 394–431.

Dirlik, A., (1994) 'The Postcolonial Aura: Third World Criticism in the Age of Global Capitalism', *Critical Inquiry*, 20: 2, 328–56.

Donovan, K., Jeffares, A. N. and Kenneally, B. (eds) (1994) *Ireland's Women: writings past and present*, Dublin: Gill & Macmillan.

Doyle, R. (1987) *The Commitments*, London: Vintage.

Driver, D., Daymond, M. J., Meintjes, S., Molema, L., Musengezi, C., Orford, M. and Rasebotsa, N. (eds) (2003) *Women Writing Africa, Volume One: Southern region*, New York: The Feminist Press.

Dubois, L. (2004) *Avengers of the New World: the story of the Haitian revolution*, Cambridge, MA: The Belknap Press of Harvard University Press.

Du Bois, W. E. B. (1969) [1903] *The Souls of Black Folk*, New York: Signet Classic.

Dubow, S. (1997) 'Colonial Nationalism, the Milner Kindergarten and the Rise of "South Africanism" 1902–10,' *History Workshop Journal*, 43, 53–85.

Durrant, S. (2004) *Postcolonial Narrative and the Work of Mourning: J. M. Coetzee, Wilson Harris, and Toni Morrison*, Albany: State University of New York Press.

Eagleton, T. (2003) *After Theory*, London: Allen Lane.

Equiano, O. (1995) [1789] *The Interesting Narrative and Other Writings*, ed. by Vincent Carretta, London: Penguin.

Fanon, F. (1967) [1961] *The Wretched of the Earth*, trans. Constance Farrington, Harmondsworth: Penguin.

—— (1986) [1952] *Black Skin, White Masks*, trans. Charles Lam Markmann, London: Pluto.

Fardon, R. and Furniss, G. (eds) (2000) *African Broadcast Cultures: radio in transition*, Oxford: James Currey.

Farrell, J. G. (1984) [1978] *The Singapore Grip*, London: Flamingo.

Felman, S. and Laub, D. (1992) *Testimony: crises of witnessing in literature, psychoanalysis, and history*, New York and London: Routledge.

Fernández Retamar, R. (1989) *Caliban and Other Essays*, trans. E. Baker, Minneapolis, MN: University of Minnesota Press.

Fiddian, R. (2000) (ed.) *Postcolonial Perspectives on the Cultures of Latin America and Lusophone Africa*, Liverpool: Liverpool University Press.

Forsdick, C. and Murphy, D. (eds) (2003) *Francophone Postcolonial Studies: a critical introduction*, London: Arnold.

Fraser, R. (2000) *Lifting the Sentence: a poetics of postcolonial fiction*, Manchester: Manchester University Press.

Friel, B. (1981) *Translations*, London: Faber and Faber.

Gabilondo, J. (2001) 'One-Way Theory: on the Hispanic–Atlantic Intersection of Postcoloniality and Postnationalism and its Globalizing Effects', *Arachne*, 1: 1, http://arachne.rutgers.edu/vol1_1gabilondo.htm (accessed 27 September 2006).

Gates, Jr., H. L. and McKay, N. (1997) *The Norton Anthology of African American Literature*, New York: W. W. Norton and Company.

Gandhi, L. (1998) *Postcolonial Theory: a critical introduction*, Edinburgh: Edinburgh University Press.

Ghosh, A. (1998) *Dancing in Cambodia, At Large in Burma*, New Delhi: Ravi Dayal.

Gikandi, S. (1987) *Reading the African Novel*, London: James Currey.

—— (ed.) (2003) *Encyclopedia of African Literature*, London: Routledge.

Gilroy (1993) *The Black Atlantic: Modernity and Double Consciousness*, London: Verso.

—— (1997) 'Diaspora and the Detours of Identity', in K. Woodward (ed.) *Identity and Difference*, London: Sage Publications, 299–346.

—— (2004a) *After Empire: melancholia or convivial culture?*, London: Routledge.

—— (2004b) 'Foreword' in H. Raphael-Hernandez (ed.) *Blackening Europe: the African American presence*, New York: Routledge, xi–xxii.

Glissant, É. (1992) *Caribbean Discourse: selected essays*, trans. J. Michael Dash, Charlottesville, VA: University Press of Virginia.

Goldberg, D. T. and Quayson, A. (2002) *Relocating Postcolonialism*, Oxford: Blackwell.

Goldie, T. (2004) 'On Not Being Australian: Mudrooroo and Demidenko', in M. Nolan and C. Dawson (eds) *Who's Who? Hoaxes, Imposture and Identity Crises in Australian Literature*, special issue of *Australian Literary Studies*, 21: 4, 89–100.

Góngora, M. (1975) *Studies in the Colonial History of Spanish America*, trans. Richard Southern, Cambridge: Cambridge University Press.

González Arias, Luz Mar (2000) *Otra Irlanda: La estética postnacionalista de poetas y artistas irlandesas contemporáneas*, Oviedo: Servicio de Publicaciones de la Universidad de Oviedo.

Graham, C. (2001) *Deconstructing Ireland: identity, theory, culture*, Edinburgh: Edinburgh University Press.

Gramsci, A. (1957) 'The Southern Question', in *The Modern Prince and Other Writings*, London: Lawrence and Wishart, 28–51.

—— (1971) *Selections from the Prison Notebooks of Antonio Gramsci*, ed. and trans. Quintin Hoare and Geoffrey Nowell Smith, London: Lawrence and Wishart.

Guha, R. (1982) 'Preface', in *Subaltern Studies 1*, Delhi: Oxford University Press, vii–viii.

Gunew, S. (1990) 'Denaturalizing Cultural Nationalisms: Multicultural Readings of "Australia"', in Homi K. Bhabha (ed.) *Nation and Narration*, Routledge: London and New York, 99–120.

Gunner, L. (2000) 'Wrestling with the Present, Beckoning to the Past: Contemporary Zulu Radio Drama', *Journal of Southern African Studies*, 26: 2, 223–37.

—— (2006) 'Zulu Choral Music – Performing Identities in a New State', *Research in African Literatures*, 37: 2, 83–97.

Gunner, E. and Gwala, M. P. (eds) (1991) *Musho! Zulu popular praises*, African Historical Sources Series, East Lansing, MI: Michigan State University Press.

Hall, S. (1996a) 'New Ethnicities', in D. Morley and K. Chen (eds) *Stuart Hall: Critical Dialogues in Cultural Studies*, London: Routledge, 441–49.

—— (1996b) 'When was the "postcolonial"? Thinking at the limit', in I. Chambers and L. Curti (eds) *The Post-Colonial Question: common skies, divided horizons*, London: Routledge, 242–60.

Hallward, P. (2001) *Absolutely Postcolonial: writing between the singular and the specific*, Manchester: Manchester University Press.

Hamilton, C. S. (1996) 'Revisions, Rememories and Exorcisms: Toni Morrison and the Slave Narrative', *Journal of American Studies*, 30, 429–45.

Hardt, M. and Negri, A. (2000) *Empire*, Cambridge, MA: Harvard University Press.

Harrison, N. (2003) *Postcolonial Criticism: history, theory and the work of fiction*, Cambridge: Polity.

Heaney, S. (2004) *The Burial at Thebes: Sophocles'* Antigone, London: Faber and Faber.

—— (2005) 'Thebes via Toombridge: Retitling *Antigone*', *The Irish Book Review*, 1: 1, 12–14.

Hegel, G. W. F. (1975) [1837] *Lectures on the Philosophy of World History*, trans. H.B. Nisbet, Cambridge: Cambridge University Press.

Highway, T. (1998) *Kiss of the Fur Queen*, Toronto: Doubleday.

Hirsch, M. (1998) 'Past Lives: Postmemories in Exile', in Susan Rubin Suleiman (ed.), *Exile and Creativity: signposts, travellers, outsiders, backward glances*, Durham, NC: Duke University Press, 418–46.

—— (1999) 'Projected Memory: Holocaust Photographs in Personal and Public Fantasy' in Mieke Bal, Jonathan Crewe and Leo Spitzer (eds), *Acts of Memory: cultural recall in the present*, Hanover, NH: University Press of New England, 2–23.

—— (2001) 'Surviving Images: Holocaust Photographs and the Work of Postmemory', *Yale Journal of Criticism*, 14: 1, 5–37.

Horne, A. (2002) [1977] *A Savage War of Peace: Algeria 1954–1962*, London: Pan Macmillan.

Hoy, H. (1999) '"Nothing But the Truth": Discursive Transparency in Beatrice Culleton' in Beatrice Culleton Mosionier, *In Search of April Raintree: critical edition*, Cheryl Suzack (ed.), Winnipeg: Portage & Main Press, 273–93.

Huggan, G. (1994) *Territorial Disputes: maps and mapping strategies in contemporary Canadian and Australian fiction*, Toronto: University of Toronto Press.

—— (2001) *The Postcolonial Exotic: marketing the margins*, London: Routledge.

—— (2002) 'Postcolonial Studies and the Anxiety of Interdisciplinarity', *Postcolonial Studies* 5: 3, 245–75.

Hughes, R. (1988) *The Fatal Shore: the epic of Australia's founding*, New York: Random House.

Hulme, P. (1986) *Colonial Encounters: Europe and the Native Caribbean, 1492–1797*, London: Methuen.

Hussein, A. A. (2002) *Edward Said: criticism and society*, London: Verso.

Hutcheon, L. (1989) '"Circling the Downspout of Empire": Post-Colonialism and Post-modernism', *Ariel*, 20: 4, 149–75.

Ingamells, R. (1969) 'Conditional Culture', in John Barnes (ed.) *The Writer in Australia: a collection of literary documents, 1856–1964*, New York: Oxford University Press, 245–65.

Innes, C. L. (2002) *A History of Black and Asian Writing in Britain, 1700–2000*, Cambridge: Cambridge University Press.

Irele, A. (2001) *The African Imagination*, New York: Oxford University Press.

Jennings, E. T. (2001) *Vichy in the Tropics: Petain's national revolution in Madagascar, Guadeloupe, and Indochina, 1940–1944*, Stanford, CA: Stanford University Press.

Johnson, R. (1979) 'Three Problematics' in J. Clarke, C. Critcher and R. Johnson (eds), *Working-Class Culture: studies in history and theory*, London: Hutchinson.

Julien, E. (1992) *African Novels and the Question of Orality*, Bloomington, IN: Indiana University Press.

Kadir, D. (1993) *The Other Writing: postcolonial essays in Latin America's writing culture*, West Lafayette, IN: Purdue University Press.

Kamboureli, S. (ed.) (1996) *Making a Difference: Canadian multicultural literature*, Toronto: Oxford University Press.

Katrak, K. H. (2006) 'Decolonizing Culture: Toward a Theory for Post-colonial Women's

Texts', in B. Ashcroft, G. Griffiths and H. Tiffin (eds) *The Post-colonial Studies Reader*, second edition, London: Routledge, 239–41.

Kennelly, B. (1990) *A Time for Voices: selected poems 1960–1990*, Newcastle upon Tyne: Bloodaxe.

Khilnani, S. (1997) *The Idea of India*, London: Penguin.

Kiberd, D. (1995) *Inventing Ireland: the literature of the modern nation*, London: Jonathan Cape.

King, N. (2000) *Memory, Narrative, Identity: remembering the self*, Edinburgh: Edinburgh University Press.

King, T. (1990). 'Godzilla vs. Post-Colonial', *World Literature Written in English*, 30: 2, 10–16.

Klein, C. F. (1995) 'Wild Women in Colonial Mexico: An Encounter of European and Aztec Concepts of the Other', in Claire Farago (ed.) *Reframing the Renaissance: visual culture in Europe and Latin America 1450–1650*, New Haven, CT: Yale University Press, 245–64.

Klor de Alva, J. J. (1995) 'The Postcolonization of the (Latin) American Experience: A Reconsideration of "Colonialism," "Postcolonialism," and "Mestizaje"', in Gyan Prakash (ed.) *After Colonialism: imperial histories and postcolonial displacements*, Princeton, NJ: Princeton University Press, 241–75.

Kneale, M. (2000) *English Passengers*, London: Hamish Hamilton.

LaCapra, D. (1994) *Representing the Holocaust: history, theory, trauma*, Ithaca, NY: Cornell University Press.

—— (1998) *History and Memory After Auschwitz*, Ithaca, NY: Cornell University Press.

—— (2001) *Writing History, Writing Trauma*, Baltimore, MD: Johns Hopkins University Press.

Lamming, G. (1992) [1960] *The Pleasures of Exile*, Ann Arbor, MI: The University of Michigan Press.

Langer, L. L. (1991) *Holocaust Testimonies: the ruins of memory*, New Haven, CT: Yale University Press.

Lansbury, C. (1970) *Arcady in Australia: the evocation of Australia in nineteenth-century English literature*, Carlton, Victoria: Melbourne University Press.

LaRocque, E. (1993), 'Preface, or Here are Our Voices – Who Will Hear?' in J. Perreault and S. Vance (eds), *Writing the Circle*: *native women of Western Canada*, Norman, OK: University of Oklahoma Press, xv–xxx.

Latin American Subaltern Studies Group (1995) 'Founding Statement' in J. Beverley, M. Aronna and J. Oviedo (eds) *The Postmodernism Debate in Latin America*, Durham, NC: Duke University Press, 135–46.

Lazarus, N. (1999) *Nationalism and Cultural Practice in the Postcolonial World*, Cambridge: Cambridge University Press.

—— (2004) 'Introducing Postcolonial Studies', in N. Lazarus (ed.) *The Cambridge Companion to Postcolonial Studies*, Cambridge: Cambridge University Press, 1–16.

Lebovics, H. (2004) *Bringing the Empire Back Home: France in the global age*, Durham, NC: Duke University Press.

Lentin, R. (1999) 'Racializing (Our) Dark Rosaleen: Feminism, Racism, Antisemitism', *UCG Women's Studies Centre Review*, 6, 1–18.

Lewis, Laura A. (1996) 'The "Weakness" of Women and the Feminization of the Indian in Colonial Mexico', *Colonial Latin American Review*, 5: 1, 73–94.

Liss, P. K. (1975) *Mexico Under Spain, 1521–1556: society and the origins of nationality*, Chicago, IL: University of Chicago Press.

Lloyd, D. (1993) *Anomalous States: Irish writing and the post-colonial moment*, Dublin: The Lilliput Press.

—— (2003) 'Editorial: Ireland's Modernities', *Interventions: International Journal of Postcolonial Studies*, 5: 3, 317–21.

Lockhart, J. and Schwartz, S. B. (1983) *Early Latin America: a history of colonial Spanish America and Brazil*, Cambridge: Cambridge University Press.

Lutz, H. (1991) *Contemporary Challenges: conversations with Canadian native authors.* Saskatchewan: Fifth House Publishers.

Lyotard, J.-F. (1988) *The Differend: phrases in dispute*, trans. by George Van Den Abbeele, Minneapolis, MN: University of Minnesota Press.

Macaulay, T. (2006) [1835] 'Minute in Indian Education', in B. Ashcroft, G. Griffiths and H. Tiffin (eds) *The Post-Colonial Studies Reader*, second edition, London: Routledge, 2006, 374–75.

McClintock, A. (1993) [1992] 'The Angel of Progress: Pitfalls of the Term "Postcolonialism"' in P. Williams and L. Chrisman (eds) *Colonial Discourse and Post-Colonial Theory: a reader*, Hemel Hempstead: Harvester Wheatsheaf, 291–304.

McKague, O. (ed.) (1991) *Racism in Canada*, Saskatoon: Fifth House.

McLeod, J. (2000) *Beginning Postcolonialism*, Manchester: Manchester University Press.

—— (2003) 'Contesting Contexts: Francophone Thought and Anglophone Postcolonialism', in C. Forsdick and D. Murphy (eds) *Francophone Postcolonial Studies: a critical introduction*, London: Arnold, 192–201.

Malouf, D. (1984) *Harland's Half Acre*, London: Chatto and Windus.

—— (1993) *Remembering Babylon*, London: Chatto and Windus.

—— (1996) *The Conversations at Curlow Creek*, London: Chatto and Windus.

Mannoni, O. (1993) [1950] *Prospero and Caliban: the psychology of colonization*, trans. by Pamela Powesland, Ann Arbor, MI: University of Michigan Press.

Mbembe, A. (2001) *On the Postcolony*, Berkeley, CA: University of California Press.

—— (2003) 'Necropolitics', *Public Culture*, 15: 1, 11–40.

Meehan, P. (2000) *Dharmakaya*, Manchester: Carcanet.

Memmi, A. (1990) [1957] *The Colonizer and the Colonized*, trans. H. Greenfield, introduced by Jean-Paul Sartre, London: Earthscan Publications.

—— (2006) *Decolonization and the Decolonized*, trans. by Robert Bononno, Minneapolis, MN: University of Minnesota Press.

Menchú, R., with Burgos, E. (1984) *I, Rigoberta Menchú: An Indian Woman in Guatemala*, trans. A White, London: Verso.

Mignolo, W. D. (1995) 'Afterword: Human Understanding and (Latin) American Interests – The Politics and Sensibilities of Geocultural Locations', *Poetics Today*, 16: 1, 171–214.

Miller, C. (1998) *Nationalists and Nomads: essays on francophone African literature and culture*, Chicago, IL: University of Chicago Press.

Millington, M. I. (2000) 'On Metropolitan Readings of Latin American Cultures: Ethical Questions of Postcolonial Critical Practice', in R. Fiddian (ed.) *Postcolonial Perspectives on the Cultures of Latin America and Lusophone Africa*, Liverpool: Liverpool University Press, 27–50.

Mills, L. (1995) '"I Won't Go Back to It": Irish Women Poets and the Iconic Feminine', *Feminist Review – The Irish Issue: The British Question*, 50, 69–88.

—— (2005) *Nothing Simple*, Dublin: Penguin Ireland.

Mishra, V. and Hodge, B. (1993) 'What is Post(-)colonialism?', in P. Williams and L. Chrisman (eds) *Colonial Discourse and Postcolonial Theory*, Hemel Hempstead: Harvester Wheatsheaf, 276–90.

Moore-Gilbert, B. (1997) *Postcolonial Theory: contexts, practices, politics*, London: Verso.

Morgan, P. (1997) 'Tales of Old Travel: Predecessors of David Malouf's *The Conversations at Curlow Creek*', *Australian Literary Studies*, 18: 2, 174–79.

Mudrooroo (1997) *Indigenous Literature of Australia: milli milli wangka*, Melbourne: Hyland House Publishing.

Mukherjee, A. P. (1995) 'Canadian Nationalism, Canadian Literature and Racial Minority Women' in. M. Silvera (ed.) *The Other Woman*: *women of colour in contemporary Canadian literature*, Toronto: Sister Vision Press, 421–44.

Mycak, S. (2004) 'Demidenko/Darville: A Ukrainian–Australian Point of View', in M. Nolan and C. Dawson (eds) *Who's Who? Hoaxes, Imposture and Identity Crises in Australian Literature*, special issue of *Australian Literary Studies*, 21: 4, 111–33.

Nandy, A. (2006) [1983] *The Intimate Enemy: loss and recovery of self under colonialism*, New Delhi: Oxford University Press.

Ndebele, N. S. (2006) *Rediscovery of the Ordinary: essays on South African literature and culture*, second edition, Pietermaritzburg: University of KwaZulu-Natal Press.

Neal, D. (1991) *The Rule of Law in a Penal Colony: law and power in early New South Wales*, Cambridge: Cambridge University Press.

Newell, S. (2000) *Ghanaian Popular Fiction: 'Thrilling Discoveries in Conjugal Life' and other tales*, Oxford: James Currey.

Newitt, M. (1981) *Portugal in Africa: the last hundred years*, London: Hurst.

Ngugi wa Thiong'o (1986) *Decolonising the Mind*, London: James Currey.

Ní Dhomhnaill, N. (1992) 'What Foremothers?', *Poetry Ireland Review*, 36, 18–31.

—— (1993) [1988]: *Selected Poems: Rogha Dánta*, trans. Michael Hartnett and Nuala Ní Dhomhnaill, Dublin: New Island Books.

Nixon, R. (1994) *Homelands, Harlem and Hollywood: South African culture and the world beyond*, New York: Routledge.

Nkosi, L. (2006a) [1967] 'Fiction by Black South Africans' in Lindy Stiebel and Liz Gunner (eds) *Still Beating the Drum: critical perspectives on Lewis Nkosi*, Johannesburg: Witwatersrand University Press.

—— (2006b) [2002] 'The Republic of Letters after the Mandela Republic' in Lindy Stiebel and Liz Gunner (eds) *Still Beating the Drum: critical perspectives on Lewis Nkosi*, Johannesburg: Witwatersrand University Press.

Nolan, M. (2004) 'In His Own Sweet Time: Carmen's Coming Out', in Maggie Nolan and Carrie Dawson (eds) *Who's Who? hoaxes, imposture and identity crises in Australian literature*, special issue of *Australian Literary Studies*, 21: 4, 134–48.

Norman, A. (1986) *The People Who Came: book one*, second edition, San Juan, Trinidad: Longman Caribbean.

Nuttall, S. (2004) 'City Forms and Writing the "Now" in South Africa', *Journal of Southern African Studies*, 30: 4, 331–48.

Nuttall, S. and Coetzee, C. (eds) (1998) *Negotiating the Past: the making of memory in South Africa*, Cape Town: Oxford University Press (Southern Africa).

O'Gorman, E. (1961) *The Invention of America*, Bloomington, IN: Indiana University Press.

Ortiz, F. (1978) [1940] *Contrapunteo cubano del tabaco y el azúcar: advertencia de sus contrastes agrarios, económicos, históricos y sociales, su etnografía y su transculturación*, Caracas: Bilioteca Ayacucho.

Palencia-Roth, M. (1993) 'The Cannibal Law of 1503', in Jerry M. Williams and Robert E. Lewis (eds) *Early Images of the Americas: Transfer and Invention*, Tuscon, AZ: University of Arizona Press, 21–63.

Palmer, C. (1976) *Slaves of the White God: Blacks in Mexico 1570–1650*, Cambridge MA: Harvard University Press.

Pana, I. G. (1996) *The Tomis Complex: exile and eros in Australian Literature*, New York: Peter Lang.

Parry, B. (2002) 'Directions and Dead Ends in Postcolonial Studies', in D. T. Goldberg and A. Quayson (eds) *Relocating Postcolonialism*, Oxford: Blackwell, 66–81.

—— (2004) *Postcolonial Studies: a materialist critique*, London: Routledge.

Pastor Bodmer, B. (1992) *The Armature of Conquest: Spanish accounts of the discovery of America, 1492–1589*, trans. Lydia Longstreth Hunt, Stanford, CA: Stanford University Press.

Paz, O. (1990) [1950] *The Labyrinth of Solitude: Life and Thought in Mexico*, trans. L. Kemp, London: Penguin.

Peres, P. (1997) *Transculturation and Resistance in Lusophone African Narrative*, Gainesville, FL: University of Florida Press.

Philip, M. N. (1993) [1989] *She tries her tongue, her silence softly breaks*, London: Women's Press.

Phillips, C. (1987) *The European Tribe*, London: Faber & Faber.

—— (2001) *A New World Order: selected essays*, London: Secker & Warburg.

Pierce, D. (ed.) (2000) *Irish Writing in the Twentieth Century: a reader*, Cork: Cork University Press.

Pitman, T. (2005) 'Chicano Muralism' in L. Shaw *et al.* (eds), *Contemporary Popular Culture in Latin America*, Santa Barbara, CA: ABC-Clio, 335–36.

Pratt, M. L. (1992) *Imperial Eyes: Travel Writing and Transculturation*, London: Routledge.

Pyne-Timothy, H. (2001) 'Reading the Signs in Pauline Melville's "Erzulie"', *Journal of Haitian Studies*, 7: 1.

Quayson, A. (1997) *Strategic Transformations in Nigerian Writing*, Oxford: James Currey.

—— (2000) *Postcolonialism: theory, practice, or process?*, Cambridge: Polity Press.

Quiñonez, N. H. (2002) 'Re(riting) the Chicana Postcolonial: From Traitor to 21st Century Interpreter', in A. J. Aldama and N. H. Quiñonez (eds) *Decolonial Voices: Chicana and Chicano cultural studies in the 21st century*, Bloomington, IN: Indiana University Press, 129–51.

Rao, R. (1967) *Kanthapura*, New York: New Directions.

Restrepo, L. F. (2003) 'The Cultures of Colonialism', in Philip Swanson (ed.) *The Companion to Latin American Studies*, London: Arnold, 47–68.

Richards, T. (1993) *The Imperial Archive: knowledge and the fantasy of empire*, London: Verso.

Rivera, T. (1982) 'Chicano Literature: The Establishment of a Community' in L. Leal *et al.* (eds) *A Decade of Chicano Literature (1970–1979): critical essays and bibliography*, Santa Barbara, CA: Editorial La Causa.

Ross, K. (1995) *Fast cars, clean bodies: decolonization and the reordering of French culture*, Cambridge, MA: MIT Press.

Ruskin, J. (1903) *Lectures on Art: delivered before the University of Oxford in Hilary term, 1870*, London: George Allen.

Russell-Wood, A. J. R. (1993) *A World on the Move: the Portuguese in Africa, Asia, and America, 1415–1808*, New York: St. Martin's Press.

Sachs, A. (1998) [1991] 'Preparing Ourselves for Freedom: Culture and the ANC Constitutional Guidelines' in Derek Attridge and Rosemary Jolly (eds) *Writing South Africa: literature, Apartheid, and democracy, 1970–1995*, Cambridge: Cambridge University Press, 239–48.

Said, E. W. (1978) *Orientalism*, London: Routledge & Kegan Paul.

—— (1993) *Culture and Imperialism*, London: Chatto and Windus.

Santiago, S. (2001) *The Space In-Between: essays on Latin American culture*, ed. A. Lucía Gazzola, trans. T. Burns, A. Lucía Gazzola and G. Williams, Durham, NC: Duke University Press.

Sarmiento, D. (1998) *Facundo, or, Civilization and Barbarism*, trans. Mary Mann, New York: Penguin.

Sartre, J. P. (1976) [1960] *Critique of Dialectical Reason*, vol. 1, trans. Alan Sheridan-Smith, London: Verso.

Seed, P. (1988) *To Love, Honor and Obey in Colonial Mexico: conflicts over marriage choice, 1574–1821*, Stanford, CA: Stanford University Press.

Seeley, J. R. (1883) *The Expansion of England*, London: Macmillan.

Shaw, R. D. (1988) *Transculturation: the cultural factor in translation and other communication tasks*, Pasadena, CA: William Carey Library.

Shohat, E. (1992) 'Notes on the "Post-Colonial"', *Social Text*, 31/32, 99–113.

Silverman, M. (2005) 'Reflections on the Human Question' in Max Silverman (ed.) *Black Skin, White Masks: new interdisciplinary essays*, Manchester: Manchester University Press, 112–27.

Skidmore, T. E. and Smith, P. H. (1992) *Modern Latin America*, third edition, Oxford: Oxford University Press.

Sklodowska, E. (2003) 'Latin American Literatures' in P. Swanson (ed.) *The Companion to Latin American Studies*, London: Arnold, 86–106.

Smith, A. (2001) 'from *The Wealth of Nations*', in Jane Samson (ed.), *The British Empire*, Oxford: Oxford University Press, 55–56.

Smith, B. (1985) *European Vision and the South Pacific*, New Haven, CT: Yale University Press.

Smyth, A. (ed.) (1990) [1989] *Wildish Things: an anthology of new Irish women's writing*, Dublin: Attic Press.

Smyth, G. (1994) 'Review of *Anomalous States: Irish writing and the post-colonial moment*, by David Lloyd', *Irish Studies Review*, 7, 44–45.

Somerville-Arjat, G. and Wilson, R. E. (eds) (1990) *Sleeping with Monsters: conversations with Scottish and Irish women poets*, Edinburgh: Polygon.

Spivak, G. C. (1987) *In Other Worlds: essays in cultural politics*, New York: Methuen.

—— (1990) *The Postcolonial Critic: interviews, strategies, dialogues*, ed. Sarah Harasym, London: Routledge.

—— (1999) *A Critique of Postcolonial Reason: toward a history of the vanishing present*, Cambridge, MA: Harvard University Press.

Stockwell, A. J. (1992) 'Southeast Asia in War and Peace: The End of European Colonial Empires' in Nicholas Tarling (ed.) *The Cambridge History of South-East Asia: volume 4: from World War II to the present*, Cambridge: Cambridge University Press, 1–57.

Tarling, N. (2001) *Southeast Asia: a modern history*, Oxford: Oxford University Press.

Therrien, M. and Ramirez, R. R. (2000) 'The Hispanic Population in the United States: March 2000', *Current Population Reports*, P20–535, Washington DC: US Census Bureau.

Thomas, H. (1993) *Conquest: Montezuma, Cortés, and the fall of Old Mexico*, New York: Simon and Schuster.

Thomas, M. (1998) *The French Empire at War, 1940–45*, Manchester: Manchester University Press.

Thurner, M. and Guerrero, A. (eds) (2003) *After Spanish Rule: postcolonial predicaments of the Americas*, Durham, NC: Duke University Press.

Torres-Saillant, S. (1997) *Caribbean Poetics: toward an aesthetic of West Indian literature*, Cambridge: Cambridge University Press.

Vera, Y. (ed.) (1999) *Opening Spaces: an anthology of contemporary African women's writings*, Portsmouth, New Haven, CT: Heinemann.

Verges, F. (2000) 'To Cure and to Free: The Fanonian Project of "Decolonized Psychiatry"', in Lewis R. Gordon, T. Denean Sharpley-Whiting and Renée T. White (eds) *Fanon: A Critical Reader*, Malden, MA: Blackwell, 85–99.

Walcott, D. (1992) *Collected Poems 1948–1984*, London: Faber.

Walcott, R. (2003) *Black Like Who?: writing black Canada*, Toronto: Insomniac Press.

Warner, M. (1996) [1985] *Monuments and Maidens: the allegory of the female form*, London: Vintage.

Wicomb, Z. (1998) 'Shame and Identity: the Case of the Coloured in South Africa' in Derek Attridge and Rosemary Jolly (eds), *Writing South Africa: literature, Apartheid, and democracy, 1970–1995*, Cambridge: Cambridge University Press, 91–107.

Wilder, G. (2005) *The French Imperial Nation-State: Negritude and colonial humanism between the two World Wars*, Chicago, IL: University of Chicago Press.

Williams, P. and Chrisman L. (1993) 'Colonial Discourse and Post-Colonial Theory: An Introduction', in P. Williams and L. Chrisman (eds) *Colonial Discourse and Post-Colonial Theory: a reader*, Hemel Hempstead: Harvester Wheatsheaf, 1–20.

Williamson, E. (1992) *The Penguin History of Latin America*, London: Penguin.

Woodhull, W. (2003) 'Postcolonial thought and culture in Francophone North Africa', in Charles Forsdick and David Murphy (eds) *Francophone Postcolonial Studies: a critical introduction*, London: Arnold, 211–20.

Young, R. J. C. (1990) *White Mythologies: writing history and the west*, London: Routledge.

—— (2001) *Postcolonialism: an historical introduction*, Oxford: Blackwell.

Yuval-Davis, N. (1997) *Gender and Nation*, London: Sage Publications.

Zamora, M. (1993) 'Christopher Columbus's "Letter to the Sovereigns" Announcing the Discovery', in Stephen Greenblatt (ed.) *New World Encounters*, Berkeley: University of California Press, 1–11.

INDEX